BLACK ARTS WEST

D1572329

BLACK ARTS WEST

Culture and Struggle in Postwar Los Angeles

DANIEL WIDENER

Duke University Press   Durham and London   2010

© 2010 Duke University Press

All rights reserved

Printed in the United States of America on acid-free paper ∞

Designed by Heather Hensley

Typeset in Minion Pro by Keystone Typesetting, Inc.

Library of Congress Cataloging-in-Publication Data appear
on the last printed page of this book.

for good friends met

and good friends lost

along the way

in this great future

you can't forget your past

CONTENTS

Illustrations   ix

Acknowledgments   xi

Introduction Acts of Culture, or, Maybe the People Would Be the Times   1

PART I **Cultural Democracy in the Racial Metropolis**

1. Hollywood Scuffle: The Second World War, Los Angeles, and the Politics of Wartime Representation   21

2. The Negro as Human Being? Desegregation and the Black Arts Imperative   52

3. Writing Watts: The Rise and Fall of Cultural Liberalism   90

PART II **Message from the Grassroots**

4. Notes from the Underground: Free Jazz and Black Power in South Los Angeles   117

5. Studios in the Street: Creative Community and Visual Arts   153

6. The Arms of Criticism: The Cultural Politics of Urban Insurgency   187

PART III **Festivals and Funerals**

7. An Intimate Enemy: Culture and the Contradictions of Bradleyism   221

8. How to Survive in South Central: Black Film as Class Critique   250

Epilogue   283

Notes   291

Works Cited   329

Index   353

ILLUSTRATIONS

1. *Jump for Joy* chorus members, 1941   25

2. Duke Ellington with Louise Franklin, 1941   27

3. Hattie McDaniel with female entertainers, not dated   43

4. Housing segregation, 1950   58

5. LAPD officers arrest Joseph Lewis at Cafe Zombie, 1947   61

6. Professor Wilkins and students, circa 1932   69

7. Mrs. Alma Hightower teaching music class, 1939   70

8. Nick Stewart publicity still, 1954   77

9. City Council members visit Ebony Showcase, 1967   78

10. Beulah Woodard with Biddy Mason sculpture, not dated   85

11. Looted surplus store, 1965   93

12. Budd Schulberg at Watts Writers Workshop, 1967   95

13. Watts Happening Coffee House, not dated   96

14. Watts Writers Workshop congressional testimony, 1966   98

15. Watts Summer Festival parade, 1968   109

16. Watts community chalk-in, 1968   131

17. Horace Tapscott playing piano, 1986   144

18. Art made from riot debris, 1966   164

19. David Hammons, "The Door," 1969   166

20. John Outterbridge, "Case in Point," 1970   167

21. John Riddle Jr., "Bird and Diz," 1973   168

22. Betye Saar, "Nine Mojo Secrets," 1971   173

23. Judson Powell with art students, 1965   177

24. Compton Communicative Arts Academy mixed-media door, 1970   178

25. Chopper show, Communicative Arts Academy, 1972   179

26. Communicative Arts Academy staff, not dated   180

27. Musical performance, Communicative Arts Academy, not dated   182

28. Julie King with trombone, Communicative Arts Academy, not dated   182

29. Performance, Communicative Arts Academy, 1970   183

30. Dancers rehearse on stage, Communicative Arts Academy, not dated   183

31. Dance class, Communicative Arts Academy, not dated   184

32. Paul Robeson Players, not dated   184

33. Communicative Arts Academy Orchestra, not dated   185

34. Musical combo, Communicative Arts Academy, 1970   185

35. Police Raid on Black Panther Party headquarters, 1969   191

36. H. Rap Brown and Ron Karenga, 1967   195

37. Black Muslim women at Communicative Arts Academy, 1970   196

38. Black Panther Party office, 1969   202

39. Judson Powell and Noah Purifoy with Mayor Sam Yorty, 1967   211

40. Emory Douglas exhibition flyer, 1969   212

41. Bob Marley at Watts Towers, not dated   222

42. John Outterbridge and Watts Towers Art Center Staff, 1980   223

43. Watts Towers at night, 2001   227

44. Watts Towers under repair, 1983   232

45. National Guard soldiers in front of MOCA, 1992   236

46. Mayor Tom Bradley with Los Angeles Olympics luminaries, 1984   239

47. Young boys at play, 1978   262

48. Crips examine peace treaty, 1988   278

ACKNOWLEDGMENTS

I can remember a graduate seminar I once took, when, in response to a particularly furious bout of criticism from students, the professor asked how many of us had ever published a book. Predictably, Robin Kelley's was the only hand raised. As the point sank in, he proceeded to explain that in the course of writing a book, one rarely felt confident that the end result had turned out perfectly. There is always something you forget, he said, something that you could have done differently or better. I hadn't really thought about that December afternoon until I sat down to try and complete these acknowledgments. This is the part of this book that I would most like to get right, and the part that I am confident will be left less than complete. In this spirit, I apologize in advance to those whose names I have omitted.

This project began as a doctoral dissertation at New York University, under the direction of Robin Kelley. Many are the students indebted to Robin for his brilliance, wisdom, and support, and I am happy to be in that number. In transitioning into a role as a teacher of graduate students, I have tried to emulate the models provided by Ada Ferrer and Nikhil Singh. Warm thanks go to Arlene Dávila and Adam Green, as well, for their support and insightful commentary. I am lucky to have had all of you as my teachers.

A legion of supportive archivists and librarians helped me to find materials. In particular, I thank Carol Wells at the Center for the Study of Political Graphics; Sarah Cooper and Alexis Moreno at the Southern California Library for Social Research; Marian Yoshiki-Kovinick and Barbara Babcock at the Smithsonian Archives of American Art branch in San Marino; Jeff Rankin, Robert Montoya, and Teresa Barnett at the University of California, Los Angeles (UCLA); and the staffs at the Los Angeles City Archives, the California African American Museum, the Bancroft Library, the Dartmouth College

Library, the Rockefeller Archives Center, and the Rutgers Institute for Jazz Studies. Thanks also to the Federal Bureau of Investigation—nothing says "openness in government" like two dozen continuous pages of completely redacted Cointelpro material.

Essential financial support for this project was provided by the Historical Society of Southern California, the Hellman Family Foundation, the W. M. Keck Foundation, and the Center for the Study of Race and Ethnicity at the University of California, San Diego (UCSD). A year spent as a postdoctoral fellow at the Bunche Center for African-American Studies, UCLA, aided the revision of the manuscript. I appreciate the support of everyone involved with the Institute of American Cultures and the Bunche Center at UCLA, including Alex Tucker, Jan Freeman, Veronica Benson, and Dean Shirley Hune. My research was assisted by a faculty career development award, a humanities center grant, and academic senate research funds from UCSD. I would never have made it to UCSD in the first place without the teaching opportunities provided by King Carter at Los Angeles Harbor College, Henry Ealy and Mattie Moon at Los Angeles City College, and David Horne at California State University, Northridge.

Artists generously shared their time, ideas, and resources as well. I am indebted to the late Horace Tapscott and the late Noah Purifoy, as well as to Alonzo Davis, Fred Ho, Marta Gonzalez, Quetzal Flores, Willie Ford, John Outterbridge, Cecil Fergerson, and Ron Wilkins.

Boundless thanks are due to the very good friends I have met in the course of becoming a scholar. Eric Avila, Jason Ferreira, and Montye Fuse helped convince me to go to graduate school in the first place. At New York University, Betsy Esch, Koray Çaliskan, Forrest Hylton, Andrew Lee, Harvey Neptune, Njoroge Njoroge, Melina Pappademos, Sherene Seikaly, Victor Viesca, Fanon Wilkins, Jeff Chang, Vijay Prashad, and Junot Díaz listened to, marched with, laughed at, and cared about a wayward Californian far from home. Sukhdev Sandhu attended the Westminster Kennel Club, saw the outermost of the outer boroughs, mocked David Blaine, and generally helped me make sense of New York City. Back in California, Luis Alvarez, Scot Brown, Katsuhiko Endo, Gaye Johnson, Scott Kurashige, Galust Mardirussian, Natalia Molina, Eric Porter, John Riehle, Denise Sandoval, Sarah Schrank, George Solt, Jason Stanyek, Don Wallace, Ted Wilkinson, and Mike Willard shared their time and ideas. Eric Avila and Eric Porter read the manuscript version, and I expect that each will recognize his interventions in the final version. Special thanks to Anthony Macías, for reading draft after draft, sharing archival gems, and helping me stay one step ahead of the University of California system.

Faculty members spread across the country helped me at many stages of this project. I extend particular thanks to Clyde Woods, Billy Woodberry, Cynthia Young, George Sanchez, Julius Scott, Teshome Gabriel, and Laura Pulido. Most academics are more than happy to share horror stories from graduate school. I have none, in no small part because of the kindness and sharp minds of Tom Bender, Michael Gomez, Walter Johnson, Karen Kupperman, Jeffrey Sammons, and Marilyn Young. George Lipsitz has given consistent mentoring and ongoing support, providing a model of what an engaged scholar looks like. Special thanks go to Mike Davis for his generosity, insight, and willingness to share. My utmost gratitude and respect go to Lisa Lowe from start to finish.

Comrades in a variety of political formations shared ideas about social life and political struggle that I have tried to translate into cultural history. Thanks go to the members of the National Congress for Puerto Rican Rights, especially the late Richie Perez; the Committee against Anti-Asian Violence; the Committee Against Police Abuse; the Labor Community Strategy Center; and the Venceremos Brigade. I am grateful to James Fugate and Tom Hamilton, whose Eso Won bookstore is worth more than all the African American elected officials in Southern California combined.

Since arriving at UCSD, I have encountered profound goodwill from an engaged and insightful scholarly cohort. Bob Edelman read multiple iterations of this work, including in the dissertation phase, making helpful suggestions all along the way. Christine Hunefeldt, Ramón Gutiérrez, Eric Van Young, Danny Vickers, Michael Bernstein, and Paul Pickowicz provided important assistance in negotiating the transition to faculty life in the University of California system. Nayan Shah, Tak Fujitani, Dave Gutiérrez, and Stefan Tanaka provided generous intellectual feedback, critical professional advice, copious sports commentary, and places to sleep during my transition from Los Angeles to San Diego. Jody Blanco, Fatima El-Tayeb, Yen Le Espiritu, Ross Frank, Rosemary George, Jin-Kyung Lee, Curtis Marez, Stephanie Smallwood, Shelley Streeby, and Lisa Yoneyama read much of this book, and I benefited greatly from their kind assistance.

Ken Wissoker drank many a cup of conference coffee in the course of shepherding this work to completion, and I am honored by and appreciative of his assistance and interest. I also thank the two anonymous readers he selected, whose comments immeasurably strengthened the final version.

Most important, my deepest love goes out to family and friends who have provided tireless encouragement. My parents, Carolyn and Michael Widener, convinced me early on that the past was a source of power and strength. Their encouragement, along with that of Edra Widener, has been unwavering. My brothers, Michael and Benjamin, have shared far more than their own ideas about art, and I am grateful to both. For Sara Johnson, my colleague, partner, and friend; boundless love, endless respect, and tremendous appreciation. I hope that you'll find your voice in here as well. Finally, since I don't have the words, I hope that life itself will grant me the opportunity to show Julián and Amaya the love I have for them.

An earlier version of chapter 3 appeared as "Writing Watts: Budd Schulberg, the Watts Writers Workshop, and the War on Poverty," *Journal of Urban History* 34, no. 4 (May 2008): 665–87.

Introduction

ACTS OF CULTURE, OR, MAYBE
THE PEOPLE WOULD BE THE TIMES

Qui et quels nous sommes?
Admirable question!
—AIMÉ CÉSAIRE

It's not what you look like,
when you're doing, what you're doing
it's what you're doing, when you're doing
what you look like you're doing.
—CHARLES WRIGHT AND THE
WATTS 103RD STREET RHYTHM BAND

This is a book about art and revolution. More specifically, it traces the interplay between efforts to develop a consciously black art and the broader African American liberation struggle. Set in Los Angeles between the Second
World War and the explosion of widespread rioting following the Rodney
King verdicts five decades later, *Black Arts West* frames the transformation of
the postwar city through an analysis of the role played by black artists and by
contrasting visions of African American culture. Taking the lives and the
products of writers, visual artists, musicians, and filmmakers as autonomous
realms of politics and as sites where material, economic, and social challenges
interconnect, *Black Arts West* assesses black efforts to forge a meaningful and
comprehensive freedom in twentieth-century urban America. Accordingly,
the narrative that follows is not meant as a comprehensive indexing of local
artists or cultural organizations or of the works they produced.[1] Indeed, any
number of subjects explored only briefly in this book, including the Inner City

Cultural Center, St. Elmo's Village, and the works of the Watts Prophets, deserve full-length monographs. Rather than offering a descriptive encyclopedic index, *Black Arts West* tracks how through the conscious activity of people—labor, in other words—the arts moved to the forefront of a multi-generational struggle for social change. With a focus on the content and form of cultural production as well as on the processes of engagement and organization by successive generations of black artists based in Los Angeles, this book presents both a cultural history of a social movement and a social history of a cultural movement.

Between 1942 and 1992, multiple visions of the politics of black culture took hold in Los Angeles. Arising over the course of a half-century, a top-down and instrumentalist approach premised on a politics of inclusionary representation encountered a parallel, and at times opposed, vision of community-based cultural politics focused on creative autonomy, collective organization, and the erasure of the border between art and life. Operating as distinct approaches to the uses of culture, each of these perspectives ultimately corresponded to and represented the interests of different segments of the black population. Exploring the postwar freedom struggle through the lens of expressive culture thus offers a critical vantage point for understanding the unfolding of both racial unity and class conflict among black Americans.

This book can be seen as two tales rolled into one. The first studies how successive organizations and individuals came to regard the arts as a central component of the black freedom struggle. The second narrative thread examines the disjuncture between the programmatic mobilization of African American culture, occasionally by artists but more commonly by outside forces, and the vision of an avant-garde emerging from and oriented toward the black working class. As Los Angeles changed from an aggressively parochial collection of small cities into a self-defined "global metropolis," contrasting solutions for regional socio-racial problems repeatedly found articulation in debates concerning black culture. Whether committed to racist exclusion, the managed inclusion of dissident nonwhite populations, or the search for radical social transformation, a wide range of political forces, including the entertainment industry, affluent liberal whites, black nationalists, elected officials, federal bureaucrats, and police agencies, saw consciously "black" art either as a possible pillar of, or as a threat to, the development of a particular vision of the postwar city.

Bringing together these viewpoints reminds us of the changes and continuities present in African American politics after the Second World War. In contrast to housing discrimination, electoral politics, or even police brutality, each of which emerged as a critical issue at a particular historical juncture, a concern with the politics of art consistently stood at the forefront of black politics after 1941. After decades during which the cinematic presentation of blackface minstrelsy had served as a major source of national integration for white Americans, the newfound contradiction between "democracy and burnt cork" constituted both a critical aspect of the black search for "double victory" and a precondition of altered postwar social relations between blacks and whites.[2] While wartime challenges to Hollywood were national in scope, Southern California occupied a critical locale where prominent sojourners such as Chester Himes and Duke Ellington joined the local civil-rights establishment in seeking a new relationship between race and representation.

Expressive culture was no less central in subsequent years. Following the Watts riot of 1965, the arts became one dimension of a wide-ranging critique of American society. In the context of a crowded field of black radical organizations, moreover, debates concerning the relationship of culture and politics emerged as a singularly divisive issue among activists committed to revolutionary struggle and radical change. While these debates waned with the eclipse of black militancy during the 1970s, cultural politics continued as a charged symbolic space throughout the multiple mayoral administrations of Tom Bradley. Between 1973 and 1993, black control over City Hall led to the development of a multicultural municipal cultural policy—described by one observer as "a gleam in Mayor Bradley's inaugural eye"[3]—that helped deflect popular pressure, masking both the economic bifurcation of black Los Angeles and the discontent of other minority populations while helping to preserve the urban peace necessary for the rise of a global city. It is critical to realize that regional economic planning and political life during the 1970s unfolded within a context in which the needs of a mobilized black community factored openly into the calculations of politicians, developers, and planners. In taking the half-century after 1942 as a period in which expressive culture served as one of the recurring issues around which local politics revolved, *Black Arts West* incorporates the idea of *cultural policy* as a central theme.

Yet this "cultural front" in the broader push for black freedom and equality is only one side of the story, for the effort to place black art in the service of black Angelenos played out differently among artists than among civil-rights crusaders, black militants, or municipal officials. A second aspect of the politicization of black culture in Los Angeles therefore concerns the rise of a distinct regional Black Arts Movement originating in the efforts of wartime cultural activists, rooted in the black working class, and characterized by an interrelated search for artistic autonomy and a persistent struggle to improve the living and working conditions of local black artists, musicians, and writers. Spread across a succession of intergenerational, overlapping groups of artists, the Black Arts Movement in Southern California constituted far more than an artistic affiliate of local civil-rights or black-power efforts. Encompassing leaders and a mass base, ideological debates and organized political campaigns, black arts activity must be seen as a social movement in its own right. A quantitative methodology would certainly concur, since the number of participants in local black arts organizations exceeded the active membership of organizations such as the National Association for the Advancement of Colored People, the Black Panther Party, or the US Organization. As informal groupings of artists increasingly turned toward formal bodies, new ideas concerning art, racial identity, and the institutional position of African American artists began to emerge. As a result, dozens of new collectives appeared, including well-known institutions such as the Watts Writers Workshop and Inner City Cultural Center and less well-known groups such as the Black Arts Council, the New Art Jazz Ensemble, and the journal *Nigger Uprising*. In following organizational histories, artistic ideas, and political struggles, *Black Arts West* explores the interrelationship between collective organization and developing ideas about content and form. In contrast to the narrative of arts policy that shaped the external mobilization of black culture, a focus on community-based cultural production raises the theme of *creative community*, or the inherent social dimension present in the production of art.[4]

Expressive culture is commonly acknowledged as an integral dimension of the postwar freedom struggle. Too often, however, the role of black artists is limited to a symbolic affiliation in which prominent figures such as Muhammad Ali and James Brown are taken as emblematic of a broader moment. Freedom songs, dashikis, Afros, and other markers of the 1960s are seen as contributive, rather than constitutive, parts of the period. This is particularly the case with the Black Arts Movement, which, alongside its spatial and temporal reduction to New York and Chicago in 1965–75, is often defined as "the cultural wing" of the Black Power Movement. Yet James Smethurst's astute observation that "one could just as easily say that Black Power was the political wing of the Black Arts Movement" can be extended across the breadth of the postwar period.[5] Doing so restores a history that questions the stark periodization between the Civil Rights Movement and the Black Power Movement, as well as the ideological division between integration and separation.

Indeed, greater attention to the lives of those who participate in social movements often forces us to reconsider our basic categories of analysis. Take William Grant Still. Among the foremost composers in American history, the redoubtable race man was simultaneously a crusader for the elimination of barriers within the expanding entertainment industry, a proponent of a racially thematic music within the compositional structures of European art music, and a participant in some of the initial community arts projects in South Los Angeles. As Steven Isoardi's insightful biography demonstrates, the pianist Horace Tapscott offers a similarly irreducible example.[6] A product of legendary South Los Angeles musical circles, the founder of one of the nation's first jazz collectives, and an active participant in the organizational unfolding of what James Forman called "the high tide of black resistance," Tapscott's five decades of cultural work belie the facile divisions of integration or nationalism, music and politics, or art and life.

Part of restoring the complexity and variety of black politics and culture during this time requires that serious attention be paid to the art that emerged. A main task of this volume consists, therefore, in assessing how the politicization of black life—or, better yet, how the massification of black political life—after the Second World War spread across various creative genres. Ideas about black liberation diffused differently across distinct artistic forms. Artists working in primarily narrative forms comparatively more open to realist aesthetics, such as poets and playwrights, found different ways to explore, perform, and articulate black radical aesthetics than sculptors or instrumental musicians did. At the same time, a sense of common questions, touching on everything from institutional placement to audience reaction, ensured that spaces for imagining a new politics of black culture across and between forms existed, as well. Thus, *Black Arts West* takes up themes raised by scholars who go beyond considering the Black Arts moment as a purely literary phenomenon to show the centrality of jazz and visual art in the development of art about and for liberation.

This "inter-artistic" view helps reframe the parameters of what one of the most authoritative voices in African American arts and letters, Henry Louis Gates Jr., has proclaimed as "the shortest and least successful" literary movement in African American history.[7] This assessment requires that we limit the Black Arts Movement to a relatively small circle of writers active in a small number of cities during a rigidly defined period of time. However, as Robin Kelley so aptly puts it, "If we can agree that the Black Arts Movement is not defined by race riots and dashikis but by a self-conscious collective effort to promote black art for black communities, art about liberation and freedom," then we are poised to unlock the politics of a story that is broader geographically, aesthetically, and intellectually than previously thought.[8]

The view that artistic expression serves as a place for organized politics is not without controversy, as, indeed, is the very notion of an identifiably "black" art. It may help clarify matters to note that the notion of "black" employed in this book is not a biological one but, rather, a mediated and contested category developed within the constantly changing exchange between discourse, law, custom, popular practice, lived experience, and everyday life. Mike Sell observes that it is possible to see blackness itself as a form of critical practice.[9] As the middle section of the book shows, ideas regarding the links between community, creativity, and race were constantly debated, theorized, and explored by local musicians, visual artists, and political activists. This alone may do little to mollify those who regard any discussion that links a racialized community with identifiable traditions or beliefs as an exercise in wrongheaded essentialism. You can't please everybody. The welcome proliferation of studies on African American art, poetry, music, and theater, however, suggests a process of historical recovery and a plurality of methodological and conceptual approaches that has done much to transcend what Kobena Mercer referred to in the transatlantic context as "the structural underdevelopment of a viable framework for black arts criticism."[10]

Central to my contribution to this critical literature is a cross-generic framing of popularly directed cultural production that privileges the voices of artists, as opposed to formal criticism of works of art. Although my analysis incorporates the aesthetic concerns of visual, literary, and musicological criticism with the biographical information common to historians, I have sought to extend Eric Porter's observation that "there is still a need for sustained, historical discussions of what African American musicians have said publicly about their music, their positions as artists . . . and the broader social and cultural implications of this" to the visual, literary, and cinematic cohorts of black Los Angeles.[11]

Privileging the ideas of politically engaged artists opens a window into an intellectual history that is closely tied to the social history of postwar black Los Angeles, for ideas about art and community, participation and politics functioned, much as Gramsci argued in his now famous terminology of the "organic intellectual," as a kind of lodestone for black radical activity. And while it may seem pedantic to point out either that artists are intellectuals or that intellectuals have ideas, focusing on how various community-oriented artists thought about what they were doing helps expose "the limits of criticism" and, more important, helps clarify the scope and stakes of attempts to take the terrain of creativity as a site of political struggle.[12]

Black artists in California developed a largely abstract, non-representational, and freeform vision of black art that connected avant-garde jazz, assemblage and "junk" art, jazz poetry, and experimental neo-realist film. Invoking thematic and conceptual tropes familiar to black audiences, these improvisations of subjectivity allowed a flexible path toward rethinking the borders of creativity and community. This is not to claim Los Angeles as the only location in which these ideas, experiments, or artistic forms developed, although the geographic particularities of Southern California do enter the story repeatedly. Nor is it to argue that all artists of African descent living in Los Angeles during this time were involved in producing a racially specific or community-oriented art.[13] Rather, it is to contend that the black liberation movement operated as both a generalized structure of feeling and a direct stimulus toward producing "street theaters with school drop-outs, junk hunts down the railroad track with pre-schoolers, back yard paintings with amateurs and professionals together" —or, put more directly, what the sculptor Noah Purifoy summarized as the "conviction that Art was an effective tool for change."[14]

Raymond Williams's notion of a social formation helps clarify the politics of this moment. In thinking through a method for exploring the politics of creative endeavors, Williams argued for the study of "social formations," which he took as "simultaneously artistic forms and social locations."[15] With its shared focus on the development of a mass-oriented and consciously black art and its parallel struggle for institutional autonomy and community control, the Black Arts Movement illuminates precisely the link between aesthetic and political radicalism. Acknowledging the centrality of art to postwar black politics, as opposed to considering culture as a facet, wing, or tributary, brings into sharper relief Harold Cruse's belief that "radical creative intellectuals" comprised a class force capable of negating the developing capitalist cultural economy. In a world where you can find 30,000 retail outlets in the People's Republic of China that sell Kobe Bryant jerseys and where Fashion Institute of Technology students slip uptown to spy on emerging sartorial trends, this remains one of the most trenchant summary statements regarding the strategic importance of African American expressive culture to the broader enterprise of black radical politics.[16] In much the same way that the program of the Organization of Afro-American Unity drawn up by John Henrik Clark and Malcolm X combined education, politics, culture, and economic affairs, Cruse argued that any move toward autonomist black politics would have to take culture, politics, and economics as one.

The positions articulated by Williams and Cruse are critical in part because they highlight the materiality of culture and therefore serve to remind us that cultural politics form an integral, rather than an ancillary, dimension of class struggle. Both Williams and Cruse strove to replace a vulgar bifurcation between base and superstructure with a more layered recognition that economic, political, and cultural matters have become increasingly intertwined amid what the more optimistic among us refer to as "late" capitalism. Several brief examples from the present study may illustrate the point. In the decade after the Second World War, musicians waged a prolonged struggle against racial segregation within the local musicians' unions. These battles were both symbolic, in that they sought to remove visible barriers to the inclusion of blacks at a time of civil-rights ferment, and material, in that membership in the white union local was considered a precondition for finding work in Hollywood at precisely a moment when television, recorded music, and the expansion of radio were combining to curtail sharply the financial position of many musicians. On another occasion, a car club affiliated with a local youth gang formed a police-monitoring project that would serve as the primary inspiration for the Black Panther Party's better-known activities several hundred miles to the north. Still later, the municipal administration of Tom Bradley developed a range of public symbols of multicultural inclusion, including the 1984 Olympiad, the expansion and consolidation of municipal cultural affairs, and the funding of ethnically based museums. These initiatives hid a shift in resources away from the black working class and toward the interests of corporate redevelopment. In each moment, both the creation of alternative cultural institutions and the cultural critique of collectively organized artists offered a popular challenge to the prevailing status quo. If, as the sociologist Dick Hebdige explains, this cultural critique often functioned as an "oblique" or hidden transcript of refusal, such is the nature of counter-hegemonic struggle. Besides, as the image of the customized cars of the Community Alert Patrol cruising along behind the police suggests, the critique was not always particularly oblique.

Thinking about black art as a place of social struggle is important for a number of reasons. In the first place, doing so facilitates the ongoing revision of African American history that seeks to transcend the spatial, temporal, and ideological partition of the postwar period into distinct and sealed moments characterized by the dual triads Southern/Civil Rights/1954–65 and Northern/Black Power/1965–75. As Jeanne Theoharis and Komozi Woodard argue persuasively, ignorance of the struggles of African Americans in the urban North and West during the 1940s and 1950s profoundly limits our understanding of the history and meaning of postwar black politics. By treating structural racism as a uniquely Southern phenomenon, one misses entirely the profundity of Northern struggles to secure basic rights to adequate housing, schools, physical safety, and transportation, if not voting rights and public accommodations. As a result, the reasons for the subsequent emergence of the Black Power Movement and, more important, the continuing salience of precisely those issues that enraged African Americans outside the South in the first place are elided by a national celebration of the self-correcting mechanisms of American democracy.[17]

Of course, the reframing of black politics away from North–South and black power–civil rights binaries can take place without using art or artists as the analytic frame. But expressive culture does provide unique paths for tracing the attempt to force "a white-dominated society to redistribute some of its power."[18] Consider the life and times of Nick Stewart, a veteran vaudevillian whose prewar success made him a part of Hollywood's small coterie of regularly working black talent. Stewart's zigzagging political trajectory saw him alternately invited to participate in patriotic wartime mobilizations, excoriated as an Uncle Tom for his participation in *Amos 'n' Andy* and Disney's *Song of the South*, and celebrated as a founder of Los Angeles's first black-owned theater company. His Ebony Showcase Theater, moreover, helped train such disparate voices as the revolutionary surrealist jazz poet Jayne Cortez; Judson Powell, co-founder and director of the Watts Towers Art Center; and the early hip hop avatars the Watts Prophets. Extending into the mid-1990s, a history of black theater and black politics told solely through his institutional and creative life would trace the shift from segregation through civil rights and black power and beyond into the rise and decline of local black municipal control. Within a solitary, ninety-nine seat non-Actor's Equity facility carved from an abandoned movie house, debates over racism in Hollywood, the necessity and limitations of integration, the existence of a specifically black culture, and the relationship between black-owned institutions, a predominantly white culture industry, and a surrounding black community—in short, the entirety of the relationship between African Americans and their host society in the postwar period—all come into focus as a continuing and evolving series of questions.

At the same time, the inclusion of creative personalities helps clarify the nature of black American social movements. Whether examining popular music or abstract painting, hairstyles or political rhetoric, expressive culture remains a pre-eminent arena of black particularity. Acknowledging that African Americans remain apart from the national polity in fundamental ways is a precondition for assessing the problems and possibilities of this particularity and for trying to think through what self-determination means in an urban, industrialized, multiracial, and globalized setting. If seemingly less acute a question than incarceration rates, the spread of HIV/AIDS, or the drowning of New Orleans, Aimé Césaire's seventy-five-year-old query remains an important point of departure at a moment when eloquent and prominent voices from across the political spectrum argue that the barriers that once divided African Americans from meaningful inclusion in the United States have essentially fallen away. Figures as ideologically divergent as Stanley Crouch, John McWhorter, William Julius Wilson, Paul Gilroy, and Adolph Reed have all, in their own way, urged us to move "beyond race."[19] Each has done so for different reasons. At the same time, all are united by their conviction that a contemporary politics of black self-determination is impossible. I disagree. An examination of creative community, cultural policy, and the cultural contours of class struggle offers one path toward recapturing what was alternately and simultaneously referred to as "nation time," "intercommunalism," and "community control."

Terms like these invoke a political vocabulary rooted in goals that emerged in the course of the radical self-activity of the black working class. Similarly, the rejection of "black" art, like the broader repudiation of black particularity of which it forms a part, constitutes an ideological position similarly loaded with class connotations. By class, it is important to note, I have in mind not a reductive focus that exclusively treats "points of production," or even exclusively labor, but the complex edifice of existence from which emerge "distinct and peculiarly formed sentiments, illusions, modes of thought and views of life."[20] Within this framework, it is possible to see "class" in terms specific to the historical experiences of African Americans.[21] To be sure, African Americans long ago began to generate language for talking about our internal schisms, perspectives, and ideas. Malcolm X's oft-repeated metaphor of house and field slaves offers one example; the equally familiar terms "ghetto" and "bourgie" add another. The narrative presented here follows a period in which black politics shifted from a cross-class alliance against racism to a sharp divergence along socioeconomic lines. Language and the broader expressive culture of which it is a part both reflected and shaped this bifurcation; thus, any study regarding the politics of black culture is simultaneously a study of class or, as one partisan put it, the effort "to fight, in the realm of ideas, philosophies, the arts, academia, the class struggle between oppressed and oppressor."[22]

Part of the conceptual utility of expressive culture lies in the issue of totality, the way that the questions raised by a social analysis of cultural production force us to reassess the limits of our perspectives and the gaps of our historical and political knowledge. "If there is no struggle," Frederick Douglass once said, "there is no progress." We can add to this: If there is no study, there is no struggle. Part of the lesson that emerges from this study is that we have ignored or misunderstood the critical contributions that female artists made to the development of a working-class black cultural radicalism in Southern California. We might recall that the first community-arts project in black Los Angeles was founded by a black woman, Frances Williams. We might also revisit the pioneering organizational work of figures such as Ridhiana Saunders, Miriam Matthews, Samella Lewis, Edna Stewart, Ruth Waddy, Beulah Woodard, and Linda Hill. We might reassess the critical theoretical, intellectual, and creative interventions of artists such as Betye Saar and Jayne Cortez. We might ask what it means that the critical figures in the longest-lasting community-arts projects more often than not worked closely with women who rarely show up in oral history transcripts, career retrospectives, biographies, or liner notes. And we might ask what role the masculine presentation of blackness played during this period, whether in film, in literature, or in the politics of style.

On a smaller level, *Black Arts West* is meant as a contribution to the expanding scholarly literature on African American Los Angeles. Southern California is a highly specific site in which the city acts as one character within the larger story. Others have shown how in locales such as Chicago; Queens, New York; and the Mississippi Delta, the social geography shapes both the forms of domination and the arts of resistance.[23] This is both a spatial and temporal process. As Michael Denning argues, tracing moments of cultural insurgency through the use of topical works requires a broader history that seeks to recreate the historical moment as a whole.[24] In the case of Los Angeles, politics and culture came to intersect, overlap, and combine in particularly vibrant and durable ways.

This was true for electoral and radical politics alike. Tom Bradley was among the first African Americans elected to head a major American city. His twenty-year tenure at the helm of Los Angeles, the country's second-largest city, makes him the longest-serving black chief executive—and one of the longest-serving mayors of any color—in American history. In a city where black voters never exceeded a fifth of the total electorate, Bradley offered a vision of black leadership unlike that taking place in other major cities with black municipal leadership.[25] As we will see, the arts played a fundamental role in municipal governance during his tenure, providing a shield against popular claims from below and facilitating a regime of accumulation and development as Los Angeles began to orient itself as a center of global investment and finance.

Los Angeles helps us to rethink the place of the arts within the realm of radical politics, as well. Los Angeles produced one of the country's largest and most influential chapters of the Black Panther Party, in part because the Los Angeles branch faced challenges that made it perhaps even more representative of the national conditions faced by the party than the Oakland headquarters. As Ward Churchill observed, more than half of all Black Panther Party members killed in the United States died in Los Angeles at the hands of police.[26] Southern California was also the base for the party's primary ideological opponents, the self-identified cultural nationalist us Organization. More important, the local history of black radical activity goes well beyond these two organizations, and this work seeks to highlight the widespread resonance and organizational multiplicity of black urban radicalism by tracing the cultural politics of less well-known local groups.

Proceeding from the assumption that Southern California deserves to be seen as an important site of black politics, *Black Arts West* asks what a history of black cultural production looks like from the vantage point of California. New York and Chicago are most typically seen as cultural capitals of Afro-America, but the interaction between demographics (mass migration, spatial concentration, and the city's multiracial makeup), the presence of the entertainment industry, and the persistent contradiction between California's shining self-image and its less savory reality altered the contours of black cultural production in Los Angeles as surely as the nexus between the auto industry and urban Detroit helped shape the music of Motown. Hollywood created opportunities and struggles unlike those that community-based black artists faced elsewhere, while the distinct spatial attributes of Southern California made an identifiable mark on black cultural forms as distinct as film and avant-garde jazz.

More generally, the intense segregation of the early postwar period facilitated the development of a black arts cohort focused on a relatively specific part of the city. Much as the factors of physical distance, the lack of public transportation, and regional political separation between Los Angeles City and Los Angeles County impeded the sorts of Third World politics seen in the San Francisco Bay Area, the infamous Southern California sprawl helped ensure the existence of parallel, and often unconnected, avant-gardes. Los Angeles reveals no figure comparable to Amiri Baraka or Bob Kaufman, capable of linking the overwhelmingly white Venice Beach beats, Ferus Gallery artists, or Echo Park bohemian enclaves with the emergent critique of black cultural radicalism in the late 1950s. Rather, Los Angeles facilitated the development of individuals such as Horace Tapscott, John Outterbridge, and Jayne Cortez, whose artistic production, political organizing, and teaching energy were aimed squarely at black Angelenos and took place largely, though never exclusively, beyond the attention, interest, or presence of politicized white experimentalists.

The inclusion of Los Angeles fills certain gaps within the study of African American life and history; the inclusion of black art helps round out the cultural history of Southern California. Richard Cándida Smith's landmark exploration of California arts and letters highlights the salience of race during the postwar period in that it points to certain stark differences between California's white and black avant-gardes. Part of the utility of Cándida Smith's exploration of Pacific modernism lies in his ability to note critical regional distinctions without arguing for Californian exceptionalism.[27] Yet whereas his predominantly white subjects pursued a mythopoetic articulation of the creative act as an individual antidote to the dehumanizing rationality of the atomic age, the successive generations of the black avant-garde sought to define creativity through a collective process and communitarian orientation. Where one group found private truths and self-narration, the other fought for collectivity and self-determination. Put another way, one group sought to interpret a world, while the other sought to change it.

It is perhaps worth dwelling for a moment on the political implications of restoring the historical distinction between California's white and black avant-gardes. As George Lewis's insightful study of what he terms "Afrological" and "Eurological" approaches to improvised music illustrates, different conceptual approaches, performance strategies, and valuations of lived individual and collective experience guarantee a gap between, for example, a John Cage and a Charlie Parker.[28] The concerns articulated by black musicians and identified by Lewis recall the interventions of several writers who highlight the limitations of adopting the culturally specific moniker "avant-garde" in relation to black artists, and, more important, who assert the need to see black culture and black people beyond the framework provided by European intellectual, political, and aesthetic models.[29] These aesthetic interventions, building as they do on works such as V. P. Franklin's landmark study of black cultural resistance, provide valuable insights that I have sought to adapt to Southern California.[30] Bound on the one hand by Ellington's comments advocating a vision of black music (and life) as integral to, yet apart from, the larger sweep of American existence and on the other hand by the desperate and joyous challenge of resurrecting community art in the aftermath of the 1992 rebellion, *Black Arts West* offers one case study in the cultural construction of a broader black radical tradition.

The final framing of *Black Arts West* engages the emerging scholarly litera-ture on black Los Angeles within the broader historiography of the city at large.[31] The book traces a history of popular struggle in a city that has shifted from "exception to paradigm" in the study of contemporary urban life.[32] The history of this politics is best understood relationally, with black politics placed within the context of a regional history where, as Carey McWilliams noted sixty years ago, "for over a hundred years, two cultural traditions—the Spanish-Mexican and the Anglo-American—have been in conflict."[33] Subse-quent scholarship only confirms the continuing aspects of this cultural con-testation, as well as its economic, political, and social dimensions.[34] That political struggles of black Southern Californians have taken place within a context of larger struggles for social justice in which the region's predomi-nantly Mexican American population plays a decisive role is axiomatic. Yet, for many observers, recent events have seemed to suggest that the rise of Latino power presupposes a coterminous drop in black access, whether to City Hall or to the hallways of the city's most storied African American schools. Given the obvious parallels between the elections of 1973 and 2005, each of which brought municipal leadership of a new color to the fore, it is perhaps unsurprising that many observers have placed the half million African Ameri-can Angelenos between two equally undesirable options: as either bystanders anxiously watching a political upsurge from the sidelines, or as ambivalent defenders of an atavistic status quo, mobilized for the electoral defense of the systematic under-representation and political exclusion of people of Latin American descent.

Yet Noah Purifoy's description of the parallels between black and Chicano cultural radicalism reveals a third way. Claiming, "It is our belief that the Community Art movement in East L.A. was also stimulated by rebellion against the authorities, as was the Watts Riot," Purifoy once sought to remind an audience of the common, if often separate, history of insurgent politics waged by Southern California's black and brown populations.[35] At times, as Laura Pulido, Scot Kurashige, and George Sanchez demonstrate, these streams have come together.[36] Political convergences, Luis Alvarez and Anthony Macías remind us, have been both anticipated and accompanied by patterns of cultural contact.[37] At other moments, postwar Los Angeles seems to resemble post-emancipation Guyana, where, as Walter Rodney wrote, "The existing aspects of cultural convergence were insufficiently developed to contribute decisively to solidarity among the working people of the two major race groups."[38]

And so, as an inquiry into one aspect of the "semi-autonomous sets of working class struggles" in Los Angeles, it is my hope that readers, particularly those outside the academy, will find themes that resonate today.[39] For the story of black cultural radicalism in Los Angeles is emphatically *not* a celebratory paean to the affective dimensions of racialized space, or even the particular importance of studying black politics through the analytic lens of expressive culture. Rather, this attempt to explore the contours of popular politics suggests a cautionary note, not simply or even principally for black people but for the city's emerging demographic majority as well. Misrepresentation and exclusion by Hollywood, the seemingly unending effort to find resources for community-based projects, and the pitfalls of having municipal leadership of the same ostensible "color" are ongoing contradictions between access and power, between representation and popular sovereignty, that touch brown as well as black lives. Indeed, if one conclusion of this volume is that the Bradley years ought to be seen, at least from the vantage point of the black working class, as a disaster, one potential implication of this study is that the subsequent rise of Latino electoral power confirms a certain German social scientist's observation about precisely how history repeats itself. By taking up the story of how the contradictions between popular pressure and electoral representation, between the street and City Hall, and between racial unity and class division all played out in South Los Angeles over the course of five decades, this book forms part of the larger, ongoing, and unresolved challenge of excavating the future in Los Angeles.

ORGANIZATION

Black Arts West is divided into three parts. Organized both thematically and chronologically, each section corresponds to a particular moment in the political history of black Los Angeles. Tracing the quarter century of activity between 1940 and 1965, Part I follows efforts to mobilize black culture in the service of racial reform against the backdrop of widespread urban discrimination. Beginning with a discussion of the Los Angeles premier of Duke Ellington's musical *Jump for Joy*, chapter 1 explores how the political instability generated by the Second World War provided an opening for a wide-ranging debate regarding the representation of African Americans by the motion-picture industry. Figures such as Chester Himes, William Grant Still, Clarence Muse, and Hattie McDaniel occupy the stage, contesting the most appropriate ways to change the representational and material circumstances of black artists. Set between 1950 and 1955, chapter 2 notes a shift from representation to access as unionized musicians, a prominent black vaudevillian, and a mostly informal grouping of black visual artists challenged segregation within the entertainment industry and throughout the city as a whole. Chapter 3 analyzes the rise and fall of cultural liberalism in the aftermath of the Watts riot of 1965, arguing that efforts to link working-class black writers and the political goals of integration and social peace revealed contradictions that found both aesthetic and organizational expression.

Part II takes up these contradictions more fully by shifting the focus away from a cultural politics of racial reform toward a community-based cultural critique. Set in the aftermath of the Watts riot, this section charts the period between 1965 and 1973. These were critical years, when, as Gerald Horne notes, a new leadership with a mass base fought to secure a wide-ranging series of changes in how black people lived; how they were policed, educated, and housed; and for whom they were willing to die.[40] Chapter 4 explores the links between free jazz, community arts, and black power through an analysis of Pan Afrikan People's Arkestra and its co-founder Horace Tapscott. The "Ark" combined aesthetic and political radicalism as it mobilized professionals and amateurs alike, pursued novel approaches to music making, and formed direct links with nationalist organizations. Chapter 5 further explores the idea of a local Black Arts Movement by showing how visual artists developed new ideas, new organizations, and new struggles within the context of widespread local urban radicalism. Artist-run organizations, assemblage art, and community-based cultural projects are the hallmarks of this cohort. The section's final chapter highlights the centrality of cultural politics for a number of black-power organizations active in Southern California in the decade after the Watts riot. Focusing particular attention on the city's two largest such groups, it traces the cultural projects, ideological debates, and style politics of the Black Panther

Party and the US Organization, exploring how similar ideas regarding aesthetics and politics developed between these bitter rivals.

The last section of the book traces the transformation of black cultural politics during the two-decade reign of African American Mayor Thomas Bradley. It represents a shift in focus, as the narrative tacks away from the arts as a site of community empowerment with artists in the fore to a more ambiguous contest over the role of black art in the governance of the multi-ethnic city. Inspired by Jayne Cortez's poem "Festivals and Funerals," this section juxtaposes radically different approaches toward black cultural politics that emanated from above and below. The post-1973 period saw heightening contradictions between an economically prosperous and politically enfranchised black middle class and the declining fortunes of black working people. Chapter 7 argues that the Bradley administration developed a co-optive multiculturalism as one means by which this intracommunal gap might be bridged.

Chapter 8 traces one response to the widening differences between African Americans under conditions of economic restructuring. In contrast to the celebration of diversity that diffused outward from City Hall, black film-makers critiqued the conditions of life in South Los Angeles in ways that spoke to the emotional, political, familial, and economic implosion of the black working class. Three films from across the breadth of the 1973–93 period, Charles Burnett's *Killer of Sheep* (1977), Billy Woodberry's *Bless Their Little Hearts* (1984), and the Hughes brothers' *Menace II Society* (1993), form the basis of this chapter. Taken together, these films suggest a distinct relationship between class and masculinity during a moment of widespread displacement and social alienation. The epilogue extends these themes, tracking the multifaceted attempt to generate a sense of community in the aftermath of the 1992 rioting, the dissolution of racially homogenous black neighborhoods, and the ossification of class cleavages among African Americans. My conclusion explores the afterlives of the Black Arts Movement to suggest how people, history, and communication, rather than place, might constitute a point of departure for a "post-civil-rights" liberation politics.

Before moving on, an explanation of the title of this introduction may be in order. The phrase "Acts of Culture" is taken from the 1970 speech "National Liberation and Culture" by Amilcar Cabral, one of the foremost thinkers of the place of culture within revolutionary struggle.[41] Cabral's twin observations that culture constitutes an integral part of revolutionary politics and his caution to recall "the decisive significance of the *class character* of culture in the development of the liberation struggle" suggest fundamental insights that I have sought to engage and, in part, adopt. The subtitle is of more local origin. "Maybe the People Would Be the Times" is the title of a song released in 1967 by the enigmatic psychedelic musician Arthur Lee, a figure stuck somewhere between Bakunin and Bukowski whose dystopian lyrics and experimental sounds suggested, a generation before N.W.A., that the City of Angels was far, far less than it was cracked up to be—especially for black people. Cut short by multiple felony convictions, Lee's career fits well within a *noir*-ish continuum bookended by figures such as Chester Himes and Easy-E.

At the same time, the idea that "Maybe the People Would Be the Times" offers a kind of black North American response to the subjectivist call of Cabral's dictum that his native Guinea-Bissau offered a fruitful terrain for armed struggle despite the lack of typical guerrilla terrain. Much as Cabral claimed, "Our people are our mountains," Lee's title describes the *how* of black revolution in North America. To the extent that a common hope in the possibility of subjective revolutionary conditions animated postwar revolutionists from Paris to Peking and from Harlem to Havana, Lee's phrase suggests the possibility that human activity might just be enough to effect fundamental change in the absence of objectively favorable circumstances. And so it is between Cabral's revolutionary optimism and the creative destruction of Arthur Lee with which we begin.

Cultural
Democracy
in the Racial
Metropolis

1

HOLLYWOOD SCUFFLE   The Second World War, Los Angeles,
and the Politics of Wartime Representation

I would rather handle everything that the Germans,
Italians, and Japanese can throw at me than to face
the trouble I see in the Negro Question.
—GENERAL GEORGE C. MARSHALL, 1943

The musical began on a Thursday. A hot Thursday. With the temperature in
the high eighties and humidity to match, a capacity crowd that wrapped
around the corner of Olympic Boulevard and Hill Street sweltered in weather
more common to Manhattan than Los Angeles. Decked to the nines, the
racially mixed crowd stood waiting in line for a performance whose blend of
sarcasm and swing also would have been more familiar to the connoisseurs of
the cosmopolitan East than the ambivalent urbanites of prewar Los Angeles.
But show up they did. Los Angeles was changing, and even with the outbreak
of war five months away, the material and social transformation of Southern
California had already begun affecting the cultural contours of local life.
    Such were conditions for the opening, on 10 July 1941, of Edward Kennedy
Ellington's new musical *Jump for Joy*. Featuring a star-studded, all-black cast,
compositions designed to evoke the breadth of African American aural history, and satirical lyrics meant "to take Uncle Tom out of the theater," the
musical signaled the realization of a longstanding ambition on the composer's
part.[1] An expansive production that included more than a dozen writers and
the stage, costume, and lighting expertise of an elite cadre of Hollywood
technical personnel, Ellington's showcase of the "sun-tanned tenth of the
nation" served as his initial foray into socially themed work. Indeed, as a
number of biographers note, *Jump for Joy* provided the opportunity for El-

lington to combine interests in creative control, racial pride, and entry into the fold of American mass entertainment.[2]

Offering a simultaneous critique of Hollywood and Broadway, *Jump for Joy* combined aesthetic and political ideas. Ellington's score blended social realism and satire, as in the number "I've Got a Passport from Georgia (and I'm Going to the U.S.A.)," while the overall sensibility of the production, described by the composer as "highly intellectual, but entertaining," sought to convey an insistence on dignity that black audiences and artists had sought for decades. Audiences were treated to an unusually serious portrayal of black romance between the co-stars Dorothy Dandridge and Herb Jeffries, while in the musical's penultimate number, "Made to Order," the veteran vaudevillians Pot, Pan, and Skillet celebrated and signified on both zoot culture and African American religiosity. Blending the height of urban style with the traditional time of year during which African Americans linked conspicuous consumption and Christian faith, the sketch featured "Mr. Luscious Beebe's" negotiations with "Fly & Dicty, Lapellists and Drapists" over the terms of his Easter suit. As the rhythm section punctuated with drum rolls and cymbal crashes, the tailors agreed to produce a "zoot suit with a reet pleat and a stuff cuff and a drape shape, shoulders extended, eighteen as intended; padding—Gibraltar, shiny as a halter; streamlined alignment; pipeline the pocket; drape it, drop it, sock it and lock it—fifty-three at the knee and seven at the cuff." The tailors then asked, "What color cloth do you want to cover your hide," to which Potts replied, "Daddy, let the rainbow be your guide!" The latter comment set up the concluding number: an Easter parade that featured pastel costumes by the Academy Award-winning costume designer René Hubert, as well as "blinding" zoot suits on Pot, Pan, and Skillet that led to uproarious applause.[3]

The show's musical selections reflected an expansive vision of African American musical culture. The singer Herb Jeffries infused his ballads with gospel inflections, while Ellington summoned the bluesman Joe Turner from Chicago to add further musical depth. Upon his arrival, Turner moved into Central Avenue's legendary Dunbar Hotel. Having commandeered an entire floor for himself and his sidemen, Ellington dictated compositions to Billy Strayhorn from inside the bath while Ben Webster, Sonny Greer, and Ray Nance played alongside from inside their rooms. Ellington's compositions ran the gamut from swing numbers and waltzes to proto-Middle Eastern/Latin jazz fusions written by the trombonist Juan Tizol, while vocals included the soon-to-become-standards "Brown-Skin Gal (in the Calico Gown)" and "I've Got It Bad (and That Ain't Good)."[4]

Musical breadth and innovative staging aside, countering common images of African Americans remained the primary aim of the production. Although Ellington described *Jump for Joy* within a longstanding African American tradition of dissimilation, claiming that the work "was well done because we included everything we wanted to say without saying it," the musical was unusual precisely as a result of its outspoken nature.[5] One scene featured "Uncle Tom" on his deathbed, wasting away despite repeated adrenaline injections from film and theater executives desperate to prolong his life. Another skit featured an African "king" and "queen" dressed in western finery. Informed by a courier that an expedition from America had arrived in search of the origins of jazz, the king laments to his wife, "We shall have to get out our leopard skins again."[6] The final number of the first act, entitled "Uncle Tom's Cabin Is a Drive-In Now," suggested the demographic, economic, and cultural shifts taking place on the eve of the war. In lyrics that connected black migration and mobility with Southern California's emerging car culture and perhaps the most famous intersection in moviemaking, the song proclaimed:

> It used to be a chicken shack in Caroline
> But since they moved it up to Hollywood and Vine,
> They paid off the mortgage with barbecued chow
> 'Cause Uncle Tom's Cabin is a drive-in now.[7]

Another skit featured the dancer Paul White followed across the stage by a white ghost that he frightened to death by turning around to shout, "Boo!" White had long danced as the "black" shadow of the white bandleader Ted Lewis, and his skit offered the veteran dancer an opportunity to demolish a humiliating previous role. As White's number ended, Ellington addressed the crowd. The composer's words spoke explicitly to the challenge that black artists and activists would face in confronting Hollywood during the coming war:

> Now, every Broadway colored show,
> According to tradition,
> Must be a carbon copy
> Of the previous edition,
> With the truth discreetly muted,
> And the accent on the brasses.
> The punch that should be present
> In a colored show, alas, is
> Disinfected with magnolia

And dripping with molasses.
In other words,
We're shown to you
Through Stephen Foster's glasses.[8]

Although Ellington had been discussing plans for a socially themed work with Paul Robeson and Langston Hughes, among others, since at least 1936, the specific impetus for *Jump for Joy* came as a result of more or less spontaneous discussions that took place amid after-hours jam sessions held in Culver City at the home of the progressive screenwriter Sid Kuller. Kuller's house parties attracted a like-minded cohort of affluent actors and writers, and the host wasted little time in raising funds from a group that included Lana Turner, Harpo and Groucho Marx, John Garfield, Paul Webster, Bonita Granville, and Tony Martin.[9] Liberal members of the "Hollywood colony" contributed $20,000 for the production, providing nearly half of its initial budget, and the cast of peripheral players associated with the project included the Popular Front icons Charlie Chaplin, Orson Welles, and Mickey Rooney.[10]

Beyond their financial contributions, progressive Hollywood personnel participated in an unusually collective creative process. While Ellington composed nearly all the music, the production involved a floating group of more than a dozen writers, leading Herb Jeffries to complain that the show had "too many chefs."[11] The ultimate result was more like a semi-improvised jazz performance than a standard musical. As Ellington noted, the show "was never the same, because every night after the final curtain we had a meeting. . . . All fifteen writers would be present whenever possible, and we would discuss, debate and make decisions as to what should come out of the show the next night."[12]

What ultimately emerged offered "a new mood in the theater."[13] This new mood targeted multiple audiences, including black Angelenos, Hollywood progressives and their employers, and the theatergoing public at large. The political core of the project, however, remained African American, with the white writer Sid Kuller describing the overall point of view as "black people looking at whites."[14] Something of the sensibility, as well as the import, of Ellington's musical is captured by reviews published in the local black press. In a joint review of competing "Negro" theatrical productions playing in Los Angeles during the summer of 1941, Almena Davis compared *Jump for Joy* to the work of Frederick Douglass and linked *Cabin in the Sky* with the political philosophies of Booker T. Washington.[15] Moreover, in addition to establishing

FIGURE 1 *Jump for Joy* chorus members, 8 July 1941. Herald Examiner Collection, Los Angeles Public Library.

a rare link between Hollywood and Central Avenue, *Jump for Joy* marked a public extension of an emerging vocabulary of urban cool unfamiliar to most whites in Los Angeles. In a move that recalled Cab Calloway's *Hepster's Dictionary* (1936) and anticipated *Dan Burley's Original Handbook of Harlem Jive* (1944), attendees received a glossary of terms intended to help them make sense of the hipster argot used in the musical. This allowed the uninitiated to follow performers who bragged about "snapping their caps" while draped in "vines" and "ice." Although Ellington viewed his principal task as demonstrating that dignity and entertainment were not mutually exclusive, his inclusion of a jive dictionary constituted a key rhetorical strategy aimed at broadening the appeal of a working-class black vernacular among consumers of mass culture. This process of translation—explicitly interracial and cross-class— reflected the exigencies of cultural politics in Los Angeles on the eve of the Second World War. At the very least, a glossary was a necessary addition to a musical program that attracted "the most celebrated Hollywoodians, middle-class ofays, the sweet-and-low, scuffling-type Negroes, and dicty Negroes as well."[16]

As Ellington's own description suggests, *Jump for Joy* sought a wide audience for its ambitious creative agenda. Throughout the course of his career, the regal race man described the production as his primary "political" work, once famously telling a group of black students accusing him of quiescence in the face of growing civil-rights activity that he had "made his statement" midway through 1941. As a militant, interracial, collective project connecting racial justice, black pride, and, however tangentially, the political left, *Jump for Joy* seems a signature example of the progressive inroads of the Popular Front period. As Michael Denning describes, Ellington spent portions of the summer and fall of 1941 lending his talents to a variety of causes, appearing at a fundraiser for American veterans of the Spanish Civil War, allowing his name to appear on statements issued by the Hollywood Democratic Committee, and performing selections from the musical on an NBC radio "Salute to Labor" broadcast. These forays attracted government notice, as well. Federal Bureau of Investigation (FBI) informers reported that Ellington's name had appeared among the sponsors of a benefit dinner held under the auspices of the American Committee to Save Refugees, the Exiled Writers' Committee, and the United American-Spanish Aid Committee.[17]

Such connections notwithstanding, *Jump for Joy* fits only so well into the typologies of the Popular Front, and a related, though distinct, framing may more accurately capture the meaning the musical held within the cultural politics of wartime Los Angeles. Premised on full creative control over the image and sound of black life, culture, and history, *Jump for Joy* offered less a celebration of the "laboring of American culture" than a cross-class, though popularly rooted, analysis of the ambiguous place of African Americans within an unstable American polity and against an openly dismissive culture industry. The idea that the musical fit within a political conversation more or less internal to African Americans was noted by journalists at the time, for the composer himself said as much. In remarks before an audience at a local Methodist church, Ellington gave his own views regarding the intersection of black culture, black particularity, and American life and history. Ellington balanced his support for Langston Hughes's call for a "democratic recognition of the Negro on the basis of the Negro's contribution" with his own observation that black America constituted something distinct that, while integral, existed apart. Terming this condition "dissonance as a way of life," he cast black Americans as simultaneously central to and indissolubly distinct from the mainstream of American life.[18]

While Ellington had been asked to take as his subject Langston Hughes's

FIGURE 2 Duke
Ellington with
the dancer Louise
Franklin, *Jump
for Joy* publicity
photograph, 15
September 1941.
Photograph
by John Reed.
Herald Examiner
Collection, Los
Angeles Public
Library.

poem "I, Too, Sing America," the composer's commentary took gentle issue
with what he saw as the limitations of discussions that linked the struggle for
racial justice to the recognition of African American contributions to the
United States. "In the poem," Ellington remarked, "Mr. Hughes argues the
case for democratic recognition of the Negro on the basis of the Negro's
contribution to America. . . . One hears that argument repeated frequently in
the Race press, from the pulpit and rostrum." Citing a litany of commonly
cited heroes, valiant military participation, and ceaseless loyalty, Ellington
added that, while "this is all well and good . . . I believe it to be only half the
story. We are more than a few isolated instances of courage, valor and achievement." Ellington's comments amounted to more than an effort to place African Americans at the center of American life and culture. They suggested a
shift away from a politics of both uplift and persuasion, opening a path toward
a framework that might simultaneously capture pride in black particularity
and demand inclusion in American liberal democracy.[19]

The dialectical vision of black life and culture as an autonomous set of practices in, but not of, the broader United States is a recurring theme of the present volume. Between 1941 and 1945, it led to a push for equal access on the representational terrain of the cultural field. Demonstrating what Harold Cruse would subsequently term "cultural democracy," this practice linked the contest over the image of African Americans with a struggle over the terms of employment within a culture industry that formed a key segment of America's domestic and export economy. In a manner distinct, though not wholly divorced, from the Italian communist Antonio Gramsci, Cruse predicated his prioritization of struggle within the superstructure on the recognition that the politics of culture reflected a strategic necessity in the context of bourgeois democracy and, most important, corresponded to the concerns, views, and demands of the masses of black people. As a practice that sought to transcend the political binaries of accommodation and protest, cultural democracy suggested a vision of pluralism that allowed creative and social autonomy as well as political and economic federation with the dominant society.[20] The framework of cultural democracy incorporated a variety of strategies, concerns, and forces, including "race" activists of varied persuasions, liberals, the radical left, and even segments of the American state. It thus had the character of a "popular front," but one that transcended the concerns of the interracial prewar left and the boundaries of postwar liberalism.

During the Second World War, Los Angeles became a key site for the articulation of a new African American cultural politics as activists and artists sought to use the unsettled landscape of life during wartime as a means for wringing rhetorical and material concessions from American society. This struggle over representation and access constituted, in essence, one inaugural element of a burgeoning struggle for self-determination that went well beyond the simple framework of "civil rights." At the center of self-determination lay self-definition, and cultural activists devoted significant attention to critiquing how African Americans appeared on stage and screen, as well as to seeking broader entry into all facets of motion-picture production. Achieving the desegregation of the culture industry—a task still incomplete at war's end—demanded new associations of artists, activists, and entertainers who recognized the strategic importance of culture as an autonomous realm of political activity. At the same time, challenging Hollywood created rifts among black entertainers, pitting those with longstanding relationships inside the motion-picture industry against those actors and activists on the outside. The cultural front thus generated both unity and struggle as it developed.

A little less than a year after the premier of Ellington's musical, a story appeared in the NAACP's monthly journal, *The Crisis*. Written by recently relocated Midwesterner Chester Himes, "Lunching at the Ritzmore" offered an account of a chance meeting during which three figures—an unemployed white laborer, a precocious white collegian, and an African American passerby—attempt to dine in a posh downtown restaurant to settle a wager concerning the relative lack of racial discrimination in Los Angeles and, by extension, the United States as a whole. Inspiration for the story was close at hand. During the spring of 1940, the head of the Los Angeles branch of the Urban League, Floyd Covington, had been refused service at one of the city's most celebrated venues, the Biltmore Hotel. Covington had been invited to the hotel restaurant by an out-of-town visitor, the Swedish social scientist Gunnar Myrdal, who was in California supervising research for his landmark study of American race relations. Following the incident, an embarrassed Myrdal wrote Covington to assure him that "I did not ask you to come there for an experiment," adding that the incident had come about because "I actually believed what several people had told me, namely, that the Biltmore had no discrimination."[21]

The fictionalized version is brief; the plot, simple. Prodded by the student, the unnamed black character agrees to seek service in the downtown establishment of his choice, thus potentially proving the student's contention that African American patronage was in actuality welcomed by nearly all businesses. As the three set out for their as yet undetermined destination, curious spectators fall in line behind, prompting a wary policeman to accuse the interracial trio of leading a communist rally. After circumnavigating Pershing Square, described fleetingly by Himes as a "Mecca of the Motley," the protagonists eventually settle on the prestigious Ritzmore, where, following a moment of confusion and panic on the part of diners and staff, the entire party orders apple pie. Although the group is served mostly as a result of the restaurant staff's inability to decide quickly how to respond, the story ends as a sardonic commentary on race relations on the coast. "And it was thus proved by the gentlemen of Pershing Square," Himes concludes, "that no discrimination exists in the beautiful city of Los Angeles."[22]

Himes's subsequent writing would extend his critique of California as a racial paradise. Drawn west by the possibility of work writing movie scripts, Himes found himself considering alternative possibilities following a summary dismissal by the head of Warner Brothers, Jack Warner, who reportedly told a subordinate, "I don't want no niggers on this lot."[23] Holding twenty-three jobs over the course of the next three years, Himes spent the war years working in a variety of physically arduous and generally menial industrial jobs. Despite his ability to read blueprints, supervise construction, and operate complicated industrial machinery, he found only two skilled positions, both on ships, and both of which forced him to work as a lower-paid "helper" to white co-workers. During this time, he continued to write both short stories and social essays that captured the deleterious racial climate and the particular difficulties Los Angeles posed for working-class black men. Himes continued these themes following his departure for New York in 1944, publishing two semiautobiographical novels centered on his experiences as a black factory worker in wartime Los Angeles.[24]

Incisive and dystopian, *If He Hollers Let Him Go* (1945) and *Lonely Crusade* (1947) have been viewed as exemplary examples of California *noir*, as pioneering examples of interethnic, cross-racial politics linking disaffected black, Asian American, and ethnic Mexican communities and as a challenging, even infuriating, effort to write seriously about the problematic boundary between race, sex, and violence in Jim Crow America. Less attention, however, has been paid to Himes's engagement with questions of the role of art and culture in the struggle for wartime democracy. Yet *If He Hollers* repeatedly demonstrates that Himes regarded the motion-picture industry as part of the broader edifice of a specifically Californian racism. After failing to find solace in cruising across town in his prized Buick, surveying Central Avenue, or sliding into a bar, Himes's protagonist Bob Jones walks out of a movie when "after about five minutes a big fat black Hollywood mammy came on the screen saying 'Yassum' and 'Noam.'"[25] On another occasion, going to the movies provides an example of the interlocking forms of representational and real discrimination his character faces:

> Take for instance something as simple as going downtown to a moving picture show. Every white person I come into contact with . . . has got the power of some kind of control over my behavior. Say if I ride the streetcar, the conductor can make me stand there waiting for my change. . . . Then when I get off and walk down the street the pedestrians can make me step aside to let them pass. The cashier can sell me loge seats when she knows there aren't any, and the doorman can send me up to the balcony, knowing there aren't any loge seats, then the usher will find the worst possible seat for me.
> And there's the picture—it's almost certain to offend me in some kind of

way. If there're Negro actors in it the roles they play will be offensive; and if it's a play with no part at all for Negroes, if you get to thinking about it, you resent the fact of seeing the kind of life shown you'll never be able to live.[26]

Although Himes remained far less optimistic about the likelihood of its realization, his wartime writings nonetheless engaged questions of cultural democracy similar to those promulgated by Ellington. Both men saw access to and employment in the creative field as a precondition for solving the entrenched problem of insulting, stereotypical depictions of blacks. Both sought to retain a space for black particularity while insisting on the full—and, for many whites, novel—recognition of the humanity of African Americans. Both captured the boundaries of black life by using humor in ways that would likely have escaped most white audiences.[27] At the same time, Himes communicated a clear unease with the burden of representing the race in the quest for collective progress. Echoing Ellington's gentle critique of Langston Hughes, Himes rejected the notion that signature black achievements—or achievers—offered a path toward racial progress. Thus, Himes's semiautobiographical protagonist bristles at his fiancée's vaguely oedipal suggestions that he assume the bourgeois pretensions of her own father, in part by concluding:

> I knew I'd wake up some day and say to hell with it, I didn't want to be the biggest Negro who ever lived, neither Toussaint L'Ouverture nor Walter White. Because deep inside of me, where the white folks couldn't see, it didn't mean a thing. If you couldn't swing down Hollywood Boulevard . . . couldn't make a polite pass at Lana Turner at Ciro's without having the gendarmes beat the black off you . . . couldn't eat a thirty dollar dinner at a hotel without choking on the insults, being a great big "Mister nigger" didn't mean a thing. Anyone who wanted to could be nigger-rich, nigger-important, have their Jim Crow religion, and go to nigger heaven.[28]

Himes framed his inability to achieve the recognition of his humanity at precisely the moment in which black progress toward fuller inclusion in American life began to gather steam in starkly geographic terms:

> Up to the age of thirty-one, I had been hurt emotionally, spiritually, and physically . . . and still I was entire, complete, functional; my mind was sharp, my reflexes were good, and I was not bitter. But under the mental corrosion of race prejudice in Los Angeles I had become bitter and saturated with hate. I was thirty-one and whole when I went to Los Angeles and thirty-five and shattered when I left to go to New York.[29]

These experiences were hardly unique, and Himes's wartime novels remain among the foremost social explorations of black life in Los Angeles. Both *If He Hollers Let Him Go* and *Lonely Crusade* are set amid the wartime transformation of Los Angeles. Both take defense workers as central characters. As a result of its proximity to the Pacific conflict, Southern California attracted nearly a tenth of all domestic defense spending, with the wages of an expanding urban workforce making up an important part of this total. Seeking economic opportunity, African Americans arrived en masse, and while migration between 1939 and 1941 was slight, tens of thousands arrived amid the expansion of defense production after 1942. Between 1940 and 1946, the black population of Los Angeles more than doubled, growing from 63,774 to 133,082. The effect of this migration on the city was immediate and long-lasting. Although far fewer African Americans moved into Los Angeles than into more traditional migration destinations in the urban Northeast and Midwest, their status as upward of one third of all new arrivals in Los Angeles made them a highly conspicuous part of a changing wartime city.[30]

Most new arrivals found atrocious housing and poor jobs. Housing restrictions consigned nonwhites to less than a tenth of available housing stock, and the homes of recently interned Japanese and Japanese Americans often constituted the only residences open to African Americans. Exclusion from highly paid industries was nearly complete. Federal investigators found only four "Negro production workers" across the entire aircraft industry during July 1941. Prospects in shipbuilding were scarcely better. At the close of Ellington's musical in September 1941, only one hundred of Los Angeles County's 8,500 shipyard workers were African American. Exclusion from jobs in the petro-chemical industry and in public transportation mirrored these trends, and both state and local defense-training programs refused to enroll African Americans. Partially as a result of these patterns, Los Angeles hosted the first hearings of the Fair Employment Practices Commission (FEPC) held outside Washington, D.C.[31]

Federal scrutiny helped facilitate a tentative foothold in local industry. Industrial employment led, for the first time, to a sizable pool of unionized black workers. On the eve of the war's end, one local leader estimated that 85 percent of Los Angeles's black workforce was involved in the manufacture of military equipment, although their status as only 5.3 percent of war workers midway through 1944 suggests continued under-representation.[32] The record of regional industrial and craft unions was mixed, and black workers were often forced to struggle simultaneously against management and their own ostensible representatives.[33] In this context, a variety of organizational forms, from established churches and extant civil-rights bodies to novel multiethnic coalitions and emergent labor unions, all became vehicles for a newly assertive politics.[34] Having braved transcontinental migration, secured adequate housing, demanded the right to equal military participation, and obtained employment amid recalcitrant industrialists and racist co-workers, Hollywood quickly became another target, and few of black Los Angeles's newly mobilized working people wanted to continue to see themselves on screen depicted only as butlers, half-naked "natives," or maids.

Such, at least, was the conviction of Floyd Covington, who included the picketing of the film *Tales of Manhattan* as part of what he termed a "proletarian upsurge" on the part of black Angelenos. In comparing the protests against the film with the rally of several thousand female workers outside the U.S. Employment Agency in July 1942, the formation of community-run produce markets, or the attendance at a Council on African Affairs rally featuring Paul Robeson, Max Yergan, and the Indian activist Lal Singh, Covington proposed an implicit link between improved portrayals of African Americans and the struggle for industrial inclusion, civil rights, and decolonization. Beyond signaling a shift toward greater political interest on the part of tens of thousands of black Angelenos, such comparisons rejected a distinction between the "cultural" and the "political," or the "representational" and the "real."

Nor was Covington alone in connecting new patterns of representational preference and cultural organization to the material reality of a newly arrived black working class. Frances Williams aimed her incipient Music Town project squarely at black defense workers, asking, "What war worker wouldn't like to dance, act in plays, learn radio technique, or form an orchestra?" Williams, a twelve-year veteran of Cleveland's Karamu House, answered her own question by organizing what in effect functioned as the city's first community-based black arts space.[35] Williams enlisted a wide variety of local talent. Benjamin "Reb" Spikes taught music classes. A Los Angeles resident since 1897, Spikes had co-founded one of the city's first jazz bands, and his music store had functioned as the original base for the city's black American Federation of Musicians affiliate, Local 767.[36] Archie Savage, a former member of Katherine Dunham's dance company, led dance workshops. Chester Himes taught playwriting, while Faye Jackson. a former youth leader with the NAACP, coordinated a creative-writing seminar. Courses in Negro history were added as a result of Williams's desire to help "our young people become more aware of their place in the scheme of things." Beyond holding classes, Music Town served as a clearinghouse for African American arts activity, hosting a ceramics and pottery workshop by the local artist Tony Hill and organizing the first local exhibition of the works of the painter Jacob Lawrence.[37]

Although short-lived, the Music Town project offers a reminder of the scope of the changes that took place after 1941. As wartime production brought both migrants and jobs, demands for inclusion in every scope of American life were accompanied by new forms of organizing. Beyond simply seeking integration, many of these forms aimed primarily at developing the capacities and options of ordinary black folks, whether as shoppers in Negro Victory Markets, workers on burgeoning assembly lines, or creative personalities in Hollywood. And while the explosion of black mobilization during the war took place across the United States, Southern California's particular relationship to entertainment, information, and propaganda ensured that creative personalities would occupy a strategic space in the broader search for racial equality unleashed in the course of the Second World War.

TOWARD A BLACK CULTURAL FRONT

Duke Ellington, Frances Williams, and Chester Himes were part of a broad local push for cultural democracy in Los Angeles between 1941 and 1945. Black migration transformed local demographics, and as employment and housing struggles mobilized thousands, entertainers, artists, and other cultural workers generated a wide-ranging cultural critique of the place of African Americans within American society. Cognizant of the link between the transformation of social conditions and the possibility of new cultural forms, each participated in the mobilization of black culture in support of the dual aims of winning the war and eliminating domestic inequality. For those activists present in Los Angeles during the Second World War, cultural politics took the form of a shifting set of shared orientations, common recognitions, and joint activities rooted in the conviction that the dual contest over representation and access constituted a core element of racial progress.

These efforts took place in part against the backdrop of a leftward shift in local politics. The political ascent of the liberal county supervisors John Anson Ford and Gordon McDonough led to a range of local initiatives aimed at fostering racial unity, marking the first organized municipal efforts to construct a more racially reconciled city.[38] Equally importantly, the war brought a decisive, if temporary, end to more than a half century of the aggressive local repression of organized labor, as the American Federation of Labor, the International Brotherhood of Teamsters, and the Congress of Industrial Organizations added tens of thousands of new members in the hundreds of defense-related factories and plants springing up throughout the region. Labor gains were also reflected in the world of cartoons, literature, and film, paving the way for the well-known postwar conflict over the place of the political left in the world of American cultural production.[39]

Beyond this, wartime Southern California emerged as an important locus of antiracist politics.[40] Inherently coalitional, this activism linked established African American, Mexican American, Asian American, and Jewish organizations with a growing cohort of activist artists, authors, and scholars such as Carlos Bulosan, Carey McWilliams, and Orson Welles. Within this milieu, black activists found no shortage of causes. Paul Robeson made frequent trips to the city, headlining benefits for Russian relief and unionization drives and launching a call for a boycott of Hollywood films.[41] The actor Canada Lee spent the second half of 1943 on the Pacific coast, joining Dalton Trumbo and Charlotta Bass at a forum sponsored by the Hollywood Writers Mobilization and joining the campaign to free the defendants in the Sleepy Lagoon trial.[42] Like Ellington and Himes, Lee acquired an FBI informant while living in Southern California, and an unnamed "Source A" told Los Angeles bureau officials that Lee had joined the Communist Party's "Northwest," or Hollywood, section.[43] Art Tatum, Billy Eckstine, Red Callendar, and Billie Holiday were among the "Stars for Democracy" who performed at an FEPC benefit co-sponsored by the Jewish Community Council, the Catholic Interracial Council, the National Negro Congress, the Congress of Industrial Organizations, and the NAACP.[44] On another occasion, an all-Negro "Benefit for Soviet Russia" was held at the Wilshire Ebell Theater, where a predominantly white audience saw a program that ran the gamut from patriotic Russian and American songs to Haitian drumming and dance.[45] Such presentations— international and interracial, politically left and consciously urbane— represented a tremendous change from the cultural and political conservatism that had dominated Southern California since the turn of the century.[46]

This iteration of a black Popular Front included organizations long accustomed to placing culture in the service of the race. Local efforts in this regard extended back decades, from NAACP protests against *The Birth of a Nation* to the staging of W. E. B. Du Bois's musical epic, *Star of Ethiopia*, at the Hollywood Bowl in 1925. An ambitious effort to showcase nearly the entire scope of known Negro history, the musical offered the first major presentation of New Negro radicalism before the city at large. A year later, Charles Johnson, a sociologist at the University of Chicago who was in Los Angeles to conduct a survey on labor conditions for blacks, convened a writing circle dubbed the Ink Slingers. Charter members included State Assemblyman Fred Roberts; the Garveyite businessman Noah Thompson; and Catherine Barr, branch founder of the Los Angeles Urban League, as well as a public-housing director, a realtor, a physician, and Gladyse Greenaway, a prominent local clubwoman known primarily for her stewardship of an annual toy giveaway. Thus, the most prominent iterations of New Negro cultural activism in interwar Southern California emerged not from creative personalities connected to the rapidly growing entertainment industry but, rather, from sojourning scholars with ties to the local ranks of the black professional class.[47]

Indeed, much of what might seem a Californian iteration of Harlem Renaissance–era activity connected artists to the most active segment of the local black bourgeoisie. One of the people involved in coordinating Du Bois's musical was Faye Jackson, vice-president of the NAACP's junior branch, who founded a literary journal called *Flash* that appeared during 1928 and 1929. With contributions from former West Coast residents Langston Hughes, Arna Bontemps, and Wallace Thurman, *Flash*, like Thurman's earlier effort, *Outlook*, provided a link between Los Angeles and parallel literary efforts taking place elsewhere. Founded in 1934, the Committee on Arts of the Negro, led by John Gray, a classical music teacher; the ragtime legend and store owner John Spikes; and Jesse Kimbrough and Thomas LeBlanc, co-founders of the black American Federation of Musicians Local 767, abolished itself after the organizers of a city-sponsored arts festival informed black participants that the event would include a separate Negro arts section.[48] Although it lasted much longer—persisting into the 1960s—the Allied Arts League was a part of this general trend. Created by a group of young women, many of them members of the Beta Pi Sigma sorority, Allied Arts sponsored lectures by Langston Hughes and W. C. Handy, participated in the first local attempts to found an African American theater company, and successfully pressured the city to give official sponsorship to an annual series of Negro History Week events. An affiliate of Carter G. Woodson's Association for the Study of Negro Life and History, Allied Arts, and its self-described "society matrons," took as a mission to "create in the city of Los Angeles an intercultural fellowship through the medium of the arts."[49]

At the outbreak of the Second World War, the use of culture in the service of racial progress remained both a pressing local concern for the black middle class and a realm in which working actors, artists, and musicians occupied a marginal place compared with local political activists. The attorney Loren

Miller furnishes an example. A critical presence during the early 1950s, when he took over stewardship of the *California Eagle* and directed hundreds of legal assaults against housing discrimination, Miller passed the 1930s in archetypical Popular Front fashion, mixing with leftist luminaries, writing for *New Masses*, and joining an internal putsch against the leadership of NAACP Director Walter White.[50] An associate of Arna Bontemps and Wallace Thurman, Miller joined a tour of the Soviet Union in 1932 with his friend Langston Hughes. Miller and Hughes were among a group of twenty-two African Americans invited to the Soviet Union by a German firm interested in making a film on racial conditions among black workers in Birmingham, Alabama.[51] Although the film never materialized, Miller returned to Los Angeles intent on challenging an industry with a global audience that depended "almost entirely on the movies for their knowledge of Negro life." Miller saw shifting the representation of blacks as a key task in the larger effort against racism. Noting that "iron clad rules" required whites be depicted as "overlords," precluded the cinematic portrayal of miscegenation, and systematically eschewed any mention of the "economic roots of the Negro question," the young attorney took the film industry as a combined political, economic, and cultural problem that linked the black working and middle classes. As an initial step toward a remedy, Miller urged greater middle-class patronage of the independent work of directors such as Oscar Micheaux and the establishment of a "second cinema" of 16 mm art films that would develop along the lines of the "little theater" movement. Miller argued that independent filmmaking would eventually produce more developed cultural criticism among African Americans. This was a twofold necessity, given both his contention that "the Negro masses will adopt a critical attitude only if organs of opinion and Negro leadership establish an adequate critique for their guidance" and his view that mass support for protest campaigns aimed at Hollywood studios could only find success following a period of political education aimed at generating widespread recognition of the strategic centrality of the entertainment industry in a larger system of American racism.[52]

Miller's ideas resonated broadly. An increasing shift toward coordinated efforts was aptly summarized in the emergence in early 1938 of two local pressure groups. Coming a year after the formation of the Associated Film Audiences, a coalition that included the NAACP, Urban League, and League for Industrial Democracy, the Los Angeles–based Committee for the Promotion of Colored People in Motion Pictures and the Cinema League of Colored Peoples took distinct approaches to solving the problem of African American discontent with Hollywood. The brainchild of Maceo Sheffield, a lieutenant with the Los Angeles Police Department, security captain at the Dunbar Hotel, and star of the film *Harlem on the Prairie*, the Committee for the Promotion of Colored People in Motion Pictures comprised prominent eastsiders seeking to develop "race capital" with the aim of financing a separate, independent, and positive "race" cinema.[53] The Cinema League of Colored Peoples, by contrast, was an activist clearinghouse committed to pressuring studios that drew members from as far away as Paris, Guyana, and the Gold Coast. The leadership of the Cinema League included T. L. Griffith, president of the local NAACP chapter; the publisher Charlotta Bass; the architect Paul Williams; John Gray; and the actor Earl Dancer. While the Committee for the Promotion of Colored People in Motion Pictures symbolized the black petit bourgeoisie's dream of marshalling its capital to take command of a defined, if not wholly captive, market, the Cinema League of Colored Peoples drew on the growth of political agitation among creative personalities and culturally oriented political radicals during the interwar period. Even the more radical formation, however, betrayed clear class sensibilities. Beyond its nearly entirely middle-class composition, the members of the Cinema League of Colored Peoples explicitly cast themselves as "intelligent colored people" eager to negotiate better roles with studio heads who in the past had been forced to rely on figures like a "studio bootblack" in answering "vital questions of race history."[54] Thus, despite the growing salience of the political left in Depression-era Los Angeles, the most visible currents of local black cultural activism remained stuck within the familiar bifurcation between a Washingtonian search for "race" capital and a Du Boisian politics of elite-based agitation.

The American entry into the Second World War provided an impetus for moving beyond these dualities. Sharpening fears regarding Negro morale imparted a particular quality to the actions of black performers, and while the mobilization for total war generated Hollywood initiatives among a wide variety of "ethnic" entertainers, reports of widespread cynicism regarding the aims of the war on the part of African Americans and federal concerns regarding the resonance of Japanese antiracist appeals allowed African American artists to imply that their efforts conferred particular strategic utility.[55] The result was an unprecedented inclusion of black entertainers in wartime propaganda.

These efforts linked a broad swath of black talent, including progressives such as Robeson, prominent Eastern celebrities such as Ellington, and members of Hollywood's small pool of regularly employed actors. Some efforts were purely theatrical, as when Humphrey Bogart, Lena Horne, and Eddie

"Rochester" Anderson allowed a detachment of the 369th New York National Guard Regiment (the famous Harlem Hellfighters) to set up antiaircraft batteries in the backyards of their homes.[56] Other events spoke directly to the emerging mobilization for victory and jobs. Known primarily for her work as an obsequious maid, the actress Louise Beavers urged a group of black female defense workers to unionize, lest they lose their jobs in the postwar period. Calling labor unions "the salvation of the worker," Beavers compared the employees of Aero Reclamation to the members of the Screen Actors Guild (SAG).[57] On another occasion, members of Hollywood's "sepia colony" headlined a war-bonds festival that filled Pershing Square and surrounding downtown streets.[58] The same informal group presided over a fundraiser and protest against the Los Angeles Railway sponsored jointly by the NAACP, the Brotherhood of Sleeping Car Porters, the American Federation of Labor, the Congress of Industrial Organizations, the Negro Business League, and Golden State Mutual Life Insurance.[59]

As American participation in the war expanded, support for integration on the part of whites associated with the entertainment industry moved from the province of the radical left to the political center. At the insistence of Bette Davis, president of the Motion Picture Academy of Arts and Sciences, one of the city's pre-eminent nightspots became the scene of public debate concerning racial mixing. Against the angry backdrop of open brawling between white servicemen and black and brown youth, Davis dismissed calls for a halt to interracial dancing at the Hollywood Canteen.[60] Around the time that Allied forces landed at Normandy, Nat King Cole's trio integrated the Sunset Strip's Trocadero club.[61] Ellington's band followed, appearing down the street at Ciro's. *Down Beat* heralded the arrival of Roy Milton's band at the formerly segregated Susy-Q club, offering "three cheers" that "attempts to keep the [L]ocal 767 boys out of Hollywood finally washed out."[62]

For artists, the retreat of segregation was as much a matter of employment opportunities as it was about ending the humiliation of discrimination. Presaging a major postwar battle, members of the racially restricted American Federation of Musicians Local 47 threatened to refuse to perform in segregated United Service Organizations (USO) venues, while the jazz promoter Norman Granz ignored instructions from the manager of the Los Angeles Philharmonic Auditorium, who insisted that black musicians make up no more than half of the faces on the bandstand. Granz was the principal force behind a "Philharmonic" that was in reality a traveling jam session that spread from the Philharmonic Auditorium to local jazz clubs, including the Hollywood club of Billy Berg. While Berg lacked Granz's racial convictions, according to the jazz historian Scott Deveaux, as a club owner he nonetheless would play a significant role as a facilitator of both the integration of local nightlife and the development of "modern jazz" in California.[63] The first local club to host the boppers Coleman Hawkins, Howard McGhee, Dizzy Gillespie, and Charlie Parker, Berg's North Vine Street club was an "unlikely oasis" for black patrons accustomed to being excluded from the Hollywood venues that were rapidly replacing Central Avenue as the epicenter of jazz in Southern California.[64]

In contrast to developments in the music world, efforts within the world of film met with less initial success. This was far more a matter of Hollywood intransigence than it was a reflection of a strategic choice by African Americans. The NAACP, of course, had vainly sought means for contesting negative portrayals of the race since 1915, when President Woodrow Wilson pronounced *The Birth of a Nation*, D. W. Griffith's interpretation of Thomas Dixon's novel *The Clansman*, "history writ with lightning."[65] Decades of marginally effective protests, boycotts, and lawsuits later, the nation's most visible racial-justice organization sought to seize on the new possibilities offered by the rapidly changing social conditions ushered in by the Second World War. The spring of 1942 saw NAACP Director Walter White joining Wendell Willkie for a series of meetings with entertainment-industry executives. Willkie, the Republican Party's presidential candidate in 1940, held posts as NAACP special counsel and as chairman of the board at 20th Century Fox and was uniquely placed to pursue a campaign aimed at fostering new practices regarding the cinematic portrayal of African Americans. White spent several months attempting to extract concessions from studio heads, although both his lack of specific directives and the film industry's longstanding ambivalence toward message movies militated against rapid or pronounced change.[66]

Indeed, the sort of message that activists demanded ran contrary to more than one established Hollywood custom. Beyond aesthetic proclivities that shied away from serious social content and the necessity of marketing films inside a segregated nation, the prevailing material conditions within Hollywood reproduced patterns of industrial exclusion found throughout Los Angeles. Employment figures revealed a motion-picture industry as committed to racial exclusion as the local oil, automobile, tire, or aerospace industries were. The pool of African Americans regularly employed in major speaking parts did not exceed two dozen. At the dawn of the 1940s, 51 African American men listed "actor" as their occupation, while the 15 black women listed by the census represented a fraction of 743 full-time actresses working in the city.

Black talent thus constituted a minuscule percentage of those actors under regular contract, and only 3 African Americans were listed among the 1,106 directors, managers, and officials in motion-picture production.[67] The bulk of those earning any wages at all were extras whose daily pay rarely exceeded the $5–$15 that automobile workers could expect. Then, as now, bit parts were the primary roles available, with hiring taking place through humiliating "cattle calls" held on the sidewalk along Central Avenue. Like the infamous "Bronx Slave Market" where black women seeking work as housecleaners were expected to show calloused knees and hands to prospective white employers, black Angelenos were selected for inclusion as enslaved field hands, unruly natives, and other crowds purely on the basis of cursory evaluations of physical appearance. For the movie industry, blacks were recognized as a source of flexible labor. This sentiment was captured most succinctly by the silent film star and renowned "Man of a Thousand Faces" Lon Chaney, who opined, "You can pull any one of them out of the mob and they can act. It is only a matter of make up and costume to create anything from a Chinaman to an Eskimo. They require no interpreters and are always available in large numbers."[68]

Whatever his cognizance of these conditions, Walter White gave scant evidence of a strategy for confronting studio executives. Indeed, his attempt to change Hollywood's racial conditions through an "attack via the luncheon table" contained an almost Washingtonian accent on persuading powerful whites of the import of treating blacks better.[69] That increasingly positive, visible, and complicated roles became more common during wartime was more properly the result of the writer Carlton Moss's role in shepherding new programming through the Office of War Information in Washington. Whatever White's ultimate role, the importance of the wartime confrontation with the culture industry was confirmed by the sight of the director of the nation's foremost civil-rights organization joining a man who had recently received twenty-two million presidential votes in making public demands for quantitative and qualitative improvements to the black situation in Hollywood.

Whether prominent members of the interracial left like Paul Robeson and Canada Lee, dedicated "race" artists like Ellington and William Grant Still, or veteran activists like Walter White and Loren Miller, the expanding pool of politicized black creative personalities constituted an identifiable political formation, a kind of black cultural front that took cultural democracy as a shared political and aesthetic imperative. This coalition rapidly found itself arrayed against two targets: the Hollywood status quo and its black defenders. The ensuing struggle would both highlight the divisiveness of efforts to harness culture in the service of racial progress and mark an important point of departure for a half century of local cultural politics split between reformist calls for representation and a radical critique based on self-determination.

AND ITS ATTENDANT CRISIS AT HOME

Despite an almost instantaneous entry into the war effort, Hollywood made little effort to involve African American entertainers in its organized propaganda work at first. Although it was founded days after the attack on Pearl Harbor, the Hollywood Victory Committee (HVC) waited eighteen months before soliciting the participation of an African American: Hattie McDaniel of *Gone with the Wind* fame. A prominent actress whose role as Mammy in the Southern epic had won her an Academy Award, McDaniel was a known quantity in Hollywood. So, too, were the eight other African Americans she added to the HVC. Citing an opportunity to "translate into action our love of country and our desire to help win the war," McDaniel, Louise Beavers, Nicodemus Stewart, Eddie Anderson, Mantan Moreland, Leigh Whipper, Fayard Nichols, Lilian Randolph, and Ben Carter were initially charged with overseeing the limited task of "entertainment of Negro troops."[70]

In describing her understanding of her mandate, McDaniel argued that the group would seek "to integrate its work with the general program of the Hollywood Victory Committee," a stance that signaled her intent to avoid supporting appeals for widespread change. Content to participate in parallel, segregated forums, McDaniel and her compatriots represented a gradual, persuasive approach favored by the small number of African Americans who were receiving regular speaking roles in major studio productions. Although formally charged with improving Negro morale to facilitate the war effort, the HVC served in fact to defend the status quo in the face of growing calls for change. After eighteen months of inaction, then, Hollywood sought to manage blacks' calls for greater inclusion in the cultural front of the war effort by relying on a cohort of loyal locals. Citing the "tremendous progress" already made, McDaniel summarized her general approach to changing the industry when she said, "I don't believe that we will gain by rushing or attacking to force studios to do anything they are not readily inclined to do."[71]

The tone of such commentary is instructive. The formation of McDaniel's committee came amid a bustle of activity. Beyond the aforementioned efforts of Wendell Willkie and Walter White, Howard Fast joined Paul Robeson in

FIGURE 3 Hattie McDaniel (center), chairman of the Negro Division of the Hollywood Victory Committee, with a group of entertainers and hostesses before a vaudeville performance and dance for soldiers stationed at Minter Field, not dated. National Archives and Records Administration.

announcing plans to begin film projects outside California. Robeson, who had long been critical of Hollywood, reiterated his call for a boycott following his disgust with the final version of the film *Tales of Manhattan* (1944). With leftist forces represented by Robeson and Fast openly discussing the possibility of forming a parallel film industry, and local activists such as Charlotta Bass and Loren Miller exploring the feasibility of launching an industry-wide boycott, White reiterated his support for the creation of an independent Hollywood NAACP bureau "conducted as to make it influential in changing the movie stereotypes of Negroes which influence scores of millions of human beings all over the earth." While the effort to transform the relationship between Hollywood and African America may not have been visible to the millions abroad who had "come to rely almost entirely on the movies for their knowledge of Negro life," the issue was a national one for black people. In addition to the three local papers, the black newspapers with the largest national circulation, including the *Courier*, the *Afro-American*, the *New York Amsterdam News*, and the *Chicago Defender*, maintained correspondents in California. As a result, hiring trends, industry gossip, and the efforts of both Robeson and White were widely reported in the black press.[72]

Widespread national interest, however, did little to engender local unity. A sharp feud set locally based stars such as Nick Stewart, Clarence Muse, and Hattie McDaniel against a diverse lot of local activists with whom they had shared a range of prewar spaces. Expanding debate brought an end to a period in which actors known for subservient roles might nonetheless maintain a respectful stature within the local community and even hold some political capital. Derided by the young libretto Harold Forsythe as "the most blankety-blankest idiot the Devil ever tossed upon the poor, long suffering Nig," Clarence Muse had served as an unofficial NAACP liaison to Hollywood since 1934. Louise Beavers, made famous as a "mammy" figure in films like *Imitation of Life*, was the niece of George and Willie Mae Beavers, local co-founders of the Peoples Independent Church and of the largest black-owned business in California, the Golden State Mutual Life Insurance Company. In the decade before her film career began, Beavers was performing in a church-sponsored youth group that counted the city's first black deputy district attorney, Leon Whitaker, and the eventual Nobel Peace Prize winner Ralph Bunche among its members. Cordial relations between Los Angeles's activist black bourgeoisie and Hollywood's sepia stars continued until the outbreak of war. Six months before the German invasion of Poland, Beavers and McDaniel joined the "race leaders" Charlotta Bass and Vada Somerville, as well as Los Angeles County Supervisors John Anson Ford and Gordon McDonough, at a gala opening of a new bathhouse and Olympic-size pool at Val Verde Park, a county-owned Negro resort fifty miles northeast of Los Angeles.[73] Thus, wartime denunciations of servile roles—and the angry rejoinders that followed—showcased the difficulties arising among the black bourgeoisie as the political winds shifted from persuasion to protest.

The production of *Stormy Weather* (1943) offers a case in point. Part of a pair of all-black musicals released amid an outbreak of summertime race riots, the film featured a galaxy of black stars, and while the story offered a fairly simplistic biography of the dancer Bill Robinson, the end result was upbeat and urbane. Proponents noted that the film marked the first time a major Hollywood studio had invested serious money in producing and publicizing a film featuring an entirely black cast. Black audiences found little that was objectionable, and *Stormy Weather* constituted the first instance in which Hollywood saw a market in representing blacks not as whites imagined them but as they understood or imagined themselves. Detractors felt otherwise. Chester Himes claimed that the entire cast, including Ethel Waters, Lena Horne, and Bill Robinson, had been refused service in the Metro-Goldwyn-Mayer (MGM) commissary. Walter White noted his discomfort with a film that ran contrary to the cinematic depiction of integration he sought, a sentiment confirmed by William Grant Still. Having quit the production following a dispute over the musical score, Still lambasted the absurdity of portraying African Americans as if they existed in a world in which whites were absent. Others decried the depiction of Cab Calloway in a zoot suit, perhaps fearing that the film and the fashion, the riots and the race, would blend seamlessly in the minds of audiences at home and abroad.

The link between domestic and international concerns constituted a critical element of wartime cultural politics. Such, in any event, was a contention argued repeatedly at a three-day conference sponsored by the Hollywood Writers Mobilization in 1943. The meeting, held at the campus of the University of California, Los Angeles (UCLA), involved the participation of an international cohort of creative personalities invested in addressing the aesthetic, political, and economic dimensions of the effort to put culture in the service of the war effort. More than 1,200 participants attended the inaugural session, which opened with a message from President Franklin D. Roosevelt. Delegations from China, Britain, Bolivia, France, and the Soviet Union joined panels chaired by communist cartoonists, exiled German writers, and progressive screenwriters. Panels explored the structure of the culture industry; debated the national cultures of the Axis powers; anticipated problems of the postwar period; discussed Pan-American Affairs; and raised formal questions about the relationship between propaganda, art, and war in radio, comedy, literature, and documentary, feature, and animated film.

Minority issues were a focus of the conference, as well. White and Willkie addressed the conference on the first day, while Revels Cayton, Clarence Muse, and Canada Lee served on the continuations committee dealing with the problems of minority groups. White's commentary described both the "enormous opportunity" and the "appalling responsibility" possessed by shapers of public opinion. The continuations committee, meanwhile, issued a ten-point declaration of principles meant "to guide the writer in his treatment of minorities." Although they never became part of a formal presentation before industry guilds or studio moguls, as the authors originally intended, the call for depictions of members of minority groups "as individuals" portrayed "in light with the scientific truth of the equality of the races" spoke explicitly to the framework of cultural democracy. The position paper linked employment with representation, domestic conditions with international affairs. The use of racist imagery was derided as a "fascist weapon," and adherents were asked simultaneously to avoid depicting "members of any race . . . as inherently shiftless, happy, miserly . . . inscrutable, subservient" and to avoid the implication "through theme, plot, incident or character that the existing order of racial relationships is complete and satisfactory." Further points asked for the elimination of employment discrimination within the entertainment industry and the expansion of subject matter to include "the infinite store of material" issuing from "the history and the current struggles for freedom of races and national groups the world over."[74]

The conference program featured two panels that spoke explicitly to the place of minorities within the culture industry. The first, held on Saturday evening, included Charlotta Bass, Carlos Bulosan, Canada Lee, Clarence Muse, Walter White, and four prominent whites: the anthropologist Harry Hoijer, the journalist Carey McWilliams, the screenwriter Dalton Trumbo, and the Bureau of Indian Affairs official John Collier. Among the film colony's most visible radicals, Trumbo offered particularly critical commentary. Echoing comments made earlier by William Grant Still, he excoriated Hollywood as more than complicit in the broadening of American racism. Noting that "the most gigantic . . . of our appeal[s] to public patronage have been the anti-Negro pictures, *The Birth of a Nation*, and *Gone with the Wind*," Trumbo added, "We have produced turgid floods of sickening and libelous treacle. We have made tarts of the Negro's daughters, crapshooters of his sons, obsequious Uncle Toms of his fathers, superstitious and grotesque crones of his mothers . . . and Barnum and Bailey sideshows of his religion."[75] Anti-black prejudice, for Trumbo, formed the last redoubt of Hollywood racism, as the previous patterns of derogatory typecasting had waned in the face of Irish political agitation, America's embrace of nationalist China, the mandates of Roosevelt's "Good Neighbor" policy, and the quiet intercession of the Mexican and Chinese governments. In contrast to Chinese Americans and Mexican Americans, African Americans remained isolated and without reliable allies in their efforts to transform their representation on screen.

In a session held the following morning, William Grant Still spoke regarding the use of music in films. Still had lived in Los Angeles since 1934, achieving widespread recognition for his compositional skills, directing the Los Angeles Philharmonic on multiple occasions, and enduring a frustrating series of false starts as he tried to find work composing film scores.[76] Still's views, while similar to Trumbo's, included both a diagnosis and a prospective remedy. Moreover, where Trumbo the screenwriter saw prejudice, Still the composer saw the profit motive, suggesting that a materialist analysis of racism was as likely to emerge from a black artist with a reputation for political conservatism as from one of Hollywood's highest-profile Marxists. Still argued that the persistence of stereotyped roles came as a result of both aesthetic conventions that impeded novelty on studio sets and the perennial search for easily estimable fiscal returns on films. Conceding "I must confess that I don't know exactly where the line of demarcation comes: what is racial prejudice and what is inherent in the business of filmmaking," Still placed his finger squarely on a dilemma that would plague black observers of Hollywood for decades to come. Having quit the picture *Stormy Weather* following repeated disagreements with a director convinced his compositions were "too good to be authentic" examples of Negro music, Still took black talent as part of the problem. He noted, "There have been many colored people who do what the men in charge command. If there had not been, there would be no problem today." The conviction that the withholding of labor could in fact force the sorts of changes that White, Trumbo, and others advocated emerged in part from Still's conviction that "there is something so fundamentally Negroid about genuine Negro music, whether it be folk or symphonic, that no white man can imitate it."[77] Still held that incorporating serious black artists was tantamount to transforming the essential structures of the cultural industry. This was more than a plea for the straightforward inclusion of African Americans into the existing order. This was more than a "laboring" of African American culture, and it moved well beyond the notion of a totalitarian culture industry "where something is provided for all so that none may escape."[78] Rather, Still turned Du Bois's notion of an exclusionary "two-ness" on its head, pointing toward black particularity as constituting a complete whole against a broader America rendered incomplete—spiritually and materially poorer—by its inability to comprehend the parameters of black culture and life.[79]

Still's notion of a genuine Negro music would, of course, have been equally familiar to a Duke Ellington or a Charlie Parker, both of whom understood the struggle over race, sound, and authenticity as one that linked the aesthetic and the material. But it was Still's caustic comment about those willing to "do what the men in charge command" that spoke most sharply to the question at hand. The actor Earl Dancer wrote an open letter to Paul Robeson and Walter White in which he argued that an "un-American" Hollywood showed no interest in altering course. For Dancer, actors like Clarence Muse, Hattie

McDaniel, and Nick Stewart were part of the problem, a colored aristocracy of cultural labor that kept Hollywood permanently unequal. Dancer's short note provoked a sharp rebuke. Hattie McDaniel, Louise Beavers, Ben Carter, Clarence Muse, Bill Robinson, and Ernest Whitman co-signed a response assailing Dancer's letter as "thoughtless," adding, "[A man] who has been given any number of glorious opportunities in Hollywood, is in no position" to argue his thesis of an "Un-American" film colony. Billy Rowe, theatrical editor at the *Eagle*, agreed, saying, "There are more people in the tinsel city for the full integration of all Americans in the nation's third largest industry than there are against it."[80] McDaniel, Beavers, and Muse were the most prominent among a group of screen personalities who denounced threats of boycotts, letter-writing campaigns, and other techniques of mass action. Having filed a $50,000 libel lawsuit after an editorial in the *Los Angeles Tribune* excoriated him as an Uncle Tom, Clarence Muse scored the "effrontery to the theatrical profession" inherent in White's decision to pursue a campaign against the studios without previous consultations with working actors.[81] Ernest Whitman concurred, noting, "Often times roles call for Paul Robeson or Marian Anderson to resort to 'dis and dat' in Negro dialect . . . yet we see no editorial tirades against them."[82] Responding to the notion of a Hollywood branch of the NAACP, Jesse Graves wondered "how in the world a man who has never been in Hollywood knows what is going on in Hollywood," while Louise Beavers retorted, "We do not have to be led by anyone." Of the talent present, only Ben Carter conceded the legitimacy of the campaign, saying, "We have a problem and I think Mr. White has something in his plan that will help us" before reiterating the predominant theme that "no layman is going to tell me that I am wrong because I make someone laugh."[83]

For the small cadre of established black actors, neither the question of political pressure nor the nature of roles could be considered as purely a social or an aesthetic matter. Noting that a torrent of angry letters to movie executives had created the perception that black audiences no longer wanted to see "our movie actors playing any parts at all as butlers, maids, cooks, coachmen, etc.," Harry Levette, a guest editorialist for the *California Eagle*, claimed that servile roles were increasingly being written as "Irish, Swedish, English, or any other nationality but Negro," with a resulting sharp decline in the number of roles available at all.[84] The claim that pressure against Hollywood was eviscerating the fortunes of the film colony continued after the war. In a lament widely replicated among her peers, McDaniel complained that the crusade against negative roles had left her able to secure only two weeks of work during the first five months of 1947.[85]

The response of Hollywood's increasingly embattled prewar black elite thus points to the emergence of an important cultural and political fault line. While artists such as McDaniel and Muse might join Robeson or Ellington for a benefit or rally, actors whose body of work had consisted primarily of trying to infuse menial roles with dignity found themselves criticized as out of step with the times. Material, social, and political circumstances were changing, and neither the hipsters in their drapes nor the thousands of black women who rallied outside the offices of the U.S. Employment Service to demand war work possessed the time or the inclination to shuffle along.[86]

Hence, both studios and the established cast of prominent black screen personalities found themselves challenged on ideological grounds. The results that followed were mixed. The *Pittsburgh Courier* cited increased employment of "race" actors and technical personnel, lauding the hiring of more than two hundred on the production of *Stormy Weather* alone. Public demand compelled the nationwide release of the wartime paean to black patriotism, *The Negro Soldier*, which originally was intended as a limited release meant to diffuse tensions among enlisted men. MGM agreed to alter scenes deemed offensive to blacks from a biography of the impeached President Andrew Johnson following protests before the Office of War Information. Most visibly, new types of films, many of which included African Americans as marginal protagonists rather than as loyal servants, began to redefine the default roles open to black actors. Both the issue of access and the question of representation began to shift ground as a result of the new context opened by the war.[87]

Many of the changes that took place as a result of wartime agitation were less readily apparent. The increasing importance of artists within debates regarding the politics of black culture offers one example. During the Second World War, figures such as Ellington, Still, and Himes became increasingly important shapers of black cultural politics, occupying ground that had been monopolized by political activists and scholars. After 1945, cultural production, reception, and analysis would continue to constitute a primary dimension of black radicalism. Aesthetic debates between artists, whether over content and form, performances and roles, or scripts and speech patterns, did more than prefigure better-known clashes of the 1960s. Rather, they suggested that Negro art and expression could simultaneously serve as an integral part of the broad fight for racial equality and constitute an autonomous zone of political action. Thus, the origins of the Black Arts Movement, in a manner of speaking, lay in the same wartime moment during which the modern black freedom movement was born.

Such, in part, was the context of *Jump for Joy*. The show's run was brief; it closed after three months. The loss of production personnel to the draft and concern that the musical's outspoken racial attitudes were polarizing audiences harmed box-office receipts. The musical was not cheap, either, and the relatively low ticket prices, combined with Los Angeles's unreliable theatergoing public, left solvency an elusive goal. Still, *Jump for Joy* reflected the efficacy of local efforts to use what William Grant Still called "the present war and its attendant crisis at home" as a staging area for a broader redefinition of the industries of mass culture and communication.[88] Ellington's musical took black history and culture as its own thematic reference point, cast the culture industry as a place of aesthetic and political conflict, proposed an autonomous portrayal of black life, and highlighted the promise of a relentless rejection of public presentations of African Americans as little more than servants, savages, or maids. As an interracial, cross-class product whose audience remained predominantly black, *Jump for Joy* demonstrated the possibilities of the self-organization of black creative talent and the existence of a substantial audience for new portrayals of African Americans.

On a national scale, the first years of the postwar period suggested a hopeful trend toward the desegregation of the culture industry. In 1946, the Screen Actors Guild passed a resolution vowing to oppose discriminatory hiring practices in the motion-picture industry.[89] In November 1950, a meeting in New York City of producers representing Paramount, RKO Pictures, MGM, Warner Brothers, and eight other motion-picture studios joined members of SAG, the Screen Extras Guild, and a representative from Central Casting at a conference sponsored by the Negro Motion Pictures Players Association. Film executives heard black actors request roles depicting "natural Americans" shown "shopping, at a ball game, or working in a factory." Conceding a "drastic oversight," William Hopkins of Columbia Pictures assured the assembly of a rapid series of improvements.[90] Similar discussions took place between black actors and television executives, who agreed to a resolution blocking discriminatory hiring practices, adding blacks to roles unspecified by race, and urging greater opportunities for black writers and production personnel.[91] Television executives vowed to "take no notice" of the insistence by Georgia Governor Herman Talmadge that television programming comply with Southern segregation laws. Responding to criticisms that television depicted "Negroes and whites talking to each other 'on a purely equal social basis,' " J. L. Van Volkenburg, president of CBS-TV, reiterated his intention to "continue to select our performers purely on the basis of their talent."[92]

After 1950, black artists, musicians, and actors fought for complete desegregation of the culture industry. These efforts would reprise wartime questions concerning the relation of politics and culture and point toward debates concerning cultural policy and cultural radicalism that would find more complete expression during the 1960s. Most fundamentally, they would find black musicians, actors, and artists pursuing new means of expression, demanding more and better jobs, and searching for an audience for a consciously black art. These activities would take place amid the extension of urban racial boundaries, setting the stage for a conflict over urban access in which African American expressive culture would play a key role.

2

THE NEGRO AS HUMAN BEING? Desegregation and the
Black Arts Imperative

In the five years that followed the end of the Second World War, signs of racial
progress appeared before all but the most jaded observers. Jackie Robinson
and Ralph Bunche became national examples of racial harmony, integrating
Major League Baseball and the highest ranks of American diplomacy, respectively. Seemingly overnight, Sambo's diners were renamed Rebecca's across the
length and breadth of Southern California. The Tuskegee Institute noted the
first consecutive years without a reported lynching, although researchers did
cite a disturbing rise in state-sanctioned killings.[1] The *California Eagle*, meanwhile, notched a novel victory in the struggle for cultural democracy. In
reviewing Donald Ogden Stewart's play *How I Wonder*, the paper led with a
simple headline: "Workshop Play Portrays Negro as Human Being."[2]

Irony aside, the *Eagle*'s headline suggested that efforts to contest depictions
of black characters had borne fruit. Between 1950 and 1955, the primary direction of black cultural politics shifted from representation to access. Efforts to
desegregate the culture industry prompted artists to forge informal communities and formal organizations, seek links to the broader black community,
and voice anew the relationship between artistic and political freedom. The
first iteration of concerted black arts activity would thus arise not from the
aftermath of the Watts riot a decade later, but from the search for civic
equality amid the plenty of postwar abundance.

Modern Los Angeles took shape between 1945 and 1960. Continued population growth, economic expansion, and a more prominent cultural infrastructure all came to the fore. Disneyland and Dodger Stadium opened their
doors. Reinvented for the jet age, Lockheed, Ford, Aeronutronics, and Hughes
Aircraft expanded research departments and assembly lines. With almost two-

thirds of federal spending earmarked for defense, newspaper want ads that had earlier sought machinists and welders now offered positions—complete with free training—for electrical engineers and systems analysts. Federal assistance led to a suburban building boom and a new system of freeways. This was a "golden age," characterized by Googie architecture, planned obsolescence, and enormous cars. The overall effect, according to one prominent chronicler, was the realization of the region's "best wartime and postwar hopes for itself."[3]

During August 1965, of course, it became clear to all exactly how few of the hopes of local African Americans had been met. In the decade preceding the Watts riot, black Angelenos experienced dramatically worsening socioeconomic conditions. Postwar re-conversion eliminated hard-won industrial jobs. The conservative climate of postwar politics traded the wartime possibility of full employment and adequate affordable housing for loyalty oaths and an aggressive, newly militarized police force. The cultural development of Southern California also reflected black exclusion, a fact epitomized equally by the rise of a racialized beach culture and the celebration of the predominantly white "cool" style as emblematic of West Coast jazz.

Against this backdrop, cultural politics that had previously considered questions of representation took on an increasingly material dimension. The years between 1950 and 1955 saw the first rise of a community-oriented cohort of locally based and politically engaged artists seeking both to join the expanding struggle for racial justice and to find collective solutions to their own aesthetic and material problems. More than a full decade before the explosion of Watts, local artists, musicians, and actors launched new challenges against segregation within and beyond the culture industry, founded the first successful community arts projects, and began processes of self-organization that would create the possibility of subsequent political and aesthetic collaborations.

CULTURES OF EXCLUSION IN THE COLD WAR CITY

In the fall of 1951, Los Angeles City Councilman Harold Harby convened a series of public hearings into the allegedly subversive elements present in a city-sponsored art exhibition taking place in a municipal park. Dozens of artists were asked to explain the intended meanings of their works, while amateur art enthusiasts derided the painters as insane, "reds," and worse. If the national context of red baiting made Los Angeles less than exceptional, the investigation into the politics of art did reveal a city somewhat out of step with the times. At precisely the moment that the abstract expressionist painting style pioneered by Jackson Pollock, a former student at Los Angeles's Manual

Arts High School, was being exhibited to Europeans as a representative example of American freedom and individuality, Californians working in similar styles were forced to defend themselves against charges that they were unconscious "tools of Kremlin propaganda."[4] Coming alongside changes in policing, housing, and race relations, the month long debate over the Griffith Park exhibition reflected the political tenor of Los Angeles during the early 1950s.

Harby's hearings took place amid a bevy of investigations into the alleged spread of subversion throughout the city, state, and nation. Between 1945 and 1960, anticommunism served as a key engine of regional economic growth, a centerpiece of local social life, and a path upward for more than one aspiring politician.[5] One result of this was a proliferation of legal hearings across three levels of government. In addition to the aforementioned hearings held by the City of Los Angeles, and the well-known activities of the House Committee on Un-American Activities (HUAC), the State of California held investigations into the spread of communist influence, as well. The state investigations were directed by State Senator Jack Tenney, former president of the American Federation of Musicians Local 47, who made his former union one of the first targets of his investigation. With the political right convinced that internal subversion, rather than external conquest, formed the primary communist threat, the arts, education, and mass communication emerged as critical arenas of concern. As a result, while investigations into civil-rights organizations, public-housing proponents, schools, trade unions, and minority communities took place, the striking convergence of federal hearings on the film industry, state hearings concerning unionized musicians, and municipal hearings on the political leanings of local artists suggest the extent to which culture became the primary site where California anticommunism played out.[6]

Offering a conjoined hostility to racial equality, modern art, and the political left, the strengthening of the political right cut across federal, state, and local levels. In Los Angeles, as in Dixie, opposition to civil rights often came from the staunchest anticommunists. Jack Tenney had led a segregated union. Freshman Congressman (and HUAC member) Richard Nixon's opposition to civil-rights legislation was a matter of public record decades before his "Southern strategy" enshrined racism as a basic pillar of Republican Party politics. Harold Harby, meanwhile, had opposed both the expansion of public housing and local desegregation ordinances. Such views formed the core sensibility of the right in early postwar Southern California. In 1949, after the City Council rejected an ordinance that would have mandated the desegregation of the all-white musicians' union local, the conservative *Los Angeles Times* identified an "echo" of the debate over public housing in the investigations into subversive art.[7] Such, at least, was the conclusion reached by the African American actor Irving Mosely, who observed caustically, "It's no accident that racial discrimination shares the limelight with blacklisting, censorship, and political persecutions."[8]

The battle over censuring painters took place within larger debates regarding public culture in Los Angeles. Competing visions of urbanity formed an important counter to the local power of the political right, and contests over the control of modern art facilities, the expansion of municipal arts and music programs, and the racial contours of popular music served as the core battlegrounds of the city's cultural life.[9] Kenneth Ross played a key role in this process. Following his appointment as director of the Municipal Arts Department in 1941, Ross's postwar tenure signaled the first concerted effort to develop a local cultural policy on the part of a city traditionally impoverished in relation to the visual arts.[10] Taking issue with rising calls for a designated arts facility that would serve as evidence of Southern California's arrival on the national art scene, Ross instead advocated a "new approach to art . . . intended to bring the enjoyment of art into reach of every person in the city." Citing the "decentralized" nature of Los Angeles, he spoke out against the building of a single showcase facility, arguing instead that an accessible program of lectures, public festivals, and arts instruction offered a more appropriate use of taxpayer funds. Despite repeated setbacks at the hands of a hostile City Council, Ross managed to enact a community-based arts program that marked the first municipal support for art by ethnic minorities in general and African Americans in particular.[11] The centerpiece of his efforts was the expansion of the city's annual outdoor arts festival into a linked set of concurrent events held at locations scattered across the city. Although Los Angeles had sponsored an annual arts exhibition since 1944, the festival in 1950 featured simultaneous events in ten locations, including Hollywood, the working-class harbor district of San Pedro, the prosaic San Fernando Valley, the affluent enclaves of Cheviot Hills and Beverly Hills, and predominantly black South Park.

The musical world arose as a second site in the struggle over the direction of municipal culture. Responding equally to the mixed racial composition of dance halls and the presumption of juvenile delinquency that surrounded, alternately, Mexican Americans, African Americans, and young people in general, the Los Angeles City Council authorized the expansion of the Los Angeles Bureau of Music from within the Municipal Arts Department. Over the course of the next decade, the Music Bureau organized classes, adult and youth choruses, symphonic concerts, and a series of neighborhood-based "community sings" that sought to realize a vision of "citizenship through music."[12] The bureau's slogan of "more music for more people" recalled the decentralized vision of Kenneth Ross, although Mayor Fletcher Bowron's clarification that "thousands of our growing boys and girls . . . will be better citizens and our city will be a better place to live" incorporated a more programmatic outcome than the one envisioned by the director of municipal arts.[13] With jump blues, boogie-woogie, and rock-and-roll bands, nightclubs, and radio shows proliferating across town, the notion of music as a defense against untoward juvenile behavior led predictably to a valorization of choral and classical music. Although trivial provisions were made for certain Mexican folk forms, the preponderance of community sings featured a range of European and American composers, including Mozart, Bach, Rachmaninoff, and Gershwin. As a result, participants and audiences were often more diverse than the programs offered to them by the city. The programs nonetheless proved popular. Between 1945 and 1952, attendance at bureau events soared from six thousand to more than four hundred thousand. Budgeting grew apace, rising from $4,000 at inception to $100,000 in the 1948–49 fiscal year.[14]

African Americans were partial participants in this emerging municipal culture. In the case of both the citywide Outdoor Art Shows and the Bureau of Music community programs, black involvement was both solicited and shunted aside. The Bureau of Music initially excluded African American neighborhoods from both the community sings and the neighborhood orchestral performances.[15] Members of the (African American) American Federation of Musicians Local 767 were likewise excluded from participation, although at least one performance by the Metropolitan Concert Band, affiliated with (white) Local 47, was held in South Los Angeles.[16] And although Ross ensured African American participation by selecting a park in a predominantly black area as one of the locations of the citywide arts exhibitions, advertisements published in the predominantly white press listed every venue except South Park. The result was a "separate but equal" situation wherein African Americans could, if they tried, imagine themselves as part of the larger city, although even dedicated white patrons were likely to miss the "black" exhibit as they traveled through Hollywood, the San Fernando Valley, San Pedro, Cheviot Hills, and the other sites of the All City Outdoor Shows.

The marginal participation of African Americans within the emerging urban culture came only partially as a result of the continuance of established local customs of racial exclusion. Rather, the dynamic novelty of postwar Californian culture and its clearly articulated racial boundaries illustrate the extent to which segregation was a system of practices and beliefs in constant evolution and reformulation rather than the legacy of a traditional past. Seen from this perspective, the development of popular culture in the 1950s did more than reflect Los Angeles Police Chief William Parker's estimation of Los Angeles as a "white spot" among American cities—it produced it. As Eric Avila has shown, the primary symbols of postwar Californian culture were racialized sites that facilitated the idea of Southern California as dominated by middle-class white ideas about public space, urban access, and social relations.[17] The invented traditionalism of Disneyland's Main Street U.S.A, for example, offered a vision of suburban order far removed from the wartime activism described as a "racial revolution" by the journalist Carey McWilliams.[18] Notwithstanding the team's pioneering role in the integration of Major League Baseball, the Brooklyn Dodgers' transplanting to Los Angeles involved erecting a stadium on the newly razed foundations of some of the city's oldest Mexican American neighborhoods. Patterns of racial exclusion grew with the city's redefinition as a surfside paradise. Housing restrictions, surf movies, and the police ensured that the city's beaches were both peopled by and represented as belonging solely to whites, while part of the "autopia" of the freeway was precisely the manner in which drivers could now glide over, rather than pass through, a darkening urban core.[19] One primary reason for trips to the city center—previously undertaken on the now defunct interurban train and trolley system—had been the patronage of black music within Central Avenue's clubs. The need for this, too, waned during the early 1950s, as the locus of the Los Angeles nightclub world shifted from Central Avenue to Hollywood and West Los Angeles.

For much of the black populace, the implications of emerging patterns of cultural exclusion paled in the face of more quotidian concerns over housing, employment, and the police. Throughout the 1950s, African American migration to Los Angeles continued to grow exponentially. Having doubled during the years of the Second World War, the local black population doubled again, rising from 133,082 in 1946 (up from 63,774 in 1940) to 171,209 by 1950. In the following decade, African American Los Angeles came close to doubling again, with the population rising to 334,916 by 1960. This vastly increased the percentage of black city residents. Making up only 3 percent of the populace in 1940, African Americans constituted approximately 9 percent of Los Angeles in 1950. By 1960, more than one out of every eight residents of the city would be an African American.[20]

As had been the case during the Second World War, few found acceptable

FIGURE 4 Racially restricted housing, Southeast Los Angeles, circa September 1950. Black migrants to Los Angeles confronted chronic shortages of housing in the face of widespread efforts to maintain urban segregation during the 1950s. California Eagle Photograph Collection, Southern California Library.

jobs or decent places to live. Far more than half of all black industrial workers lost their jobs after the war, and the manufacturing, aerospace, and defense production that remained in Southern California increasingly shifted away from the urban center and into distant and segregated sections of Orange County and Southeast Los Angeles.[21] The slackening of industrial opportunities came as a result of more than these geographic and demographic trends. As one recent study notes, the evisceration of the political left inside the constituent unions of the Congress of Industrial Organizations (CIO) radically diminished the willingness of labor unions to engage in struggles over racial equality.[22] In the absence of either mass pressure from African Americans or the broad milieu of Popular Front–era antiracism, the most visible dimension of the struggle for racial justice shifted decisively from the shop floor to the classroom and the realtor's office.[23] The result was a string of civil-rights victories regarding housing, education, and political representation that did little to meet the growing needs of a black working class inhabiting neighborhoods that saw little of the surrounding postwar economic boom.

While insufficient housing and underemployment remained ongoing concerns, a different matter constituted a daily problem for African American Los Angeles. After 1950, relations between African Americans and the Los Angeles Police Department (LAPD) worsened dramatically. A series of administrative reorganizations, capped by the selection of the former Marine Corps officer William Parker as chief of police, inaugurated a half-century of strained relations between black Angelenos and the police force charged with their protection. Parker arrived as an internationally recognized figure. Rated by *Life* magazine as the nation's second most popular law-enforcement officer after his unspoken rival, FBI Director J. Edgar Hoover, Parker had been made honorary captain of the national police force of South Korea in recognition of his assistance in setting up the far-right Republic of Korea's national police.[24] This pedigree served Parker well locally, where he received repeated commendations by conservative powers, including the Chamber of Commerce, the Manufacturer and Merchants Association, and the *Los Angeles Times*. Parker reshaped the Los Angeles Police Department, transforming a force with a reputation as one of the nation's most corrupt into a paramilitary body modeled on his beloved Marine Corps. Discipline, physical endurance, sophisticated intelligence gathering, and technological advancement were the hallmarks of a force defined within and beyond Los Angeles by its endemic patterns of racism and its dogged independence from municipal oversight.

Present throughout the history of Los Angeles, these patterns of racist behavior became entrenched within the department after 1950. Gerald Horne records that as much as a third of the force was estimated to belong to the radically conservative John Birch Society.[25] Although Los Angeles had been among the first American cities to hire "Negro" officers, these policemen were often restricted to traffic duty inside heavily black precincts and were always paired with white partners. Many of the white police officers were openly racist, arbitrarily detaining African Americans who wore tennis shoes or drove expensive cars, wantonly beating black people, and reportedly setting quotas concerning the number of blacks to be arrested and charged every month. The last practice reflected Parker's proclivity for what he termed "scientific policing," and he dismissed concerns regarding the targeting of blacks as "ridiculous" while claiming that policing based on race "was a tool, not an attitude." Describing the police in the anticommunist language of containment, Parker warned that a "thin blue line" was all that promised protection "for family and home" in a city expected to become nearly 45 percent "Negro" by 1970. Contrasting this vision of a city overrun with the popular slogan of Los Angeles as the "white spot of the great cities of America today," Parker repeatedly raised the ire of black residents with his offhanded references to "Congolese hordes" and "monkeys in a zoo."[26]

Widely despised among African Americans, Parker's men generated particular opprobrium among black musicians. As was the case in Oakland, the Los Angeles Police Department and Sheriff's Department recruited transplanted Southern whites, few of whom were likely to respond favorably to the displays of attitude and affluence for which jazz musicians were known. The presence of significant numbers of white patrons inside Central Avenue nightspots added another dimension. Having sought to concentrate vice within the spatial boundaries of black Los Angeles, and convinced that the presence of interracial couples could only indicate prostitution, police officers increasingly acted as if suppressing the musical life of South Los Angeles might eliminate crime. Police raids provoked a response from across the class spectrum. As Mike Davis notes, the record-shop owner John Dolphin organized a protest of one hundred and fifty black business owners following a police blockade aimed at interdicting the interracial clientele who patronized his twenty-four-hour rhythm-and-blues emporium.[27] A longstanding pattern in American social life, the use of force to forestall relationships among blacks and whites—particularly among black men and white women—entered a crisis phase in the context of postwar spatial patterns, new policing regimes, and the increasing impoverishment of South Los Angeles.

Such, at least, were the conclusions reached by musicians in the area. The trombonist Clara Bryant recalled intrusive searches along Central Avenue, noting that male officers would grope female detainees, while male suspects would be forced to stand or kneel in humiliating positions. Searches for drugs provided a pretense for invasive encounters, and amid a sharp rise in the number of narcotics-related arrests, police made a clear decision to target the nightclub world and, by extension, the musicians around whom it was built.[28] Buddy Collette described the police as "the only trouble" on Central Avenue.[29] The pianist Coney Woodman claimed that the police "harassed us all the time," a sentiment corroborated by his brother Britt.[30] Art Farmer recalled being stopped three times in the course of a single evening as he walked between gigs.[31] Armed police drew down on the trumpeter Bobby Bradford and the saxophonist Ornette Coleman, threatening to shoot Coleman for rolling his window down too slowly during a traffic stop.[32] The cumulative effect was perhaps best captured by Coleman's description of Los Angeles as "a police state."[33] Harassment was a concern for black folks without instruments,

FIGURE 5 LAPD officers arrest Joseph Lewis during a raid at Cafe Zombie at 5434 Central Avenue, 31 March 1947. Musicians often encountered unwanted attention from police, especially as the police attempted to suppress interracial mixing in nightclubs. Such scenes were critical to reestablishing urban segregation after the Second World War. *Herald Examiner* Collection, Los Angeles Public Library.

as well. Having recently driven west from New York, the artist John Garay was told by police that they had stopped his car because it had "foreign" (that is, New York) license plates, because "no Negroes lived" in the section of the city he was driving in, and, finally, because they wanted to find out "the last time he had been in jail."[34]

Constant contact produced mutual antipathy. Police beat the blues singer Jimmy Witherspoon badly enough that he required hospitalization.[35] Johnny Otis was arrested for asking police to loosen a juvenile detainee's handcuffs.[36] Glendale police customarily escorted black musicians to the city limits at the end of gigs; blacks, whatever their talents, were unwelcome in the city after sundown. The white bandleader Jimmy Wright's integrated band was arrested or prevented from performing across a wide swath of Los Angeles County, including Hollywood, West Hollywood, Downey, and South Gate. While the latter two locations formed part of the "Alameda Curtain" of southeastern Los

Angeles suburbs known for their hostility toward African Americans, the Hollywood sites were racially contested spaces that were becoming increasingly important as centers of nightlife.

The physical exclusion of African American musicians took place alongside a more subtle symbolic excision. Although migration from Louisiana and Texas had ensured an early beachhead for what the jazz pioneer Reb Spikes called "Louisiana-style or ragtime or jazz or whatever you want to call it," it was not until the early 1950s that a distinctly "West Coast" style of jazz became widely known as such.[37] Reaching the height of its popularity between 1952 and 1956, West Coast jazz emphasized small combinations, elaborate scores, a narrow improvisational range closely tied to written compositions, and a playing style celebrated (or derided) as relaxed, understated, and unhurried. As the jazz author Robert Gordon notes, many of the participants in the emerging West Coast sound were white veterans of the big-band era whose considerable formal training led them to believe that Southern California would provide opportunities for earning additional money as studio session musicians.[38] The West Coast style arose amid the economic decline of Central Avenue, and the primary venues for the new style were to be found in predominantly white sections of Hollywood, Hermosa Beach, and West Los Angeles. The imagery that surrounded the West Coast sound was playful and airy, captured in photographs and album covers that featured musicians sailing, emerging in scuba gear from the surf, strolling across golf fairways, or playing their instruments astride a merry-go-round.

And it was white. Notwithstanding figures such as the pianist Hampton Hawes, nearly all of the avatars of the West Coast sound were Caucasians, including Shorty Rogers, Gerry Mulligan, Chet Baker, Art Pepper, Bob Cooper, and Shelly Manne. By 1954, *Time* magazine had proclaimed the pianist Dave Brubeck its "man of the year," easily the highest honor ever bestowed on a jazz musician. Brubeck's apotheosis recalled the insults of a previous generation, when the composers Cab Calloway, Duke Ellington, and Count Basie had watched the white bandleaders Paul Whiteman and Benny Goodman crowned "kings" of swing. An interview between the bassist and composer Charles Mingus and Leonard Feather, a white columnist for *Down Beat*, suggests something of the ire felt by many black musicians at the time. Asked to participate in a blind review, Mingus refused to award a record by Lee Konitz even a single star—the coin of the realm of Feather's "Blindfold Tests." He instead ridiculed Konitz, Paul Desmond, and Dave Brubeck. Dismissing Konitz's combo as sounding like "five dead men," Mingus concluded, "If they play jazz, I don't play jazz."[39] Despite the presence of a growing pool of musicians working in the emerging "hard bop" idiom that combined bop's modernist forms with established African American musico-religious sensibilities, California's black musicians were all but absent from jazz criticism, journalism, and recording during this time. Indeed, the tenor saxophonist Harold Land languished in obscurity for four decades as a result of his decision to stay in Los Angeles, despite the fact that his rare stints in New York earned his playing nearly universal acclaim. Accolades notwithstanding, Land remained severely under-appreciated until his death in 2001, despite recording with Max Roach, Clifford Brown, Thelonious Monk, and Elmo Hope.[40] Mina Yang attributes the invisibility that plagued Land and others to the demise of Central Avenue, noting that the *Down Beat* columnist Hal Holly confined his "Los Angeles Band Briefs" to discussions of performances held in Hollywood, Culver City, and the South Bay. *Metronome* and *Record Changer* did so as well, proclaiming Los Angeles bereft of a jazz history, a bop genesis, or a distinctive sound until the arrival of the style associated with Dave Brubeck, Shorty Rodgers, Chet Baker, Bob Cooper, and Shelly Manne.[41] Ultimately, the exclusion of black performers from the musical landscape of Southern California came as the result of more than the demise of a black central business district, the laziness of the jazz press, or the efforts of a racist police force. Exclusion served as the capstone of a larger culture of whiteness-in-formation enacted not only through housing discrimination and policing, but also through architecture, mass entertainment, and intellectual production.

It is to the response of black artists to this exclusion that this chapter now turns.

ACHIEVING AMALGAMATION

During the spring of 1952, a small group convened a series of informal meetings to explore the possibility of ending the practice of maintaining segregated locals among unionized musicians. Racially mixed bands and nightclubs had become more common locally during the Second World War, and although the presence of separate union locals had been at issue more than once during the postwar period, little movement had been made toward changing a long-established practice. Yet with unemployment rising among unionized musicians of all colors, many black musicians viewed desegregation as both an urgent material imperative and a long-overdue recognition of their equal talent and ability.

A year before the merger, few observers would have bet that white musicians would vote to integrate their local. The beneficiaries of preferential hiring by local film and television studios, Local 47 had moved toward the political right following accusations of communist influence made by Jack Tenney. Between 1950 and 1953, both the American Federation of Musicians' monthly magazine, *International Musician*, and Local 47's journal *Overture* published regular denunciations of communist influence in the labor movement. Indeed, with the exception of vociferous opposition to the Taft-Hartley Act, anticommunist broadsides constituted the preponderance of non-musicological items published in both periodicals.

An AFL affiliate founded at the tail end of the nineteenth century, the American Federation of Musicians (AFM) followed the common craft-union practice of maintaining racially exclusionary locals. Black and white musicians in the AFL's more than five hundred locals, with exception of those in Detroit and New York, shared little beyond occasional social contacts. This general pattern held in Southern California, where a separate black AFM branch, Local 767, had existed since 1918. By the time merger talks began thirty-five years later, Local 767 maintained a paying membership of between four hundred and eight hundred. Originally chartered in 1897, the racially restricted Local 47 counted between thirteen thousand and fifteen thousand white members in the decade after the Second World War. Accurate numbers for both locals were difficult to come by, as a substantial number of musicians who lived elsewhere maintained paid union memberships in Southern California to take advantage of industry conventions and union rules favoring locals for lucrative work in film and on television.[42] Estimates by informed observers, however, portrayed two locals that were actually far closer in size than their paper membership suggested. Local 767 election returns suggested that at least four hundred members were present within Los Angeles at any given time, a factor that suggests a higher actual membership. A subsequent battle over the administration of union dues, moreover, revealed that less than one tenth of Local 47's membership reported earning any income from music, thus placing the active membership of the local closer to three thousand, a number confirmed by the general number of votes cast in the various referenda regarding integration.

As was the case with actors and writers, musicians were drawn to the West Coast by the possibility of work in film and television. Working on a television or film score offered five or ten times nightclub rates with residual payments afterward, thus promising an important source of income in an industry that had continued to shed jobs with the successive introductions of sound movies, recorded music, radio, and television. Lucrative studio work remained scarce, however, especially for black musicians forced to compete against racist perceptions and better-connected white musicians.[43] Discrimination in studio work was endemic, with the argument that blacks were unable to read music serving as a primary exclusionary excuse. When forced to concede the fallacious nature of this claim, employers commonly asserted that black musicians lacked the ability to "double up," or play multiple instruments during a single recording session. This reason, too, had little factual basis, since African American multi-instrumentalists were common. The Dorsey High School and Los Angeles City College alumnus Eric Dolphy, for example, was unable to find either studio or orchestra jobs, despite the fact that he had classical training on the flute and oboe in addition to the alto and tenor saxophone. Individual examples aside, the practice of doubling up remained relatively rare, as it required studios to pay musicians a premium.[44]

Exclusionary studio practices were compounded by the efforts of Local 47 members, who kept choice parts of a rapidly diminishing pie to themselves whenever feasible. Such, in any case, was the view of most black musicians. Red Callender claimed that "all the work" went to the white local, while Buddy Collette recalled that the most common experience for black musicians was a temporary call when an entire black band was required to "sideline," or play over, music previously recorded by white musicians.[45] Even mixed gigs were a humiliating proposition. Lionel Hampton reported being paid as little as one fifth of the wages paid white musicians on the same bandstand.[46] Racially based inequalities affected the social identity of musicians. Anthony Macías notes instances of black musicians' claiming "Creole" status in seeking entry into Local 47, as well as Mexican American musicians arguing for a racial designation of white even as they were excluded from employment in the Los Angeles Symphony Orchestra.[47]

Talks about unifying the two unions began informally among black and white musicians. The timing of such a move seemed fortuitous. Mixed bands and integrated nightspots had become more common during the war, and supporters of amalgamation introduced an unsuccessful City Council resolution demanding an end to union discrimination in 1949.[48] The AFM's main journal, *International Musician*, had recently dropped the identifier "colored" from its listing of nonwhite union locals, and even Local 47 officials who expressed skepticism about the proposed federation conceded that the practice of maintaining separate locals purely on the basis of race was "un-American."[49] Thus, despite the conservative political leanings and acute financial fears of many unionized white musicians, both the growing salience and the increasing acceptability of civil-rights activity during the early Cold War formed part of a context within which new social conditions and arrangements became both imaginable and achievable.

The unfolding process of union amalgamation highlights the leading role of black musicians in the symbolic and actual contest for integration in Los Angeles in the 1950s. This by itself is unsurprising. As both the preceding (wartime) and following (post-Watts riot) historical moments illustrate, musicians often occupied the forefront of black politics. Indeed, as Amiri Baraka and Sterling Stuckey note, historical experience and aesthetic valuations had made music, like religion, a cornerstone of black identity along both racial and class axes.[50] As such, it was almost a given—an overdetermination, in other parlance—that musicians would occupy the forefront of the struggle for integration, just as they would stand at the pinnacle of both wartime cultural democracy and the post-1965 search for self-determination. Integration and self-determination, of course, emerged as demands from within distinct and sometimes antagonistic segments of African America, and if one were to hold that consciously black music formed a core sensibility of the black working class, one might well argue that musicians would have been unlikely to stand at the forefront of the struggle for integration, given the firm association between civil rights and the black middle class. Insofar as they possessed unique skills that allowed them a degree of autonomous labor power and occupied a cross-class appeal as symbols of dignified autonomy, black musicians ultimately held a strategic position as activist intellectuals whose self-activity nearly always had broader social repercussions.[51] It was thus fitting both that they would occupy a leading role in integration and that integration would demonstrate its limits through their example.

As an initial step, a petition asking members of the white local to support desegregation was circulated at Los Angeles City College, where several members of Local 47 held teaching positions. This effort met with little success. More helpful to the cause of amalgamation was the formation of the interracial Community Symphony Orchestra (cso) by the high-school friends Charles Mingus and Buddy Collette. Prodded by Mingus, an outspoken critic of union segregation, Collette made known their intention to found an interracial orchestra. According to Collette, public cso rehearsals attracted a wide spectrum of resident and visiting musicians and conductors. This in turn attracted media drawn by the image of an interracial band playing classical music in parks and schools. Although formally unaffiliated, the cso came together as the City of Los Angeles Music Bureau began sponsoring the aforementioned series of free concerts, music education programs, and other public events. The group thus became a part of the growing urban culture developing in postwar —and pre-riot—Los Angeles. With the added participation of the famous music teachers Lloyd Reese and Samuel Browne, the cso also began a series of jazz jam sessions that involved teenage African American musicians such as Eric Dolphy and Horace Tapscott, as well as older white members of Local 47 with little experience playing improvised music. Thus, in addition to providing black and white musicians a public stage, the cso contributed to a broader opening for white musicians seeking to open spaces for alternative musical genres in a union local dominated by symphony musicians.[52]

The cso brought together an interracial group eager to end segregation. Comprising roughly equal numbers of blacks and whites, approximately two dozen participants attended the initial meetings held to plan the merger campaign.[53] In addition to Mingus and Collette, the African American musicians Benny Carter, Gerald Wilson, Marl Young, Red Callender, Britt Woodman, John Anderson, Gerald Wiggins, and Bill Douglas played important early roles in coordinating the amalgamation campaign. Beyond using the bandstands of the cso as an improvisational pulpit, this group solicited statements of support from prominent black musical celebrities, including Josephine Baker and Nat King Cole, while planning a press campaign and a series of public events designed to pressure leaders in both locals.

A key figure in prewar jazz, the saxophonist, trumpeter, and composer Benny Carter, had won acclaim both as a bandleader and as an arranger for Fletcher Henderson's orchestra. After living for a time in Europe, Carter had moved to Southern California, where he had composed musical scores for several films, including *Stormy Weather*. Partially as a result of his prominence and reputation, Carter was selected as the chairman of the integrated amalgamation committee. A sideman of Carter's during 1943 and a respected composer in his own right, Gerald Wilson played an active role in the amalgamation effort, as well. Arriving from one of the two major cities without segregated musicians unions, Wilson, a Detroit native, initially proposed submitting the question to a membership vote against the wishes of Local 767's president, Leo Davis.[54]

The pianist Marl Young played an even larger role. A Chicagoan by way of Virginia, Young arrived in Los Angeles with a law degree and experience dealing with a powerful white union. Chicago's all-white Local 10 was led by James Petrillo, who would launch the wartime ban on recorded music following his election as president of the entire AFM. Although initially uninterested in working in an integrated union, Young was annoyed by what he saw as the quiescence of the black union leadership. Condemning the union's small size and inaccessible geographic location relative to Hollywood, Young criticized the tendency of union officials to ask whites across town for administrative assistance. Noting that the vice-president of Local 47 had written the black union's bylaws, Young opined, "Well, hell, if I'm running a union, I don't want you calling anybody for advice. . . . It looks like the man is taking care of your business. That's bullshit."[55] In addition to serving as a trustee for Local 767 during the merger, he negotiated the eventual compromise on seniority and benefits and served as an official in the integrated union after 1957.

The elected leadership of Local 767 strongly resisted amalgamation. Wariness was neither a matter of political conservatism nor, as some disingenuous observers held, evidence of black support for segregation. Rather, the desire to maintain longstanding patterns of autonomy was rooted in a rich history of collective organization and mutual assistance among area musicians who had long adopted practices aimed at turning "segregation into congregation."[56] During the interwar period, Local 767 and the Los Angeles chapter of the National Association of Negro Musicians (led by the music educator John Gray) had served as bridges linking cultural education, economic development, and political leadership. Gray, a graduate of the École Normale de Musique in Paris, wrote the weekly newspaper columns "Pianology" and "In the Music World," which offered perhaps the most eloquent local articulation of racial uplift ideology, concerned as they were with what he termed "the mental development of a people" and the "outline of their culture" provided by their songs.[57] Musicians Protective Union Local 767 had originally met in a record store owned by the local jazz pioneers John and Reb Spikes, whose shop floor doubled as a booking agency and a primary conduit for work in Hollywood, amid shelves filled with instruments and drawers crammed with sheet music. Thus, both of Los Angeles's active music associations could trace their efforts—and thus their constituencies—back decades.

Whatever criticisms can be made today of the scholarly focus on culture as a category of analysis, the fact remains that culture in general, and music in particular, formed a mainstay of the quest for respectability that stood at the heart of prewar black politics.[58] Music instructors constituted a formidable section of the local black petit bourgeoisie, accounting by one estimate for between a third and a fifth of the city's black professionals between 1920 and 1940. In 1900, one out of every hundred black Angelenos was a music teacher.

FIGURE 6 Professor Wilkins and piano students, circa 1932. Shades of Los Angeles Archives, Los Angeles Public Library.

Two decades later, the proportion had declined, but absolute numbers had more than tripled, growing from 78 to 226 by 1930.[59] The top level of musical instruction included both men and women, with the pianists William Wilkins, John Gray, and Genevieve Barnes Lewis; the violinist Bessie Williams; and the choir director Elmer Bartlett the most prominent. Each founded or acquired his or her own music school at some point; thus, the teaching and composing of European art music rested on strong institutional foundations among black Angelenos. Care was taken to envision music instruction as both a legitimate vocation for specialists and something useful for all "Negro" youth. In this vein, an article in the *Los Angeles Sentinel* noted that "children of average talent are able to . . . give recitals, sight read, and [possess] a working knowledge of elementary harmony" following a short period of study under Professor Gray. The number of local music students reached into the thousands, and with the most prominent schools enrolling an interracial student body, both the willingness of whites to send their children to study music under the tutelage of blacks and the obvious quality of the city's black piano, violin, and choral instruction could not but, in the words of one observer, "help mould sentiment for the uplift of the race."[60]

Traditions of mutualism and racial uplift were strongly embedded within

FIGURE 7 Music class, 13 December 1939. The piano player, Mrs. Alma Hightower, taught music to many youth in the Los Angeles area, including a number of professional musicians. Such scenes were typical of the rich music education opportunities open to black Angelenos in the pre–Civil Rights period. Photograph by Fred William Carter. *Herald Examiner* Collection, Los Angeles Public Library.

the educational networks that fostered much of the city's youthful jazz talent. John Gray, William Grant Still, and W. C. Handy served as guest instructors in the Jefferson high-school orchestra led by Samuel Browne. Private instructors included Lloyd Reese, whose students included Mingus and Eric Dolphy, and Alma Hightower, who taught Sonny Criss, Dexter Gordon, Melba Liston, and others. When one considers both the sharp contests over black access to public spaces during this period and the likely impression that a high-school student might take away after a classroom visit by a Duke Ellington or a Nat King Cole, it is hardly difficult to imagine that the primary constituency for maintaining high-school classrooms, union halls, and even after-hours nightclubs as more or less entirely black spaces was likely to come from among the most outspoken proponents of racial pride. Among musicians, the shift from independent, if segregated, institutions to integrated groupings—in other words, from mutualism to civil rights—promised greater individual opportunities at the expense of established patterns of collective self-help. Ultimately, even the promise of the former would prove chimerical, and the widespread exclusion of area musicians from work assignments by the newly integrated locals would serve as one catalyst for the emergence of new forms of place-based collective organizing among musicians in the decade to follow.

But that would come later. At the time, resistance to folding Musicians Protective Union Local 767 was cast as a defense of intergenerational instruction, financial autonomy, and decades-old patterns of racial solidarity. Indeed, the leading voices of opposition to the proposed merger were area musicians with longstanding local ties. The pianist Florence Cardrez "Tiny" Brantley, a former student of John Gray and the recording secretary, had worked to integrate local USO shows during the war. A former sideman for Jelly Roll Morton, Paul Howard, the treasurer, was the co-founder of the Quality Serenaders, a jazz orchestra founded in Los Angeles in 1924.[61] Aided by the financial secretary, Harvey Brooks, Brantley and Howard marshaled both material and emotional appeals against the merger. Conceding inferior facilities and fewer opportunities than those open to whites, the elected leaders of Local 767 argued that these negatives were more than counterbalanced by the autonomy of a separate union. Claiming that Local 767 was an independent body rather than a "colored auxiliary," they argued that amalgamation would cost members a building, substantial bank deposits, and, possibly, their identity in the face of a much larger white local.

Charging that union officials sought only to preserve their jobs, amalgamation advocates launched a fierce struggle for control of the local.[62] Incumbent forces won an initial vote rejecting further negotiations, prompting proponents to publish a series of editorial advertisements concerning the campaign in the *California Eagle*.[63] A second election, held four days later, ended inconclusively. The pro-merger candidate Benny Carter lost to the incumbent president, Leo Davis, by a bare thirteen votes, or less than 1.5 percent of votes cast. Buddy Collette and Marl Young won election to the union's three-member board of trustees, giving that body a two-to-one majority in favor of amalgamation. The larger board of directors was split down the middle, with the *Eagle* reporting four candidates in favor and four against. Internal divisions paralyzed the union for six weeks, at which time the membership of Local 767 would vote to join Local 47 by a vote of 274 to 127.[64]

Seesaw votes and rancorous internal debates point to the deep ambivalence regarding integration felt by a substantial section of black musicians. Accustomed to both autonomy and prestige within their community, many musicians regarded the promise of additional work as insufficient justification for relocating—physically and symbolically—from South Los Angeles to Hollywood. The vote approving the merger, moreover, came on the heels of a vote in favor of amalgamation by members of Local 47, who after substantial debate, particularly over the question of seniority and benefits, had voted 1,608 to 1,375 in favor of merging with Local 767.[65] Majority support for integration thus came only after it became clear that a plurality of white musicians also preferred a change.

This decision capped almost a year of public agitation. African American advocates of the merger had rejected repeated offers from Local 47's board of directors, largely as a result of demands that the black local dissolve itself so that former members could apply for individual entry into Local 47.[66] Recognizing that this would result in lost seniority and death benefits, and that it would require longtime union members to pay a second initiation fee to the AFM, pro-merger forces demanded that Local 47 members be allowed to vote solely on the issue of joining together the two unions in their entirety.[67] Amalgamation advocates also sought to check the main argument advanced by their white opponents—namely, that the merger would cost the white local lost revenue. Noting that a merger would involve the transference of all the assets and property of Local 767 and add nearly six hundred dues-paying members, advocates of the merger countered that amalgamation would constitute a windfall for the organization. In the end, their logic and persistence were rewarded.[68] Under the final merger terms, black musicians entered Local 47 with full seniority and benefits and without having to pay an initiation fee.[69]

The fate of efforts to establish a single union for studio musicians constituted the most visible local civil-rights issue in the winter of 1952. On a day that the *California Eagle* reported on a spate of police killings, the successful passing of the lieutenant's exam by Police Sergeant Thomas Bradley, and the winding path of the court case *Oliver L. Brown v. The Board of Education of Topeka (KS)*, the paper also carried two articles and an advertisement detailing the struggle against "Jim Crow" within Local 47. Editorial commentary connected developments among musicians to local efforts to end racially restrictive housing covenants, integrate the fire department, and contest the worrying shift from lynching and other vigilante violence to police brutality and "legal" killings. Against this backdrop, advocates of maintaining separate institutions based in, controlled by, and aimed predominantly at a spatially bound black community found themselves on the wrong side of a newly emergent civil-rights consensus. In this vein, the *Eagle* columnist Wendell Green argued that the struggle within Local 767 had national implications, since the "pro-segregation" efforts of the anti-merger forces in black Local 767 had attracted national media attention among foes of integration.[70]

Nationally, the example of Los Angeles provided a model for the complete desegregation of the American Federation of Musicians. Amalgamation also marked a turning point in the entertainment industry. Although black entertainers and musicians would continue to complain about a dearth of opportunities, amalgamation removed the last official vestige of racial exclusion in radio, television, and film. Amalgamation represented the confluence of two factors, both of which illustrate the importance of cultural politics. On the one hand, artists successfully organized themselves into a political campaign aimed at winning a collective improvement in their conditions. This form of artist self-organization would return again in South Los Angeles after 1965. Moreover, the nature and degree of attention given to the struggle against segregation in the entertainment industry—every significant development in the unfolding process made the front page of either the *Sentinel* or the *Eagle*—presaged the prominence of cultural struggles after 1965.

At the same time, the experience of black musicians between 1950 and 1955 illustrates the uneven and contradictory process of urban desegregation beyond the South. In a pattern that would confound black elected officials in decades to come, formal barriers fell even as overall material conditions worsened. In the years following the Supreme Court's decision in 1948 declaring restrictive housing covenants unenforceable, rising levels of urban poverty actually increased residential segregation in several heavily black areas of Los Angeles. Few musicians of any color could make a regular living recording for radio, television, or film, and both the westward shift of the city's nightlife and the increasingly draconian policing of Southern California's spatial boundaries hampered opportunities for black musicians. When combined with the symbolic exclusion of cool jazz, these socioeconomic realities would increasingly suggest the limits of integration as a framework for addressing either the material or aesthetic interests of black artists.

STEWART'S SHOWCASE

The attempt to democratize the musicians' unions took place in public view. Newspapers announced union gatherings and recorded vote tallies. Open meetings were held where partisans rallied converts to their positions, and the final result was widely celebrated as a victory against racial discrimination. Other engagements in the effort to desegregate the entertainment industry unfolded more quietly, however. West of the former Local 767 headquarters, now an informal social club for black musicians, a newly opened theater was busily preparing its first offering. The founding of the Ebony Showcase Theater, owned and operated by the actor and entertainer Horace Winston (Nick) Stewart, a participant in one of television's most familiar and controversial shows, would in its own way prove as important in the cultural history of black Los Angeles as the integration of Local 47.

Born in 1910 in Harlem to Garveyite parents of Barbadian descent, Stewart made an important career choice early in his adolescence. Dismissing the career wishes of his parents with the pointed observation that "everybody with an education was a Pullman porter," he left school at fourteen. Working as a custodian in the dance halls and vaudeville theaters surrounding his Harlem home, he rubbed shoulders with black America's performing elite, including Bill Robinson, Cab Calloway, and Duke Ellington. Watching led to learning, and after pilfering a few steps and the odd wisecrack, the teenager found a job as part of the vaudeville troop of the comedian Danny Smalls. Although Smalls liked the young Stewart's steps, he was less impressed by the youngster's name. And so, shortly after taking the job, Horace Winston became "Nicodemus."[71]

A quick study, Nicodemus landed prized jobs at the peak of Harlem's time as the entertainment capital of the black world. Working with Smalls led to an introduction to Cab Calloway, who got the sixteen year old a job alongside Lena Horne in the Cotton Club's chorus line. Fearing himself insufficiently handsome for a dancer, Stewart gravitated toward comedy and by 1933 was touring nationally with the Franchon and Marco vaudeville troupe. Three years later, he rejoined Calloway as his featured comedian, a role Stewart would also fill for Ella Fitzgerald and Louis Armstrong.[72]

Appearing as part of such prestigious ensembles brought Stewart into contact with black and white celebrities, facilitating an initial foray into Hollywood. After seeing him perform with Calloway at the Palladium Theater in Los Angeles, the actress Mae West sent word inviting him to try out for a part in *Go West Young Man*. He did, and in 1937 Stewart made his cinematic debut. The promise of further roles prompted a permanent move to Los Angeles in 1941. Over the course of a decade, Stewart landed significant roles in eighteen films, including *Stormy Weather* and *Cabin in the Sky*. One of the most visible black actors in Hollywood, he was among the cohort of established black actors selected by Hattie McDaniel for participation in the Hollywood Victory Committee.[73]

Stewart's career in the entertainment industry continued to grow. In 1951, the veteran of vaudeville, theater, radio, and film was cast as Lightnin', the dimwitted custodian on the soon to be televised *Amos 'n' Andy* show. Switching *Amos 'n' Andy*, the most popular program in radio history, to television posed a significant challenge for studio executives. Radio episodes had featured white actors imitating black characters. This form of "aural minstrelsy" proved unsuited to the new visual medium of television, for while the content of postwar episodes remained the same, changes in the racial landscape made the idea of white actors appearing in blackface on television implausible. Forced to hire blacks as a result, executives at CBS made *Amos 'n' Andy* the first all-black show on television.[74]

The odd spectacle of "blacks imitating whites imitating blacks" did little to mollify the show's longtime critics. *Amos 'n' Andy* had been a source of ongoing irritation to black newspapers, civil-rights organizations, and progressive activists since its inception on radio in 1928, and protests against the televised version began soon after the premier on 28 June 1951. An NAACP Bulletin entitled "Why the Amos and Andy Show Should Be Taken off the Air," issued in August 1951, blasted the portrayal of blacks as clownish, lazy, dumb, and dishonest. Specific complaints were lodged against the show's portrayal of black women as "screaming shrews," of black lawyers as unethical, and of black doctors as quacks. The campaign against the show, and the companies that advertised during the show, continued until the final network broadcast two years later. Although black newspapers with national circulation, including the *Pittsburgh Courier*, *Chicago Defender*, and *Baltimore Afro-American* were instrumental in building the campaign against the show, local newspapers were quiet. Having proclaimed the decision to feature black cast members a sign of progress, the *California Eagle* covered the first television debut of CBS's "classic comedy" in a short article that mentioned the broadcast time but said nothing about the controversy surrounding the program. The *Eagle* greeted the show's demise even more meekly. The final broadcast merited mention only as an aside, noting the show's move into syndication in the fall of 1953.[75]

The protests against *Amos 'n' Andy* marked a return to controversy for Stewart. As a resident Angeleno, Stewart had participated in wartime debates between established African American performers and their critics. Many of those opposed to the *Amos 'n' Andy* show had previously denounced Disney's cartoon version of antebellum life *Song of the South* (1946), for which Stewart provided the voice of Br'er Bear. Several years earlier, Stewart had run into what he termed a "funny situation" during a broadcast as a result of his reluctance to change the lyrics to his ditty "If You'd Only Let Me Sleep an Hour More." The song, which told the story of a black barber dreaming of cutting the throat of Adolf Hitler, only to be awakened prematurely, was dropped, along with Stewart, at the insistence of the headliner, Paul Robeson, who saw the portrayal of a homicidal and somnolent Stewart as a wrongheaded contribution to the war effort. Although Stewart generally responded publicly to complaints about his portrayals by paraphrasing Hattie McDaniel's rejoinder that she preferred to "play a maid than be one," Stewart's choice to open his own theater came partially as a result of his own dissatisfaction with the nature of the roles open to him and other black actors.[76]

Along with his wife, Edna, Nick Stewart opened the Ebony Showcase Theater in 1950. One of three black theaters in Southern California, the Ebony Showcase Theater began humbly.[77] Stewart located a small building on the increasingly integrated Crenshaw Boulevard, which he opened as a ninety-nine-seat venue. The small site proved unsuited to the institution Stewart envisioned, however, and with money saved from his television paychecks, he and Edna purchased a dilapidated movie theater several miles north, on the corner of Western and Washington boulevards. Using lumber salvaged from a studio construction site, and performing all labor themselves, the Stewarts transformed the 1,200 seat movie theater into a 300-seat venue with offices and a small lounge. Exceeding one hundred seats required participation in the Actors' Equity Association. Although Stewart was a member of both Actors' Equity and the Screen Actors Guild, his novel vocation as a theater owner incurred additional expenses, principally insurance payments and the requirement that he cast only those performers who paid Actors' Equity dues. Conscious that he was training young talent with little experience and even more limited means, Stewart initially subsidized the payment of these performers' union dues with his salary from CBS.[78]

The contradiction of directing and managing a black-owned theater while acting on a show many blacks found reprehensible was not lost on Stewart. Nor did it escape the notice of CBS executives, who, citing concern that his split efforts were affecting his performance, notified Stewart of the studio's decision not to renew his contract for the upcoming season.[79] His termination came but a few weeks before *Amos 'n' Andy* went off the air after seventy-eight episodes. The move to a larger theater promised to partially offset the loss of revenue resulting from the end of the television show, provided that audiences could be found. Here the support of the industry publications *Daily Variety*

FIGURE 8
Publicity still
of Nick Stewart,
founder, Ebony
Showcase Theater,
5 May 1954.
Herald Examiner
Collection, Los
Angeles Public
Library.

and *Hollywood Reporter* proved invaluable. Both carried reviews of Ebony Showcase openings, providing publicity that later community arts projects would find difficult to garner. Both periodicals generally eschewed any special mention of the theater's ownership or composition, although they did note productions that featured casts composed entirely of African Americans. Further assistance came from the local television station KTTV, which produced a short-lived weekly variety program entitled *Ebony Showcase Presents*. The show featured artists who had performed in the regular talent shows held at the Ebony Showcase Theater.[80]

Between the opening of its doors in 1950 and the Watts riot in 1965, the Ebony Showcase Theater attracted predominantly white audiences. Attendance during the inaugural season was estimated at 95 percent white, and while Stewart had little interest in running a community theater, he did concede that his initial audience demographics were "far from being a healthy sign."[81] A crash campaign aimed at black social clubs led to increased ticket purchases for

FIGURE 9 Group photo of Ebony Showcase Theater cast members in whiteface, circa 1967. Billy Mills (left) and Gilbert Lindsay (center), members of the Los Angeles City Council, are also pictured. Photograph by Rolland Curtis. Los Angeles Public Library

the production of *Anna Lucasta*, although the episodic patronage of the Merry-Go-Rounders, Bronze Mannekins, and Dahlberg's Chicagoans did little to offset the general makeup of audiences.[82] A subsequent "*Eagle* Night" marked a more serious effort in this direction. Sponsored by the newspaper, this "sparkling night of fun and gaiety" sought to raise the profile of the theater among black Angelenos through a star-studded, interracial benefit. Attendees included a cross-section of visiting and local politicians, actors, activists, and middle-class social notables, including the civil-rights leader A. Philip Randolph; the *Eagle*'s publisher, Loren Miller; the liberal white County Supervisor Kenneth Hahn; the black City Councilman Gilbert Lindsay; and the Allied Arts president, Dorothy Johnson. A full-page illustrated spread published in the *Eagle*, however, named a majority of attendees as members of local black social clubs, as independent professionals (doctors, real-estate brokers, and caterers were listed by name and occupation), or as Allied Arts affiliates.[83] Thus, as in the case with the emerging cohort of locally active visual artists, the cultural activists affiliated with the Ebony Showcase struggled to find an audience in South Los Angeles beyond either the small professional class or, more pointedly, the society pages of the local black press.

Despite periodic efforts to attract a larger pool of black ticket buyers, Stewart later estimated pre-1970 crowds as up to 80 percent white. The composition of the crowds had multiple explanations. Stewart gave little initial indication that he intended to consciously seek out black audiences. Both the decision to locate the theater on Washington Boulevard, at the northernmost border of what could then be reasonably considered a part of "black" Los Angeles, and the nature of Stewart's connections—which ran more to Sunset Boulevard than Central Avenue—militated against the notion that he was creating a community institution of any sort. The black theatergoing public in Southern California during 1950 was relatively small, in any event, owing to the presence of the film industry and the absence of the sort of theatrical infrastructure present in New York and Chicago. Diminishing coverage in the black press further hampered audience growth. Unlike *Variety* or the *Hollywood Reporter*, the black Los Angeles newspapers *Sentinel* and *Herald-Dispatch* provided episodic coverage, at best. Although the reviews of Ebony Showcase plays published in the *Eagle* were overwhelmingly positive—the paper described the play *Anna Lucasta* as "the talk of the film city"—the paper's single theater page actually covered the entire entertainment industry. Thus, readers were as likely to find concert announcements, nightclub schedules, and discussions of new films as they were to see theatrical listings or reviews of plays.[84]

At its inception, the Ebony Showcase Theater maintained a focus on a relatively narrow set of aims. Attracting black audiences was not an explicitly stated goal. Nor was providing an exhibition space for the work of black writers. Of the eighteen plays performed during the theater's first decade, only one was by a black playwright. Stewart deliberately chose to present works by white playwrights, maintaining that showcasing blacks in roles from which they had traditionally been excluded would provide more relevant experience and was more likely to convince observers that particular actors should be cast in their plays or films. Indeed, Stewart tailored his programming toward reinforcing his central goal of showcasing the wealth of black acting talent then residing in Los Angeles. Whatever its later community links, the Ebony Showcase would exist first and foremost in order to train black actors and technical personnel.

Whether despite or because of this focus, Ebony Showcase plays offered more than the opportunity to see working black actors. Comedies made up a slight majority of theater offerings, and Stewart regularly presented works dealing with sexuality. Early plays performed included the aforementioned

Anna Lucasta, a play about a streetwalker that ran for three years on Broadway before coming to California, and the *The Moon Is Blue*, a "frothy" boy-meets-girl story, the film version of which had been banned as indecent under the production code the previous year.[85] These productions allowed Stewart to direct men and women in roles where they could display more complex portrayals of black sexuality than were familiar to most black or white audiences. This was also the case with *Norman, Is That You*, a play about a gay interracial couple that had bombed on Broadway but ran for seven years under Stewart's direction.[86]

Stewart regarded the development of acting talent as the primary mission of his theater. Providing stage experience, he argued, opened possibilities for further work in film and television that would otherwise elude black actors. Stewart offered individual and group instruction in acting, dance, and stage direction. The only institution of its kind in Southern California before 1965, the Ebony Showcase offered initial breaks for many of the first black actors to land significant television roles during the 1960s and early 1970s.[87] Beyond the intentions of its founder, the Ebony Showcase facilitated the development of later community arts efforts, as well. The poet Jayne Cortez, for example, trained with Stewart. Not all actors who performed at the Ebony Showcase were seeking an initial break. Indeed, early participants such as Jimmy Edwards, Maldie Norman, and Juanita Moore had already established stage and screen careers by the time they appeared in *No Exit*. Nationally regarded entertainers, including Frank Silvera, Sammy Davis Jr., and Louise Beavers, also appeared in Ebony Showcase productions.[88]

The Ebony Showcase adapted longstanding black strategies for achieving greater access to cultural institutions to the new openings created by the expansion of television and film and by the improving racial climate. Committed to the idea of demonstrating the capabilities of black actors given more demanding scripts, Stewart saw his theater as challenging the idea that black actors were incapable or only suited to marginal roles. Stewart was also committed to maintaining financial independence and creative control. As an iteration of cultural democracy, his vision ran more toward pluralism than, strictly speaking, integration, as he sought to build an autonomous space from which blacks might enter Hollywood as equals.

As a privately funded organization making use of extensive contacts throughout the entertainment industry, the Ebony Showcase served as an inspiration both for those who desired financially self-reliant community institutions and for those who saw the possibilities of bridging the access gap between Holly-wood and South Los Angeles. Linking entrepreneurship and black arts, the Ebony Showcase Theater thus became important as a model of one sort of institution that developed in South Los Angeles. Stewart's vision of an institution capable of providing experience while developing skills necessary for success in theater, film, and television would be taken up by post–Watts riot institutions such as the Inner City Cultural Center and Watts Writers Work-shop. At the same time, Stewart's determination to eschew offerings by black playwrights would increasingly seem out of step after 1965, leading him to conclude that the Ebony Showcase would need to transform itself to survive.

THE UNLIKELY WELLSPRING

The early 1950s were a time of increasing visibility and significance for black visual art, as well as for theater and music. Between 1950 and 1955, informal networks of local artists began coalescing into an identifiable community. This cohort exhibited together, organized "Negro Arts" festivals, gained a toehold in local museums and galleries, and generated the first widespread enthusiasm for black visual culture among local African Americans. Despite its impermanence—and subsequent lack of a historical record—the creative community of black visual artists that took hold in the early 1950s constituted a novel, collective effort to think through questions regarding black creativity, to establish new organizations for and by artists, and to develop an arts infrastructure in South Los Angeles. These efforts paralleled the growth of a postwar literary, musical, and visual modernism that took hold among Afri-can Americans across the United States, presaging the proliferation of com-munity arts as a mass phenomenon after 1965.

The development of a creative community of black visual artists in Los Angeles was not a given. In contrast to theater, music, and dance, the visual arts lacked an established local audience and an ongoing institutional base among African Americans in Southern California. Indeed, prior to the 1950s, African American visual art was largely confined to the same pages of black newspapers that announced social balls, fashion shows, and the marriages of prominent figures. Once this began to change, however, it changed rapidly. During 1952 and 1953 alone, African American artists living in Southern Cal-ifornia produced at least a half-dozen group exhibitions, including an event that opened with a lecture by revolutionary and scholar C. L. R. James, who spoke on the subject of "the Negro and American Culture." This event featured an exhibition of oil paintings by William Alexander, Beulah Woodard, Alice Gafford, Constance McClendon, and Lenora Moore; watercolors by Bill Pajaud and William E. Smith; and sculptures by William Blackman.[89]

This postwar visual avant-garde was actively rooted in the lived experiences of the black working class. Both Curtis Tann and Bill Pajaud worked in industrial design, although by 1957 Pajaud had taken a post in the public relations department of the Golden State Mutual Life Insurance Company. A former riveter on a wartime assembly line, Ruth Waddy spent much of the 1950s cleaning houses, a job also held by the sculptor Beulah Woodard. While a few local artists such as Noah Purifoy and Betye Saar, both of whom had worked as social workers, were part of the professional class, most of the emerging community of black visual and plastic artists was working class in origin. This by itself was not unusual. Some of California's most important painters, poets, and assemblage artists had been dockworkers, and while too few scholars of the white avant-garde today make the link, neither Southern California's art scene in the early 1960s nor the San Francisco Beat milieu would have looked the way it did without the labor struggles of the preceding decade.[90] Time liberated from the clock became time given to organized creativity. If the working-class composition of black bohemia was hardly unusual in the larger history of California avant-gardes, it did mark a sharp change in black Los Angeles, where visual arts had been the more or less exclusive preserve of the black middle class.

Although both the riot and the subsequent proliferation of cultural and political radicalism would mark Watts as the signature black community of Los Angeles, the spatial center of the black visual and plastic avant-garde lay elsewhere. By the middle of the 1950s, Altadena, a sleepy hamlet of tree-lined streets and single-family residences adjacent to Pasadena, had become the epicenter of black arts activity. Home to Charles White, Curtis Tann, Noah Purifoy, and John Outterbridge, Altadena was close to the childhood home of Betye Saar, as well. Multiple factors explain why Altadena became the temporary epicenter of black creativity in Southern California. The San Gabriel Valley offered better housing stock than South Los Angeles, and as long as one avoided certain sections of Glendale, Monrovia, Eagle Rock, Pasadena, and San Marino—everywhere, that is, save Altadena, a single section of Pasadena, and the uninhabited Angeles National Forest—one was also likely to avoid the sort of trouble with neighbors or police that was commonplace almost everywhere else. Altadena, moreover, offered access to the cultural infrastructure of nearby Pasadena, whose amenities during the early 1950s exceeded those of the larger city of Los Angeles. Although most exhibitions by local African American artists during this time were held in city parks, the businesses in which the artists worked, or the living rooms of their homes, Pasadena's museum and gallery world opened, at least partially, before Los Angeles's did. Curtis Tann participated in the show "California Design" held at the Pasadena Museum of Art that also featured the black ceramicist Doyle Lane, and Tann held his first one-man show in the notoriously racially exclusive South Pasadena during 1954.

The San Gabriel Valley remained a somewhat paradoxical center of black arts activity even after the Watts riots. New arrivals energized the black arts community of Pasadena, and both a satellite project of the Watts Writers Workshop and one of Southern California's only black literary magazines, *Nigger Uprising*, were founded inside the city. Like the Venice Beats and the avant-garde galleries along La Cienega Boulevard, black arts activity in pre-1960s Los Angeles had a geographic center. But this center was neither South Los Angeles nor its soon to be infamous district, Watts.

The key association for this early 1950s visual arts community was a short-lived gallery named Eleven Associated Artists. A collectively run space, Eleven Associated had originally been founded by Curtis Tann, a painter and ceramicist who had relocated to California from Cleveland in 1946. Taking up residence in what he described as a "hut made of beaverboard," Tann worked as a tie painter before finding a job designing sewing machines. His job brought him into contact with the painter William Pajaud, who worked as an industrial designer for a rival sewing company. Freshly discharged from the army, Tann endured an unhappy stint at the nearby Chouinard Art Institute, where, confined by a policy restricting blacks to night classes and unable to relate either to disinterested teachers or a younger, more affluent, and overwhelmingly white student body, Tann found arts education in Southern California a far cry from what he had known.[91]

Having arrived from Cleveland, Tann had previous experience combining arts education, experimental works, and creative community. Cleveland was a site of pioneering black arts activity as a result of the founding in 1915 of the Karamu House Theater. A member of both Karamu House and its theatrical affiliate, the Gilpin Players, Tann spent much of the Great Depression teaching art at an integrated Cleveland settlement house under the auspices of the Works Progress Administration. While acting and working on set design at Karamu, Tann was part of a milieu that involved visiting luminaries of the Harlem Renaissance such as Langston Hughes and Zora Neal Hurston. Other Midwestern transplants affiliated with Eleven Associated had similar histories.

A fellow Ohioan, William E. Smith, knew Tann from their time together at Karamu House. William Pajaud and the painter and printmaker Ruth Waddy arrived in Los Angeles by way of Chicago, where both had participated in Southside community arts projects affiliated with Margaret Burroughs and Richard Wright. Pajaud was also a close friend of John Biggers, the painter and muralist whose aesthetic and historical interests and personal journeys had positioned him at a crossroads of American regionalism, Mexican muralism, the Popular Front, and midcentury black modernist debates. Waddy, like Beah Richards, Frances Williams, and Beulah Woodard, had a variety of left connections, and by the mid-1960s she would accompany a selection of her prints on tours of Eastern Europe and the Soviet Union. Hence, even before the arrival in 1955 of the graphic artist Charles White, Southern California's small cohort of black visual artists possessed clear links to the politicized cultural projects of the Harlem Renaissance, the New Deal, and the interwar Popular Front. Both the experiences and subsequent trajectories of these figures serve to remind us that neither a creative genealogy centered entirely in New York nor a history of black Los Angeles that tracks only Southern migration suffices to explain the development of local cultural life.[92]

Several longtime residents of Los Angeles were affiliated with Eleven Associated as well. The painter Alice Tayford Gafford was a pioneer among black California artists. Born in 1886 in California, Gafford was among the first African American students to attend the Otis Art Academy and to exhibit at Earl Stendahl's Wilshire Boulevard gallery. She was also a co-founder of one of Southern California's few prewar arts festivals. Beulah Ecton Woodard also joined Tann's gallery. Born near Frankfort, Ohio, in 1895, Woodard had attended Otis and the Los Angeles Art Institute following her family's move to the southeastern Los Angeles suburb of Vernon before the First World War. Woodard's paintings had been featured in a one-woman show held at the Los Angeles Central Library in 1935, a show that marked the first time a black artist had participated in such an event. Woodard was also a driving force behind the short-lived Los Angeles Negro Art Association, which began sponsoring lectures on "Negro Art" in 1937. Woodard and Gafford were members of the Our Authors Study Circle, a book club affiliated with Carter G. Woodson's Association for the Study of Negro Life and History that invited guest lecturers and organized public presentations on black history and literature.[93] In persuading Mayor Bowron's office to enact the city's first Negro history week celebrations, this all-female club opened the initial space for black inclusion within Los Angeles's municipal culture.

FIGURE 10 Beulah Woodard (left) shows her Biddy Mason sculpture to Gladys Owens Smith, great-granddaughter of Biddy Mason (right), and to Harriet Fritzhand, not dated. Mason, born a slave, successfully obtained her freedom after filing a lawsuit in 1856 against her master, a Mormon who had moved from Utah to California. Mason became the owner of lucrative real estate in downtown Los Angeles. Los Angeles Public Library.

Before her untimely death in 1955, Woodard was the primary link between African American Los Angeles and the attempt by the Municipal Arts Department director Kenneth Ross to expand city-sponsored cultural programming into South Los Angeles. Located on 51st Street and Avalon Boulevard, approximately halfway between downtown and the Watts district, South Park was set within a predominantly black neighborhood of mixed economic composition. The primary site for public exhibitions of African American culture until the restoration of the Watts Towers during the following decade, South Park hosted summertime classical concerts sponsored by the city's music department, as well as lectures, jazz concerts, and "Negro history week" events. One of these, held in February 1950, featured an arts exhibition and a panel discussion on "Negro Art Today." The event, coordinated by Beulah Woodard, involved fourteen local black artists, including Tann, Pajaud, and Moore. The October art festival demonstrated the potential audience for similar events, with attendance estimates topping 3,500. Woodard was also instrumental in persuading Los Angeles County Supervisor John Anson Ford to support the county-funded exhibition "Negro Art" at the County Museum of Art.[94]

Woodard's example highlights the importance of black women within the expanding population of local visual artists. In addition to Woodard, Gafford, and Waddy, a young Betye Saar, the painter Henrietta Craft, and the sculptor P'lla Mills were active in both the informal associations and formal organizations that made up the city's early black arts circles. Women were significantly better represented among the visual and plastic arts community than among musicians or actors. The reasons for this are complex and have to do, in part, with a feminization of the visual arts compared with genres such as music and film, and a close connection between applied and fine arts among California-based black artists. While vocational training was by no means limited to women—the male artists Pajaud, Tann, and Purifoy all held jobs in industrial design or decoration—the link between work and art provided opportunities for women with interior decorating (Saar), welding and weaving (Mills), and other industrial arts experience. Indeed, Saar credited her subsequent facility in assemblage art to both her experience with interior design and educational tracking that shifted black students from fine to manual and industrial arts.[95] The result, as the art historian Judith Wilson notes, was "an amazing proliferation of talent" that stands in sharp contrast to continued critical invisibility.[96] This invisibility was contemporary before it was historical. Even if few observers, black or white, noticed the efforts of pioneers such as Woodard and Mills, their role in fostering a larger community of black women artists ensured that as the 1960s progressed, black visual artists would develop a critique that linked aesthetic freedom with a political practice that treated the "black" and "women's" liberation movements as one and the same. Such, in any case, is one reading of the 1970 exhibition "Sapphire (You've Come a Long Way, Baby)." The title combined a common derogatory term for an allegedly overbearing black woman with an advertising slogan that constituted a bête noir of the predominantly white women's movement; the all-female exhibition of a half-dozen contemporary California black artists, held in Suzanne Jackson's Gallery 32, marked a pioneering effort at realizing a specific black feminist cultural critique.[97]

Female artists were similarly critical in founding the collective spaces that were central to the creation of community among and between artists. Although Eleven Associated Artists was originally the brainchild of Curtis Tann, both Beulah Woodard and P'lla Mills were important in the founding of the gallery. Betye Saar collaborated with Tann in another partnership, Brown and Tann, which sold enamelware out of the artists' homes.[98] A decade later, the printmaker Ruth Waddy would organize Art West Associated, the first mass organization of local black artists, and a few years later still, the dancer and painter Suzanne Jackson would open Gallery 32, one of only two artist-run, black-owned galleries in Los Angeles during the 1960s. Following her arrival in 1964, Samella Lewis founded a local Museum of African American Art, although her ultimate role in fostering creative community through her academic writing went well beyond her curatorial project. Thus, while male artists were generally hired to run community arts projects affiliated in some way with the city or state, the collective milieu of the black arts would simply not have occurred without the institutional and creative efforts of women. This pattern was not limited to the visual arts. The Underground Musicians Association (UGMA) associated with Horace Tapscott originally met in the house of the pianist Linda Hill, and it is doubtful that this institution, perhaps the signal achievement of the California black arts movement, would have taken hold without her early participation. Jayne Cortez co-founded the Studio Watts workshop a year before the riots, and the Pasadena resident Ridhiana Saunders published and edited the literary journal *Nigger Uprising*.[99]

The early creative community of postwar African American artists shared a number of similarities with the coterminous white avant-garde with whom it had little direct contact. The spatial segregation of the fragmented metropolis contrasted with prevailing patterns in San Francisco and New York, and Los Angeles produced no figure capable of linking the city's black and white bohemians. Still, a number of similarities between the white and black vanguards of the pre-counterculture are worthy of note. A preference for informal connections over formal membership bodies offers one example. Moreover, like their white counterparts to the west, local black visual and plastic artists were experimenting within and across forms. In contrast to white avant-garde circles such as the Ferus Gallery and the Venice Beach Beats, however, no single genre or form predominated among Los Angeles's unnamed black arts milieu.[100] P'lla Mills worked simultaneously in metal sculpture and textiles, mixing work on a handmade loom with pieces welded from salvaged steel. Daniel LaRue Johnson produced assemblage pieces that contained text and found images on painted canvas. Curtis Tann preferred ceramics and batik. Bill Pajaud worked primarily in watercolors. Ruth Waddy made prints. Betye Saar's early work involved a variety of visual media, including serigraphs, oil paintings, and collage. Beulah Woodard's sculptured busts were studiously realist, concerned as she was with showing "the natural beauty and dignity" of continental and diasporic Africans.[101]

Amid such stylistic variation, a specific set of aesthetic concepts among this group of pioneering artists is difficult to locate. The difficulty in uncovering their ideas is exacerbated by a lack of materials in museums, archives, or texts. At the same time, a number of tentative extrapolations can be made. Bebop aside, the first decade of the postwar period remains an underappreciated moment of black cultural history, a critical interregnum between the Harlem Renaissance and the 1960s. Part of this midcentury modernism was a search for a black art divorced from either a specific political program or a notion of art as autonomous and unrelated to surrounding social forces. Bill Pajaud's prolific depictions of the contours of everyday (black) life and Woodard's quest to "record as many types" of African features as part of an effort to achieve what she termed "an authentic Negro art" speak to a sensibility distinct from that we commonly associate with the 1930s or 1960s. Moreover, the anticipatory outlines of what the art historian Richard Powell terms "an emphasis on a blackness . . . that derived its form not from painted or sculpted black humanity but, rather, from a marshalling of symbolic or conceptual strategies" is present in Tann's folk enamels, Saar's early spiritualist abstractions, and young Melvin Edwards's abstract "lynch fragment" sculptures, drawing as they did on European avant-garde, West African, and Southern Californian sensibilities.[102] Comparable, if largely unconnected, to parallel groupings present in Chicago, Philadelphia, New York, and, undoubtedly, other as yet unstudied locales, the experiences of California's postwar black artists highlight the extent to which efforts to realize a distinctly African American modernism would necessarily involve collective organization, the crossing of forms and genres, and an expansive exploration of the meaning of community.

Between 1950 and 1955, African American musicians, actors, and visual artists occupied a central place in urban antiracist politics. In significant part, this came as a result of the strategic context of public expression at a moment of urban expansion and developing civic culture. The attempt to find a place for improvised music among studio musicians, the increasing inclusion of African imagery and protest themes in the sculptures of Beulah Woodard and Mel Edwards, and the debates about content that accompanied the casting of all-black casts at the Ebony Showcase theater all pointed to future debates regarding the possibility and parameters of an identifiably black art.

These efforts took place against the backdrop of a growing contradiction between the promise of unbridled affluence and the failure of white Californians to include their black counterparts in their postwar dreams. The resulting resolution—from the explosion of August 1965 to the decade of black radicalism that followed—would shift the focus of black politics away from the cross-class struggle against racism and toward a working-class-led redefinition of the meaning of black freedom. Expressive culture would prove central in this regard again. As the second section of this project will argue, the dominant thrust of this mass movement gravitated toward themes of creative and political autonomy grounded in the experiences and aspirations of the black working class. Themes taken up during the post-1965 mass phase of black arts activity would move well beyond the rhetorical pluralism of wartime cultural democracy or integrationist cultural politics of the early 1950s. Before this, however, a coalition of forces would offer a final attempt to use black expressive culture in the service of racial reform.

3

WRITING WATTS   The Rise and Fall of Cultural Liberalism

If not quite, as one participant termed it, "the greatest continual literary success story in America," the Watts Writers Workshop undoubtedly emerged as the most visible of the community-based cultural institutions to develop in Southern California after the Watts riot of 1965. By the group's first anniversary, thirty participants were preparing an anthology for publication, NBC had produced an hour-long television special, and essays by workshop writers had appeared in *Esquire*, *Harper's*, and *Time*. By late 1967, a permanent location had been found, rented, and renovated; six satellite projects had opened throughout Southern California; and possible expansion into the Pacific Northwest (Seattle), Central California (Fresno), the Northeast (Harlem and Washington, D.C.) and the urban West (Denver) was under consideration. A repertory theater group joined the writing workshop, and participants began writing for local film and television studios, testifying before congressional panels debating social policy, and entertaining an expanding pool of celebrities drawn to what was increasingly seen as a model of urban reform through arts education.[1]

Using creative writing as a path toward social equality suggested a novel vision of local antipoverty politics, best understood as a kind of cultural liberalism that sought to combine political and aesthetic goals. As with the broader war on poverty, job training, education, and racial reconciliation remained foremost among the aims of cultural liberals. In contrast to more familiar remedies, like the job corps or Head Start, the poems, essays, and plays produced under the auspices of the Watts Writers Workshop offered those targeted by antipoverty efforts an opportunity to assess, in writing, their feelings about the process of urban reform and the broader social context in which antidiscrimination efforts took place. As a result, the attempt to generate support for integration among African Americans through the facilitation of expressive culture involved no small measure of ideological contestation over the direction and nature of black writing.

The development of a community-focused interracial cultural politics marked a shift from earlier patterns. In a reversal from the war years, Hollywood now came to South Los Angeles, and African Americans were asked to represent themselves instead of being forced to contest externally produced images. Unlike efforts to integrate the culture industry, moreover, the aims of cultural liberalism aimed less at bettering the conditions of working creative personalities than at creating new artists committed to a particular vision of the relationship between art and politics. Thus, while the integrationist aims and industry links suggested points of commonality between the cultural politics of the 1940s, 1950s, and mid-1960s, the mass focus and timing of the post-riot project guaranteed that the workshop would serve as a kind of bridge between distinct moments of cultural activism.

Retracing both the initial success and the rapid decline of cultural liberalism is important for understanding the shifting ground of urban politics during the second half of the 1960s. While the vision of using art as a means of generating a greater investment in American society among working-class blacks produced widespread enthusiasm, the limits of reform in a radicalizing moment generated contradictions as well. Expressed both aesthetically and organizationally, these differences would spell the end of a period in which local cultural politics aimed primarily at facilitating black entry into the culture industry and the broader city as a whole. The fissures that divided Watts writers thus provide an opportunity to note a transition in the primary thrust of black cultural production away from the organization of black creativity toward the reformist goal of increased access. In its place would grow a poetic, musical, and sculpture cohort—extending well beyond the members of the Watts Writers Workshop—dedicated to an autonomist, grassroots vision that linked political and aesthetic liberation. The Watts Writers Workshop, then, remains a critical, if short-lived, institution through which to measure the changing role of culture in postwar black politics in Los Angeles and beyond.

FROM THE ASHES

The Watts Writers Workshop was the brainchild of the author and Academy Award–winning screenwriter Budd Schulberg, the son of a studio executive. Schulberg's storied resume included the novel *What Makes Sammy Run*, a stint as a successful boxing promoter, and writing credits for the film *On the*

Waterfront. Like many white Angelenos, Schulberg was taken aback by the explosion of South Los Angeles in 1965. Stunned at the ferocity of what he termed "the unscheduled spectacular" unfolding across his television screen, the longtime resident took the rioting as a personal challenge to his intellectual and emotional understanding of Southern California. Shortly before the riot, Schulberg had completed a new introduction to Nathaniel West's *Day of the Locust*, a novel set in Hollywood that features a protagonist whose masterpiece is a painting entitled "The Burning of Los Angeles." Conceding that he, like millions, had been unprepared for this sudden confluence of art and reality, he cast his initial forays into the devastated areas of South Los Angeles as part of a quest to understand "a full scale revolt years in the making."[2]

Years in the making, the rioting nonetheless caught much of the city unprepared. Following an ill-fated traffic stop by a highway patrolman, South Los Angeles erupted in anger at decades of neglect. Rioting spread rapidly beyond the boundaries of what any reasonably familiar observer would have described as Watts, and the ultimate curfew area established by police agencies and the California National Guard was larger than either San Francisco or Manhattan. Six days of violence left thirty-four dead, thousands injured, and hundreds of millions of dollars in property damage. Subsequent research placed the number of active participants and "close observers" as high as seventy thousand—or as much as two-thirds of the adult male population of the curfew area—and the numbers of police and military units sent to quell the violence exceeded those used in the American invasion of the Dominican Republic in 1965.[3]

The precise timing of the violence offered an eloquent and ironic commentary on the public perception of a northward shift in the black freedom struggle. The riots took place less than a week after the signing of the Voting Rights Act and less than seventy-two hours after the conclusion of locally held federal hearings regarding the problems plaguing antipoverty efforts in Los Angeles.[4] The riots also made international news—with the *Economist* pointedly comparing the clash between African Americans and Jewish American shopkeepers to rioting taking place on the other side of the globe between Indonesians and ethnic Chinese merchants.[5] Given this publicity, it is unsurprising that powerful voices from across the political spectrum felt compelled to weigh in with opinions. Although his public commentary was measured, President Lyndon Johnson took the riots as a personal affront, privately telling aides that "Negroes will end up pissing in the aisles of the Senate . . . as they had during Reconstruction."[6] Johnson's comments stemmed in part from

FIGURE 11
Security guard
stands over a
looted war surplus
store on Avalon
and 108th streets,
13 August 1965.
Herald Examiner
Collection, Los
Angeles Public
Library

the stinging criticism of LAPD Chief William Parker, who initially sought to deflect responsibility away from his department by claiming that violence was inevitable when "you keep telling people that they are unfairly treated and teach them disrespect for the law."[7] When a common target of Parker's ire, Martin Luther King Jr., arrived in Los Angeles to survey events firsthand, the civil rights icon encountered repeated heckling by black youths who punctuated his entreaty to "join hands" with the exclamation "and burn!"[8]

The restoration of order following nearly a week of severe unrest elicited contradictory responses. Having denounced the violence, established civil-rights leaders pondered the difficulty in shifting antidiscrimination efforts beyond the segregated South. As the historian Lisa McGirr notes, among the most enduring legacies of the violence was a conservative backlash evident in everything from a run on local gun stores to the subsequent gubernatorial triumph of Ronald Reagan.[9] At the same time, the rioting spawned almost a decade of local black radical activity, symbolized equally by the presence of large chapters of national groupings such as the Black Panther Party and by dozens of local projects, such as the US Organization, Self-Leadership for All Nationalities Today, and the Community Alert Patrol.[10]

At the same time, the uprising provided a temporary upswing in the fortunes of liberals seeking to broaden the focus of social spending from a preoccupation with juvenile delinquency to a wider-ranging urban renewal. Indeed, proponents of the War on Poverty were quick to point to increased social spending as an antidote to possible outbreaks elsewhere. Among those committed to this vision, employment, education, and health remained central concerns. A vocal minority, however, argued for the inclusion of cultural programs within the larger antipoverty crusade. These proponents of cultural liberalism saw the arts as a key element of urban reform, insisting that writing, music, and other creative endeavors could provide opportunities for blacks and heal the divisions reflected in events like the Watts riot.

Reviewing the rise and decline of cultural liberalism in Southern California offers a reminder of the underappreciated centrality of cultural analysis, explanation, and politics within the Great Society and the War on Poverty. As the postwar "rediscovery" of poverty shifted attention from rural destitution to urban decay, cultural factors became prominent among competing explanations of socioeconomic inequality.[11] So-called culture of poverty arguments, of course, were not universally taken up, and proponents of varied forms of environmental causality argued trenchantly against the idea of an intergenerational pathology that constituted a "self-perpetuating world of dependence."[12] Cultural patterns were often taken as an explanation for poverty—that is, as a problem; cultural production, however, was less often seen as a possible solution to the problems that the varied programs of the Office of Economic Opportunity sought to address. Yet it was precisely these issues that Budd Schulberg took up through the practice of creative writing and the promise of employment in Hollywood. The Watts Writers Workshop reminds us that neither academics nor politicians maintained a monopoly on the terminology or use of culture during the War on Poverty. Beyond this, and in line with the broader task of explicating the place of cultural politics in postwar black Los Angeles, the Watts Writers Workshop demonstrates that the multifaceted struggle for "access" was as much a matter of pursuing an ideological debate concerning black culture and life as it was a question of securing entertainment jobs or producing less odious depictions of African Americans on stage or screen.

The progenitors of this cultural liberalism within Southern California included black artists and community activists, sympathetic (and generally affluent) whites, and representatives of major philanthropic organizations.[13] The framework of cultural liberalism linked politics and aesthetics as clearly as subsequent Black Arts Movement and Black Power activists did. Preventing

FIGURE 12 Budd Schulberg with Watts Writers Workshop members, circa 1967. Courtesy Dartmouth College Library.

further urban unrest emerged as a central preoccupation, and, as we shall see, proponents held to a distinctive ideological viewpoint that conceived of expressive culture as providing what were variously described as "nonviolent," "communicative," and "hopeful" alternatives for frustrated urban youth otherwise susceptible to militant appeals.[14]

The organization of a creative-writing workshop by a well-known Hollywood screenwriter with a wealth of media connections guaranteed the Watts Writers Workshop, as it came to be known, a visibility much greater than comparable efforts elsewhere. Initial press interest touched on both Schulberg's ability, as a white outsider, to communicate with residents of post-riot South Los Angeles and the efficacy of arts education as a component of urban reform. The first published works by Watts Writers Workshop members appeared as part of an educational supplement in *Time* magazine dedicated to the educational reform of "ghetto dropouts," and the initial television documentary produced by NBC-TV was titled *The Angry Voices of Watts*, despite

FIGURE 13 Desireo Edwards, owner of the Watts Happening Coffee House, chats with a customer, not dated. The coffeehouse site hosted performances by the Watts Writers Workshop, the Pan African People's Arkestra, the New Art Jazz Ensemble, and others. Photograph by James Jeffrey Jr. Security Pacific Collection, Los Angeles Public Library.

workshop participants' protests that, beyond anger, they also sought to convey thoughtfulness, critical self-analysis, memory, and humor.[15]

Widespread publicity drew additional participants. This growth prompted a search for a new location. At its inception, the workshop had met in the offices of the Westminster Neighborhood Association. A community service project founded by the Presbyterian church in 1959, Westminster had by the time of the riot become a major provider of social services for residents of South Los Angeles. In the months that followed the riot, Westminster became a primary conduit of outside spending, and by 1966 its annual budget of $1 million and its one-hundred-person staff made it the largest private employer in the curfew area.[16] Simultaneous expansion of both the Westminster Neighborhood Association and the Watts Writers Workshop created a dearth of space for each, and in the spring of 1966, the Workshop moved to the Watts Happening Coffee House. Located on 103rd Street, a commercial strip that had been the epicenter of looting the previous summer, the converted supermarket hosted a variety of poverty programs administered by the federal Office of Economic Opportunity as well as a multiplicity of cultural groupings.[17] The latter included weekly rehearsals and performances by the New Art Jazz Ensemble; the Pan Afrikan People's Arkestra; painting, sculpture and drawing classes; and parallel poetry and theater workshops conducted by Jayne Cortez and Stanley Crouch.[18]

The move to the new location coincided with the first ideological criticism leveled at the workshop. Noting that a year after the riot "the (white) Man was still a target for abuse and I was the only one present," Schulberg decried the "other angries" who "would bang the piano or the bongos to drown out the poets."[19] Workshop meetings faced hecklers who questioned the motivation of a white outsider instructing blacks. As the premier venue for community arts performance in post-riot South Los Angeles, the coffeehouse featured performances by musicians and poets sympathetic to nationalist ideas, including Elaine Brown, Jayne Cortez, Stanley Crouch, and Horace Tapscott. Occasional interruptions subsequently gave way to more serious critiques of Schulberg's project of liberal-arts instruction. A visiting official from the Rockefeller Foundation reported that James Woods, co-founder of a nearby collectively run performance space called Studio Watts, had "no kind words" for the workshop, while the jazz critic Frank Kofsky attacked the "liberal paternalism" that facilitated and publicized interracial literary activity while ignoring the indigenous musical talent present in South Los Angeles.[20]

Damned or praised, Schulberg's presence shaped the fortunes of the Watts Writers Workshop during its first year of existence. In addition to contributing funding and intellectual guidance, his contacts within and beyond the entertainment world provided opportunities well beyond those enjoyed by comparable arts projects elsewhere. Although it is precisely this status that subsequently came under internal and external criticism, there is no question that Schulberg's participation largely explains the ability of the workshop to attract thousands of dollars in donations, and it is difficult to imagine NBC filming *The Angry Voices of Watts* or the presence of the writers Johnnie Scott and Henry Dolan before a congressional subcommittee on urban affairs in the absence of his connections.

The latter case illustrates something of the highly particular nature of the Watts Writers Workshop vis-à-vis other black arts groups. A former "friendly witness" in the HUAC hearings on communist influence in the motion-picture industry, Schulberg was familiar to and comfortable with congressional panels.[21] At a moment when the best-selling and most visible black poets were increasingly popularizing insurrectionary paeans calling for social revolution, Schulberg, Johnny Scott, and Henry Dolan were discussing the promise and possibilities of urban reform with appreciative and attentive members of the U.S. Senate. Dolan read a letter describing Watts and answered questions on

FIGURE 14 Harry Dolan, Budd Schulberg, and Johnny Scott (seated at table from left to right) testify before Congress, circa December 1966. Courtesy Dartmouth College Library.

the mood in the city, while Scott read portions of his autobiographical essay, "The Coming of the Hoodlum." Although Schulberg made a brief statement advocating the creation of an "arts corps" as an element of urban reform, the comments of all three men primarily addressed urban blight; the limited transit, health, and employment picture in South Los Angeles; and the likelihood of further unrest.[22]

Lengthy comments by Johnnie Scott revealed the workshop's broad social mission and concerns. Scott, for example, took issue with previous statements made by Los Angeles Mayor Sam Yorty. In response to Yorty's dogged insistence that the single-family homes, palm trees, and "nice buildings" precluded the definition of Watts as a "ghetto," Scott responded that "the ghetto is not the houses. It is the people, not the physical environment. . . . It is created in the mind." Scott addressed further comments to the process of transforming the mental attitudes that hampered black advancement. Arguing that creative writing could shift African American attitudes toward American society by opening new linguistic vistas, Scott continued by asserting that community members were, in fact, demanding greater intellectual stimulation. Telling members of the Senate of a conversation with a black social worker demanding that concerned parties not send "any more baseball players or prize-fighters," Scott further added that cultural programming needed to be put in context. Watts lacked both substantial educational facilities and a comprehensive transportation network, while the nearest hospital was more than ten miles away. Members of the Senate committee asked Scott and Dolan for general commentary on the social conditions in South Los Angeles, and the responses of the two men appeared less as the statements of artists or the successful progeny of urban antipoverty funding than as experts on urban conditions. Indeed, all three men repeatedly cast their discussion of cultural efforts as part of a broader approach to urban reform. This was a role not often reserved for African American artists, especially authors without national reputations or familiar audiences. Nevertheless, both men read from their work, prompting the chairman of the subcommittee, Abraham Ribicoff, to declare somewhat hyperbolically that their portrait of life in Watts was "as moving and memorable as anything that has come before the U.S. Senate on the floor or in committee."[23]

WRITING WATTS

A prolonged crisis of understanding followed the devastation of August, when, in the words of Stanley Crouch, South Los Angeles "burst like a Mexican piñata stuffed full of statistics about economics, racism, and frustration."[24] Although rioting had hit New York City a year earlier, both the scale of the violence and the manner in which participants spoke variously of an uprising, insurrection, or rebellion suggested that events in Los Angeles could not be understood fully within the familiar language of race riots. The effort to comprehend, define, and frame the uprising rapidly became a site of ideological conflict in which the members of the Watts Writers Workshop offered high-profile and relatively unmediated black voices. In this way, Scott's and Dolan's commentary before the Senate offered a tactical intervention within a broader battle over the production of knowledge in post-riot Los Angeles.

Michel Foucault's observation that "the exercise of power itself creates and causes to emerge new objects of knowledge and accumulates new bodies of information" is helpful for clarifying the politics of this process.[25] This was visibly true for black Los Angeles, as the clipboards of social scientists replaced the armored personnel carriers of the National Guard. Less than two weeks after the start of the riots, Governor Edmund "Pat" Brown appointed a commission of inquiry led by the prominent industrialist and former CIA Director John McCone. Entitled "Violence in the City—An End or a Beginning?," the report cast the rioters as a minority within the larger black population, rejected police brutality as a major concern, and cited the "superior conditions" of living in Los Angeles relative to "the conditions under which Negroes live in most other cities."[26] Reception of the report was decidedly mixed, with civil-rights activists such as Bayard Rustin, liberal academics such as Robert Blauner, and the co-founder of the *New York Review of Books* denouncing the report's methodology, questions, and conclusions.[27]

Within the context of the War on Poverty's focus on the generation of social-science expertise regarding the poor, the literary production of workshop authors acquired a distinct import.[28] Insofar as they took issue with both the notion of a "culture of poverty" and a wholly structural view that removed African Americans as active agents, the comments of workshop participants offered a set of ideas beyond the most common debates regarding the reasons for socioeconomic inequality. More locally, the Watts Writers Workshop repudiated both the conservative conclusions of the McCone commission and the commission's liberal detractors. As part of their battle over the production of knowledge, local poets provided critical answers to questions such as, "What do Negroes want?" and "Will there be another riot?" by challenging the sorts of questions that were being posed in South Los Angeles in the first place. Thus, Johnny Scott's declaration that the members of the workshop sought to convey more than anger and his insistence that the "ghetto" was less a physical location than a mental state suggested that the transformation of South Los Angeles was less a matter of an effective antipoverty or police counterinsurgency program than a rethinking of sociological and psychological research that took black Angelenos as an undereducated, spatially confined, enraged mass. In place of questions that sought to elucidate the precise relationship between unwed motherhood, employment opportunities, and attitudes toward the police, poems like Scott's "Chaos in a Ghetto Alley" offered the insistent humanity of a black couple:

> The two who are one
> whose genitals match perfectly
> and whose fruits are ugly statistics.[29]

K. Curtis Lyle offered a differently styled repudiation of W. E. B. Du Bois's famously formulated query, "How does it feel to be a problem?" Eugene Redmond's comparison between Lyle and the fellow (for a time) Californian surrealist poets Bob Kaufman and Jayne Cortez is apt, for Lyle's improvisational language "half-way between mechanized jawbones and ancient skullcaps" created a similarly styled aural and textual call and response between sound and text.[30] Lyle also took up the Afro-surrealist focus on anti-imperialism and madness. Set within the Ventura County mental institution where Charlie Parker spent the last six months of 1946, Lyle's "Sometimes I Go to Camarillo and Sit in the Lounge" counterpoised images of "yellow trumpets of starving blues / against a piece of body that used / to hold some Vietnamese mother's breast" with

they (the inmates)	propped in gutters of cafeteria
their (funk)	bowels running thru America's
	kitchen ascending minds transcending
	the walls of room 305

before coming to rest with

	God himself
himself	an irrepressible sound blowing
	nuclear heroes
	into the
	rivers of time
	and
	space[31]

Other poets framed the contestation over representation, knowledge, and meaning making through a more material language of employment, transportation, and policing. Harry Dolan's "Sand Clock Day" took as its subject the combination of underemployment and transit dependence faced by many black Angelenos. In the decade before the riot, the Los Angeles "autopia" lacked a cohesive public-transportation network, and the city was alone among major metropolitan areas in its refusal to subsidize public transportation. Transfers from the Atkinson Transportation Company, which served South Los Angeles, were not honored on the citywide busses of the Rapid Transit District, forcing tens of thousands of black commuters to pay twice if they sought to travel beyond South Los Angeles. East–west routes were few, preventing access from overwhelmingly black South Los Angeles to the racially restricted beach cities of the South Bay. Indeed, transit dependence for working-class Angelenos of color would remain a major civil rights issue decades after the riot, forcing an activist campaign and federal lawsuit that concluded with a consent decree in 1996.[32]

Written as a dialogue in the protagonist's head, and later filmed as a short included in the *Angry Voices* television broadcast, Dolan's short story told of a daylong search for work across the landscape of Los Angeles. Dolan narrated two journeys. The first told of an ambitious (for South Los Angeles) effort to get to a job interview in the suburban, predominantly white San Fernando Valley using public transportation. Riffing on spatial distance, post-riot white anxiety, and the link between economic security and domestic bliss, Dolan's narrative spoke to the unsuitability of narrowly focused efforts to create economic opportunity in the face of the sorts of interlocking problems confronted by the urban working class:

> Try one of these job-hunting expeditions into the frightened, frustrated white man's world. Bring your lunch, and if you're real smart bring your dinner, because it's an all-day trek. Having an appointment for a job is only half the battle, 'cause job-hunting in the wide-open spaces ain't like in the city, the Windy City . . . or even old Bean Town. At least there you have rapid transit, speeding underground trains that cross cities in minutes, but not in the west. Man, I swear those buses don't even have engines, they got real horses for power, plow horses at that. Forty-one cents to ride three miles, ain't that a gas? And not even a transfer?

Disembarking downtown, the protagonist rushes toward a bus stop several blocks away, arriving only to watch his bus take off, even after he makes eye contact with the driver. Unable to spare the change to call the job to say he will be late, the protagonist shells out another "eighty-one cents, damn," before arriving in the valley to be told that, despite the early hour, the job has been filled.

Folded within this physical journey is an emotional passage from optimism to despair. As he waits for the bus, he asks himself, "How many times can a man fail? How many times can his children cry of hunger? How many times before his wife walks out?—and that's all I got, baby, my wife, my kids." From a beginning proclamation that "this is it, this is that once-in-a-lifetime" chance, Dolan descends to a conclusion that "this was my day. The last grain in the sand-clock."[33] While Dolan's narrative is, in a sense, fairly conventional, the unremarkable and inescapable banality of his day recalls other local efforts to untangle the mix between employment, masculinity, and racial pride. Dolan's story parallels both the portrayals of black workers produced during his wartime sojourn by Chester Himes, noted earlier, and the interventions of films such as Charles Burnett's *Killer of Sheep*, as we will see. Dolan's story can thus be read both as a response to the social-science, governmentalist language produced to "explain" South Los Angeles after 1965 and as an intertextual dialogue with other working-class black cultural production focused on the deleterious effects of racial capitalism on the self-image and life opportunities of black men.

To be sure, other early Watts poetry went beyond a discussion of local conditions or personal exploration. In "To Mister Charles and Sister Anne," Ojenke's vision of the middle passage in which

defiant blacks /
hang like anchors
and chandeliers in Neptune's mansion

touched on subjects largely absent among the initial cohort of workshop poets.[34] Harry Dolan's attempt to answer one question posed ad nauseum throughout 1966, "Will there be another riot in Watts?" offered Sam Greenlee–like images of urban insurrection, including "church meetings with no one on their knees . . . stumbling winos who drink colored water and practice runs past storage tanks . . . locksmiths who make two keys," while Johnny Scott's "Watts 1966," included as its stark conclusion

The man named fear has inherited half an acre,
and is angry.[35]

On the whole, however, neither *From the Ashes* nor *The Angry Voices of Watts* offered the cross-generic collaborations, freeform experimentalism, or musical, historical, and spiritual thematic reference points that would animate subsequent jazz poetry, the parallel avant-garde jazz community, or the cohort of assemblage artists working throughout Southern California during this time. Indeed, later workshop participants, such as Kamau Da'ood, Quincy Troupe, and K. Curtis Lyle, would fall more comfortably into the category of a grassroots, jazz-oriented, historically referenced black art that this work will argue for in subsequent chapters. During the workshop's first year, however, the production remained focused primarily on exploring the social conditions of Watts through highly personal poetry and prose.

Yet it would be a mistake to conclude that the writings of the workshop represented conformity with the social vision of cultural liberalism articulated by Schulberg, the Westminster Neighborhood Association, or the Rockefeller Foundation. The first cohort of Watts writers wrote, read, and published within a dialogic process where multiple influences and inferences were coming together, and where local writers sought to explain themselves and their surroundings in the face of outside efforts to do the same. Their writings thus highlight the liminal nature of the Watts Writers Workshop as a whole. On one hand, the project represented another effort to mobilize black culture for a clearly defined social purpose. As had been the case during the wartime confrontations with Hollywood studios and with the push to desegregate the cultural infrastructure in the early 1950s, individual entry into previously closed spaces emerged as a central goal. At the same time, Johnny Scott's explanations of the poetry, alongside and somewhat at odds with Schulberg's depictions, illustrated authors moving internally toward recognizing a distinct, and highly variegated, vision of black working-class life in which a collective creative process, spatially bound neighborhood, and assertion of broader liberation could come together. Caught between an established pattern of cultural democracy and an emergent "self-determination music," the Watts Writers Workshop would ultimately encounter serious internal contradictions. But those would come later, following a period of increasing success.

THE CULTURAL WAR ON POVERTY

Congressional testimony, published anthologies, and television specials rapidly increased the visibility of the Watts Writers Workshop. Until this point, most of the workshop's expenses had come from Schulberg's deep, but hardly unlimited, pockets. The solicitation and dissemination of antipoverty funds involved no small measure of jockeying between competing groups, and Schulberg's willingness to cover expenses using his own means impressed both potential funding sources and local residents. Citing a need to maintain local control, one workshop member, Amde Hamilton, had repeatedly criticized the selection of blacks from outside the Watts area for administrative positions in community cultural institutions. Commenting on the trustworthiness of Schulberg, however, Hamilton observed, "He wasn't a poverty pimp. He was already rich."[36] A similar perception of Schulberg's trustworthiness extended to New York, where officials of the Rockefeller Foundation expressed interest in helping the organization. Noting that in-kind assistance, donations of equipment (NBC-TV had donated cameras and editing equipment), and individual contributions had come only after Schulberg had demonstrated his willingness to pay the workshop's expenses himself, observers from the Rockefeller Foundation suggested that additional small grants might continue to supplement funds raised from private donors.[37]

The most reliable source of funding for what federal officials and private foundations agreed was a program "with direct application to the country's social problems" remained individuals whom Schulberg knew personally.[38]

Here, the massive amount of positive publicity the workshop had generated was put to good use. Schulberg solicited donations from a wide pool of associates, including James Baldwin, Robert F. Kennedy, Richard Burton, Irving Stone, Elia Kazan, Truman Capote, Steven Allen, Art Buchwald, and John Steinbeck. Steinbeck's assistance proved particularly helpful, as he procured funds from the National Foundation for the Arts and provided the group's initial recommendation to the National Endowment for the Arts. By October 1967, the National Foundation for the Arts had contributed $25,000, an amount ultimately matched by private donors.[39]

Visiting officers of the Rockefeller Foundation described the workshop as "the most impressive single cultural effort mounted in Watts following the revolt." An initial recommendation of $25,000 in matching funds was proposed, and an ongoing relationship between the Watts Writers Workshop and the Rockefeller Foundation began. Foundation officials also reported that Robert Walker, an official with the National Foundation for the Arts, had encouraged Schulberg to submit a request for $268,000 for the 1968 fiscal year.[40] Rockefeller charities had long funded African American projects, including a number of historically black colleges and universities, as well as the American Negro Theater, the Free Southern Theater, and the Cleveland-based Karamu House. In Schulberg's workshop, they found an ideal candidate for support.

Dedicated to providing a creative outlet and to increasing the opportunities open to disadvantaged blacks, Schulberg also hoped to exclude "extreme nationalism" and the "most militant" viewpoints circulating in Watts. Schulberg spoke out against what he considered extreme points of view in both closed writing sessions and reports prepared for the Rockefeller Foundation. Although this position would create internal strife as the workshop expanded, Schulberg's political moderation undoubtedly facilitated the organization's initial growth. External financiers could be assured of a level of moderation and oversight at a time when many philanthropic organizations openly worried that grants were being used to underwrite militant activity or were simply disappearing into the coffers of corrupt or incompetent poverty-program administrators.[41]

Schulberg's antipathy toward displays of "extreme nationalism" arose from multiple sources. Publicly committed to racial justice and integration, he may well have shared the sense of exclusion and despair other whites sympathetic to civil-rights activity described when faced with black nationalism. Moreover, his personal experience with "political art" had been decidedly negative.

In his testimony before HUAC, he cited efforts by Communist Party officials to alter portions of his novel *What Makes Sammy Run?* (1951) as the reason he began to question his affiliation with the radical left. Firmly entrenched within the noncommunist "liberal" left, Schulberg viewed art as capable of tremendous social transformation but equally susceptible to ideological manipulation. As a result, among the aspiring writers of Watts, Schulberg encouraged works that revealed individual experience rather than programmatic statements and that proffered a generalized goal of communication while leaving aside the question of what ultimately might be communicated.[42]

The framework of cultural liberalism extended well beyond the figure of a single screenwriter. Similar concerns, for example, occupied the Inner City Cultural Center (ICCC) during its first year. Formed in the aftermath of the riots by two African American academicians affiliated with the University of California and intended as a consciously interracial body, the ICCC counted a prominent cast of Hollywood figures among its patrons; aimed to develop an audience among blacks, whites, Mexican Americans, and Asian Americans; and cast the arts as an antidote to social upheaval. The ICCC, too, was envisioned as an educational institute that would help provide opportunities for actors seeking work in Hollywood. And like the Watts Writers Workshop, the ICCC received major foundation funding—in this case, some $330,000 from the Ford Foundation. Most critically, however, the ICCC's location at the edges of the curfew area and its stated mission of bridging the presumed "communication gap" between white and nonwhite residents of Los Angeles highlighted the deep ideological continuities between the two institutions.[43]

As they had in the Watts Writers Workshop, questions of content and mission proved internally divisive among those seeking a theatrical version of cultural liberalism. Repeated skirmishes took place between the ICCC's founder, C. Bernard Jackson, who argued for "relevant" plays featuring "representative" themes and casts, and the actor Gregory Peck, who countered with a call for "plays of merit" aimed at students, including classics that "would hopefully create a much greater interest . . . on the part of the students for their classroom work."[44] Peck, the most prominent of the ICCC's early patrons, further laid out his vision of cultural politics in a fundraising letter that argued, "We, in Los Angeles, can make a dramatic contribution to the entire nation . . . to affect positively the lives of the people in the minority and economically deprived areas."[45] Peck had been instrumental in convincing the prominent theater director Andre Gregory to relocate to California to act as the artistic director of the theater, despite internal resistance to the naming of a white artistic director for a theater explicitly dedicated to serving a nonwhite constituency. Peck persuaded a skeptical board of directors to create a partnership with area high schools, the Educational Laboratory Theater Project, in which more than thirty-five thousand students attended plays hosted at the ICCC. Peck also agreed with Gregory's decision to employ a majority of white actors (only nine of the twenty-five members of the repertory company were people of color) and his selection of five plays, *Richard III*, *Tartuffe*, *The Glass Menagerie*, *The Seagull*, and Bertolt Brecht's *Caucasian Chalk Circle*, for the ICCC's inaugural season, despite objections that the lack of works by minority playwrights was out of keeping with the goal of providing plays of interest to the surrounding community.[46]

Initially, the vision of an integrationist cultural politics presented by Schulberg and Peck generated widespread enthusiasm among black artists. The members of the Watts Writers Workshop chose to name the permanent site the Frederick Douglass House. In selecting the abolitionist autodidact as their symbol, the writers aligned themselves with perhaps the most famous integrationist in American history before the rise of Dr. Martin Luther King. Sonora McKeller, a participant in the workshop and an official of the Westminster Neighborhood Association, argued that the workshop, like the teen posts springing up throughout Los Angeles, might prevent young blacks from joining "militant" organizations. On a visit to Chino prison, James Thomas Jackson observed that the "inmates are there for some of the same reasons many of us here at the Douglass House are not. . . . We were stopped in time, by someone who cared."[47] Johnny Scott claimed that the workshop filled an urgent need in an area where the senior high schools often lacked adequate speech and English departments. Scott argued the validity of both oral traditions and what he termed "street speech" but argued forcefully that greater technical instruction could transform black attitudes toward mastering the English language from "homework, which nobody does, to something that is meaningful."[48]

Throughout 1967, this vision met with increasing success. New workshops began in Altadena and San Bernardino, a sprawling county east of Los Angeles. Inmates at the California Institute for Men in Chino founded a site, while an initial public event held to announce the founding of a Long Beach branch drew eight hundred spectators and participants. Regular membership in the Long Beach group grew to approximately seventy active members by the summer of 1968. Summer marked the debut of a predominantly Chicano East Los Angeles Branch directed by Guadeloupe de Saavedra, who had been a member of the Watts group since early 1967. The East Los Angeles branch began preparing a bilingual anthology and a theater workshop. The "breakthrough" of the workshop to East Los Angeles was viewed with particular pleasure by Rockefeller Foundation officials, who had earlier lamented that, with the exception of staff, the Watts, Altadena, Chino, and San Bernardino workshops were "exclusively black" and that "so far it has proved difficult to bring in Mexican Americans, Japanese Americans, and American Indians."[49]

Conceived as a parent organization comprising the Watts Writers Workshop, the Douglas House Theater, and associated branches, the Douglas House Foundation provided funding and administrative guidance to these satellite projects. Associated branches planned and held autonomous local events, although members of the Altadena and Long Beach branches participated in the Watts Summer Festival in 1968. Incorporated as a nonprofit corporation, Douglas House oversaw the distribution of funds throughout the various branches. For the 1968 fiscal year, expenses totaled just over $125,000, an amount representing more than double the amount spent in 1967.[50] Of the amount budgeted for 1968, almost $99,000 went to the Watts project, with smaller amounts ($11,679) budgeted for Altadena and San Bernardino and for Chino ($4,490). Costs for the Watts project included rent, food, and other housing-related expenses; a travel budget; and additional monies for administrative coordination and supplies.[51]

Workshop activities throughout 1968 highlight the key areas of emphasis as envisioned by Schulberg. In addition to composition classes, the workshop hosted courses in screenplay writing, acting, television and film editing, motion-picture-camera operation, and film production. The U.S. Department of Health, Education, and Welfare (HEW) contracted the Douglass House to write pamphlets with the stated purpose of explaining HEW programs in terms "people in ghetto communities can understand."[52] Workshop participants were encouraged to pursue and master skills that would allow them to survive on their craft. Generally, this meant writing poems and prose for paid publication, although the project's strategic location in Southern California made possible a wide range of paying pursuits. By 1968, at least five workshop participants were regularly writing for three local television studios. Others had secured fellowships at Stanford, the University of Iowa, and the University of Ghana. Workshop alumni held teaching positions at the Ohio State University, George Washington University, and at two local state university campuses in California. Columbia Records released an album of poetry read by members of the group, and plans were under way for additional television performances.[53]

FIGURE 15 Watts Summer Festival parade float sponsored by Douglas House Foundation/Watts Writers Workshop, 1968. Photograph by Rolland Curtis. Los Angeles Public Library.

Cultural liberalism was born as an ad hoc response to the explosion of South Los Angeles in 1965. The goal of using creative writing and drama as a path to racial integration, social inclusion, and nonviolence generated excitement, publicity, and public and private support. Operating as a kind of "cultural front" in the broader war on poverty, cultural liberalism took the creative process as a form of job training and cast the exclusion of black nationalist politics as an aesthetic and political imperative. The fortunes of this vision illustrate the difficulties of reformist ideas at a moment of increasing urban radicalism.

THE LIMITS OF LIBERALISM

Despite the growth of the theater project, the addition of talented new members, and continued positive press attention, the workshop confronted three major difficulties. The first major crisis was financial. As early as November 1967, Schulberg warned Rockefeller officials of imminent budgetary problems. Noting that estimated expenditures exceeded revenues by nearly $99,000, he asked that the Rockefeller Foundation consider an annual funding commitment of $100,000. The arrival of proposed funds would have done little more than delay further crises, as budget estimates for 1968 showed expected expenditures exceeding $250,000. Although Schulberg had been encouraged to apply for more than this amount by Robert Walter, an official with the National Foundation for the Arts, confidential correspondence between Rockefeller Foundation officials revealed that Schulberg was unlikely to see such a large grant. Opining that Schulberg might see as little as $50,000, one official argued that, as "B.S. is apparently the sole force in Watts now working for the arts and Equal Opportunity, his needs should be supported." Despite this favorable assessment, annual Rockefeller funding would come nowhere near this amount, instead hovering around the $25,000 mark. Although the conferral of tax-exempt status for the Douglass Foundation helped matters somewhat, National Endowment for the Arts and National Foundation for the Arts funding, private donations, and grants from the Rockefeller and Randolph foundations left the Douglass project short nearly $57,000.[54]

The Douglass Foundation initially sought to meet these challenges by relying on the same contacts used to procure funding for the original Douglass House site. A celebrity billiards tournament was organized that featured Willie Shoemaker, Shirley MacLaine, Walter Matthau, Groucho Marx, Jack Lemmon, and Janet Leigh. Although such star power demonstrated Schulberg's continuing ability to translate positive press and personal connections into concrete financial support, the event failed to close a budget gap that worsened with every Watts Writers Workshop and Douglass Foundation success. The decision to encourage independently organized affiliates now became a liability, as new ventures on the Westside and in Fresno sprang up. As had been the case with the first satellite project in Altadena, these workshops also expected financial support, creative coaching, and a measure of organizational guidance.[55]

Rapid expansion thus created budgetary constraints as funding sources began to slow. This trend extended well beyond Watts, as national affairs increasingly seemed to suggest that five years of concerted antipoverty funding had accomplished little. Following the assassination of Martin Luther King Jr. in April 1968, riots tore across more than one hundred cities. This was followed by the fifth year of major summer riots, including the violence that accompanied the Democratic National Convention. Growing conflict between police and urban radicals further eroded support for antipoverty funding, as conservative critics denounced what they saw as little more than federal subsidies for insurrectionary activity. By year's end, the election of Richard Nixon on a platform highlighting support for "law and order" signified a further curtailing of spending on urban reform. In keeping with these general trends, the Rockefeller Foundation announced a temporary suspension of funding for equal-opportunity programs.[56]

Competition from similar projects throughout South Los Angeles arose as a second concern. While the size of South Los Angeles certainly justified multiple cultural institutions, donors who had earlier described Schulberg as operating the "sole," "only," or "most impressive" cultural effort in an area larger than Manhattan now became aware of the tremendous energy, breadth, and ability of parallel local programs. Noting that foundation funds were limited, Rockefeller Foundation officials expressed hope that closer working relationships between the Watts Writers Workshop, Studio Watts, and the unaffiliated poets of the Watts Happening Coffee House might be forged. Perhaps unaware of the contrasting visions that lay at the heart of different individuals and organizations, visiting Rockefeller Foundation officials seemed puzzled and somewhat taken aback by the seeming lack of interest in greater cooperation.[57]

Earlier, of course, the fact that Schulberg came from outside Watts had been precisely the point of supporting his endeavor. The presence of a famous white author willing to facilitate the development of black creative talent suggested possibilities for racial reconciliation and black advancement. The ambivalence of the coffeehouse poets; the critical comments of Jim Wood; and the growth of new organizations sympathetic to precisely the "extreme nationalism" attacked by Schulberg signaled more than competition for resources. The success of openly nationalist projects such as the Performing Arts Society of Los Angeles, the arts journal *Nigger Uprising*, and the Underground Musicians Association led by the pianist Horace Tapscott highlighted the expanding salience of black demands for control over the organization and direction of black cultural activity. By 1968, Los Angeles boasted one of the most active black arts scenes in the nation, with more than thirty community arts projects linking more than a thousand artists, musicians, and writers. Foundation agreement with the argument that local groups should be prioritized over the efforts of a sympathetic, but external, white celebrity might therefore be seen as evidence of external recognition of a cultural turn toward "maximum feasible participation" and community control.[58]

Given the greater ideological confluence between Schulberg, the workshop, philanthropic organizations, and government officials, public and private donors might well have continued to prioritize the Watts Writers Workshop over other groups. Both the workshop's high overhead and Schulberg's desire to reduce his own commitment to the organization militated against this. Following the publication of *Sanctuary V*, a novel about political persecution in Latin America, Schulberg moved permanently to New York.[59] Although Rockefeller Foundation officials noted with sympathy that three years of focus on the workshop had left Schulberg insufficient time to write, they showed little inclination to provide substantial support to a workshop led by a new director, Harry Dolan. The workshop continued to enjoy critical success, particularly with its theatrical productions. Increasingly, however, the community-service aspects of the workshop were supplanted—at least in the minds of some—by the work of other organizations. Hence, one observer argued that the nearby Mafundi Institute demonstrated greater "vitality," and that both Mafundi and Studio Watts had more flexible facilities, especially for experimental theater, than did the Douglass Foundation. By 1970, visitors from the Rockefeller Foundation were suggesting that either Mafundi or Studio Watts might put limited donations to better use.[60]

A third major crisis to hit the Watts Writers Workshop came in the form of an internal schism. In the fall of 1968, thirteen members of the group left, citing "subtle censorship" and "literary sharecropping."[61] The emergence of Watts 13, as the new group elected to call itself, exposed divisions along ideological, generational, and aesthetic lines. With several notable exceptions, those writers who chose to remain at the Watts Writers Workshop tended to be older, more politically moderate, and less given to experimenting across artistic genres than the members of the new foundation. Following the example of the Douglass Foundation, Watts 13 rented and refurbished a nearby house for use as a residence and performance space. From this base, dubbed "the house of respect," the new group issued a series of press releases announcing a benefit concert, plans for a theatrical production, and the publication of a new anthology.[62]

The new anthology, *Watts Poets* (1968), signaled a clear move away from the ideological underpinnings of *From the Ashes*. In place of positing literature as a vaccine against social upheaval, Milton McFarlane's introductory sentence in *Watts Poets* proclaimed, "There can never be a successful adjustment of black people to the American economic system."[63] *Watts Poets* also represented a wider selection of local writing. Whereas *From the Ashes* contained works only by authors affiliated with Schulberg's workshop, *Watts Poets* included works by experienced writers who had been published elsewhere. In addition to former members of the Watts Writers Workshop such as Quincy Troupe, Ojenke, Emmery Evans, K. Curtis Lyle, and Vallejo Kennedy, contributors to *Watts Poets* included Elaine Brown; Stanley Crouch; Linda "Lino"

Hill, co-founder of the Pan Afrikan People's Arkestra; and Ridhiana Saunders, publisher of *Nigger Uprising*. Driven by these additions, the contributors to *Watts Poets* devoted greater attention to issues of black musicality, nationalist politics, and international affairs than the earlier anthology had.[64]

By the time the Watts Writers Workshop ceased effective operation in 1973, more than a few of its members had become important figures in an increasingly radical community arts milieu.[65] The poet Kamau Daáood had transitioned from the Watts Writers Workshop to the Pan-Afrikan Peoples Arkestra and Underground Musicians Association. The former workshop stalwarts Amde Hamilton, Richard Anthony Dedeaux, and Otis O'Solomon combined to form the Watts Prophets, a pioneering proto-rap music trio whose albums *Black Voices on the Streets of Watts* and *Rappin' Black in a White World* heralded the arrival of a Californian counterpart to the lyrical radicalism of New York's Last Poets.

Watts Writers Workshop members would also intervene in the sectarian polemics between the Black Panther Party and its cultural nationalist rivals, the US Organization, excoriating the latter as "traitors and fools" after a shootout between the two groups on the campus of the University of California, Los Angeles. The latter commentary is instructive, for the terse statement warning both groups against "an all out jam-bang gangland bloodbath . . . with the masses of black people on the sidelines, ambivalent and not really understanding," suggested an organization increasingly oriented toward the internal schisms undermining the Black Power Movement and away from the earlier integrationist projects aimed at Hollywood as much as Watts.[66] Perhaps the ultimate confirmation of the Watts Writers Workshop's shift toward a stance more in keeping with radical peers such as the Black Panther Party and the Underground Musicians Association came in 1973 when Darthard Perry, a former Army intelligence officer turned FBI informant, infiltrated the organization, committed repeated acts of sabotage, and finally burned down the building that housed the workshop.[67]

Yet these ultimate affiliations with precisely those "most extreme" elements decried by Schulberg should obfuscate neither the distinct origins nor the early history of the Watts Writers Workshop. Founded as an explicitly reformist body dedicated, as Schulberg described it, to establishing a connection between Watts residents "and what you might term the outside world," the project initiated a novel attempt to develop a unique model of urban reform through arts education.[68] By inaugurating a vision of cultural liberalism that brought together black authors, sympathetic white outsiders, and significant private funding, the effort to use creative writing as a path to individual progress, racial reconciliation, and gainful employment represented more than a failed experiment in urban cultural policy. The internal challenges facing the Watts Writers Workshop illustrate the extent to which the primary political chasm of the 1960s was less that of right and left than the gulf between American liberalism and its radical detractors. Most significantly, the internal metamorphosis of the Watts Writers Workshop from access to autonomy aptly symbolized the broader change under way locally as black artists began to articulate anew the conviction that the creative, social, and political problems of South Los Angeles might be solved using the creative, social, and political resources located within South Los Angeles. This revolutionary chrysalis forms the second section of this book.

PART II

Message

from the

Grassroots

4

NOTES FROM THE UNDERGROUND Free Jazz and Black Power
in South Los Angeles

An author who has carefully thought about the condition
of production today . . . will never be concerned with products alone, but always, at the same time, with the means
of production. In other words, his works must possess an
organizing function besides and before their character as
finished works.
—WALTER BENJAMIN

> The first place we went, before I got to my house, my mother told the driver
> to stop the car. Our suitcase was still in the trunk. And I said, "This is where
> we live?" She said, "No, this is not where we live. I want to introduce you to
> your first music teacher." She'd already picked him out. We hadn't gotten to
> the house yet. I don't know where I live. . . . That's the first person I met in
> Los Angeles, Harry Southard. . . . He said, "I'll be seeing you son." The next
> day I was at music lessons.[1]

Eventually finding his way home, Horace Tapscott spent much of the next
half-century blending visionary music and communitarian politics. Forsaking
Manhattan for Watts, he spent the better part of four decades as part of a
South Los Angeles musical and political underground. He is marginal in jazz
historiography, and many of his compositions are equally difficult to locate on
the shelves of record stores. Despite a burst of posthumous attention, Tapscott
remains obscure almost everywhere beyond the local community in which he
worked and lived.

This is unfortunate, for his life opens a critical window into the cultural
politics of black Los Angeles, illustrating the key role played by local artists in

the growth of insurgent urban politics. A veteran of Los Angeles's music-education circles, a witness to the decline of Central Avenue, and an out-spoken critic of the aftermath of union amalgamation, Tapscott and his life gave eloquent testimony to the evolving efforts made by artists seeking to address the material, social, and aesthetic limitations of cultural liberalism and racial integration. As a key figure in the development of community-based musical institutions, as a partisan of "the new music," and as someone whose career linked the worlds of expressive culture and radical organizing, the six and a half-foot "Papa," as he was widely and affectionately known, was literally a local giant.

Repeatedly rejecting entreaties aimed at drawing him east, as his contemporaries Eric Dolphy, Charles Mingus, and Ornette Coleman had been, Tapscott instead established a legacy aptly symbolized by a decade of free weekly concerts held in a ramshackle church. Like the Watts Writers Workshop and Inner City Cultural Center, the Underground Musicians Association that Tapscott co-founded functioned as a teaching institution, providing a critical source of musical instruction at precisely the moment when aspiring musicians faced worsening economic prospects, declining playing opportunities, and the evisceration of music programs in area schools. Like Budd Schulberg and C. Bernard Jackson, Tapscott saw aesthetics and politics as linked. Yet where the screenwriter and psychologist suggested a *response* to the 1965 riot, Tapscott offered an *affirmation*. In response to cultural liberalism's blend of interracial universalism, job training, and societal investment writ large, Tapscott's vision of a self-determination music proposed a sonic translation of the black liberation movement's directive to "serve the people." As a radical democratic vision rooted jointly in experience and experiment, Tapscott's politics of culture constituted a kind of emancipatory epistemology based upon the possibility of defining freedom in multifaceted, open-ended, and comprehensive terms.

Horace Tapscott was the most recognizable member of a combined community orchestra and jazz collective known variously as the Underground Musicians Association (UGMA), the Union of God's Musicians and Artists Ascension (UGMAA), the Community Cultural Arkestra, and the Pan Afrikan People's Arkestra. Founded in 1961, the Arkestra continues to perform today, despite the passing of founding members such as Tapscott and Linda Hill, the departure of high-profile alumni such as Arthur Blythe, and the inevitable turnover of forty years. This chapter takes up the Arkestra during its first dozen years, a period bookended by the growth of a politicized community arts cohort and the waning of widespread social radicalism in the context of police repression, the election of Mayor Thomas Bradley, and the end of American involvement in Vietnam.[2] During this period, the Arkestra occupied a distinct political and aesthetic space that combined a focus on local community, creative control, musical experimentation, and support for the broader project of black liberation.

The historical moment that facilitated the emergence of the UGMA ensured the emergence of peer organizations elsewhere in the United States. In Chicago, Detroit, St. Louis, New York, and elsewhere, community-oriented musicians made attempts at collective organization, freeform musical experimentation, and support for radical politics. Seen from the broadest angle, the politics of black improvised music after 1950 is a national, even international, story. At the same time, Tapscott and his ilk emerged from a specific local context, a web of musical and social life that led logically to an orientation premised on the theory and practice of community control. Based physically in South Los Angeles, Tapscott had a vanguard vision based less on the charismatic model of Huey Newton or Martin Luther King than on the radical participatory democracy of Ella Baker. Thus, while trained instrumentalists made up the bulk of the of the Arkestra, many of the more than two hundred individuals who passed through the Ark were poets, young musical apprentices, or simply interested people from the surrounding community. Band members ranged in age from seven to seventy, and one of the band's first records featured several compositions written by Herbert Baker, a student at nearby Dorsey High School. Having come out of schools, union locals, and informal networks dedicated to affirming African American cultural life, the UGMA operated as a unique local resource.

The conscious choice to obliterate the distinction between professional and amateur had revolutionary aesthetic implications that are taken up in the succeeding section. The performative dimensions of the band's activity, as we shall see, connected to parallel efforts of visual artists and political radicals. As a partisan of "the new music," "avant-garde," or "free" jazz, Tapscott formed part of a nationwide cohort whose rejection of clubs, studio work, and other traditional venues in favor of far less remunerative gigs in parks, at festivals, and in churches constituted a vision of self-determination through collective expression and worker control. If the ironclad association between free jazz and black radicalism has been helpfully rendered more complex by recent scholarship, Tapscott's tale offers one of the most direct historical links between black cultural and political avant-gardes.[3] As Andre Gorz used to say, worker control is always more than that, and Tapscott's "self-determination music" was voiced equally through the development of new forums for an avowedly politicized jazz, through musicological choices made measure by measure and year by year, and through his common cause with a variety of insurgent political forces.

The timing of the UGMA, which was founded four years before the explosion of Watts, is significant, as well. Its early history highlights the need to see the ideas of self-determination associated with black power as arising alongside, rather than in response to, the more familiar struggle for civil rights. In the case of cultural activism, the community musical ensemble co-founded by Tapscott and Hill, like the Studio Watts workshop of Jayne Cortez and Jim Woods, the Art West Associated project led by Ruth Waddy, and the early Watts Towers Art Center of Noah Purifoy and Judson Powell, suggests that the "Watts Renaissance" began before, and could therefore not be a response to, the riot of 1965. One implication stands out clearly: The rise of a creative community of committed, politicized, cross-generic artists in 1960s South Los Angeles was motivated not by the presence of federal, state, or local resources, or even by the local growth of the Black Power Movement. It was motivated by the indigenous creative and organizational capacities of black Los Angeles.

ROOTS OF THE DARK TREE

For a family that considered finding a music teacher on a par with finding a place to live, Los Angeles had much to offer. Although key members of the Los Angeles jazz avant-garde moved west as adults, a larger group had migrated either as children during wartime or had been born and raised in Los Angeles. While the saxophonist Ornette Coleman (Fort Worth), trumpeter Bobby Bradford (Cleveland, Mississippi), composer and clarinetist John Carter (Fort Worth), drummer Ed Blackwell (New Orleans), and bassist Charlie Haden (Shenandoah, Indiana) first came to Los Angeles as young adults, an important cross-section of local free players were the products of Southern California's musical community. In addition to Horace Tapscott, the list of native sons included Eric Dolphy, Charles Mingus, Hampton Hawes, David Bryant, Don Cherry, George Newman, Billy Higgins, and, later, Arthur Blythe and James Newton. All benefited from a combination of public and private instruction, a thriving nightclub scene, and the touring opportunities that accompanied life in a center of popular music.

Educational networks constituted a singularly important resource for the development of a jazz community in 1960s-era Los Angeles. Southern California spawned at least three prominent music-education circles, each based within a specific geographic locale. Tapscott was an alumnus of the most celebrated of these, Samuel Browne's classroom at the predominantly black Jefferson High. Browne was himself the product of local music-education circles, having studied with the legendary composers William Wilkins and John Gray.[4] Browne's teaching career at Jefferson lasted more than two decades, during which time his students included a wide cross-section of local jazz talent. Among his students were Dexter Gordon, Chico Hamilton, Ernie and Marshall Royal, Tapscott, Don Cherry, Frank Morgan, and Roy Ayers. Browne's rehearsals often included former students such as Sonny Criss; students from other schools, including Eric Dolphy, Charles Mingus, and Buddy Collette; and the occasional visiting professional. Indeed, the trumpeter Bobby Bradford met Don Cherry and George Newman in Browne's classroom.[5] Visitors ranged from W. C. Handy and Nat "King" Cole to Lionel Hampton and William Grant Still. Browne's interests were wide-ranging, encompassing everything from proto-free experimentation to classical and operatic scores. The most common curriculum, however, consisted of big-band arrangements that highlighted Browne's affinity for complex arrangements, demanded the inclusion of talent at varied levels, and incorporated compositional themes rooted in African American history and life.[6]

Where Browne's influence was both philosophical and organizational, sources of technical instruction abounded. One particularly important teacher was Lloyd Reese. A trumpeter and alto saxophonist, Resse taught students from both Jordan and Jefferson, including Tapscott, Collette, Mingus, Gordon, and Eric Dolphy, as well as the Chicano saxophonist Anthony Ortega. Area players were effervescent in their praise for Reese. Charles Mingus acknowledged that many of the local players who eventually achieved fame were students of Reese, adding that Eric Dolphy earned the money to pay for lessons from Reese by cutting his grass and clipping his hedges.[7] Britt Woodman described Reese as "probably the greatest all-around teacher in LA," while Horace Tapscott decided that, after Reese, he would never again need lessons. Reese insisted that students play piano and learn to compose, whatever instrument they preferred. And, as Tapscott noted, "he really focused on how to make sounds and his ear was incredible. He had one of those terrible ears that would hear everything. . . . He would give me something to work on for maybe two weeks, wouldn't tell me how to work on this, but for me to find a way to do it."[8] As was the case with Browne's classroom, Reese's home was a place both to learn and to make contacts. Tapscott, for example, first met Duke Ellington there. Reese's sessions also spanned something of an age gap, as Collette and Mingus, born in 1921 and 1922, respectively, belonged to a prewar and wartime scene unfamiliar to younger players such as Tapscott (born in 1934) and Don Cherry and Billy Higgins (both born in 1936).

However important, these intergenerational networks go only so far in explaining the subsequent political orientation of Tapscott and the Arkestra. After all, many musicians who had benefited from the same networks relocated to New York, found other work, or remained in Los Angeles without choosing to make developing a community orchestra their life's work. Part of the social basis of the Arkestra lay outside South Los Angeles, and it is possible to see both a community orientation and a willingness to affiliate with "nationalist" forces as one byproduct of Los Angeles's tentatively integrated music world of the 1950s. The end of formal discrimination against musicians brought deep disappointment. In the context of a rapidly expanding local cultural infrastructure, symbolized by the public campaigns for a major music performance hall and the nation's second-largest art museum, both Eric Dolphy and Charles Mingus made little headway in the search for orchestral work, with the latter managing only a short stint in the local junior philharmonic. While he was enrolled at the University of Southern California, Dolphy had been dropped from the university orchestra after faculty members complained that he "ruined the color scheme."[9] The musicians' union—which had boasted about the standard of living enjoyed by its members only a few years before amalgamation—now offered living wages to a small group of musicians, most of whom were white. Many black musicians saw continued exclusion as deliberate, and it is worth recalling that amalgamation took place alongside the official "whitening" of Southern California jazz during the early 1950s. Indeed, forums such as *Down Beat* magazine's panel "The Need for Racial Unity in Jazz" in 1963 emerge less as evidence of a sincere commitment to equality than as a running critique of black assertiveness when we recall the active role of jazz periodicals in repositioning jazz as an increasingly white musical form.[10] Not for the first time, black musicians had reason to doubt the sincerity of the commitment of whites faced with the demand that they carve the turkey into different portions. A sizeable minority of Local 47, it should be remembered, opposed the federation. Among these was a significant section of the music department at Los Angeles City College, where Tapscott enrolled after graduating from high school. Banned from multiple classrooms for offenses that ranged from soloing "with funny styles and shit" to pointing out that college instructors were not teaching anything about European classical composition that Samuel Browne was not teaching high-school students at Jefferson, Tapscott finally decided to leave City College following a dispute with a teacher who had dismissed Duke Ellington's *Black, Brown and Beige* as "written wrong." Concluding that "this school was a waste of my time," Tapscott instead opted for the postgraduate curriculum offered by what he called "the U of S, University of the Streets."[11]

On the sprawling campus of the university of the streets, older musicians played a critical role in developing young talent. Buddy Collette's and Bill Green's Progressive Musicians Organization (PMO) held weekly jam sessions with the aim of providing a regular forum for developing musicians. Held at the Crystal Tea Room on 50th and Avalon, these sessions included such notables as Sonny Criss, Frank Morgan, Eric Dolphy, and David Bryant. Other young participants included the eventual Arkestra members Walter Benton, Ernest Crawford, and Sweetpea Robinson. The PMO was one of a trio of exploratory, socially themed orchestras formed by Collette in the early postwar years. Each linked an aesthetic and political practice. The Community Symphony Orchestra offered jazz and classical musicians an experiment in peaceful coexistence even as the formation facilitated the broader quest for union amalgamation. Later, Collette would co-found a Black and Brown orchestra that linked Chicano and black musicians interested in exploring the spaces between the problematic categories of "jazz" and "Latin" music. Another influential mentor was the composer and bandleader Gerald Wilson, who made a point of hiring young musicians for his big-band bop orchestra. Indeed, it was Wilson who originally brought Tapscott into the musicians' union, while Eric Dolphy described how the older man "would take me around to hear all the musicians and explain things to me." Wilson, like Browne, possessed an expansive vision of jazz that sought, in particular, to meld the virtuoso-showcasing advantages of small combos with the wider assortment of arrangements made possible by larger ensembles. Writing shortly before his death in 1964, Eric Dolphy opined that Wilson's band had "been making the modern sounds since the war years. He had a band in 1944 that would be considered modern today."[12]

This mentorship proved invaluable to young musicians, who often found that an affiliation with Reese, Collette, or Browne was enough to secure entry into one of the more than thirty local nightclubs, after-hours spots, and informal sessions dotting South Los Angeles. Many of these sites were within walking distance of each other, with clubs such as the Downbeat, Club Alabam, the Last Word, the Turban Room, and Jack's Bird Basket located within a few blocks. Although crowds had begun to thin after the end of the Second World War, as the local club scene shifted westward, even a declining Central Avenue offered young musicians a platform. Many emerging local players secured their first serious musical employment following unscheduled club appearances. Like Charles Mingus and Dexter Gordon before them, initial jobs with big-band tours came to Dolphy, Tapscott, Hawes, and others largely as a result of reputations earned on late night bandstands.[13]

The participation of these individuals in big bands raises an important point—namely, the need to see the free jazz players who became identified with aesthetic and social radicalism as emerging from the broader jazz community. Given the historiographical tendency that treats the jazz avant-garde as either emerging full-blown from Ornette Coleman's horn or focuses over-much on the ire that free jazz provoked among a sizable number of musicians and critics, acknowledging the continuing interconnections between figures like Tapscott and Wilson demonstrates the fallacy of reducing jazz to a fixed set of stylistic categories. People spread culture, and as the interpersonal and inter-corporeal networks of cultural transmission continue to come to light, it is critical to acknowledge that local representatives of the jazz avant-garde shared experiences, bandstands, and ideas with musicians working in other styles.[14] The drummer Billy Higgins and the trumpeter Don Cherry, after all, were playing in a bop combo when they first met Ornette Coleman. The interventions of musicians "playing out" often rested on rearticulating and transforming previously developed ideas. Tapscott's album *Songs of the Unsung*, for example, contained a big-band composition written by Sam Browne, as well as an arrangement of an Elmo Hope piece, *Something for Kenny*, that Tapscott and Hope had played as part of Wilson's band in 1958. Furthermore, while free jazz is sometimes taken as the antithesis of "West Coast" or "cool" jazz, the avant-garde Chicagoan Anthony Braxton identified the "cool" jazz saxophonist Paul Desmond as an influence, while the bassist Charlie Haden worked as a sideman for Chet Baker. This is not to deny the marked hostility of critics such as *Down Beat*'s John Tynam, who excoriated Ornette Coleman's compositions as "anti-jazz," or to deny that musicians like Horace Tapscott and Bobby Bradford offered something new. Rather, it is meant to suggest a degree of continuity between the avant-garde and musicians identified with other styles.[15]

The early 1950s represent a moment of critical musical maturity in Southern California. The tremendous innovation of the period deeply influenced local musicians, including the youthful members of the emerging avant-garde. Eric Dolphy toured with Roy Porter's big band, a bop outfit that included the brothers Art and Addison Farmer, Chet Baker, Teddy Edwards, and Jimmy Knepper. Many musicians met Dolphy at his home. Although Dolphy was well under thirty years old, his house was akin to the Minton's of Los Angeles, a largely audience-free spot where musicians could work out ideas in jam sessions held in Dolphy's soundproofed garage. Resident local players included the pianist Hampton Hawes, whose father was pastor and musical director of a church attended by Dolphy's parents, as well as Buddy Collette, Charles Mingus, Elmo Hope, Sonny Criss, and, especially, Harold Land.[16] The saxophonist Lester Robinson, a close friend of Dolphy's and an important member of the UGMA, was a frequent presence, as well. Episodic visitors included Max Roach and Clifford Brown, then living in Los Angeles, as well as John Coltrane.[17] Within the context of a rich musical scene that included expanding hard bop and Latin music combinations, as well as more familiar "West Coast" sounds, an experimental community began to take hold. In such a milieu, stylistic proclivities should be seen as tendencies, at best, for most serious players were invested more in crossing boundaries than in inventing new ones.

A similar story could be told for those "out" musicians arriving in Los Angeles during the middle and late 1950s. Veterans of Southwestern rhythm-and-blues circuits, the Texans Ornette Coleman and John Carter spent their teen years as "stone boppers" before coming west. Fellow Texan Bobby Bradford's return west offers as much a tale of a bygone era as does Tapscott's reminiscence of meeting his music teacher the very day he arrived in Los Angeles.[18] In a city regarded as the epicenter of the private automobile, Bradford ran into Ornette Coleman on the soon-to-be defunct system of street trolleys known as the red car. "Lo and behold," Bradford recalled, "I couldn't have been in town more than 90 days and here I'm on the red car where we live, and who's on the car with me? Ornette Coleman."[19] These chance meetings helped stitch together an experimental cohort that included Coleman, Dolphy, and Bradford, as well as musicians such as Wardell Gray, Harold Land, and Sonny Stitt, who, while not generally considered "out" players, could often be found sharing bandstands with "free" jazz musicians. Other additions in the early 1950s included the drummer Ed Blackwell, the Chicano altoist Anthony Ortega, the pianist Andrew Hill, the bassist Charlie Haden, the flautist Prince Lasha, and the pianists Paul and Carla Bley. Thus, in the half-decade that preceded the founding of the Arkestra/UGMA, Los Angeles began to develop a distinct, if small, cohort of experimental musicians.[20]

While experimentation with different musical styles facilitated the development of new musical sensibilities, changing financial patterns also transformed area jazz. Following the decline of Central Avenue, a process irreversibly evident by 1950 and largely complete by 1955, the locus of Southern California jazz shifted northwest to Hollywood, toward the beach cities of Santa Monica, Venice, and Manhattan Beach and to the Mid-City area west of downtown.[21] Smaller bands and fewer clubs reduced playing opportunities, increasing musicians' reliance on club owners. Significantly, this spatial shift contained a racial component, since most of the new clubs opening to the west were owned and operated by whites. Many of these owners proved openly hostile to "playing out." Few club owners had the space or the inclination to book performances by Horace Tapscott or Sun Ra's Arkestras, since they might easily involve dozens of musicians, dancers, and poets. Most patrons bought drinks between songs, and some owners felt that the longer compositions inaugurated by the jazz avant-garde's move away from using popular standards as the basis of compositions weakened liquor sales, the primary raison d'être of clubs. Others blamed dwindling crowds on a style many audiences found difficult to understand. Others were perhaps responding to the increasingly assertive denunciations by musicians of the world of booking agents, club owners, and underappreciative crowds.[22]

Such critiques on the part of musicians were vocal and widespread. One of Ornette Coleman's ablest biographers observes that "the very conditions of the jazz business were antithetical to the creation of fine art."[23] Few, John Litwiler charges, would expect classical musicians to put up with the substandard acoustic conditions, intermittent compensation, and generalized disrespect that jazz musicians experienced nightly. Echoing sentiments from the prewar heyday of swing, Coleman complained about regularly earning less than white musicians, despite attracting larger crowds. Dismissing jazz nightclubs as "whorehouses," Coleman added that "the nightclub is still built on the same two things: whiskey and fucking." Coleman's comments, although broadly applicable, may well have specifically referenced his situation. Many of his initial performances in Los Angeles with Bobby Bradford took place in adult cabarets inside a disreputable area of downtown Los Angeles known as "the nickel." More reputable nightclubs seldom seemed better. The critic Frank Kofsky described patterns of harassment directed by management toward performers at the Manne-Hole, a Hollywood club owned by the drummer Shelly Manne. In addition to a bevy of instructions concerning song and set length, management sought to dictate which local sidemen could be used and encouraged musicians to purchase alcoholic beverages while surreptitiously deducting the cost of the drinks from paychecks. Mismanagement extended to allegations of racially biased bookings and a clear unwillingness to book local avant-garde players such as Bradford, Tapscott, and Carter. In discussing bookings, Bradford claimed that style was at least as important as race. "You can forget about black clubs," he told Kofsky in an interview. "The black clubs that are open are interested in selling the drinks and getting the cover."[24]

Nor were club owners the only focus of performers' ire. Many artists expressed tremendous frustration at what they perceived as ignorant and rude audiences. Miles Davis's solution for dealing with problematic audiences is well known. But he was not alone. Charles Mingus and John Coltrane lamented the cacophony generated by conversations, the clinking of drink glasses, and the ringing of cash registers. For his part, Tapscott complained about being transformed into a court jester, revealing his disgust at being asked to play songs such as "Bill Bailey, Won't You Please Come Home." Bradford called the ignorance of listeners "amazing," noting that they seemed to care little about the music they were paying to hear. For him, the issue spoke to the entire purpose of playing. "I don't mean the form and what the technical things are," he clarified. "They don't know whether the music is memorized or not. They don't care whether we play the same thing every time or if that's what we're trying to do. They have no understanding of what's going on."[25]

As a result, the move toward formal collective organization among local musicians interested in experimental music was grounded in a simultaneous set of shared aesthetic and material concerns. Tapscott's twofold critique of the lives of touring musicians illustrates the connection. While on tour with Lionel Hampton's band, Tapscott had visited New York, observing with displeasure the penurious lives of cutting-edge artists such as John Coltrane and Eric Dolphy. Road life, moreover, seemed to impose unwanted limitations on what musicians could play. Lamenting that "the music was getting lost, as far as I was concerned," Tapscott abandoned touring.[26] Similar convictions animated other early Arkestra members. David Bryant referred to his work with the UGMA as helping him to keep his sanity amid the boredom and stagnation of playing commercial music, while the bassist Al Hines claimed, "We wanted to preserve the black arts, to keep them alive."[27] As we shall see, the group that ultimately emerged adopted twin goals of preserving and extending what it saw as consciously black music and transcending the material and emotional limitations confronting professional musicians.

After leaving Hampton's band in 1961, the twenty-seven-year-old Tapscott joined with the pianist Linda Hill to plan the organizations that became the Underground Musicians' Association and the Pan Afrikan People's Arkestra (PAPA). The former group included the entire range of associated community artists, while the latter referred more specifically to the avant-garde big band conducted by Tapscott. The former moniker was typically used for small group ensembles and political events, although the names were often used inter-changeably. Gatherings were called "jam sessions," since, as Tapscott noted, "no one comes if you call a meeting." Interested musicians were invited to informal practice sessions held at Hill's home, which Tapscott commemorated with a composition entitled "Lino's Pad." The group grew quickly, counting by the end of the first year a rotating membership of thirty active members.[28]

The timing of their efforts was apt. The founding of the Ark coincided with Samuel Browne's departure from Jefferson High. After two decades of facili-tating the development of student musicians, Browne relocated to a newer, more affluent, and overwhelmingly white high school located in hilly, beach-side Pacific Palisades. Although Browne's primary reasons for moving were personal—he cited a lack of interest among students as the reason for cancel-ing his sixth-period band class—his exit coincided with the broader shift of the black middle class out of South Los Angeles.[29] In the decade that followed the Supreme Court decision in 1948 declaring racially restricted housing cove-nants unenforceable, new sources of housing stock opened to middle-class African Americans.[30] This migration was further facilitated by the expansion of a freeway system that sliced through the elevated Adams Avenue district that had formerly housed many affluent blacks. This movement, coupled with the lingering effects of post–Second World War re-conversion, left South Los Angeles poorer in 1960 than it had been at the end of the war.

Although the Arkestra emerged in part from these specific local circum-stances, the broader turn toward collective organization among jazz musicians took place throughout the United States. The early 1960s saw increasing politi-cization among jazz musicians simultaneously inspired by the black freedom movement and pressed by declining sales, closing clubs, and the rise of rock and roll. Organization took two general forms. On one side stood groups like the Arkestra and Chicago's Experimental Band, which by 1965 had become the Association for the Advancement of Creative Musicians (AACM).[31] Like the AACM, the UGMA was less an organization aimed at addressing issues of specific concern to professional musicians than an ongoing clearinghouse aimed at expanding the musical resources open to the black communities of South Los Angeles. Nevertheless, shared compositional duties, a collective decision-making process, and a general desire to circumvent the world of nightclubs and record companies linked the Arkestra to efforts like that of the Jazz Artists Guild and the Jazz Composers Guild. These groups, both centered in New York, saw collective organization as a means to confront structures of economic inequality within the nightclub, recording, and festival circuit. The collective organization of the Arkestra was less an economic strategy than a social one. Most Arkestra members, for instance, maintained other occupations, a necessity given that the majority of performances were free affairs held in public spaces. Free public performances formed a key aspect of the avowed mission of the band, which Tapscott described as the preservation and showcasing of the work of unknown and under-appreciated black composers. These composers were often locals, with the band regularly performing the music of Tapscott's mentors Gerald Wilson and Samuel Browne, as well as that of William Grant Still.[32]

A multifaceted articulation of community became a defining element of the group's mission. Having emerged from a context of creative community and ongoing mentorship, PAPA and the UGMA in turn became multigenerational organizations that combined high-school students, members of local junior-college bands, and professional musicians. As one constellation in what Aldon Nielsen describes as "the omniverse of jazz and text," moreover, Tapscott and the UGMA worked with numerous poets, including Jayne Cortez, the Watts Prophets, and various Watts Writers Workshop members.[33] Furthermore, both the constant participation of the UGMA and PAPA at arts festivals and the importance given jazz by black artists working in other mediums and genres ensured that Tapscott would develop relationships with authors, playwrights, visual and plastic artists, and cultural critics of every stripe. In addition to incorporating community members and showcasing the work of local composers, Tapscott made the surrounding community a compositional motif. Noting "most of my songs deal with people I've known," Tapscott composed songs dedicated to acquaintances from Houston ("Sketches of Drunken Mary") and Los Angeles ("Lino's Pad"), as well as family ("Sandy and Niles") and his musical mentors ("Ballad for Samuel").

The collective leadership of the Arkestra participated in two distinct, though overlapping, creative communities: the world of Los Angeles–based free jazz musicians and a broader tendency of community-oriented artists united around issues of collectivity, experimentation, political commitment, and a conscious relation to African American history, culture, and life. By 1964, the principal members of both bands had become increasingly affiliated with the developing black arts scene. The first community arts organization the UGMA became involved with was the Studio Watts Workshop. The principal initial organizers of Studio Watts were Jayne Cortez and James Woods. Cortez, born in Arizona but raised in Watts, had been involved in a variety of local black cultural circles, including an acting workshop at the Ebony Showcase Theater. Extremely familiar with the work of the jazz avant-garde, Cortez had performed with the clarinetist John Carter and had been married for a short period to Ornette Coleman. During the early 1960s, Cortez was experimenting with incorporating music into her poetry, and she originally met Tapscott while collaborating with the tenor saxophonist Curtis Amy on a one-woman show. It was Cortez who suggested basing the project in Watts, and Woods found a vacant furniture outlet located on 104th Street and Grandee Avenue. Woods called a meeting of interested parties, and a group of area artists began planning what became Studio Watts. Though not a practicing artist himself, Jim Woods was a determined proponent of the idea that art could accompany political work. In this vein, he acted, in the words of John Outterbridge, as a "spearhead into getting over the cautiousness" of artists.[34] Although donations from private parties and funds from poverty programs became more readily available after 1965, Woods, who worked at a local savings and loan, and his wife, a probation officer, paid the initial operating expenses. Studio Watts served a dual purpose, hosting a wide range of classes and providing working space for practicing artists. Educational projects included design classes taught by Bob Rogers, as well as classes in sculpture, painting, and dance. Tapscott taught a host of music classes, while Cortez directed an acting workshop that became the Watts Repertory Theater.[35]

The financial support of Margo Woods raises a dimension of cultural politics that often goes overlooked. In a number of instances, black women provided the material support that allowed autonomist and uncompromising cultural institutions to subsist. Horace Tapscott's wife Celia acted as the family's primary breadwinner. Further support, of course, came in the form of Linda Hill's decision to allow her house to become, in essence, a communal living and rehearsal space. "Lino's Pad," as the composition dedicated to the house on 75th Street east of Central was called, quickly became a place where "the guys would just get together and have sessions. We'd play and then just hang out. Some guys would spend the night there, then wake up and play."

FIGURE 16 Chalk-in champion Richard Wyatt Jr. The Studio Watts founders Jim Woods and Jayne Cortez began the chalk-ins as a way to foster community participation in the arts, 1968. Los Angeles Public Library.

Hill, a single mother of one who worked as a nurse's aid at a local hospital, was a brilliant and largely self-taught musician. As Steven Isoardi notes, Hill possessed a basic musical education but nothing approaching the training or experience of a professional. Within two years of co-founding the Arkestra, however, she was playing piano, singing, and arranging compositions for the band. Equally importantly, however, she was providing a place for the UGMA's experimental fusion of music and politics to take place. In a context where, as the Arkestra member Al Hines recalled, "Horace wouldn't get no job and I wouldn't get no job," it is critical to remember that Linda Hill, like Celia Tapscott and Marla Gibbs, had a job. Gibbs, who sang with the Arkestra, offered critical support. In 1976, Gibbs, who was starring in the television show *The Jeffersons*, purchased a building for $85,000 that became the site of the group's community arts projects and a practice space. Seen in this light, the Arkestra's core mission of complicating the boundary between art and life, in the final analysis, rested on the labor of black women.[36]

At the same time, Cortez's work illustrates the need to see black women as providing aesthetic direction as much as a material underpinning. The surrealist fusion of working-class, feminist, and consciously black themes of Cortez, a critical figure in African American arts whose voice has only recently garnered sufficient critical attention, made her poetry unique well beyond California. A former garment worker, Ebony Showcase alumnus, and self-described "jazz fanatic," Cortez found her increasing political commitments taking her to Greenwood, Mississippi, as an organizer with the Student Non-Violent Coordinating Committee (SNCC) and prompted her to co-found, with the designer Bob Rogers, a Friends of SNCC chapter in Los Angeles. Art and politics, sound and text, class and gender all formed points of intersection for a woman committed "to an array of art possibilities, a variety of forms, different images, political ideas, an exposition of dreams, a juxtaposition of attitudes, familiar and unfamiliar behavior patterns and references."[37] Cortez was active both individually and collectively, performing with Tapscott and other local musicians, participating in Studio Watts, directing the Watts Repertory Theater, and performing one-woman shows of literature and jazz.

Two additional parallels between Cortez and the jazz avant-garde are worthy of mention. First, much like Horace Tapscott and John Carter, Cortez was actively committed to the idea of creative and financial control over her artistic production. Following her move to New York, Cortez founded Bola Press. Named after the Yoruba word for success, Bola allowed Cortez to release her written and recorded works with minimal interference from the publishing or recording industry. As Nielsen notes, having her own imprint allowed Cortez control over the visual presentation of her material, most of which included art by her husband Mel Edwards.[38]

As with musicians, moreover, Cortez actively criticized the structures of the jazz industry. Much as Bradford, Tapscott, and their peers criticized the ignorance of audiences and the perfidy of club owners and record companies, Cortez's poem "How Long Has Trane Been Gone" tracks the continuing exploitation of black creativity:

all you wanta do
is pat your foot
sip a drink & pretend
with your head bobbin up & down
what do care about acoustics
bad microphones or out of tune pianos
and noise
you the clubowners and disc jockeys

made a deal didnt you
a deal about Black Music
& you really dont give
a shit long as you take[39]

Throughout her poem, the critique of white power is inseparable from a critique of black people's complicity in their continued oppression. Counterpoising the revolutionary figures Malcolm X and John Coltrane, another stanza of Cortez's poem casts black art as an integral part of black collectivity that affirms the bonds between community, art, and revolution. Kimberly Benston describes the elegy to the altoist as "an unheard sacral wisdom or undelineated communal meaning" dispelled through a "circuit of cognition and recognition." As with Malcolm X, Cortez's Coltrane offers "a final sermonic exhortation" to the "lost-found Nation/within a nation" made up of "all black people, so-called Negroes, second-class citizens, ex-slaves."[40]

The link between Malcolm and Coltrane, asserted so forcefully by Cortez, hints at the holistic and comprehensive engagement with transformation that was at the heart of the cultural project of black liberation. Beyond her role as activist, writer, and community arts administrator, Cortez stands out as one of the first black Angelenos pursuing a serious and ongoing fusion of music and poetry. Part of a group that includes the longtime Arkestra collaborator Kamau Daáood, the Watts Prophets, and Stanley Crouch, to name only a few, Cortez writes poetry whose combination of internationalist politics, surrealist imagery, and highly personalized intersections of race, class, and gender marks her as distinct among black writers of the period. At the same time, her deep investment and inclusion of musical themes and subjects, her collaborations with musicians, and her attempt to cast her spoken voice as a musical instrument links her to both her peers in Los Angeles and a broader tradition of black writers for whom black music comprised a primary compositional, aural, and thematic referent.[41]

A similar blend of music and text infused the work of Linda Hill. While the democratic structure of UGMA life ensured that many of the band's works emerged from a truly collective process, Hill's generally underappreciated role deserves mention. Having passed away prior to the critical resurgence regarding Horace Tapscott, Hill remained long absent from discussions of the UGMA. Yet beyond providing material support for the organization, she was responsible for writing or arranging many of the group's early compositions and arrangements. Several of these, including "Little Africa" and "Why Don't

You Listen," as well as "Warriors All" (co-written with Tapscott), became Arkestra standards. Hill sang in, and later directed, an expanded version of the Arkestra's choir. An active writer, Hill published poems in the anthology *Watts Poets* as well as in the Pasadena-based journal *Nigger Uprising*. In this, like Cortez, Ruth Waddy, R'Wanda Lewis, and Ridhiana Saunders, Linda Hill played a critical role in sustaining a cultural movement whose archival existence, community memory, and historical record all remain primarily peopled by more famous male figures such as John Outterbridge, Noah Purifoy, Cecil Fergerson, Budd Schulberg, C. Bernard Jackson, Alonzo Davis, and Horace Tapscott.[42]

Each of these men and women was linked to a particular community arts project. Lewis ran a dance company; Cortez, a theater project. Waddy was the core of Art West Associated; Hill, an underappreciated pillar of the Arkestra. Purifoy, with Judson Powell, had directed the Watts Towers Art Center. Outterbridge joined Powell at the Compton Communicative Arts Academy. Schulberg founded the Watts Writers Workshop; Woods founded Studio Watts. Tapscott and Jackson were the public faces of the Arkestra and the Inner City Cultural Center, while Alonzo and Dale Davis ran the Brockman Gallery. Fergerson, along with Claude Booker, had co-founded the Black Arts Council. By 1967, a given afternoon might well have found many of them in a single space. By this time, the locus of community arts efforts centered on Studio Watts had shifted a block north, to the Watts Happening Coffee House. Housed in an abandoned supermarket burned during the riot, the new site hosted a variety of poverty programs administered by the Office of Economic Opportunity in addition to its cultural offerings. By 1967, the coffeehouse had become the pre-eminent cultural site in South Los Angeles, hosting the Watts Repertory Theater, the Watts Writers Workshop, the Pan Afrikan People's Arkestra, Bobby Bradford and John Carter's New Art Jazz Ensemble, and a variety of painting, sculpture, and drawing classes.[43]

By the end of the decade, the UGMA had become a cultural institution in its own right. A retiring merchant familiar with Tapscott's mission donated a three-story building that the group occupied between 1969 and 1974. The building included a number of functioning printing presses, with which the UGMA foundation publicized Arkestra concerts and community-service classes. In addition to dance classes and musical instruction, Linda Hill taught remedial reading and composition classes. The actors William Marshall and Ted Lange taught acting classes, as did Marla Gibbs. Discussions between actors and musicians led to the film *Passing Through*, a fictionalized action adventure film directed by Larry Clark. A clear allegory to the work of the UGMA, the film follows two musicians separated by a generation as they attempt to "rescue" improvised music from a mob-controlled recording industry. Featuring a score by Tapscott, *Passing Through* represented a rare link between community-based cultural radicals and the "Los Angeles School" of independent black and Third World filmmakers active during the mid-1970s at the University of California, Los Angeles (UCLA).[44]

Passing Through brought together artists working in three distinct contexts: the community-based avant-garde; the emergent body of independent black filmmakers associated with UCLA; and politicized black talent working inside the entertainment industry. Horace Tapscott's role in the film is not minor, and he appears as the musician most sympathetic to the ideas of creative control and political autonomy championed by the protagonist, Warmack. The Arkestra provides most of the music depicted on screen in the film, including an introductory montage shot in stark primary colors that features Tapscott's hands moving across the keys of a piano as other musicians dissolve and reappear on screen. Charles Burnett served as one of the cameramen, while Julie Dash assisted with the sound. The film used both diegetic and nondiegetic sound, the Arkestra providing the former while the latter appears as an index of the jazz avant-garde, including Dolphy, Coltrane, Sun Ra, and the AACM. Ultimately, Clark's film questions the conceptual separation between the two uses of sound, since part of the film's resolution is a mystical transference in which the distance of "Miles" is journeyed by "Trane" to the land of the "Pharaohs." Clark's film is serious about taking jazz as a vehicle for liberation. Literally.

Like Marla Gibb's ongoing financial support and teaching work with the Arkestra, or Nick Stewart's strategy of simultaneously working inside and outside Hollywood, *Passing Through* linked black actors working inside the monster, so to speak, with the black avant-garde. The octogenarian Clarence Muse played the sagacious Poppa, whose ethical clarity, mystic sensibility, and technical proficiency were lifelines for the angry, spiritually nomadic Warbuck. Muse, as noted earlier, had been among the actors criticized during the Second World War for the nature of his portrayals of African Americans. The screenplay was based on a story written by Ted Lange, an actor best known for his television role as a gregarious bartender on the endlessly cruising *Love Boat*. For Lange, casting the recording industry as synonymous with the mafia served as a means of signifying on the mores of the entertainment industry.

Although the film mobilizes a wide range of allegories, including the Attica prison rebellion, Yoruba religion, and the liberation struggles on the African continent, *Passing Through* is in many ways the story of the Pan Afrikan People's Arkestra. Clark's film posits jazz as a revolutionary creative form central to the past, present, and future of black Americans, while creative control over the playing and recording of improvised music functions as a proxy for national liberation. *Passing Through* casts the intergenerational transfer of knowledge from Poppa (note the references to PAPA and Tapscott's nickname) to Warmack through a kind of "Sun Ra meets Samuel Browne" looking glass. Both this intergenerational connection and the portrayal of the complex emotional relationship between Warmack and Maya stand in marked contrast to depictions of intimate relationships in subsequent films set in South Los Angeles. The film captures a distinct moment, not simply in black cultural production, but also in the external points through which black people referenced and defined themselves. Much as the Arkestra moved through a milieu populated by Panthers and members of the US Organization, *Passing Through* incorporates documentary footage of the guerrillas of the Partido Africano da Independência da Guiné e Cabo Verde (PAIGC), newsreel images of Attica, and a montage of African liberation–movement leaders. In the case of Attica, we are shown an incarcerated Warmack, jailed after coming to the defense of a musician attacked by mobsters. The blurring of the boundary between the depicted and the "real" suggests something along the lines of the complication between "art" and "life" present in the Arkestra's inclusion of nonprofessionals, its selection of alternate venues, and its participation in nonmusical projects. Above all, the primary themes engaged by *Passing Through*—history, community, creativity, experimentation, liberation, love—operate as an index of the consciousness of the politicized musical avant-garde. In this way, although it was completed at the end of the historical moment that it sought to champion, *Passing Through* might well be said to constitute a key document for understanding the importance of the Arkestra, its musical choices, and its community concerns.

The UGMA/Pan Afrikan People's Arkestra occupied a critical part of the cultural infrastructure of post-riot Los Angeles. Articulating a triadic mission, the group operated as an educational resource, a working body dedicated to the preservation and performance of the work of unknown black composers —including those yet to develop—and a vital force challenging the distinction between cultural and political radicalism. Each of these efforts was premised on the notion of *creative community*, a multigenerational milieu of expression and exchange characterized by a constant effort to renew and extend bonds between artists and the surrounding neighborhoods. The goal of developing a bond between the cultural and the political drew on a strategy that rejected any separation between the two, and the tactics intended to bring this narrowing about were both representational and real.

The kind of rubric advocated by Arkestra members required an ongoing and evolving link with community attitudes and mores. Tapscott cast the decision to change the name of the Underground Musicians' Association to the Union of God's Musicians and Artists Ascension as an effort to develop a vocabulary more grounded in the cultural life of—and thus presumably more accessible to—working-class African Americans otherwise separated from the language of nationalist agitation. In his autobiography, Tapscott claimed, "We chose the name because black cats in my age bracket were all brought up in segregated America . . . and we still had a respect for that type of feeling that the religion's supposed to have been fostering."[45] Yet while the Arkestra worked to develop a language that would resonate with working-class African Americans, the band was conscious of its desire to foster and facilitate change among the same population. Adding that the decision to include the moniker "Afrikan" in the band's title offered a challenge to ordinary black Americans making the complicated transition from "Negro" to "black" and "African American," Tapscott held, "those seemingly tiny, minute things that people hardly think about were what we were working on."[46]

Tapscott's lived experience created a worldview that privileged community, a worldview in which locality was equated with growth. As the primary ideological force in the Arkestra, Tapscott repeatedly sought to turn the group inward, opposing proposals to tour or record. Forays outward were conceived as threatening aesthetic stagnation, penury, and racist hostility. It is certainly possible to see such a view as doggedly provincial, as a kind of insistent localism that betrays an atavistic fear of the world beyond. From this vantage point, the Arkestra's continuous years of free concerts in churches, community centers, and parks might resemble a circle that spins endlessly without going anywhere. Seen from the vantage point of Tapscott's conscious effort to advance a creative and political agenda, however, a different dialectic emerges. The local musicians who came of age in the shadow of Watts needed new solutions for old problems. Union amalgamation failed to answer their aesthetic or material concerns, even as the aftermath of wartime struggles for cultural democracy revealed that the terrain of representation could advance the overall struggle of black artists only so far. Even before the explosion of Watts, Tapscott and the UGMA proposed to address these by participating in a multigenerational process of creation and renewal based on the collective mobilization of the resources and people of South Los Angeles. This was a vision of self-determination that went beyond the certainties of nationalism, separatism, or militancy and into a creative and open-ended call to liberation. In the end, this call proposed a practice that proclaimed that the only way forward was to stay in one place.

THE FOREST OF CYMBALS

The soil of Los Angeles is often regarded as questionable for the flowering of creative endeavor and artistic inquiry. This perception historically has been shared by both city residents and outside observers and has proved as true for music as for dramatic and visual arts. Following suit, jazz historiography generally assigns the West Coast a prosaic space encapsulating the insipidity of cool jazz and the repeated failure of the region to sustain the creative talent it was able to produce. Revisionist works, meanwhile, remain for the most part narratives of declension, even when they praise the rich history of local clubs and personalities. Whatever the conceded contributions, the ultimate end remains shuttered windows, closed doors, and migrating musicians.

The story of the jazz avant-garde furnishes a representative example. Key works on the history of jazz in California end with the departure of the jazz avant-garde from Los Angeles at the end of the 1950s, while seminal accounts of the jazz avant-garde begin with the arrival of Coleman, Mingus, and Dolphy in New York.[47] The continuing presence in California of musicians such as Albert Ayler, Don Cherry, Charlie Haden, Paul Bley, Billy Higgins, Ed Blackwell, Bob Bradford, Prince Lasha, and John Carter is taken as a temporary interlude or a historical coincidence. Particularly marginal are those who chose to stay in Los Angeles. Yet as this chapter demonstrates, musicians based in Southern California continued to pursue the musical and social interventions of free jazz even as their brethren found fame elsewhere. The remainder of this chapter focuses on the musical interventions of the UGMA and the New Art Jazz Ensemble of Bob Bradford and John Carter. All three featured dedicated experimentalists committed to transcending what they perceived as the limitations of the established jazz canon. All three were committed to the idea of expanding the financial and organizational resources of musicians. And all three saw the two pursuits as linked.

Whether referred to as "avant-garde," "free" jazz, the "new music," or by a host of other, fairly problematic terms, the music that concretized into a style during the "long '60s" permanently transformed the jazz canon; divided audiences, musicians, and critics; and helped secure the importance of jazz within discussions of black politics and culture at a moment of intense nationwide mobilization.[48] As John Gennari argues, the partition of jazz into distinct and successive styles obscures as much musical history and analysis as it reveals.[49] In the case of free jazz, the problem is further complicated, first by the deeply partisan debates surrounding the music, and second by the difficulty posed by a definitional phrase made up of two equally insubstantial words. Alan Merriam and Fradley Garner hold that an etymological search for the roots of the term "jazz" quickly turns into a debate about the music itself, while DeVeaux observes pointedly that "freedom is a goal that can only be approached asymptomatically."[50] Most treatments of the subject acknowledge as much, noting that the variation present in the work of musicians like Coleman, Dolphy, Cecil Taylor, and Albert Ayler raises the question of whether or not a distinct stylistic category of free jazz exists. Still, the innovations associated with Coleman, Dolphy, Taylor, John Coltrane, the AACM, Albert Ayler, Archie Shepp, and others represented a general shift in orientation that, while characterized by tremendous internal variation, nonetheless signaled a departure from the predominant jazz styles of the preceding decades. "Playing out," moreover, constituted a set of practices whose political overtones were difficult to elide. Bobby Bradford's comments are instructive. Describing Ornette Coleman's impact on the Los Angeles music scene, he noted, "I think you'll find an urgency and a dead seriousness in Ornette's music that said things weren't going to be about Jim Crow or a resigned black man or West Coast Cool any longer."[51]

Taken together, the core elements of free jazz augured a shift away from prevailing patterns of modal jazz and hard bop. One aspect of the new music was a novel approach to time, including the abandoning of rhythmic patterns based on subdivisions of a beat, a decision that freed the drummer from functioning as a timekeeper. Many musicians associated with the style began to incorporate new instrumentation, including instruments that generally had been marginal during the bop era, including the clarinet and flugelhorn, as well as percussive, string, and woodwind instruments drawn from Indian, Far Eastern, and African cultures. Free jazz broke decisively with the use of popular songs as a compositional basis and took up patterns of simultaneous or collective improvisation in place of the sequential and chord-based improvisations common to bop.

Many of these elements were present in both Arkestra compositions and Tapscott's solo playing. The latter reflected both the tutelage of the big-band composers Gerald Wilson and Samuel Browne and Tapscott's determination to work simultaneously through a wide range of stylistic ideas. Arrangements for the full Arkestra were often of an advanced modal nature. This framework allowed relatively new musicians to adhere to relatively simple chord progressions while allowing more experienced Arkestra members greater freedom to improvise in the absence of expected harmonic structures. UGMAA pieces include a wide range of musical forms, including familiar structures based on popular songs, marches, and blues progressions, as well as more freeform collective improvisations. As in other improvisational contexts, these collective improvisations prioritized *listening* and interacting with others over *reading* (music), an aesthetic practice that shares much with the broader orality of African American intellectual, spiritual, and poetic tradition. Tapscott's writing, moreover, demonstrated wide rhythmic variation. Working in an avant-garde musical milieu known for rhythmic openness, Tapsccott's compositions swung despite, or because of, his propensity to use four or five time signatures in a given piece. As the bassist Roberto Miranda observed, "Horace not only had no difficulty in playing many odd time signatures, he excelled in odd time signatures. I remember many times feeling . . . astonishment at how hard this man was able to swing in 5, 7, 11, or 13."[52] The time signatures of a number of Arkestra pieces highlight this variation: "Lino's Pad" tacks between 7/4, 8/4, and 4/4, giving the piece an unusual thirteen-bar structure. "Ballad for Deadwood Dick" shifts from 5/4 to 6/8 back to 5/4 and finally to 4/4. "Breeze," a composition from the *Flight 17* album, includes a rare use of 3/2 clave time, as well as of 6/8 and 4/4.

In the context of an ensemble that often included up to three dozen musicians divided into multiple kit drummers, percussionists, guitarists, "god knows how many saxophones," and a "phalanx" of woodwind players, producing a sound that professional musicians found interesting, audiences found engaging, and amateurs found possible to play, demanded considerable organizational and musical acumen. Roberto Miranda provided a succinct description of how the Arkestra achieved its sound. Noting that Tapscott "always approached the Ark as though it were a small group . . . whether it was five or thirty musicians, whether the music was modal or based on changes," he added that musicians were expected and encouraged to privilege developing their own sound over trying to fit together.[53] With a membership that fluctuated considerably over decades, moreover, the longtime members of the Arkestra incorporated new members at varied musical levels. The trumpeter Will Connell cited the influence of the saxophonists Lester Robinson and

Calvin Henry in helping him to find contrapuntal "chains of rhythm" that anchored a section of "At the Crossroads" in which every horn player was expected to "solo" at the same time.[54]

Connell's reminiscence offers a reminder that the Arkestra saw itself as a multigenerational teaching project whose commitment to preserving and extending black music began with the band members themselves. Viewing their music as part of a continuous "black art form" that captured "the essence of our existence" presupposed a connection between the Ark's music and other genres. A similar point could be made for "playing out" in general. Although many saw the stylistic changes identified with the jazz avant-garde as new— and, often, unwelcome—many of these innovations had been tried before. Indeed, as John Litweiler notes, Lennie Tristano's sextet had produced multiple recordings in 1949 that featured something akin to collective improvisation and that eschewed compositional themes and harmonic structures.[55] Ornette Coleman readily admitted as much, conceding that many of the tenets of his emergent style had been tried in isolation previously.[56] The critic A. B. Spellman went further, arguing of Coleman: "Once past his radical innovations in tone and tonality, one can hear shuffles, stomps, hollers and certainly blues in his music."[57] Nor were such sentiments limited to proponents of the style. When Charles Mingus asked Duke Ellington if he wanted to collaborate on an avant-garde record, the elder statesman demurred, replying that he was not interested in going that far back into the past.[58] Closer to home, Horace Tapscott noted that many of the rhythmic interventions of free jazz had been tried in Samuel Browne's classroom workshops at Jefferson High. From this vantage point, the "new music" was as much an attitudinal as a musical framework.

One of the ideas questioned by the Arkestra was the separation between music and other forms of art. In place of the practice of collective improvisation used by smaller combinations such as Coleman's, Arkestra pieces were often based on prearranged sketches loosely coordinated by Tapscott. During rehearsals, Tapscott would provide suggestions regarding possible changes and progressions, including interchangeable series that could be directed nonverbally during performances. Arkestra performances often featured poets and dancers, an inclusion Tapscott cast as necessary to understanding the totality of a particular musical piece. Often these presentational ideas fused with the social mission of the band. The Arkestra developed a musical program for Cecil Rhodes's play *Three Brothers*, a mostly improvised theater piece based on the idea of a trio of siblings whose ideas correspond to contrasting programs within the black liberation movement. Written dialogue was minimal and replaced by stage directions "like a chord progression" meant to facilitate improvisation between the actors.[59] The Arkestra played throughout *Three Brothers*, often walking behind the actors while improvising short pieces meant to evoke the thoughts of the protagonists during the play's many unscripted moments. Another series of compositions, *Daddy Goodness*, formed part of a play adapted from the writings of Richard Wright.[60] One particularly fruitful collaboration between the Arkestra and the actor William Marshall came in the form of the musical play *King Christophe*. Featuring a script by Aimé Césaire, whom Marshall had met while living in France during the early 1960s, *King Christophe* featured a number of Arkestra compositions that became band standards, as well as live stage performances that featured Marshall and Tapscott playing leading speaking roles.[61] Other events were more routine but no less important. Bobby Bradford recalled another Arkestra performance that featured an unnamed poet who did "a piece called 'hey man, got any works' meaning needle and spoons and lighter. He'd turn the thing into what that [heroin] was about and why you like it and why you shouldn't and he was moving his body as he did it and it went on like that and it was like 'ba-boom, ba-boom, ba-ba-boom,' like that unbelievable."[62]

As might be expected from a band that eschewed recording while performing in a dizzying variety of community locales, live performances formed a central aspect of the UGMA's work. Open to a variety of performers and performance styles, taking place in nontraditional venues such as churches, parks, community centers, and even a flatbed truck, and asking people to participate and contribute to the experience, the Arkestra was primarily a vehicle for enacting a vision of community in public. In this way, the Arkestra's live concerts—like experimental theater, happenings, be-ins, and other events based on the idea of reclaiming creativity as a universal human property—served as an aural and visual staging of the opposition between the "universal" fact of creativity and the "particular" fact of blackness. Kimberly Benston suggests that a central argument of the Black Arts Movement was the conviction that the dialect between universal and particular—as it related to the lives and culture of black people—could be resolved on "a ground internal to African-American discourse itself." Within this conceit, it is possible to see the Arkestra pursuing a project of self-definition that was simultaneously resistant "to totalization, critical recuperation and ideological closure,"[63] set within the aesthetics of an autonomist black radical tradition,[64] or part of an evolutionary, revolutionary "changing same."[65] Amid this related language of

African American criticism is a critical point: The project of self-definition is a critical building block of self-determination. Whether encapsulated in the moniker "Underground," the refusal to record a product that reflected a lack of full creative and financial control, or the decision to develop a community orchestra open to and aimed at the specific location of South Los Angeles, the UGMA/PAPA embodied the idea that black people possessed the capacity to solve their own problems without outside help. Like the Arkestra's notion of an expansive musical tradition that transcended the limitations of "jazz," this was a vision of politics that went beyond the terminology of nationalism, separatism, or black power.

Tapscott, too, sought to articulate a vision of what the Chicago-based members of the AACM termed "great black music." Consciously expansive by definition, Tapscott cast his efforts as an attempt to preserve and extend African American musical traditions. The Arkestra played originals by Tapscott and other band members, as well as rethought standards and works by unknown black composers. Both freeform experimentation and more structured big-band compositions were part of this, as were ostensibly non-jazz popular forms including soul, rhythm and blues, operatic scores, and hip hop. Indeed, like his contemporaries in Chicago, Tapscott couched his rejection of the term "jazz" as musically insufficient as well as politically problematic.[66] In much the same way that free jazz constituted a point of view as much as a distinct musical style, the notion of great black music existed as a profoundly "social" concept rooted in a collective production of art based on the recognition of common elements at play.

Often these common elements were musical. Occasionally they were not. Tapscott took transatlantic history and contemporary politics as part of the assumed knowledge of a surrounding community. Of course, the use of history as a vehicle for the articulation of an a priori communitarian sentiment rapidly slides into tautology.[67] The Arkestra's response to this problem was dual. One the one hand, the Arkestra was an interpersonal affair in which ideas spread through human contact. This contact served to democratize the creative and expressive process, as demonstrated by the inclusion of new works as well as the band's eventual decision to record. At the same time, Tapscott's community was not so much imagined as in formation, based on a common discursive language and an ongoing set of collective experiences. Put another way, the music of the Arkestra was meant to extend, as much as to reflect, a set of musical and social practices that together would constitute something akin to a tradition in formation. Such, at least, was part of the idea

FIGURE 17 Horace Tapscott playing piano, Los Angeles, 1986. Los Angeles Times Photographic Archive, circa 1918– (Collection 1429), Department of Special Collections, Charles E. Young Research Library, University of California, Los Angeles.

behind the practice of playing free weekly concerts, year after year, featuring compositions by a diverse group of composers such as James Weldon Johnson, Thelonious Monk, and Aceyalone.

For members of the jazz underground, dissatisfaction with the aesthetic status quo was matched by a marked antipathy toward the financial and organizational structure of the world of jazz. Often, the problem was a lack of exposure. Carter noted dryly that "the U.S. is not overrun with places to play new music." Tapscott and the UGMA, as noted earlier, often had difficulty finding paid work. Although Carter and Bradford occasionally performed in area clubs, fans were far more likely to encounter the group at venues such as the Ash Grove, a counterculture nightspot that predominantly featured folk music, at community festivals, or at nontraditional spaces such as the Watts Happening Coffee House. While partially a choice of musicians actively seeking alternate spaces, this marginality contributed to the notion that the region lacked a serious jazz scene, a perception further fostered by the general paucity of recorded works released by members of the local jazz avant-garde. Often, this was a deliberate reaction to the economic structure of artistic life. Tapscott, in particular, resisted recording. He argued against participating in the sessions that produced the album for Flying Dutchman in 1969, and the session dates were arranged only after other Arkestra members outvoted him. Following this date, it would be a decade before the Arkestra issued another album, largely due to Tapscott's insistence on total creative control, including the selection of particular recordings, the final word on everything from sound engineering to cover art, and sufficient payment. Indeed, much like their peers on the East Coast, Bradford, Carter, and Tapscott complained that the recording industry was often as exploitative as the world of nightclubs. "Many of the Arkestra's live concerts have been recorded," noted Tapscott, "but we have chosen not to release them until the proper deal is made." Carter concurred, adding, "I just never have gotten on to the idea of getting ten percent of something that is all mine." Partially as a response, Carter founded his own recording label, on which he released a single album.[68]

For the jazz avant-garde, greater self-organization emerged as the solution to both acute economic problems and the lack of suitable venues. Having played with both Coleman and Dolphy, Bobby Bradford, John Carter, and Horace Tapscott were well aware that the negative critical response to "playing out" was often accompanied by financial penury. One response among musicians during this time was to form jazz collectives—collectively run and managed enterprises wherein musicians shared compositional duties, booking responsibilities, and publishing and recording credits and otherwise sought to develop both creative and financial autonomy. Although both the New Art Jazz Ensemble and the Pan Afrikan People's Arkestra functioned in this manner, the effort to achieve greater independence was constrained by the increasingly anemic jazz infrastructure in Southern California. Los Angeles proved incapable of developing anything that resembled the avant-gardists' alternative loft scene in New York. It did musicians little good to act as their own booking agents when they lacked locations or consistent audiences. For those experimentalists who chose to remain in Los Angeles, two possibilities emerged. Carter and Bradford maintained their sense of artistic autonomy by selecting alternative careers, recording sporadically, and performing only under acceptable financial conditions. Tapscott, meanwhile, brought his music to his audience, making the Arkestra and the UGMA a part of the South Los Angeles community during years of intense cultural transformation and political ferment.

The new music formed an important aspect of black radicalism in Southern California. Amid the proliferation of radical organizations, the Arkestra became less a musical group linked conceptually to the local black freedom struggle than a part of the organizational fabric of the movement itself. Beyond incorporating themes about black liberation into their music, or playing benefits for revolutionary organizations, Arkestra members participated in efforts to develop a working unity among Southern California's divergent radical groupings. Active participation in meetings, strategy sessions, and ongoing campaigns placed the Arkestra in a select group of the most committed members of a musical avant-garde known in part for their association with revolutionary activists across the United States. Retracing something of this moment thus helps demonstrate the breadth of cultural radicalism in South Los Angeles after 1965, providing an example of local historical importance and serving to illustrate a larger conceptual point. Beyond simply highlighting the gap between community-based radical musicians and the efforts of C. Bernard Jackson and Budd Schulberg, an accounting of the exchanges between black musicians and black radicals complicates the strict separation between politics and culture as sites of thought or activity.

Perhaps more important, recalling the political participation of the Arkestra illustrates the extent to which the Black Power Movement and Black Arts Movement shared a vocabulary and, at times, a set of organizational orientations. Certainly, many black radicals became deeply invested in the idea that music constituted an organic part of the overall black freedom struggle. The reasons are easy to see. The musicians associated with the new music and the political figures associated with what Gerald Horne calls "the new leadership" shared a terminology, tactics, and, above all, an entrenched set of contradictions related to their status as African Americans living in areas where neither the goals nor the outcomes of the freedom struggle were easily agreed upon.[69] As noted earlier, both musicians and activists adopted a worldview that linked individual transformation with collective political progress. Both groupings adopted the vocabulary of a self-proclaimed vanguard, shown equally in the struggle for pre-eminence among black radical factions and in titles such as *The Shape of Jazz to Come* and *Tomorrow Is the Question*. Both saw the need for some form of communal, collective autonomy. While their title was intended as a reference to their artistic choices, Bob Bradford's and John Carter's notion of "self-determination music" traded on a set of terms reminiscent of concomitant efforts to rename Watts "Freedom City." Both cohorts shared an orientation that included a healthy suspicion regarding the benefits of the so-called free market. The extent of hostility to the market differed among proponents of black power and the members of the jazz avant-garde, and the formation of jazz cooperatives was hardly the same as the League of Revolutionary Black Workers' or the Black Panther Party's calls for the overthrow of American capitalism. The sense of connectedness to a broader nonwhite world both unified and divided, as well, and neither John Coltrane's incorporation of Indian instruments nor Randy Weston's inclusion of African-derived rhythms was precisely the same as the Black Power Movement's attempt to transpose Senghor or Mao. Neither musicians nor activists held singular ideas concerning the nature of black American connections with the world beyond, and certain artists might find themselves closer to radical activists than other musicians, and vice versa. The presence of common keywords such as "freedom," "self-determination," "new," "Third World," and "Africa" among both groups created problems, including the reductive argument that avant-garde jazz was intrinsically linked to black nationalism. At the same time, as we will see, a common language created opportunities for collaborations rooted in the common awareness of the difficulty posed by the effort to make freedom mean something concrete in the politically ambiguous spaces outside the segregated South.

Tapscott's first album as a bandleader, *The Giant Is Awakened*, demonstrated the general influence of the times on his creative output. Inspired by John Coltrane's album *Giant Steps*, as well as by the High John the Conqueror figure of African American folklore, Tapscott's giant was a symbolic figure representing the slumbering potential of African America. Subsequent album titles included *Songs of the Unsung*, *Dissent of Descent*, *At the Crossroads*, and *The Call*. Although Tapscott listed friends, neighborhood associates, and other personal relations as his most common compositional subjects, Africa, African American history, and political struggle provided the titles for many of his works. African-themed compositions included "Niger's Theme," "Ancestral Echoes," "Little Africa," "Thoughts of Dar es Salaam," and "Akirfa." Movement-inspired titles included "The Giant Is Awakened," "Songs of the Unsung," "Struggle X: An Afro-American Dream," "The Black Apostles," and "The Call."[70]

In evoking history, liberation, and place, Tapscott's compositions linked him to a broader community of jazz composers inspired by and interacting with African music and cultural life.[71] Whereas many musicians found generalized inspiration in the transatlantic struggle for black liberation, Tapscott and the members of the UGMA/PAPA developed ongoing formal links with radical forces operating locally. The Arkestra assisted many of the most important organizations active in South Los Angeles during this time, and Tapscott seems to have made a conscious effort to ensure that it remained a nonsectarian body. This was both difficult and vital, given that internecine conflicts among movement organizations occasionally proved fatal in Southern California. Queried on this point, Tapscott replied that music served as a unifying force capable of bridging the differences among local organizations, all of which recognized the UGMA as a neutral yet committed force. The Arkestra, moreover, contained black radicals of widely variegated stripes, including independent radicals, black Muslims, orthodox (Sunna) Muslims, and at least three Black Panther Party members. Finally, both the group's local origins and its long history—the UGMA was, after all, older than both the US Organization and the Black Panther Party—may also have served to mitigate sectarian encounters at Arkestra gigs.

Arkestra representatives participated in the ongoing meetings of the Black Congress. Active during 1967 and 1968, the Black Congress drew together a disparate cast of two dozen organizations active in Southern California. Participating groups represented a wide variety of political orientations and ideological ends. Despite the participation of established moderate forces, including the Congress of Racial Equality and the National Association for the Advancement of Colored People, the general thrust of the Black Congress was as a nationalist clearinghouse broadly representative of the emergent leadership of the mobilized black working class. This included familiar national bodies such as SNCC and the Black Panther Party; local black draft-resistance coalitions; welfare-rights organizations, including the Los Angeles County Welfare Rights Organization and Citizens for Creative Welfare; and progressive clergy such as the Immanuel Baptist church and Black Unitarians for Radical Reform. Among the most critical forces were those who self-identified as cultural nationalists, including Ron Karenga's US Organization, the Sons of Watts, and Self-Leadership for All Nationalities Today. Cultural organizations included representatives from the Watts Happening Coffee House, independent poets, and the Arkestra. The two most important projects of the Black Congress were the attempted secession and incorporation of Watts as a renamed and independent "Freedom City" and the coordination of a major black power rally, held in February 1968 at the Los Angeles Sports Arena, meant to showcase the ongoing merger talks between SNCC and the Black Panther

Party.[72] In addition to participating in the ongoing Black Congress coalition, UGMA members attended the Western Regional Black Youth Conference in November 1967. This event brought together more than one hundred and fifty delegates representing a broad range of activist organizations dedicated to developing broader unity among competing black radical organizations.[73] In a similar vein, the UGMA held repeated benefits for the Black Student Alliance, an umbrella organization that linked black student unions on local university, junior-college, and high-school campuses. Finally, participation in the meetings of the integrated Peace Action Council added a specifically antiwar dimension to the Arkestra's work, while connections with the Ash Grove nightclub and performance space added a link to the predominantly white counterculture of Hollywood and Echo Park.[74]

A particularly close relationship arose between the Arkestra and the Southern California chapter of the Black Panther Party. The chapter's leader, John Huggins, had been a member of the Arkestra's choir. Acknowledged as one of the most capable and popular Panther cadres on a national scale, Huggins had done much to shape the early fortunes of the Los Angeles chapter, and his murder in 1969 by members of the US Organization proved debilitating to local party operations. Tapscott also connected with Elaine Brown, the party's deputy minister of information, whom he met through the poet and essayist Stanley Crouch. Brown was working as an administrator at the coffeehouse while Crouch was active in Watts cultural circles, performing and recording jazz poetry and directing the Watts Repertory Theater following Jayne Cortez's move to New York.[75]

Tapscott and Brown recorded two albums together. The first, recorded in 1969, was released at the height of sectarian violence between the Panthers and the US Organization. Titled *Seize the Time*, the record featured the Arkestra mainstays Everett Brown and Lester Robinson, as well as a host of other locally recruited players. The record featured ten songs written by Brown and reflected a broad range of styles, although the mix of ballads, rhythm and blues, and jazz compositions used more conventional instrumentation and arrangements than Tapscott's *The Giant Is Awakened*, which was released by the same label the same year. Brown and Tapscott rehearsed together regularly, and Brown's soaring and somewhat operatic vocal style dominated the mostly subdued arrangements. While a number of songs featured Tapscott "playing out," the record generally demonstrated little of the link between radical politics and unconventional aesthetics that politicized free jazz players sought to convey.[76]

In addition, the Arkestra played repeatedly at Panther benefit events. Most of these were designed to raise funds for legal defense, an ongoing struggle for an organization forced to pay several hundred thousand dollars in nonrefundable bail costs in 1970 alone. Arkestra benefit concerts took place for the national Panther leaders Angela Davis, Bobby Seale, and Huey Newton, as well as for the local leader Geronimo Pratt. Tapscott also attended a fundraising event held at the visual artist Suzanne Jackson's Gallery 32. This event, which took place several months before the release of *Seize the Time*, featured a performance by Elaine Brown and an art exhibit by the Panthers' minister of culture, Emory Douglas.[77]

In the context of widespread surveillance, these connections ensured that Tapscott and the band would eventually come to the attention of law enforcement. By December 1967, the FBI had added the UGMA to a growing list of "black nationalist hate groups" targeted for surveillance and disruption. That the UGMA came under such scrutiny is hardly surprising, given Southern California's importance as a center of black nationalist activity and the matching degree of organized government repression directed against local activists. Federal counterintelligence (Cointelpro) activities are documented as a result of the release of files under the Freedom of Information Act. Less accessible, and consequently less well known, are the clandestine activities of the Criminal Conspiracy Section (CCS). Likewise tasked with disrupting subversive organizations, the CCS was one of host of secretive bodies at work within the LAPD. By 1969, it had become clear that Los Angeles was ground zero in FBI Director J. Edgar Hoover's war against the Black Panthers. As Ward Churchill notes, a majority of party members killed nationwide by police were killed in Los Angeles. Despite generally poor relations, federal and local police agencies remained united in their antipathy toward what the FBI termed "black nationalist hate groups," and both the FBI and the LAPD participated in clandestine efforts to foster differences between groups and to bury party members under an avalanche of specious charges, expensive trials, and lengthy prison sentences. Occasionally, police went further. On at least one occasion, animal-control officers working with the secretive CCSS dumped rattlesnakes caught in the nearby Santa Monica mountains through an open window in the Black Panther Party's headquarters on Central Avenue. These efforts paled in comparison with the ultimate confrontation between the party and the police: a raid on 8 December that featured simultaneous attacks on three Panther facilities in South Los Angeles, including a six-hour attack by the LAPD's newly developed Special Weapons and Tactics (SWAT) team—the nation's first—armed with assault rifles, dynamite, helicopters, and a military-surplus armored personnel carrier.[78]

Within this wealth of police activity, however, surveillance remained the sine qua non. Police officials spoke openly of their mission as a form of counterinsurgency, invoking a type of warfare predicated on intelligence gathering. Observation and infiltration intimidated suspects into becoming informers. The presence of informers generated paranoia. And paranoia created conditions in which the daily work of organizing—serving the people, in Panther parlance—could not take place. The FBI followed more than one hundred organizations in Los Angeles alone, and police officers and informants implemented a well-documented program of surveillance, infiltration, intimidation, harassment, false conviction, and even assassination against local political activists. Cultural radicals in the area faced government hostility, as well. Tapscott, the visual artist David Hammons, and the poet Amde Hamilton all recounted repeated stops and searches by hostile policemen, although it is unclear whether such interactions were the result of a deliberate effort to target them as individuals or came as a result of a more generalized racism among the police. Federal agents maintained dossiers on Tapscott and the UMGA, as well as on the Watts Writers Workshop, Watts Happening Coffee House, and Mafundi Institute. Police did more than watch, however. Local police testifying before Congress named the Inner City Cultural Center among a list of ostensibly subversive groups active in Los Angeles. Officers conducted repeated raids on the Watts Happening Coffee House, and the Arkestra's rehearsal space on Figueroa Boulevard was stormed more than once. More seriously, as noted earlier, were the actions of the arsonist and informant Darthard Perry, who almost singlehandedly brought the Watts Writers Workshop to a close when he burned down the Douglass Foundation building.[79]

As is often the case in such matters, it remains difficult to assess the precise effect of government attention on the lives and careers of Tapscott and the other members of the Arkestra. Tapscott's home and telephone were monitored, and he was familiar enough to police that agents were able to identify his presence at a variety of events. Tapscott remembered being shadowed by suspicious figures, and coming home to "two guys in Hawaiian shirts and dark sunglasses" became a regular occurrence. Although Tapscott recalled such surveillance as having lasted a year, more or less, FBI file entries describe slightly more than six years of intermittent attention. While excisions make conclusive statements impossible, available dates suggest that FBI screening began following the release of the first of Tapscott's two albums with Elaine Brown. FBI agents requested and received selective service, Department of Motor Vehicles, and voter-registration records. These revealed no criminal information. Nor was anything found following background checks conducted by the Los Angeles Sheriff's Department and the LAPD. As a result, even though Tapscott performed at several Panther rallies, agents recommended in March 1971 that his file be closed and further investigations suspended. Although at least one special agent held that "it is apparent that Tapscott is not associated in any substantive manner with militant or dissident groups in Los Angeles," additions to his file continued until late 1973. Most of them noted conversations between Tapscott and various Black Panther Party functionaries. FBI files reveal little more than surveillance, although the possibility remains that LAPD officers took a more active role in suppressing the UGMA. Tapscott believed as much, claiming that police had attempted to infiltrate the UGMA and had spread rumors of his radical affiliations as a way to impede his ability to secure paying work.[80]

Whether as a result of police activity or not, paid performances represented a small percentage of Arkestra activity over the course of the next two decades. The end of FBI surveillance during 1973 offers a fitting epitaph for the period of close cooperation between the UGMA/PAPA and the city's most visible black nationalist organizations. Throughout the preceding period, the band, in the words of its principal founder, had always been "in the middle of it," providing both a soundtrack and a distinct view toward the possible fusion of political and cultural revolutions.[81] Witness to the rioting in Watts, the Arkestra had also overseen the complicated and brief effervescence of revolutionary nationalist struggle in black Los Angeles. By 1973, the Black Panther Party had collapsed under the conjoined pressures of police violence, internecine violence, and internal division, leaving a void that competing formations proved incapable of filling. Millions of African Americans, too, had moved on. With the end of widespread American involvement in Vietnam and the implosion of organized radical activity into anarchist "groupuscules" like the Symbionese Liberation Army, the Weather Underground, and the Black Liberation Army, armed struggle offered considerably less than the promise of economic and political opportunity suggested by the mayoral triumph of Thomas Bradley in 1973. By then the criticism of arms no longer found local adherents, although as a later section of this work will show, the Arkestra continued to play a part in the critique of Bradley that developed among working-class black artists during his two decades in office.

5

STUDIOS IN THE STREET   Creative Community and Visual Arts

The art of American Negroes began when [they] emerged
as a group and it will continue as long as they think of
themselves as a group, which they will do for generations
after they are full partners in their native democracy. . . .
They do not think of themselves "simply as American
artists," whose primary tasks are to seek fuller "integration
in American life."

—CEDRIC DOVER

Midway through 1970, the suburban enclave of Glendale, California, hosted the exhibition "Black Artists on Art." Reviews published in the local newspaper instructed visitors to prepare for a journey of learning and self-discovery, advising them that attendees risked becoming "better people." While the eager correspondent of the *Glendale News-Press* perhaps overstated the possible benefits of museum attendance, the display of more than sixty works by twenty-two mostly local artists marked a milestone for a city that had seen the bombing of a local fair-housing organization and where, as late as 1964, African Americans were reputed to be unsafe on city streets after nightfall. Black art, in its own small way, was moving Glendale forward.[1]

One figure whose work was shown was John Outterbridge. Outterbridge, whose comments on art narrated a nationally distributed film that shared the exhibit's name, contributed several pieces, including "Song for my Father," a five-foot welded steel utility truck without wheels dumping a pile of manure (replaced with wood chips by the museum) onto the gallery floor. Homage to a man whose work as a junk hauler had educated and fed five children in the Jim Crow South, the truck offered rich symbolism. The lack of wheels signified "work without satisfaction, movement without progress," while the manure signified the lack of choice and degree of unpleasantness inherent in the work that Outterbridge's father, John Ivery, had done. Parts of the truck were left unfinished, meant to rust and grow old "as John Ivery had," while a mirrored cab drew viewers, through their images, into the piece itself. Using a title borrowed from the Horace Silver composition that conjured images of labor and family, jazz and class, "Song for my Father" captured themes that ran through many of the works Outterbridge would produce throughout his career. The truck certainly struck a chord with someone: It was stolen soon after the exhibit from the yard of his home in Altadena.[2]

By the time of the Glendale exhibition, Outterbridge was part of a cohort of like-minded cultural activists. An easygoing and prolific man, he was the co-founder and visual arts director of the Communicative Arts Academy in Compton, as well as a key figure in local efforts to shape a relevant and identifiable black art and, in the attempt to develop a multi-generic community arts movement throughout Southern California. The career of John Outterbridge thus highlights the role played by black visual and plastic artists in the cultural and political struggles taking place in postwar South Los Angeles.

Much as with Horace Tapscott, John Outterbridge's tale cannot be understood in isolation. Part of an initially small and informal grouping of local visual artists, Outterbridge's cohort mushroomed to include hundreds whose work as artists and cultural activists influenced thousands. This group included known artists such as Charles White, David Hammons, and Betye Saar, as well as more obscure local figures such as Van Slater, Gloria Bohanon, and Dale Davis. Working in dozens of community institutions and linked by gallery affiliations, informal conversations, and artistic sensibilities, artists working and living in Southern California made the visual arts a critical component of the larger fight for political and aesthetic liberation.

Visual arts were critical to the broader enterprise of black cultural politics. In searching for new means of expression rooted in and relevant to the communities from which they came, black artists such as Outterbridge, Judson Powell, Betye Saar, and Noah Purifoy pushed the parameters of consciously black art while building a variety of community arts projects. These projects, which in essence sought to "serve the people" by offering a fundamental reevaluation of the meaning art could have in black lives, paralleled and often intertwined with similar efforts in music and literature. Moreover, much as was the case with those working in other genres, visual and plastic artists found themselves struggling to reshape the conditions and circumstances of their own work. The result, in Southern California and nationwide, was an attempt at greater collective organization, including the establishment of membership organizations and artist-run galleries. These institutions, in turn, provided an organized base from which to launch struggles for both greater access to and viable autonomy from the cultural landscape of Southern California's museums, festivals, and galleries.[3]

WAY OUT WEST

To a large extent, initial efforts to formalize links between likeminded artists came about with the recognition of the absence of spaces for discussing, exhibiting, or selling their work. Despite the overall expansion of the Southern California art world during the early 1960s, museums, schools, and galleries remained indifferent to the presence of black visual art. With the notable exception of Joan Ankrum's gallery, few art dealers in Los Angeles handled the work of local black artists other than Charles White.[4] The region's premier art school, Chouinard Art Institute, enrolled fewer than a dozen black students, and continuing allegations of racism dogged an institution that had long limited the enrollment of African Americans to night classes.[5] Although the underfunded County Museum of Art had exhibited the works of local black artists before moving from Exposition Park in 1965, the newly expanded museum initially sought to demonstrate the arrival of Southern California on the national cultural landscape. As a result, new museum management favored exhibitions of established artists over those of more obscure local artists of any color.

This indifference is all the more striking when set alongside the proliferation of black artists' organizations in Southern California after 1960. As noted earlier, the 1950s saw the birth of several groups of black visual artists. In the decade that followed, these sorts of efforts expanded. Melvin Edwards exhibited with a semi-formalized cultural collective called the Seekers.[6] The prolific figurative painter Walt Walker opened the LeJan gallery on Crenshaw Boulevard and 48th Street. The most successful effort to draw together black artists came as a result of the efforts of Ruth Waddy, who founded Art West Associated. Meeting sporadically in Waddy's home during 1960 and 1962, Art West (as the organization was also known) evolved an organizational structure, with elected positions and defined tasks, that formalized previously casual networks.[7]

The concretization of a collective body among local artists allowed for simultaneous discussions of form, the influence of the black liberation movement on art, and the material circumstances of black artists. Art West affiliates held several shows in nontraditional venues, including Los Angeles City Hall; secured a small National Endowment of the Arts grant; began advertising in *Essence* magazine; and paid for Waddy to travel cross-country soliciting prints for a locally produced book on black printmaking. Meetings took place in homes or in the back room of a local black-owned savings and loan. Participation spurred Waddy's own artistic development, since, tired of being asked questions about form that she could not answer, she enrolled at Otis Art Institute. Following Waddy's relocation to San Francisco after 1965, Art West Associated melted away as key personalities left to pursue opportunities elsewhere. For some, New York exerted a powerful pull, and, like much of Southern California's homegrown jazz talent, visuals artists such as Camille Billops and Mel Edwards made permanent moves east. Nevertheless, Art West Associated played a key role between 1960 and 1965, beginning a process of artistic challenges to the municipal arts establishment, providing a space for growing numbers of black artists to meet and share ideas, and helping link talent based in Northern California and Southern California.[8]

The experience of Art West Associated illustrates particular difficulties that the Black Arts Movement's imperative toward greater collective organization posed for visual artists. On the one hand, artists' collectives were no harder to form for painters and sculptors than for musicians or poets. Poets and playwrights, however, could perform in any number of places, and it was far easier to open a new repertory theater or music venue than a museum. Publishers and nightclub owners may have been difficult, but they could be circumvented through small presses and independent record labels. Allies like Broadside Press and Flying Dutchmen Records were often willing to take modest chances on unfamiliar subjects, thus providing writers and musicians with alternative production and distribution channels. Beyond this, theater and music were long-accepted pastimes in black communities, and people were accustomed to paying money to hear music or see plays. Books and records were generally cheaper than artwork. All of this left visual and plastic artists comparatively more dependent on the surrounding world of critics, galleries, and museums than artists working in other forms. As a result, the process of self-organization involved not simply the creation of spaces for discussing issues germane to artists or the attempt to change one's material circumstances, but also the attempt to build a base for the appreciation and support of black visual culture more generally.

In the decade that followed the Watts riot, an expanded community of black visual and plastic artists in Southern California took up these tasks.

Exhibition catalogs, collected interviews, and published biographical sketches review a loosely connected community in the hundreds. A casual estimate by Cecil Ferguson put the number of practicing visual artists, arts administrators, and arts educators participating in black arts organizations in the thousands, and while this number seems higher than archival materials record, a number closer to five hundred seems plausible. Although the broad community of black visual artists was (and continues to be) a multigenerational one, the post-Watts moment saw the emergence of a distinct cohort. Born between 1939 and 1946, most had come to Los Angeles as the children of wartime migrants. Many were graduates of area community colleges and state universities, although both Suzanne Jackson and Alonzo Davis had studied at local arts institutions. All were beginning careers as artists at a moment when debates concerning black liberation—and the presence of organizations seeking to transform these debates into political action—were altering the landscapes of the urban north and west.[9]

Much more than jazz, poetry, or theater, black visual art in Southern California developed against a backdrop of lack of interest from the mainstream white community. Black visual culture attracted little of the attention directed at black writing, theater, or music following the riot in 1965. The Watts Writers Workshop and Inner City Cultural Center operated with six-figure budgets; black visual artists confronted continued indifference on the part of gallery owners, museum directors, and the press. Indeed, the main art reviewer for the *Los Angeles Times*, William Wilson, had never reviewed the work of a black artist before being publicly challenged to do so by John Outterbridge.[10] As a result, new galleries owned and operated by local black artists presented the overwhelming majority of works shown by black artists.

As with institutions like the Underground Musicians Association and the Inner City Cultural Center, the collective organizations formed by visual artists were often the brainchild of a primary or singular figure. Suzanne Jackson's Gallery 32 offers a case in point. Jackson arrived in Los Angeles from the Bay Area. An abstract painter and published poet with a background in dance, she regarded being defined as a black artist as the "somewhat accidental," byproduct of the company she kept. Jackson lived in Echo Park, a bohemian enclave northeast of downtown, and initially knew little about South Los Angeles. "All I knew were the Watts Towers," she recalled. "I didn't understand that there was a whole black community that lived there." Jackson's first connection with local artists came when she took a drawing class with Charles White. An invitation to enter her works in the Watts Summer Festival arts competition followed. Jackson's initial decision to open a gallery came from a desire to foster community. Seeking to replicate previous experiences of San Francisco bohemianism, Gallery 32 was intended less as a business than as a place for the exchange of ideas and philosophies "over a pot of coffee and a big piece of jack cheese." Jackson funded the gallery without assistance, largely with money earned teaching and working as an exotic dancer. The gallery made little money but became an important place, in the words of the artist Dan Concholar, "for building a black base that supported black artists." Showing "anything and anybody who fell off the street," Gallery 32 shows included a group exhibition of the work of local black female artists and an exhibition of works by the Black Panther Party's minister of culture, Emory Douglas.[11]

In comments made to the interviewer Karen Anne Mason, Jackson discussed the relationship between artists' own organization and the development of an audience for black art. Noting that one first had to have a space to bring people to, Jackson explained how artists concluded that "it was important for black people to know about the artists' work and to stop hanging cheap posters that they actually paid more for than they would for a piece of art."[12] Writing in the 1930s, Loren Miller had lamented the lack of a critical apparatus for disseminating information about black art to black audiences. This is a concern that subsequent artists such as Charles Burnett would raise in the 1980s and beyond. That black visual artists—along with musicians and theater people—achieved some success in fostering a wider critical appreciation for black art during the late 1960s and early 1970s should be seen as one of the intellectual victories of this moment. When one recalls that Jackson articulated the primary point of a kind of spontaneous arts education as fostering a sense that people were investing not in something of monetary value but in something of authentic quality, then we can see how the Black Arts Movement's effort to develop a new art was part of a wider milieu of social, political, and aesthetic development on the part of black people more generally.

The most successful local black gallery was the Brockman Gallery. Founded in 1967 by the brothers Alonzo and Dale Davis, Brockman became the primary venue for exhibiting black art in the city. Like Gallery 32, Brockman served as a place for the exchange of artistic ideas, hosting regular forums and serving as an informal gathering space. John Outterbridge told the interviewer Elton Fax about Brockman's importance as a meeting place. "We discovered common ground," he noted, adding that "some strenuous problems and questions have been strenuously thrashed out right here at the Brockman Gallery." By the early 1970s, Brockman had become a multifaceted community arts space, as well, hosting a festival in nearby Leimert Park; sponsoring classes in yoga, drawing, painting, photography, and commercial art concepts; and administering a series of mural projects funded through the federal Comprehensive Employment and Training Act.[13]

Several factors contributed to Brockman's success. First and foremost, the gallery had a wide pool of local talent from which to draw, as well as owners willing to suspend their own creative work in the interest of completing administrative tasks. Equally important, however, was the gallery's location. Positioned in the Leimert Park area, Brockman was able to attract distinct populations of African Americans. Leimert Park lay in the shadow of the "black Beverly Hills," as the middle-class areas of View Park, Ladera Heights, and Baldwin Hills were colloquially known. Access from working-class neighborhoods of South Los Angeles, however, was easy, given the quick-moving Santa Barbara, Adams, and Vernon boulevards. Leimert Park lay within the larger Crenshaw district, which had formerly consisted of a mixture of Japanese Americans, whites, Jewish Americans, and middle-class blacks. By the mid-1970s, newly mobile segments of a black working class rising on a tide of municipal employment joined the remnants of this mixed-income, integrated neighborhood. With crowds built through consciously black shows, community festivals, and film screenings, Brockman could build a diverse social base, including a nearby population that could afford to buy art. As a result, Brockman prospered, if temporarily. By the time the gallery closed in the late 1990s, it was the oldest black-owned art gallery west of the Mississippi.[14]

Many artists affiliated with Brockman became members of two arts organizations formed during 1968. Following the demise of Art West, the Black Artists Alliance (BAA) and Black Arts Council (BAC) became the two major forums for bringing together visual artists of African descent in Southern California. Whereas the BAA, which came partially out of the Brockman Gallery, focused on addressing formal concerns relating to art, the BAC took as a mission creating opportunities for artists and generating broader interest in the arts in the surrounding black community. Two workers at the County Museum of Art, Claude Booker and Cecil Fergerson, founded the BAC. Booker was a veteran of the Korean War and a former LAPD officer turned shipping clerk. Fergerson was a former custodian who had mastered the successive job descriptions within the lower rungs of the museum hierarchy, becoming, in order, an art preparer, a museum helper, a museum assistant, and, finally, a curatorial assistant. After thirty-seven years of full-time employment at the Los Angeles County Museum of Art (LACMA), Fergerson held the position of curatorial assistant, which made him the highest-ranking black staff member. As a result of the museum's lack of interest in hiring African Americans for curatorial and other professional posts, the initial membership of the BAC consisted primarily of museum security officers, a majority of whom were black.[15]

The BAC grew quickly. Its origins lay in a struggle with museum management. Although Fergerson had a particular interest in French modernist art, the absence of any commitment on the part of the county museum to exhibit works by black artists bothered him. Fergerson began holding meetings aimed at embarrassing the museum into hiring more black staff and showing more black artists. Alonzo Davis, Outterbridge, Ruth Waddy, Timothy Washington, and David Hammons were among those who turned up for initial public forums. Stan Saunders, a former Rhodes Scholar and planner of the annual Watts Summer Festival, served as the group's attorney, drawing up papers of incorporation. Gradually, the BAC began to attract a loose membership that included many of the black artists in the city. Fergerson claimed a high point of three thousand members, although he noted that none of them was willing to serve as the group's secretary.[16]

Producing a more relevant LACMA remained an elusive goal. Forming an organization that counted significant numbers of museum security guards among its membership allowed a certain degree of flexibility and militancy when planning actions. Angry that a major Cubism show ignored that form's debt to African art, a number of Black Arts Council affiliates decided to remove several works from the museum's walls. "A lot of black artists worked as guards," recalled John Outterbridge, "so we knew how to do that without damaging the paintings." The guards "were in the movement," he added, "so we figured they wouldn't shoot us." Rather than pursuing this avenue, however, the artists decided to picket the show.[17]

Under duress, museum management agreed to a series of lectures on black art. These paired local artists and included musical performances and visits by the US Organization's Taifa Dance Troupe. Taifa generally performed an "Afro-Americanized" version of the polyrhythmic stomping boot dance of South African gold and diamond miners.[18] Lecturers included Samella Lewis, a professor of art at the Claremont Colleges and a visual artist in her own right; John Riddle; Bernie Casey; and Charles White. The third lecture in the series, which began with a series of Paul Robeson ballads broadcast across Wilshire Boulevard, drew upward of one thousand spectators, far more than the three hundred or so expected by the museum.[19]

Despite the success of the series, which did begin to draw more blacks to LACMA, the museum continued to eschew local artists. A partial capitulation came in early 1971 with the exhibit "Three Graphic Artists," which featured works by Charles White, David Hammons, and Timothy Washington. The exhibit, which took place in a basement room generally reserved for art rentals, demonstrated the fissures within the visual arts community. The BAC demanded a Charles White retrospective in the main gallery, charging that a recognized master of American modernism should be exhibited separately from two younger artists. Fergerson and Booker grew angry that museum staff had gone directly to Alonzo Davis at Brockman rather than to them in organizing the show. Claude Booker and Cecil Fergerson organized picket lines outside the museum, and David Hammons reportedly tried to pull one of his works off a museum wall. Partially as a result of continuing pressure from local artists, LACMA agreed to host a six-week exhibition featuring fifty-one local black artists. Most of the works were by emerging artists. Of the seventy-six works shown, only five had been lent by galleries, and only one was privately owned. The exhibit, "Los Angeles 1972: A Panorama of Black Artists," thus provided a rare opportunity for artists who otherwise were struggling for recognition and demonstrated the possibility of creating a more receptive museum.

Although it was primarily an advocacy organization, the BAC also served an educational purpose. Fergerson gave periodic lectures on art throughout Los Angeles. The Black Arts Council received repeated invitations from local black student unions eager to host black art shows. Fergerson occasionally demurred, worried that shows in student centers risked pigeonholing black artists who belonged in museums and galleries. University shows did take place, however, and the BAC was on the verge of mounting a major show at a new gallery at UCLA until the killing of two Black Panthers by US Organization members put the plans on hold. Even the federal government called on the Black Arts Council. When racial tensions erupted on a nearby air base, the Air Force asked Fergerson to help organize a show aimed at calming tense nerves. One can only imagine the reception the donated works received. "Boy it was a trip," remarked Fergerson. "They sent trucks, Army Air Force trucks with these rigs that open up like a whole living room. And they were putting John Riddle's 'The Operation' into the side of the truck and the side of the truck has this big eagle on it and 'The Operation' was two steel figures with one white figure taking the brain out of a black figure."[20]

The BAC folded in 1974. Its demise came partially as a result of the tremendous amount of work involved for both Booker and Fergerson. Financing the group was difficult, as well. Periodic fundraisers helped, but Suzanne Jackson commented that much of the BAC's funding came from Booker's and Fergerson's household budgets. Neither could maintain the organization, keep his day job, and hold together a reasonable family life. But the BAC also drifted apart as a result of the partial successes of the organization. LACMA's mandate had been significantly broadened, and by 1976 the museum hosted a major exhibition, "Two Centuries of Afro-American Art," guest curated by David Driskell. Although local artists were largely excluded from planning or contributing in any way to the show, many were also tired of perennial confrontation and began to focus their energy on establishing the institution that became the California Afro-American Museum.

The evolution of collective organization on the part of local visual artists illustrates the dialectic between aesthetic and political critique. As in the case of Eric Dolphy's parents' house, the private homes of Ruth Waddy and Noah Purifoy began as places for informal discussions about form. Speaking of his own home, Purifoy recalled, "Here was a place where we could discuss our lives in connection with art. . . . We could experience the past and plan for the future."[21] "In Noah's house," Outterbridge said, "we'd go and get into big fights at times, almost physical fights and drink good wine and solve the problems of the world, and then critique our work."[22] A "constant flow" of politics, philosophy, psychology, and art similarly took place in more formally organized spaces such as Jackson's Gallery 32 and the back offices of the Golden State Mutual Life Insurance Copmany building, provided by the watercolorist Bill Pajaud.

Part of the passage from informal meetings to organized gatherings came about precisely as black artists began to critique their positions as artists trying to survive and as black people intent on doing the same. Collective organization provided one road toward addressing the latter concern. Assemblage art provided another.

REDEMPTION SONGS

Redemption is the great overriding myth explored in
assemblage art: what shall survive of what we are?
—RICHARD CÁNDIDA SMITH

The desire to foster an engagement between the growing black liberation movement and new aesthetic ideas posed specific challenges for visual and plastic artists.[23] Despite the rapid diffusion of radical visual images, the call for the development of consciously revolutionary black art often cast aspersions on the visual arts, particularly painting. The most widely distributed contemporary source of essays on competing conceptions of black expression, Addison Gayle's edited volume *The Black Aesthetic*, contained sections examining cultural theory, fiction, drama, poetry, and music. Only five of the book's more than thirty contributors made any mention of painting. This brief mention did little to erase the marginal position held by the visual arts relative to other genres. As Lorenzo Thomas notes, jazz, despite its predominantly instrumental form, was more likely to be seen as useful to potential black revolutionaries than the visual or plastic arts because of the political activity of jazz musicians, the tendency to view music as possessing an inherent racial authenticity, and the circulation of ideas that held jazz, particularly "free jazz," as therefore revolutionary in form.[24]

As noted earlier, musicians had themselves sought to dismiss the notion of a reflective correspondence between music and politics. In this regard, the belief that particular artistic genres either possessed a revolutionary character or were inherently irrelevant in the struggle for black liberation proved as problematic for visual artists as it had for musicians. Despite their desire to avoid being typecast, and notwithstanding the relatively more marginal responsibility assigned visual artists in the struggle for racial revolution, the black liberation movement exercised a powerful influence on black visual artists. In his survey of twentieth-century African American art, Richard Powell argues, "Betye Saar, along with fellow Los Angeles artists Houston Conwill, David Hammons, Senga Nengudi, John Outterbridge, and Noah Purifoy[,] began to redefine black consciousness in art."[25]

Mixed-media assemblage became a key form for enacting this transformation. Given the towering influence of Simon Rodia, this was unsurprising. As Sarah Schrank and Cécile Whiting show, the triangular link between the Watts Towers, the junk art form, and the ethno-demographic affiliation to black Angelenos took time in developing.[26] Beyond South Los Angeles, assemblage, junk art, and other nontraditional sculpture forms had become an important part of the California avant-garde, drawing the energy of, among others, Wallace Berman, George Herms, Ed Keinholz, Bruce Conner, Fred Mason, and Clay Spohn. Peter Plagens called assemblage "the first home-grown California modern art," noting that, although its roots lay elsewhere, assemblage art became emblematic of the postwar confluence of bohemianism and mass culture. In the specific social context of Southern California, assemblage,

FIGURE 18 Artwork made from riot debris displayed at Watts Renaissance of the Arts, 1966. Los Angeles Times Photographic Archive (Collection 1429), Department of Special Collections, Charles E. Young Research Library, University of California, Los Angeles.

junk, and found art became a means "for recycling the discards of postwar affluence into defiantly deviant configurations."[27]

Certainly, the form seemed particularly suited to the needs of black artists. Much as musicians like John Carter combined blues structures and phrasings with freeform improvisation, assemblage art mixed folk-art traditions and avant-garde experimentation. Assemblages transformed the familiar, forcing new looks at old objects. In a neighborhood surrounded by junkyards and plagued by infrequent garbage collection, junk art asked the community to reexamine the true value of the objects around it.[28] Whether one used hair (Hammons), riot debris (Purifoy and Powell), or rags and steel (Edwards, Outterbridge, and Riddle), assemblage offered the possibility of creating images familiar to black audiences without the constraints of pure realism. A form given to juxtaposition, assemblage allowed for the exposition of both irony and contradiction. That it did so relatively inexpensively was a bonus. That it blended a highly intellectual process of selection with an improvisational, even spontaneous, method made for a jazz-like sensibility. Thus, like jazz, assemblage art suggested the possibility of a non-essentialized form of black creativity whose racial codings might be deciphered by black audiences whether or not white artists or audiences sought to replicate, extend, or consume the end result.

The use of familiar images, objects, or, in the case of David Hammons, one's own body allowed for the creation of pieces that were highly symbolic, deeply personal, and largely abstract and yet often carried explicitly political overtones. Edwards's "Lynch Fragments" blended African masks, abstract expressionism, intense sexuality, and omnipresent force and violence in a work that he began shortly after the police raid on a South Los Angeles Nation of Islam mosque.[29] The art historian Samella Lewis described Purifoy's "Sir Watts" as a "commemoration of the struggles of a people in battle."[30] Part of a collection of pieces forged from salvaged riot debris, "Sir Watts" had come together as a result of Purifoy's and Judson Powell's ongoing work creating found art with local residents of Watts. Saar's iconic "Liberation of Aunt Jemima" offered a riff on the oft-reproduced portrait of Huey Newton as an armed potentate perched inside a wicker throne, while suggesting that, as in Vietnam, even the most unthreatening figure could rapidly become a warrior. Though the armed centerpiece of Saar's composition commands immediate attention, her parallel inclusion of cotton along the base of the box, with a notepad featuring the image of the Jemima mammy caring for a white child, offers a work-centric ethic much like Outterbridge's "Song for My Father." David Hammons's body print "Injustice Case" incorporated his own bound and gagged body, surrounded by a border made from an American flag, in a posture that recalled the gagging of the Black Panther leader Bobby Seale during the trial of the Chicago Eight. Another piece, "The Door (Admissions Office)," featured an inked body outline of a face, arms, and torso pressing against a closed door. Outterbridge's "Traditional Hang-up" featured a steel cross with a stars-and-stripes pattern running across the top, bisected by a post filled with small, skull-like objects. Part of the larger *Containment* series, the work for Outterbridge symbolized the problematic historical relationship between African Americans and Christianity, as well as the violent disjuncture between the American promise of equal treatment and the violent repression of black Americans.[31] These ideas were extended in *Containment*, where a series of metal frames and stretcher bars were broken apart in a comment on the limits of enclosure while mixed polished and unfinished surfaces were juxtaposed in an effort "to suggest the unrealized potential or raw talent within his community."[32]

FIGURE 19 "The Door (Admissions Office)," by David Hammons, 1969. Wood, acrylic sheet, and pigment construction. Collection of California African American Foundation. Courtesy California African-American Museum.

Speaking generally, it is difficult to miss the political content that adheres to a work of art that features a cross, skulls, and an American flag. Other pieces, however, achieve a similarly affective link to the social through a less confrontational pose. Outterbridge's "Case in Point," part of his *Rag Man* series, features a series of cylindrical rags sewn together and bound with leather straps. Baggage tags adorn the surface of the piece, and one tag bears the phrase, "Packages travel like people." As with the truck he left exposed to the elements, the sense of distressed and worn materials is palpable, with the sewn rags showing uneven coloration and obvious wear. The piece reflects a kind of historical materialism, suggesting the critical experience of migration in African American life and reminding how the process of collecting discarded items has been—and remains—a central strategy of survival for economically marginalized urban black men. As the *Rag Man* series progressed, Outterbridge developed more figurative creations embellished with mirrors, beads, cloth, nails, and boards. Divided between objects that give power and those that display, the latter pieces of the *Rag Man* series reflect an increasing en-

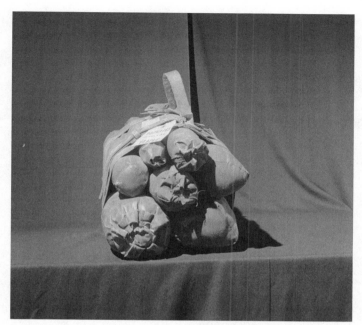

FIGURE 20 "Case in Point," *Rag Man* series, by John Outterbridge, 1970. Mixed-media assemblage. Photograph by Willie Ford. Compton Communicative Arts Academy, California State University, Los Angeles Library.

gagement with spiritual themes drawn from West African cultural idioms as well as from rural Southern African American outsider art.

Evocations of mobility, work, spirit, and struggle are similarly present in the work of the assemblage artist and sculptor John Riddle. A Los Angeles native who had attended Los Angeles City College before moving on to the campus of California State University, Los Angeles, Riddle described his art in part by noting, "There are very few avenues of communication open to black people."[33] He added, "Every black person in America must engage in the struggle or see the struggle controlled by the beast."[34] One work that took up the linked question of communication and struggle was "Bird and Diz." Part of a series alternately entitled *Made in Mississippi* and *Spirit versus Technology*, "Bird and Diz" is set within the rectangular frame of an ammunition box manufactured in Mississippi. Riddle's piece simultaneously engages questions of organized violence, black migration, and the centrality of jazz within an oppositional African American culture. As part of what Clyde Woods calls "the blues tradition of explanation," Riddle's piece offers musicality (and the

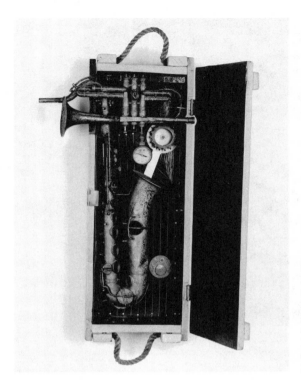

FIGURE 21 "Bird and Diz," *Spirit vs. Technology* series, by John T. Riddle Jr., 1973. Mixed-media assemblage. Collection of California African American Foundation. Courtesy California African-American Museum.

hidden labor of playing) as a central component of African American efforts at self-definition and political subjectivity.[35]

At a formal level, Riddle's piece is less spontaneous and playful than, for example, the Dadaist absurdity of Purifoy's "Sir Watts." Part of this difference emerges in the distinction between the "found" nature of the former and the "constructed" status of the latter, although these are distinctions that emerge more in the interpretive act than in the actual circumstances of production. Beyond this, Purifoy's piece seems to capture a moment—the paladin is charred but standing—where Riddle engages a longer sense of historical time through the formal properties of the distressed materials used as well as through the link to the bebop generation.

Riddle's piece, too, is open to a "materialist" reading. Dizzy Gillespie and Charlie Parker are signified by, perhaps even reduced to, their means of producing. Part of the larger *Made in Mississippi* series, Riddle's "Bird and Diz" posits the binaries spirit–technology and black culture–America as unfolding within the confines of a militarized space. These are ideas he had touched on previously in works such as "There's More at Stake than Just Attica." In both cases, the creative response to the threat of technological annihilation—a core concern of the postwar Californian white avant-garde—is answered through the assertion of a coded language of ethnic particularity signified most clearly by jazz. Thus, Riddle's piece, like Outterbridge's "Song for My Father" or Larry Clark's film *Passing Through*, posits a cross-generic, socially referenced, jazz-centric aesthetic of cultural politics as the key to black collectivity.

With the exception of the muralist Charles Freeman, who moved to Los Angeles as an organizer with the Black Panther Party, none of the principal figures involved in the visual arts community belonged to any of the competing nationalist organizations in South Los Angeles. Despite this, the black liberation movement exercised a powerful, if diffuse, influence. In describing her Aunt Jemima assemblage, Saar quipped, "Extreme times call for extreme heroines," adding, "My intent was to transform a negative, demeaning figure . . . into a warrior ready to combat servitude and racism."[36] Though more temporally specific, Outterbridge's mixed metal and fabric "Pig Painted Blue," like John Riddle's sculpted tribute to the memory of prisoners killed in the Attica prison uprising, reflected the ongoing engagement with the black freedom movement. "In a way," claimed Outterbridge, "we were all Panthers." At times it appeared that the police agreed. During the exhibition of works by Emory Douglas, police issued citations to every car parked near Gallery 32, where the exhibition opening was being held, while on another occasion, officers providing a comical example of jurisdictional confusion threatened the gallery's owner, Suzanne Jackson, with a tax audit because of their displeasure with the subject matter in her gallery. Although the intrusion of police into Los Angeles art galleries had been a recurring issue during the 1950s, these activities took on a new tone in the context of open violence between the police and radicals after 1962.[37]

Within the social context of black liberation, black artists developed a wide range of ideas on art. Some, like Marvin Harden, rejected the notion of black art or any particular affiliation with groupings of black artists. Many artists whose works evoked nationalist themes or who referred to themselves as "black artists" critiqued the idea of a singular "black art."[38] Van Slater derided the term "black art" as "meaningless." Alice Gafford maintained that she saw no contradiction between her insistence that art was universal and her commitment to nurturing both individual black artists and facilitating the broader appreciation of consciously black art.[39] Despite the openly political message of an armed Aunt Jemima, Betye Saar described her primary interest as creating an occult sensibility that would be vague enough to unleash the imagination of viewers. Saar summarized her position in a poem:

I never had the / stroke for "mainstream"
it went against my
flow
From the past remnants / of lost ceremonies the
loosening and unwrapping
of mystery emergence / from the shadows to face /
the unknown / purification
(these works are what I leave behind).[40]

Indeed, part of the extraordinary vitality of Saar's art was the way in which, like Horace Tapscott, she moved easily between antiracist confrontation, historical allegory, communal spirituality, and interior, familial life.[41] Purifoy saw art as a process for both self-discovery and communication. Citing the need for "more than the creative act," Purifoy called the group show "66 Signs of Neon," which featured sixty-six separate pieces constructed from riot debris, a means for fostering collective responsibility and communication between individuals. Indeed, Purifoy argued that the essence of art was communication:

If junk art in general, and 66 in particular, enable us only to see and love the many simple things which previously escaped the eye, then we miss the point. We wish to establish more. . . . There must be a ME and a YOU, who is affected permanently. Art of itself is of no value if in its relatedness it does not effect change, a change in the behavior of human beings. And changes in behavior are effected through communication.[42]

Purifoy's and Powell's "66 Signs" illustrates the complex vision of community-oriented assemblage artists working in the context of social upheaval. Initially casting their efforts as a comment on the limits of the McCone commission report on the riots, the duo described their desire "to reflect the August 11th event on a symbolic level and to demonstrate . . . if the community of Watts found itself in the midst of something—something like junk—value could be placed on it to far exceed the few cents paid at the junk yards on Monday morning." He continued, "Here the Junk Art concept becomes one of many artistic expressions which begins to describe and symbolize the act of doing, transferred into an art of being and becoming: a format which symbolizes human existence." In his commentary, Purifoy conjured a Dadaist vision of a creative process that, in the words of Anne Ayres, was "more life than art."[43] The actual process of scavenging and assembling the debris used in the show, moreover, combined hard labor—salvage efforts took three months of daily work—with a performative spontaneity that saw art "not as a particular thing in itself, but as a reason to establish conversation and communicate one on one." The show was never intended to be permanent, as Purifoy wrote in the introduction to the book of poetry that accompanied it: "We now stand ready to throw '66' back into the junk pile." At the same time, Purifoy's and Powell's vision explicitly rejected the suggestion that "66 Signs," or any of their other art or teaching, reflected a view of "art for art's sake." Rather, they affirmed the "wish to establish that there is more to art than the creative act, more than the sensation of beauty, ugliness, form, color, light."[44]

The way artists spoke about the relationship between political questions and artistic expression attests to the interaction between individual consciousness and social life during a moment of mass activity. For Outterbridge, art during this moment became "socially oriented, not because of your choosing as an artist, but because we were sensitive and active and open during a period when the skin of America was reeking of little abscesses."[45] That artists began "taking their studios to the street" was an inevitable result of their recognition that "we began to understand art's potential for social change."[46] David Hammons saw the place of politics in art as unavoidable. Citing a "moral obligation" to document the things he felt socially, Hammons nonetheless saw politics as something of an unfortunate creative intrusion. "I'm still political at times," he noted, "but I don't want to be; but there are . . . issues which come up, and . . . they bother me."[47]

One result of the widespread social engagement among visual artists was the development of a new formulation of black art that combined insurgent political themes with familiar cultural tropes regarding music, migration, and spirituality. Augmented by an inter-artistic, cross-generic engagement with sound and text, this bricolage avoided the formal limits of realist representation. Much as Horace Tapscott, John Carter, Charles Mingus, and other members of the jazz avant-garde incorporated non-Western musical themes, diverse religio-magical imagery, African American history, and social themes into their music, visual artists developed an abstract language of blackness that, while hardly self-evident or propagandistic, could nonetheless be spoken about by artists as confirming the broader effort to bring the questions posed by the Black Power Movement's cultural critique of American life into the world of visual art.

Works often incorporated spiritual imagery. Betye Saar's mixed-media box construction "Black Girl's Window" combined pictures, objects, and a central silhouette with an outline of hands (designed to recall a palmistry chart) pressed against the multi-paned window. Other compositions of hers combined mystic symbols, bones, household objects, and miscellaneous talismans together in a powerful symbolic blend. Her mixed-media assemblage "Nine Mojo Secrets" (1971) features an open, red palm print embossed with the all-seeing eye over a photograph of an African religious initiation. External panels feature painted phases of the moon, while patches of wheat, a lion, skeletons, and a small head of indeterminate origin (Exú?) provide a sense of grounding and rootedness. One overall effect of this piece is to heighten a vertical cosmological sensibility—stars and moon above but connected to Earth, dirt, and that which lies under it. Beads, fibers, and seeds hang alongside the bottom of the painted window frame, further incorporating conjure elements. At the same time, Saar places Africa at the center of a mystic ensemble that nonetheless radiates specific African American magico-religious ideas. Beyond its finished fixity, Lizette LeFalle-Collins describes how the process of creating the assemblage revealed a spiritual practice partitioned into the distinct steps of dreaming, ritualistic searching for items, the bringing together of the found items, the production of the given work, and its public release.[48] The process of assemblage was thus envisioned through a series of steps in which private revelations were revealed and confirmed through public exposition and circulation.

Noah Purifoy's "Burial Ground," "Zulu #4," *and* "The Sound of One Hand Clapping" blended feathers, rags, chains, washers, and pieces of tin into unique magical fetishes. Spiritual concepts used a range of West African images and symbols. While these attempts were occasionally criticized for collapsing together the vast complexity of the continent's constituent populations, the actual works generally revealed attention to regional and ethnic specificity. Saar's "Homage to Eshu" (the Yoruba deity of manifestation and choice) and Greg Edwards's "Praise for Shango" (the Yoruba Orisa associated with lightning, rain, and royal authority) and "Prayer for Olodumare" (the Creator) worked within a specific cultural complex. Even when black artists deliberately transformed African elements, they often did so in conscious homage or with deliberate Pan-African aims. John Outterbridge's iron pots fell within recognizable parameters of Yoruba aesthetics even when filled with objects familiar to black Americans. Or so it seemed to Brazilian followers of the Yoruba-derived Candomblé religion, who took Outterbridge for an Ogun devotee when he exhibited at the São Paulo biennial in 1994. Although more gener-

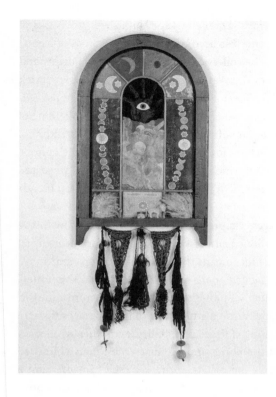

FIGURE 22 "Nine Mojo Secrets," by Betye Saar, 1971. Mixed-media assemblage. Collection of California African American Foundation. Courtesy California African-American Museum.

alized spiritual and African elements were often incorporated into larger works in ways that changed their context or meaning, it hardly follows that this process was essentialist or haphazard. Part of the benefit of assemblage art was the extent to which it allowed cultural characteristics common throughout the African diaspora—selective appropriations and the alteration of meaning through new juxtapositions—to find a place in the visual and plastic arts.[49]

Black popular music formed another important reference point for visual artists. Many were themselves musicians and found ways to incorporate musical themes or ideas into their work. Ruth Waddy, Camille Billops, John Outterbridge, and Cecil Fergerson all had musical backgrounds. Riddle, Hammons, and Purifoy incorporated musical instruments into their assemblages and collages. Mel Edwards cited a deep engagement with jazz in his work, while Outterbridge conceptualized the entire creative process through a musical prism, referring to the rhythm of his tools and all his art as a type of musical composition.[50]

Visual artists incorporated poetry into their work, as well. Jayne Cortez wrote a series of poems to accompany the growing body of "Lynch Fragments" pieces by Melvin Edwards. Suzanne Jackson published two books of poetry.[51] A book of sixty-six poems also accompanied the "66 Signs of Neon" project by Purifoy and Powell. The collection included poems by Purifoy and Powell, as well as by members of the Watts Writers Workshop, the Frederick Douglass House, and the Watts Towers Art Center poetry workshops. *Untitled*, as the "66 Signs" volume was called, offered a cross-generic blending of poetry, assemblage, and collage. The ultimate product was predicated on an interchange between the intersecting forms. "Each page," wrote the editors, was intended as a "form poem" in which an "informal wedding of verse and graphics" was meant to elicit a mood "transferable from poetry to art; Freudian slips; protest; affirmation."[52]

The proliferation of cross-generic projects, connected as it was with the emergent confluence of musicality, spiritualism, and poetry, thus linked visual artists with artists working in other forms. Both Camille Billops and Betye Saar made films, with Saar's *Colored Spade* serving as a cinematic counterpoint to her other work recasting racist imagery. Taking its title from a song in the musical *Hair*, *Colored Spade* features a montage of racist images that are gradually replaced with depictions of Klansmen, police, and other symbols of racist (dis)order.[53] Lasting eighty seconds and having cost less than a hundred dollars to make, the film shares the collage form, a bevy of images, and a generalized context with the unfinished film *Repression*, made as a joint project between the Los Angeles Newsreel collective and the Los Angeles Chapter of the Black Panther Party.

Revisiting connections between artists working in distinct creative genres helps clarify the outlines of the heterodox and unprogrammatic art developed by musicians, writers, visual artists, and others during this time. Richard Powell notes how David Hammons's use of his own body, as well as of products and elements familiar to black Americans, helps form a representational field where spaces of coded communication are created between artists and audiences.[54] At times, this communication was directly political, urging mobilization and more. Often, however, this representational field is abstracted but clearly comprehensible and deeply attuned to affective constructions of communal identity.

In an early review of Saar's magico-religious assemblage boxes, the curator Marcia Tucker argued that Saar's transition from bold, ironic, and directly political pieces such as "The Liberation of Aunt Jemima" to more intimate, symbolic, and mystic assemblages represented an effort to explore "the roots and residues of black folk culture."[55] While instructive, her comment is incomplete. For much as Tapscott's decision to shift from the militant language of the "Underground Musicians Association" to a more accessible "Union of God's Musicians and Artists Ascension" was meant to reassert the popular, community-based focus of the jazz collective by using language accessible to everyday black folks, I would argue that Saar's shift toward works that foreground a spiritual collage shows a continuing interest in precisely those forms of widespread mobilization and political advocacy that an earlier, more openly militant language had sought to engender. In her discussion of black female writers and filmmakers, Judylyn Ryan argues for a conception of "spirituality as ideology" in which creative producers provide multifaceted engagements with racially coded sacred imagery as a way to establish truth claims, an intertextual "ethic of connectedness," and a larger sense of common purpose across historical time.[56] Among others, Eric Hobsbawm has written about the problems inherent in considering religio-ethnic linkages or the past as pillars on which a collective identity might be based.[57] Although he was clear about revealing its historically contingent and indeed inherently ahistorical aspects, Benedict Anderson's examination of the subject argued persuasively that nationalist sentiment was first and foremost a conscious intellectual act.[58] From this perspective, it is possible to see music, history, spirituality, and even concepts such as "improvisation," "soul," or "blackness" as forming the outline of a creative, oppositional culture set within the boundaries of a "nation to be." This "nation" was less a physical space than a conceptual orientation and less a pragmatic political statement than a commentary on the necessity of refusing things as they were. It wasn't "national" in the sense of collapsing the class spectrum of African Americans into a singular grouping. It was, rather, "national" in placing black Americans within the political geography of a rapidly decolonizing world. In marshalling an index of the particularistic —whether through music, black religious distinctiveness, or the physical bodies of artists themselves—black artists advanced an aesthetic strategy concomitant with the larger project of artists' organization, community linkages, and social transformation.

Thus, visual artists working principally in the mixed-media assemblage form sought to develop an expansive, open-ended, yet socially committed abstract art that, in the words of John Outterbridge, while "open to anyone" was first and foremost "always relevant to us as black people."[59] As in the case of avant-garde jazz and poetry, informal meeting places expanded into organized sites for political struggle and aesthetic debate. Beyond this, visual artists would prove central to the broader effort to develop a working-class cultural politics across South Los Angeles. The central role of local visual artists in developing community arts projects across South Los Angeles, discussed hereafter, thus offers a third link between the visual, musical, and literary segments of the black avant-garde.

COMMUNICATION AND COMMUNITY IN COMPTON

Beyond their development of open-ended, racially referenced aesthetics and their widespread move toward collective organization, visual artists played a major role in transforming cultural activism into a mass movement with a wide social base. New community-based arts organizations constituted the critical vehicle for this process. Aided in part by new sources of government funding, the period between 1965 and 1973 saw the expansion of groups such as the Watts Towers Art Center, Studio Watts, and the Ebony Showcase Theater, and the emergence of the Performing Arts Society of Los Angeles, the Inner City Cultural Center, the Brockman Gallery, the Mafundi Institute, and the R'Wanda Lewis Dance Company.[60] While each of these organizations described its focus and goals in distinct ways, all incorporated some form of outreach, teaching, and political content in the overall mission. This was as true for new projects like the Inner City Cultural Center as it was for more venerable bodies like the Ebony Showcase Theater.[61]

The trajectory of community arts in the City of Compton highlights something of this process. In contrast to Los Angeles, where the direction of municipal cultural policy after 1973 demonstrated the class cleavages and political struggles within the regional elite, the residential suburb of Compton had little cultural policy at all. As had been done in other industrial suburbs of southeastern Los Angeles, such as Bell, Lynwood, Huntington Park, and South Gate, boosters of Compton had originally marketed the city as a white enclave.[62] For Compton, this would prove a losing proposition. Located directly southeast of the predominantly black Watts and Willowbrook districts of Los Angeles, the incorporated City of Compton was estimated at 40 percent black at the time of the Watts riot. Soon after, Compton became the first majority-black city in the state.

Community arts came to Compton through something of a backdoor. White flight and the accelerating decline of heavy manufacturing caused a sharp decline in local tax revenue while population growth, particularly among working-class African Americans, created expanded demand for housing and educational, medical, and other social services. Recognition of this fact led federal officials to declare Compton a "model city" eligible for federal

FIGURE 23 Judson Powell, art instructor, with two students against the background of the Watts Towers, 1965. Los Angeles Times Photographic Archive, circa 1918– (Collection 1429), Department of Special Collections, Charles E. Young Research Library, University of California, Los Angeles.

aid. The Compton–Willowbrook Community Action Council was among the institutions charged with developing an action plan for spending federal assistance.[63] Judson Powell, former director of the Watts Towers Art Center, served as deputy director of the organization. His duties included coordinating a host of poverty programs, and he asked Outterbridge to consider developing an arts education program for the Compton–Willowbrook agency. His initial desire to create an arts program with Outterbridge met with skepticism from staff members concerned with prioritizing more practical pursuits, although the logic of such a program seemed undeniable. In a school district with thirty-seven thousand students, there were only nine music and three art teachers.[64] Van Slater, an art instructor at Compton Community College, argued that arts education might reduce violence among youth, a belief that dovetailed neatly with Outterbridge's and Powell's contention that the power of art to facilitate communication gave arts education a critical social importance. Certainly, Outterbridge, the art director of the new Compton Commu-

FIGURE 24 Mixed-media assemblage door, Compton Communicative Arts Academy, 1970. Photograph by Willie Ford. Compton Communicative Arts Academy Collection, California State University, Los Angeles Library.

nicative Arts Academy (CAA), anticipated answering the query he had posed in the academy's bylaws. "How many painters, sculptors, writers, actors, dancers and musicians," he asked, "are working their magic in the street?" The academy would bring them in and see.[65]

The Communicative Arts Academy grew rapidly, exchanging a house donated by the Salvation Army for an abandoned skating rink. Because no willing insurer could be found, the broken and boarded windows were replaced with murals. Elliot Pinkney, who happened to ride by on his bicycle, helped in this effort, as did John Riddle. Symbolically titled "Something from Nothing," the murals at the CAA were unique mixed-media compositions blending relief sculpture, assemblage, and paint.[66] Insurers probably should not have worried. The CAA shared a storefront with a local motorcycle club that provided revenue and a measure of informal security. The relationship involved a degree of symbiosis: On at least one occasion, the academy hosted an event organized by a club member called Sugar Bear that was billed as a "combination trade show and interaction between community and bike club members."[67]

The CAA's reach extended beyond the world of choppers and hogs. A concert held in 1973 in recognition of the electoral victory of Mayor Doris

FIGURE 25 Chopper show, Compton Communicative Arts Academy, 1972. Photograph by Willie Ford. Compton Communicative Arts Academy Collection, California State University, Los Angeles Library.

Davis (who had become the first black woman in the country to head a major city when elected mayor of Compton in 1970) featured performances by Benny Powell and his wife, the pianist and vocalist Petsye. Events held in conjunction with the Black Arts Council provided a space for the public exchange of ideas about art. One such event featured an African art exhibit composed of objects lent by UCLA and installed by BAC representatives from the County Museum of Art (LACMA). The centerpiece of the event was a panel discussion featuring members of the CAA, other local black artists, and representatives from the Mechicano Art Center, a predominantly Chicano cultural center and gallery in East Los Angeles.[68]

These events raised the agency's profile. Two local television networks ran short programs covering the aims and projects of the CAA. A National Endowment for the Arts conference held in greater Los Angeles brought approximately five hundred observers to see the center. Such publicity aided ongoing fundraising efforts that gained new urgency as the academy sought to expand its offerings. During the first years of its existence, the CAA had been funded primarily as a project of the larger Compton–Willowbrook Community Action Council. As programs expanded, however, funding needs grew. Budget estimates for CAA expenditures in 1971 and 1972 totaled $50,000 and $100,000, respectively. Budgets increased during the next two years, with the California

FIGURE 26 Communicative Arts Academy staff on railroad tracks, not dated. Photograph by Willie Ford. Compton Communicative Arts Academy Collection, California State University, Los Angeles Library.

Arts Commission ($20,000), Office of Economic Opportunity ($30,000), private contributions ($25,000), and in-kind donations ($40,000) equaling a budget in 1973 of $115,000. Operating revenue for the following year came from the National Endowment for the Arts and the Compton Model Cities program, as well as from the Los Angeles Brotherhood Crusade, the Cummins Engine Foundation of Indiana, and the Salvation Army. In-kind donations also increased, with the Salvation Army donating use of a nearby facility in Willowbrook and more than seventy individuals, including Cecil Fergerson, Claude Booker, Elliot Pinkney, Gloria Bohanon, Alonzo and Dale Davis, Bill Pajaud, and the musician Charles Wright contributing time, money, and expertise.[69]

In-kind donations illustrate the essence of community arts as social movement. Although nearly every significant cultural institution in Los Angeles had one figure, or possibly two, whose dedication allowed it to survive, community artists such as Horace Tapscott, Noah Puriofy, and R'Wanda Lewis were equally dependent on the hundreds of volunteers and the smaller number of paid staff who functioned, in effect, as the cultural cadres of the community arts movement. At the Inner City Institute for the Performing and Visual Arts, the training component of the Inner City Cultural Center, approximately one hundred sixty courses were offered annually by forty teachers, many of whom, like the actor Beah Richards, the composer Margaret Bonds, the photographer Marion Palfi, and the mime Antonin Hodek, were significant figures in their fields.[70]

Nonetheless, for the CAA, costs expanded more quickly than revenues, and state funding began to decline even as programming expanded. Staff salaries and costs of materials grew. In essence, success proved fatal, as increasing participation from neighborhood residents necessitated new hiring and greater material costs. Serving a regular population of approximately two hundred children and six hundred teenagers and adults, the CAA held classes in music, theater, writing, graphic arts, photography, audiovisual production, and interpretive and ethnic dance.[71] An orchestra comprising students at nearby high schools, Compton Community College, and the University of Southern California performed original compositions. A separate jazz workshop included some seventy-five students working in eight different combos. The trumpeter Donald Byrd took several of the academy's jazz students to perform with him at UCLA. The CAA also developed a theater program. Directed by Robert Browning, the Paul Robeson Players performed a mix of classic and original plays. Browning's trajectory suggests the continuity of the local black cultural infrastructure. In addition to a degree from a local junior college and a stint studying fine arts at the University of Judaism, he had studied acting and drama with Charlie Polacheck at the Ebony Showcase Theater and with Yaphet Kotto at the Watts Writers Workshop. While at the CAA, he participated in the founding of the Compton Community Theater and the Compton Ethnic Arts Association.[72]

The Compton Communicative Arts Academy folded in 1975. Closure was the result of processes familiar to cultural activists and arts administrators nationwide. A changing political climate and worsening economy reduced the availability of public and private funds. Deindustrialization and a weakening tax base aggravated by "white flight" hamstrung municipal budgets. This combination spelled the end for many organizations and forced those that survived to curtail class offerings and other programs. Concerned artists who sought to maintain a connection with local black communities could still do so, although they found fewer institutions where such efforts could take place. One survivor was the Watts Towers Art Center, the first multi-generic arts education project in South Los Angeles and the first dedicated community

FIGURE 27 Musical performance with intergenerational audience, Compton Communicative Arts Academy, not dated. Photograph by Willie Ford. Compton Communicative Arts Academy Collection, California State University, Los Angeles Library.

FIGURE 28 Julie King with trombone, not dated. Photograph by Willie Ford. Compton Communicative Arts Academy Collection. California State University, Los Angeles Library.

FIGURE 29
Performance,
Communicative
Arts Academy,
1970. Photograph
by Willie Ford.
Compton
Communicative
Arts Academy
Collection,
California State
University, Los
Angeles Library.

FIGURE 30
Women rehearsing
on stage,
Communicative
Arts Academy,
not dated.
Photograph by
Willie Ford.
Compton
Communicative
Arts Academy
Collection,
California State
University, Los
Angeles Library.

FIGURE 31
Dance class,
not dated.
Photograph by
Willie Ford.
Compton
Communicative
Arts Academy
Collection,
California State
University, Los
Angeles Library.

FIGURE 32 Paul
Robeson Players
performing *Man's
Best Friend*, not
dated. Photograph
by Willie Ford.
Compton
Communicative
Arts Academy
Collection,
California State
University, Los
Angeles Library.

FIGURE 33 Arts Academy Orchestra on stage, not dated. Photograph by Willie Ford. Compton Communicative Arts Academy Collection, California State University, Los Angeles Library.

FIGURE 34 Musical combo, 1970. Photograph by Willie Ford. Compton Communicative Arts Academy Collection, California State University, Los Angeles Library.

arts center in South Los Angeles following its founding in 1961. After 1975, the newly renovated Watts Towers Art Center again became the principal site of community arts in South Los Angeles, this time under the directorship of John Outterbridge. For the most part, those least dependent on outside funding, including the Pan Afrikan People's Arkestra, the Ebony Showcase Theater, and the Brockman Gallery, proved most adept at surviving the uncertain financial climates of the 1970s and 1980s.

Between 1960 and 1975, Los Angeles witnessed the rise of a new community of black visual and plastic artists. Comprising several dozen activist artists, this cohort shared many experiences familiar to the informal networks of underground jazz musicians and radical poets living in Los Angeles during this time. In both cases, black artists sought to develop new institutions to ameliorate financial and creative concerns. Musicians, writers, and artists alike engaged in a search for distinct means of expression rooted in the concerns, historical experiences, and pre-existing cultural lexicon of African American audiences. New institutions drew these audiences in as participants, and visual artists played a critical role in transforming the Black Arts Movement into a social movement with a mass base. Finally, the centrality of the desire to maintain a dialogue with the residents of South Los Angeles brought visual artists and musicians into contact with new social forces that viewed black expressive culture as a strategic tool for effecting a widespread transformation of South Los Angeles and the world beyond.

6

THE ARMS OF CRITICISM   The Cultural Politics
of Urban Insurgency

All art is propaganda, but not all propaganda is art.
—ATTRIBUTED TO MAO ZEDONG AND
GEORGE ORWELL AMONG OTHERS

During the fall of 1969, the two most visible black radical organizations in Los
Angeles recorded and released jazz albums. Hitting shelves even as the fratricidal feud between the US Organization and the Black Panther Party intensified,
Kawaida and *Seize the Time* represented something relatively rare. While
collaborations between musicians and activists had long been a feature of
black political life, the albums signaled an unusually direct attempt to translate ideological positions into music. The effort to produce records that would
express the competing ideals of cultural and revolutionary nationalism in
both content and form marked more than an isolated curiosity or a historical
footnote. Rather, the projects revealed the mutual recognition on the part of
competing nationalist organizations that the battle for the hearts and minds
of potential black revolutionists would be waged in no small part on the
terrain of cultural expression.

Taken together, *Kawaida* and *Seize the Time* illustrate the complex interplay
between expressive culture and black radicalism in Southern California. Although the lyrical content of the albums revealed sectarian differences over
questions of strategy and tactics, the similarities between the production and
the formal properties of the two records demonstrated the unmistakable affinities between the Black Panther Party and the US Organization. Bitterly
divided over how to achieve social transformation, the two groups viewed the
relationship between politics and art in essentially the same functionalist,

utilitarian manner. They developed a similar range of cultural practices, infusing apparel, hairstyles, and other stylistic choices with political content. Each group sought connections to established artists. The inclusion of allies who brought their own ideas about black culture, politics, and art forced each group to sharpen its ideological positions, a process that often revealed considerable differences between politically conscious artists and culturally concerned political activists. In the end, both organizations came to rely more on developing their own initiatives than on building their alliances with sympathetic outsiders. Retracing the cultural strategies and programs of black nationalist organizations thus reveals how the attempt to bring black art to black communities created different imperatives for political radicals than for either community-oriented artists or the proponents of a cultural war on poverty.

At the same time, *Kawaida* and *Seize the Time* remind us that political activists were a part of the Black Arts Movement, as well. At the time, Amiri Baraka acknowledged being deeply impressed with Karenga's seriousness, calling the focus demonstrated by US activists a "next step" compared with the Spirit House project with which Baraka was involved in Newark.[1] Ron Karenga reciprocated, suggesting that Baraka add the title "Imamu," or spiritual leader, before his name. Karenga, the founder of the group responsible for *Kawaida*, Kwanzaa, and a host of other cultural initiatives, was part of the board of directors of the Mafundi Institute, one of the largest and best-funded of community arts centers in South Los Angeles. Karenga's organization had links with a number of cultural bodies across Southern California and had been well represented in the leadership responsible for creating the Watts Summer Festival and its parallel art exhibition. As noted earlier, the Panthers were linked to the Pan Afrikan People's Arkestra, with both John Huggins and Elaine Brown performing on occasion with the band. The Panther artist Emory Douglas had contacts among Southern California's visual arts community, and cultural and political activists often hailed from the same network of neighborhoods, churches, and schools. These examples suggest, rather than exhaust, the multiple linkages between cultural and political formations present in the years after the Watts riot, and they point to a need to see patterns of cultural and political activity as inextricably linked.

This chapter examines the relationship between expressive culture and radical nationalist politics in Southern California between the Watts riot and the eclipse of widespread radical activity after 1973. Focusing on the Southern California chapter of the Black Panther Party and the Los Angeles–based US Organization, it traces how political activists viewed the relationship between expressive culture and political liberation.[2] Assessing the theorization, cultural production, and performative aspects of post-1965 activists is important for three reasons. First, doing so reminds us how and why fights over rights and resources inevitably require cultural work. Second, the cultural strategies of black radicals complicate the separation of "culture" and "politics" into distinct, sealed categories. In much the same way that cultural organizations such as the Watts Writers Workshop and the Underground Musicians Association participated in political mobilizations, coalitions, and debates, ostensibly "political" forces expended considerable effort in developing cultural complements to their visions of radical social change. Maintaining a partition between cultural and political activism is made more difficult once we recall the range of movement activities.

Finally, the "culturing" of black radicalism illustrates the limitations present in a scholarly literature dependent on terminology borrowed from movement organizations and theorists. While the academic appropriation of the terms "revolutionary" and "cultural" nationalism reflects real debates within the black liberation movement, the wholesale use of these categories fails to capture the fluidity and complexity of either those debates or the practices that accompanied them.[3] Despite the presence of contemporary accounts that challenged this bifurcation, a stark separation pervades the literature on postwar black politics in Southern California. In his study of Amiri Baraka, for example, Komozi Woodward holds that "in the aftermath of the . . . Watts Rebellion in Los Angeles, two rival political styles were generated in California: the *cultural nationalism* of us and the *revolutionary nationalism* of the Black Panther Party."[4] Gerald Horne's extensive work on the aftermath of the Watts riot identifies revolutionary, cultural, and religious nationalism, contending that the latter two emerged to fill a vacuum left by the decline of the Communist Party–led left.[5] Manning Marable's critical and wide-ranging study of postwar black politics critiques, yet ultimately uses, the terminology of revolutionary and cultural nationalism, as well.[6] Yet anti-imperialist internationalism and collective economic strategies held a central place for religious and cultural forces as surely as they did for those who openly identified with Marx and Mao. During the early 1960s, the Nation of Islam's weekly paper, *Muhammad Speaks*, offered widespread coverage of national liberation struggles throughout the world. Ron Karenga's us Organization opposed the Vietnam War, advocated draft resistance, and called for a violent social revolution aimed at generating a system of economic cooperation among blacks. At the same time, Black Panther cultural politics were far more than "an unrelenting barrage . . . to bludgeon black people into adopting their politics and joining their revolution."[7] As we shall see, the Panthers' approaches toward culture demonstrated flexibility and forethought, as evidenced by the breadth of their collaborations, while offering an overall cultural policy in line with the party's broader para-statist orientation. Ignoring the limitations of the categories of cultural and revolutionary nationalism generates a form of historical incomprehension that stifles our understanding of the chronology, contours, and concerns of postwar black radicalism.

ELEMENTS OF STYLE

Style is the area in which the opposing definitions clash
with most dramatic force.

—DICK HEBDIGE

In the predawn hours of 8 December 1969, several hundred Los Angeles police officers launched simultaneous raids on three of the four field offices of the Black Panther Party in Los Angeles.[8] The main office, located on the busy Central Avenue thoroughfare that had once served as the epicenter of jazz on the West Coast, absorbed particular violence. Using assault rifles, armored vehicles, and other tactical military equipment, police unleashed a daylong attack on the mostly teenage occupants of the building. Refusing to surrender until it was clear that the hundreds of spectators gathered beyond police lines would provide some measure of protection against summary execution in the street, thirteen Panthers traded fire with the police for nearly five hours before laying down their weapons.

All charges against the Panthers arrested that Monday morning would eventually be dropped. The destruction of the central headquarters, however, would mark a turning point in the local fortunes of the organization. In the three years between the founding of the Southern California chapter and the destruction of the central office at the hands of the police, the Los Angeles chapter, like Black Panther Party chapters elsewhere, had developed a wealth of ideas, initiatives, and programs aimed at fostering a community-based, internationalist, and anti-imperialist vision. As with most successful radical projects, the Panthers acted as if this transformation was already underway. Police monitoring projects, breakfast and elder-care programs, anti-narcotic campaigns, and arts projects were all part of a para-statist orientation that sought to provide an alternative model of how black life might be organized in the absence of a directly repressive state. Indeed, Nikhil Singh attributes the

FIGURE 35 Aftermath of the police raid on Black Panther Party headquarters, 4100 block, Central Avenue, Los Angeles, circa December 1969. Los Angeles Times Photographic Archive (Collection 1429), Department of Special Collections, Charles E. Young Research Library, University of California, Los Angeles.

violent repression of the Panthers in significant part to the challenge they offered to the idea of the American state either as a legitimate source of coercive authority or as a guarantor of the survival of citizens. Such a view helps explain why the police often seemed as incensed by the party's breakfast program as by the specter of armed blacks confronting patrolmen on the street. Faced with a rapidly growing social movement that pointed out to people that what political scientists called "the monopoly on the legitimate use of force" was little more than bureaucratically organized murder, the government swung into action. Activists across the country found themselves hunted by city, state, and federal police, and in the aftermath of the raid in December, the Los Angeles Panthers rapidly went from "seeing like a state" to running for their lives.[9] As the incarcerated New York Panther Dhoruba Bin Wahad told Ward Churchill, "We'd achieved a genuine mass base of support for our organization. But people were scared. Nobody wanted to go to jail for a million years or become just another pop-up target for the death squads. . . . People began to distance themselves from us. They saw it as a matter of self-preservation."[10]

Revisiting the style of the Black Panther Party illustrates how and why the organization became both a leading element of the postwar black liberation movement and a main target for government repression. In his landmark study of postwar English youth, Dick Hebdige writes of youth subcultures as providing "an oblique challenge to social consensus."[11] This challenge, based on an internal language of recognizable signs, acquires political import partially through its demolition or repudiation of the symbols of everyday order and their replacement with an improvisational bricolage. Although Hebdige's primary concern rests with teasing out sublimated forms of politics that take place in the absence of widespread movements for change, his framework adapts easily to situations of mass political activity. Recalling that a generational loss of respect for the symbols of authority was a central feature of the 1960s illustrates the connection between, for example, the Sex Pistols' determined vandalizing of the Queen's picture and the depictions of Nixon and Uncle Sam as bloodsucking vampires. Order requires its symbols, and the demolition of the indices of authority was a harbinger of the collapse of authority in Watts, Chicago, Kent State, or Orangeburg. From this point of view, the politics of style signified the rupture from which a new politics would emerge.[12]

For the Panthers, however, rejecting outdated images of colored servitude or Negro quiescence wasn't enough. Jane Rhodes writes powerfully of the determined effort at self-representation made by the Black Panther Party, noting how imagery and language formed core parts of the group's effort to demonstrate the fissures opening within American society.[13] Nikhil Singh describes the Black Panther Party's affinity for the political use of deliberately cultivated spectacle, from the occupation of the California State Capitol building by armed activists to the more commonplace monitoring of police patrols. In the context of widespread resistance to both American foreign policy and the bureaucratic administration of domestic life, the Panthers "revealed black visibility as the defining antithesis of national subjectivity in the United States."[14]

While the Panthers proved particularly adept in its use, they hardly pioneered this politics of performativity. Wartime boppers and zoot suiters, after all, had offered a similar rejection of the purportedly national ideals of sacrifice, patriotism, and conformity.[15] Two decades later, this "style warfare" had become characteristic of the black liberation movement as a whole. Along with musicians, athletes, and other icons of popular culture, urban radicals were recognized as initiators of new patterns of behavior and belief that captured the imaginations of millions of African Americans.[16] Indeed, radical organizations grew in part because they were able to make participation in political activism a precondition of accessing blackness. On the other side of the ledger, being seen as beyond the stylistic pale often meant marginality and ridicule, as when Jesse Jackson and Carl Stokes criticized Newark's mayoral candidate Kenneth Gibson as dangerously ignorant of the appearance and ethos required of candidates trading on black aspirations for municipal control. Denigrating both his short haircut and unfashionable shoes, Jackson and Stokes warned Gibson that winning a contested election required that "he slick up a bit."[17]

In Southern California, however, being slick could come at a price. For more than a half-century, the clash between nonwhite youth and police has been a central element of the racial order of everyday life. Three major moments of local urban unrest—the zoot-suit riots of June 1943, the Watts uprising of August 1965, and the Rodney King rebellion in April 1992—came as a direct result of police violence directed at minority youth. As a result, considerable scholarly attention has been devoted to explicating the seemingly intractable conflict between the Los Angeles Police Department (LAPD) and nonwhite youth. But the zoot-suit riots, the Watts uprising, and the Rodney King rebellion illustrate a different sort of continuity, as well, since wartime debates regarding the purportedly "unpatriotic" zoot suiters, the alleged "delinquency" of Watts youth, and, above all, the "gang" menace of the mid-1980s all touched on the relationship between clothing, youth behavior, and social order.[18] For the police, charged by an anxious citizenry with policing the internal racial boundaries of a city defined in part by the automotive mobility of its residents, a preoccupation with the physical appearance, clothing, hand gestures, and other coded communications of young people remains an integral part of a policing project invariably discussed using the language of counterinsurgency. For the policed, by contrast, the dialectic between cultural practices and ongoing repression forms a centerpiece of the "dispositions acquired through experience" that condition and structure patterns of urban living.[19] In a city where what you wear can get you frisked, beaten, or killed, clothes and hairstyles, custom cars and urban gaits (from the Slauson shuffle to the Crip walk) are a testament to the materiality of culture.

Both the possibilities and limitations of black style politics can be seen in the case of hair. For the period under discussion here, no single symbol conjures the symbolic protest politics of the post-1965 period like the Afro, or "natural." In popular memory and contemporary parlance, the natural serves as the pre-eminent marker of black solidarity, radical affiliation, and the tenor of the times. Of course, as observers have pointed out, such a view is beset by numerous problems. In a fascinating essay, Kobena Mercer notes the falsity of many of the basic assumptions that attend the style. Hairstyles, he argues, are "never just natural" but always "stylistically cultivated and politically constructed in a particular historical moment." Moreover, the rapid passage of the natural from symbol of rebellion to a marketable commodity raises the issue of whether or not the "nature" invoked by the "natural" was less a potential space of autonomy from Western values than "an ideologically loaded idea created by binary and dualistic logics within European culture itself."[20] As arguably the figure most associated with the style, Angela Davis has decried the reduction of the radical complexity of the time, lamenting that the nostalgic appropriation of the Afro has led to an ahistorical and depoliticized "politics of fashion."[21] Robin Kelley's historicization of the natural challenges the automatic association between radical politics and the hairstyle, noting that the commonsense association between the Afro and the post-1966 black power period ignores successive phases, from a "partial origin in bourgeois high fashion circles" through an early association with a pre-1966 bohemian anticolonial arts community of women that included figures such as Nina Simone, Miriam Makeba, Abbey Lincoln, Odetta, and Margaret Burroughs.[22]

These are important contextualizations that offer a multifaceted caution against taking any given cultural practice as a straightforward form of political resistance. At the same time, Mercer, Kelley, and Davis agree in recognizing black bodies as one of the key places where black politics happens. In seeking to answer the question, "Why do we pour so much energy into our hair?" Mercer argues that hairstyling constitutes "a popular art form articulating a variety of aesthetic 'solutions' to a range of 'problems' created by ideologies of race and racism."[23] In his discussion of the natural, Kelley maintains that attention to both the style and the "texts" that surround it reveal the natural as its own site of politics, beset with struggles over meaning, markets, representation, and economic control.[24] While we should take pains to avoid a politics of style that reduces hair, or clothes, or dances, or songs, to representations of rebellion or substitutes for mass politics, all can be seen as sites of actual struggle wherein the material and symbolic interconnect.

For the emerging cohort of black radicals active in Los Angeles after 1965, the subcultural structures of clothing, personal stylization, and naming were key aspects of the radical turn. Indeed, what Gerald Horne terms "the new leadership" was novel in part because its style departed so forcefully from existing modes of "Negro" leadership. The Black Panther Party's dark sunglasses, leather jackets, and berets contrasted with the shaved heads, carved amulets, and neo-African garb of the US Organization, as well as with the

FIGURE 36 H. Rap Brown and Ron Karenga at a Black Power rally, 14 August 1967. Los Angeles Times Photographic Archive (Collection 1429), Department of Special Collections, Charles E. Young Research Library, University of California, Los Angeles.

pressed suits and bowties of the Nation of Islam. Each group sought to develop a clearly identifiable uniform. In addition to apparel, changing naming patterns became a common element of the rhetorical practice of black nationalism. During the 1950s, the Nation of Islam had popularized the practice of dispensing with surnames, characterizing them as the unwelcome inheritance of enslavement. Taking new names recalled blues and jazz traditions, gangster movies, street life, and the broader milieu of Third World radicalism. US activists chose mostly Swahili names meant to symbolize their affiliation with an East African lingua franca in a manner consistent with their Pan-African aims, while the monikers of Panther cadres conjured up folk traditions (Michael "Zinzun"), domestic resistance figures (Elmer "Geronimo" Pratt), and international revolutionary solidarity ("Toure" Pope).

These practices were national in scope. At the same time, local cultural geography made particular contributions to the development of nationalist style politics on the part of African Americans. Many of the nicknames acquired by local activists had their genesis in the street life of area gangs. The Panther leader "Bunchy" Carter and the SNCC activist "Crook" Wilkins had belonged to separate sets within the Slauson gang. Then, as now, gangs often served as the incubators of stylistic innovation in Southern California. The

FIGURE 37 Black Muslim women at a Communicative Arts Academy event, 1970. Compton Communicative Arts Academy Collection, California State University, Los Angeles Library.

Slausons, based several miles north of Watts, maintained a number of distinct cultural practices that included styles of dress, hand signals, and a dance step. All were eventually commemorated on a record called *The Slauson Shuffle*. The hand signal of Watts-based gangs, typically formed by tucking the thumb while crossing the middle and index finger to create a "W" shape, increasingly became popularized as a way to symbolize support for the Watts riot.[25]

As contemporary observers noted, former members of these street gangs participated disproportionately in post-rebellion nationalist organizations. The riot and its aftermath led to a near-cessation of violence between black gangs, with conflict resuming with the decline of nationalist radicalism during the early 1970s.[26] Members of the Watts-based Businessmen and Sons of Watts gangs developed close working relationships with political and cultural activists in Watts, including Karenga, and the Sons of Watts provided security for the inaugural Watts Summer Festival, held on the first anniversary of the riot.[27] On at least one occasion, Slausons intervened when whites began beating an interracial group of protesters seeking to integrate a local diner, while the Slauson set leader Bunchy Carter brought dozens of former gang members with him into the Southern California chapter of the Black Panther Party, at one point taking almost an entire teen post into the organization.[28]

Ron "Crook" Wilkins, a member of the Student Non-Violent Coordinating

Committee and former Slauson, helped form the Community Alert Patrol (CAP), an organization that illustrates the link between style, Southern California's unique car culture, and the counter-hegemonic aspects of black radical performance. Founded as an oversight agency shortly after the rebellion, CAP became the first in a long line of community-based anti-police-brutality organizations in South Los Angeles. In a city where police malfeasance was among the most common complaints of local residents, CAP activists armed with two-way radios and legal codes tailed police cruisers in a highly visible challenge to the behavior and legitimacy of the authorities.[29]

Cars were more than a means of transportation for CAP activists. Wilkins maintained both a 1938 Plymouth and a 1931 De Soto. Before using his cars to monitor the police, Wilkins had been a member of a car club limited to owners of pre–Second World War vehicles.[30] During 1966, the group wrote grants seeking funding to open a garage and body shop in an effort to use funds available for job training to further their political organizing and police-monitoring activities. The members of CAP stenciled "To Protect and Observe" on the sides of their rides, turning Oldsmobiles and Buicks into customized symbols of alternative authority. CAP cars illustrated the extent to which popular culture had the ability to envision alternative social relations. In addition to appropriating the phrase "to protect and to serve" from the panels of LAPD squad cars, CAP activists placed lights and sirens on their cars and sometimes followed police through red lights. Law-enforcement officials considered such behavior highly offensive. In addition to arguing before Congress that CAP members were armed, dangerous, and subversive, police and municipal officials sought to block the disbursement of Office of Economic Opportunity funds to the group.[31]

Police-monitoring projects are emblematic of the intricate linkage between culture and politics that was at the heart of black nationalist organizing in Los Angeles. For some, the specter of customized cars shadowing the LAPD across the wide boulevards and through the narrow alleys of South Los Angeles might be taken as a form of guerrilla theater that had little lasting impact. Certainly, neither the Community Alert Patrol nor the Black Panther Party was rewarded with legislation confirming the right of concerned citizens to follow the police around to ensure that the police performed their duties in compliance with the law. But to evaluate these efforts purely on the basis of their outcome is to miss both the intent and the effect of the aestheticized practice of black power. For black Angelenos, the politics of style symbolized by berets and leather jackets, Afros and shaved heads, and customized cars constituted a step toward self-definition that led logically to programs aimed at curtailing the power of what they considered an oppressive state. To be sure, the public display of firearms and the tailing of police cruisers were often theatrical. But, then, most guerrilla armies consider armed propaganda a fundamental part of political organizing. Critics of cultural politics and those who see civil rights or liberal democracy as the only appropriate framework for political conduct inside the United States simply cannot comprehend the effect—on participants or spectators—that efforts such as CAP's had on working-class African Americans for whom humiliating traffic stops were a feature of everyday life.

As in the broader range of cultural politics from which they are drawn, the elements of style and the politics of performance are shifting, open to multiple interpretations, and hard to pin down. Guerrilla tactics always are. Emerging as a multilayered radical style, police-monitoring projects, free breakfast programs, and the open display of firearms offered an insistent inversion of official monitoring and coercive powers that the state found difficult to ignore. The counter-hegemonic activities of black activists succeeded partially because of their cultural dimensions. The public display of arms was made more alarming by the presence of uniforms that suggested an alternative social order. Breakfast programs were simultaneous spaces of music and dance, and J. Edgar Hoover considered Panther propaganda effective enough that the FBI spent both time and money circulating fake newspapers and children's books in an effort to damage the party's image.[32]

At the same time, the styles adopted by Black Power activists formed only one part of a larger vision of the relationship between aesthetic and political liberation. As terms such as "self-determination" began to gain wider currency among working-class African Americans, a wide-ranging debate on the place of art within a changing African America emerged. Among activists eager to distinguish themselves from competitors, the place of cultural politics within the struggle for social transformation constituted a central preoccupation even as cultural practices became one of the primary ways to distinguish between rival claims of radical leadership. Examining these ideas provides an important link between the politics of style and the larger push for self-determination.

THEORIZING REVOLUTIONARY CULTURE

The cultural politics of black nationalism transcended the stylistic and performative. Both the Black Panther Party and the US Organization devoted considerable energy to theorizing the relationship between cultural transformation and political struggle. These arguments became critical to their unfolding internecine struggle and to the cultural initiatives that both developed after 1965. Revisiting them illustrates the centrality of cultural politics within a larger moment of urban insurgency.

From its local origins in Oakland, California, the Black Panther Party for Self-Defense grew into one of most important radical movements in U.S. history. Although the Black Panther Party was never as deeply folded within the fabric of everyday organizing as SNCC, lacked the strategic clarity of the League of Revolutionary Black Workers, and cannot be said to have pioneered Third Worldist Marxism among African Americans (a distinction that belongs to the Revolutionary Action Movement), the Panthers became arguably *the* emblematic expression of 1960s-era black radicalism. The party grew more rapidly than any black organization had since the Universal Negro Improvement Association, expanding from thirty-one members in May 1967 to more than ten thousand active participants by the end of 1969. Chapters could be found in twenty-six states, the District of Columbia, and more than a few foreign nations. The Panthers' rise to national prominence can be explained in a number of ways, from their skillful manipulation of the national media to their style politics and the manner in which they posed new answers to long-standing challenges facing a minoritized, subject population. Yet while the Black Panther Party was national in scope, critical variations shaped the particular orientation of chapters and branches in distinct locales. These ran the gamut, with international connections, media strategies, gender relations, military tactics, and cultural patterns showing sufficient variety that one might well conclude that the Panthers themselves are best seen less as an organization than as a movement in their own right.[33]

Although the Black Panther Party is remembered today primarily for its social-service programs and armed activism, attempts to forge a radical culture formed a centerpiece of its theory and practice. As self-defined "revolutionary nationalists," the Black Panthers sought to foster a "revolutionary culture" that would emerge in the course of political struggle. Culture was thus envisioned both as a process and as an outcome. Emory Douglas, the party's minister of culture, linked the two, claiming that the party's survival programs heralded a new form of cooperation that would assist in fostering new relationships between individuals and communities. In addition to changing interpersonal relationships, this struggle would transform cultural production. "Out of the struggle for liberation," Douglas continued, "comes a new literature and art."[34] George Murray, the party's minister of education, expressed similar sentiments, defining black culture as the totality of creative output of black people while arguing that only those elements that contributed to political struggle would be retained. Murray took a section of "Listen Here" by Eddie Harris as an illustration, noting, "Where you hear actual screams coming from a Black Saxophone, those are the battle cries of mad, crazy black men."[35]

The idea of a liberation *art* that would form part of a broader liberation *culture* was a central idea within the Black Panther Party even before the founding of the Southern California chapter. Although he figures less prominently than Huey Newton, Eldridge Cleaver, and Bobby Seale, the graphic artist Emory Douglas was both an early member of the party and present at many of its most memorable events, including the armed demonstration at the California State Capitol building and the standoff with rival militant groups over the protection of Malcolm X's widow, Betty Shabazz. Moreover, although the Panthers are rarely linked directly to the Black Arts Movement, Douglas had been a student activist in the San Francisco State University Black Student Union, where he had studied theater with Amiri Baraka and come into contact with critical Black Arts Movement figures. And while the subsequent expansion of sectarian differences would divide many Panthers from former colleagues, Douglas had been part of a Bay Area black arts scene that included Sonia Sanchez, Marvin X, and the editors of the influential literary journal *Soulbook*. The Panthers' ideas about a liberation art that would transcend racial and national communities thus developed precisely in the context of both the intercultural radicalism of San Francisco and under the tutelage of several of black America's most visible cultural nationalists.[36]

Resistance formed the centerpiece of this new revolutionary art. Douglas, responsible for the vast majority of images circulated by the organization and for a majority of party statements on cultural affairs, published more than a dozen articles discussing the relationship between art and politics.[37] Conceding that his visual works were essentially propagandistic, Douglas argued that the role of the black artist was twofold. On the one hand, art had the power to educate by "giving the people the correct picture of our struggle." Douglas saw his images as helping to "create an atmosphere" where "the vast majority of black people" would "feel they have the right to destroy the enemy." Noting elsewhere that "revolutionary art gives a physical confrontation with tyrants," Douglas argued that art formed an integral element to the important counterhegemonic work of community-service programs and armed confrontations with the police.[38]

This culture of resistance was global. From its inception, issues of the *Black Panther* included pages of revolutionary poetry drawn from sources outside the United States. The paper reprinted the works of activists and poets from abroad, including poems by Nicolas Guillén, Ho Chi Minh, and Mao Tse-tung. This global culture of resistance was compared to a narrow, racially based affinity with Africa. An essay titled "The True Culture of Africa and Africans" featured four pages of photographs taken at guerrilla base camps in Angola, Mozambique, Guinea-Bissau, and Zimbabwe. The text of the article discussed educational programs, agricultural achievements, and the development of the armed struggle against the Portuguese and Rhodesians. Absent, however, was any discussion of the cultural dimensions of these struggles, despite the fact that—at least in the case of Guinea-Bissau—conceptions of cultural transformation had been of primary theoretical import to the revolutionary leadership offered by Amilcar Cabral. In the pages of the *Black Panther*, the position that blacks "have no nation without a fight against those who oppress us [and] no culture but a culture born of our resistance" held true on both sides of the Atlantic.[39]

Party writings on culture thus subordinated both content and theory to the command of politics. Form followed function. Holding that "the types of skills that can be useful to the world liberation movement are as varied as the skills employed in the complexity of this society," Frank Jones argued that only the development of revolutionary ideology allowed the successful deployment of individual creativity. In the context of art, this required that "politics guide the brush." Recognizing that many artists felt uncomfortable with the limitations certain to emerge from this policy, Emory Douglas denied that revolutionary art required any greater sacrifice than drawing for the oppressor did. Perhaps recognizing that this contention might not find universal agreement, he advocated for a "united front" of art whereby artists would devote a particular amount of their energy to the type of artwork the Black Panther Party considered useful.[40]

Although the cultural theory and production of the Black Panther Party has been criticized as dogmatic and unpopular, the party's notions of revolutionary art actually shared many features with the ideas and cultural production of community-oriented artists who were not members of nationalist organizations. Both groups held, for example, that galleries were ill-suited as spaces for the exhibition of consciously black art. Douglas's contention that "the gallery for revolutionary art becomes the streets themselves" was similar in effect to David Hammons's practice of spontaneously creating junk sculp-

FIGURE 38 Black Panther Party field office, reopened following the LAPD raid, December 1969. From left to right: Virginia Harris, her daughter Kerrie, Bob Duren, and Steve Harris (on the phone). *Herald Examiner* Collection, Los Angeles Public Library.

tures on the street corners and in the alleyways of South Los Angeles, or, for that matter, the coterminous proliferation of muralism championed by Judy Baca and other Chicano activists across Los Angeles. In addition to physically seeking to locate art on the walls, sidewalks, and telephone poles of urban areas, Douglas and other party cultural theoreticians contended that any relevant art should emerge from the community itself. This view created common ground with artists such as John Outterbridge, Noah Purifoy, and Betye Saar, whose vision of black culture rested in part on the inclusion of physical elements from the community and who dedicated a significant measure of their time to participating in arts education projects. Prioritizing the communicative and educational aspects of art over the notion of creativity as the expression of a privately held truth created a measure of common ground between nationalist radicals and community-oriented artists. Such was the impression of Outterbridge, who, asked to evaluate the impact of political radicals on his art, made the observation noted earlier that "in a way, we were all Panthers."[41]

Beyond seeking to consolidate a common program among politicized African Americans, the members of the Black Panther Party concerned with group cultural policies took steps to build links with prospective allies. Addressing the simultaneity inherent in the imagined community of a revolutionary globe in formation, party activists proposed the existence of a nonracial culture rooted in the global process of political resistance. Arguing that "solidarity with the revolutionary people all over the world has brought about a common culture to people who know nothing of each other," the Panthers sought a cultural approach mirroring their belief in the efficacy and necessity of interethnic coalitions. Douglas held that "this new born culture is not peculiar to the oppressed Black masses but transcends communities and racial lines."[42]

The concept of a culture of resistance that transcended racial sentiment was used to distance the Black Panther Party from ideological rivals who rejected cooperation with whites. During 1967 and 1968, elements of the Black Panther Party were conducting merger talks with SNCC and working in Los Angeles with both SNCC and US. At the time, both SNCC and US refused contacts with predominantly white organizations, and efforts to forge an ongoing coalition between elements of the three organizations stalled. The collapse of merger efforts and the outbreak of violent hostilities between US and the Black Panther Party during the first months of 1969 led to a rise in the publication of attacks on figures and practices seen as the primary threat to the growth and vanguard status of the Black Panther Party.[43]

Cultural nationalists were the primary targets of this ire. Invective and caricature were used to ridicule those who argued that learning Swahili, wearing African clothes, or taking new names served a valid political purpose. In the midst of a worsening internecine context, cultural manifestations of black radical sentiment were increasingly seen as wrongheaded or even counter-revolutionary. While conceding that "the police fear brothers and sisters who wear naturals," George Murray nonetheless countered that no matter how beautiful the natural, it could never convey the liberating potential of a gun. Frantz Fanon's argument for a strategic essentialism rooted in his belief that cultural nationalism formed almost an inevitable state in the development of black radical consciousness was rejected, and Huey Newton, Bobby Seale, and David Hilliard expended considerable energy attacking what they identified as cultural nationalism within and beyond the organization. The tenor and tone of party attacks on cultural nationalism revealed the party's recognition that ignoring the widespread diffusion of evocations of black pride throughout African America threatened the group's status as the most advanced segment of the black liberation movement. Noting that black pride had become the order of the day, Emory Douglas argued, "The question confronting Black people today is not whether or not he or she is 'Black,' but whether he or she is a revolutionary." In this formulation, the cultural nationalist Ron Karenga was no more revolutionary than others who had gone on record as supporting a vaguely defined black power, a list that included James Brown, François "Papa Doc" Duvalier, and even President Richard Nixon.[44]

Although the Black Panther Party succeeded in marginalizing US, the depoliticization of cultural nationalism cost revolutionary nationalists as well. Divorcing the development of revolutionary consciousness from the cultural heritage of a given people went against the grain of the organization's most important intellectual influences. Figures such as Frantz Fanon, Che Guevara, and Mao Zedong had elsewhere written about the importance of national culture in developing revolutionary sentiments, and party theoreticians noted the importance of culture to the movements with which the Panthers sympathized. Although he observed that the Palestine Liberation Organization, Cuba, North Vietnam, and other Third World forces all possessed "some type of revolutionary art" grounded in the extant traditions of their people, Douglas spent little energy examining the content of these projects. Other activists sympathetic to armed struggle, socialism, and Third World solidarity took issue with the Panthers' strident bifurcation of cultural and political radicalism. Ernest Allen, writing in *Negro Digest*, denied that culture and nationalism could be separated, arguing that the revolutionary struggle for state power would require cultural policies and practices. Allen further warned that denunciations of cultural nationalism might easily become a generalized attack on both black nationalism and black culture.[45]

For one thing, it was easy to see the Black Panther Party adopting unmistakable elements of precisely the sort of cultural nationalism they criticized their rivals for adopting. Ignoring criticism from the Party's Oakland-based founders, New Yorkers such as Assata Shakur, Dhoruba Bin Wahad, Sundiata Acoli, and Sekou Odinga took African and Muslim names and commonly wore African-style clothing. Such practices were only partially explained by Harlem's longstanding and complicated nationalist traditions. Californians displayed similar proclivities, as demonstrated by "Masai" Hewitt and "Toure" Pope. The most commonly reproduced image circulated by the Black Panther Party leadership in Northern California featured a uniformed Huey Newton seated in a wicker chair holding a spear in one hand. Another commonly sold image, attributed to Douglas but based on an earlier print by the Cuban graphic artist Lazaro Abreu, depicted a woman clad in traditional African regalia balancing an infant and a rifle. The cumulative effect of these practices was a recurring strategic essentialism aimed at channeling growing

African affinities among U.S. black people into the desired revolutionary framework.

Such imagery, contested within the ranks of the Black Panther Party, constituted the sine qua non of the group's primary ideological rivals. Cultural nationalism, a fluid and shifting set of ideas and practices with a long history in African American life, became increasingly identified between 1966 and 1969 with the US Organization. Under the philosophical banner of what Karenga termed Kawaida, members wore African clothing, studied Swahili, took African names, adopted dietary restrictions, and otherwise sought to convey their participation in a transoceanic African culture. Under the guidance of Karenga, US argued that a cultural shift away from adherence to white beliefs and norms was a precondition of black social advancement. Decrying elements solidly entrenched within African American culture, Karenga argued that black cosmetic preferences, Christian religiosity, and linguistic dependence on English revealed the outlines of a white cultural hegemony that would continue to enthrall African Americans. Repudiating this domination was envisioned through a process in which the changing of ideas would lead logically to a change in social reality. The contours of this prospective transformation were encapsulated in seven principles known as Nguzo Saba that covered issues of faith, self-determination, collective work, collective economics, purpose, creativity, and unity. This common set of values would be developed through daily practices and through the acceptance of newly developed mythology, history, and ethos.[46]

Although one might take Karenga's focus on consciousness over conditions as evidence of a neo-Platonic, or perhaps Hegelian, approach to change, it is not too difficult to see the intellectual outlines of a certain Sardinian in his thinking as well. In his landmark study of the US Organization, Scot Brown argues that Karenga adopted a Leninist approach to building a vanguard party that stood in marked contrast to the more open recruiting process of the Panthers. While this view captures the difference in how each group organized among prospective new members, it is worth recalling that Karenga emerged from the same Revolutionary Action Movement–affiliated study group that included critical figures such as Huey Newton, Ernie Allen, and Cedric Robinson.[47] This gave Karenga at least a passing familiarity with Marxist thought explored in a structured context—something that few of most influential Panthers in Los Angeles initially had.[48] To the extent that both the Panthers and US adopted a "subjectivist" position toward revolutionary possibility—a view that put them, as Robin Kelley and Betsy Esch note, in the mainstream of those postwar movements that looked to Cuba, China, and other sites of "impossible" revolution—both sides of the revolutionary–cultural nationalist divide might be said to have displayed an unacknowledged engagement with Western Marxism.[49] This was a point that was somewhat obvious at the time, given the ties between figures such as Angela Davis and Herbert Marcuse, the attempt to concretize a theory of revolt that could include both the Third World and the dissent of white youth on two continents, and the lingering presence of figures such as Jean-Paul Sartre and Jean Genet on the periphery of black radical activity.

In the case of the US Organization, the insistent attack on hair straightening, Christian faith, Western clothes, and the English language formed part of a real effort at what Ngugi wa Thiong'o calls "decolonizing the mind."[50] That doing so became seen as an either–or proposition when placed against the parallel need to end police terror in black communities partly explains why the revolutionary organizations of the 1960s are no longer around. In contrast to those in other sites of protracted resistance—Northern Ireland and Palestine provide perhaps the best comparisons—black activists in the United States proved unable to unite armed struggle, class analysis, and cultural nationalism. With the acuity of hindsight, it is easy to see how Karenga, like the Panthers, was engaged in a search for a means by which the implicit assumptions of the dominated could be revealed as a step toward breaking with "the 'spontaneous' consent given by the great masses of the populations to the general direction imposed on social life by the dominant classes."[51] Put another way, both Karenga and the Panthers were engaged in struggling for cultural hegemony within the world of black nationalist radicalism.[52]

Karenga sought both the widespread diffusion of his ideas on art and the establishment of links with artists and cultural activists sympathetic to cultural nationalism. Many artists demonstrated a relatively generalized interest in the particular ideological principles expounded upon by US, lauding the organization's practice of granting creative personalities respect and deference, even as they expressed reservations regarding the more inaccessible particularities of the group's political line. Such was the view of Amiri Baraka, who became closely affiliated with Karenga after their initial meeting in 1967. As Baraka noted in his autobiography, this affiliation proved mutually beneficial. The doctrine of *Kawaida* provided an organizational framework for the sort of cultural nationalism Baraka sought to develop in San Francisco, Harlem, and Newark, while a link to one of black America's most influential voices—and the organization he directed in Newark—allowed US to claim the status of a national organization for the first time.[53]

Karenga spread his notions of *Kawaida* during numerous speaking tours across the United States, although the most commonly encountered organizing tool was a booklet of quotations covering his views concerning art, history, and politics. *The Quotable Karenga* served as a coincidental comment on the similarities between the US Organization and the Black Panther Party. Openly derisive of Marxist theory during this period, Karenga nonetheless cast himself in the style of one of the Black Panther Party's key intellectual sources when he bogarted his title from Mao's famous collection of aphorisms. Seemingly divided over questions of strategy and tactics, the two groups developed essentially identical positions on the relationship between aesthetics and politics. Both Douglas's short article "Revolutionary Art/Black Liberation" and Karenga's "Black Cultural Nationalism" claimed an affiliation with the ideas of the poet and activist Amiri Baraka. Both essays rejected evaluative criteria based on questions of form or the notion that artists might be involved in autonomous struggles. Both authors demanded that artists devote their creative output to nationalist political outcomes, and both argued that the measure of artistic quality should be a given work's social effect. Finally, in defining their cultural goals, both displayed a willingness to dispense with African American history and cultural traditions, Karenga in favor of a mythologized Afrocentrism and Douglas in favor of a vaguely defined socialist utopia.

Unsurprisingly, politically committed black artists criticized both views. Sometimes this criticism came as a gentle rebuke. Suzanne Jackson, for example, told an interviewer that black artists based in Los Angeles preferred Emory Douglas's personality to his art.[54] In private comments in her journal, Jackson criticized the Panthers' art as unable to acknowledge that African Americans might have creative and political views different from those advanced by the party. Jackson framed this partially as a question of political viewpoint and partially as a limitation of realist art, writing, "I'm not interested in putting in every hair and eyelash."[55] The narrow views and overbearing style of the US leadership were criticized in *Nigger Uprising*, a monthly journal of literature, politics, and visual art published by the Pasadena resident Ridhiana Saunders.[56] In a debate published in *Negro Digest*, James Cunningham, a member of the Organization of Black American Culture in Chicago, challenged Karenga's call for a "functional, collective and committed" art judged on the basis of its ultimate utility to the black revolution. Cunningham held that Karenga's argument missed the very aspect of the creative act that had revolutionary potential. This potential came not as a result of art's collective nature or social utility but precisely because it offered a path toward individual growth and change. Self-determination, Cunningham maintained, was an individual matter, while art, given its unique potential for effecting such a transformation, was inherently revolutionary.[57]

One manifestation of this supposed oversimplification was Karenga's denigration of the blues as "music of resignation." Writing a few years earlier, Karenga's erstwhile confidant Amiri Baraka had proposed the blues as a foundational pillar of working-class black ontology, a view that others have subsequently taken up.[58] Karenga, by contrast, excoriated the blues as premised on the passive acceptance of a reality that revolutionary artists sought to change. The latter position quickly proved unsustainable. Whether one saw the blues as a socially themed artistic form, as a musical idiom that provided both structure and improvisational possibilities central to black American musical and linguistic culture, or simply as a core element of the avant-garde jazz that the US Organization, like many in the black arts milieu, took as the clearest example of a revolutionary sound, it is clear that jettisoning the blues as a "music of resignation" suggested only a passing familiarity with the social and musical development of the form and the musical ideas of black artists of the time. As noted earlier, the rejection of the blues simply did not enter into the intellectual or artistic framework of Angelenos such as Horace Tapscott, Jayne Cortez, Stanley Crouch, Bob Bradford, and John Carter, all of whom referenced the blues as inspiration and as a compositional basis.[59]

Despite these difficulties, Karenga proved adept at developing links that gave the US Organization widespread access to the developing cultural infrastructure of South Los Angeles. He worked closely with the black Rhodes Scholar Stan Sanders and Tommy Jacquette, a member of the Westminster Neighborhood Association staff. Among the most visible and influential activists in South Los Angeles, Saunders and Jacquette joined Karenga and the *Los Angeles Sentinel* columnist Booker Griffin in planning the inaugural Watts Summer Festival.[60] Karenga's ideas deeply influenced Vantile Whitfield, founder and director of the Performing Arts Society of Los Angeles (PASLA), which was established as an all-black theater company. PASLA's members took African names, as was the custom with the US Organization, and were encouraged to view themselves as surrogate family. Whitfield explicitly confirmed his tilt toward cultural nationalism, telling an interviewer that he regarded PASLA as "tending to agree" with the substance of Karenga's ideas.[61] Karenga also maintained ties to Bernard Jackson and J. Alfred Cannon, professors at UCLA who co-founded the interracial Inner City Cultural Center. Together, these three co-founded the Mafundi Institute, a multi-generic space located on 103rd Street, the main commercial thoroughfare of Watts. The Mafundi Institute, in operation between 1967 and 1973, functioned as both a community arts center and a training academy for those seeking jobs in the entertainment industry. Like the Inner City Cultural Center and the Watts Writers Workshop, it attracted celebrity participation and significant foundation funding. Unlike these, however, the Mafundi Institute also held classes in history and political theory, cast itself as black rather than multicultural, and, because of the presence of members of the Sons of Watts and the US Organization, was seen as a partisan in the conflicts between nationalist organizations.[62]

PRACTICING CULTURAL REVOLUTION

Beyond seeking influence as interpreters of black culture, both US and the Southern California chapter of the Black Panther Party developed a wide range of their own cultural initiatives. The Panthers produced poetry, records, graphic images, and a film meant to foster the development of anticapitalist revolutionary sentiment. Activists affiliated with US released two albums, formed a dance troupe, and publicly celebrated newly minted holidays. The latter efforts formed part of the attempt to extend the concepts of *Kawaida* and *Nguzo Saba* into the consciousness of the residents of South Los Angeles. Both groups devoted considerable resources to their cultural production, and a discussion of the politics of black nationalism or local Third Worldism is incomplete without at least a brief assessment of these initiatives. Beyond this, the parallel nature of these projects again points to the core similarities between the two organizations. Finally, and perhaps most importantly, they demonstrate the extent to which radical organizations increasingly came to see artists as unreliable allies in the search for a revolutionary culture.

This vanguard sensibility could be seen in the cultural projects developed by US. Each member of the organization received specially made amulets incorporating multiple African motifs, visual representations of Nguzo Saba, and individualized symbols reflecting a given member's attributes or role. More visible were what Karenga termed *Dhabihu*, or holidays meant to commemorate the lives of significant persons of African descent. The first of these, held in 1966 in honor of Malcolm X, marked the public debut of the organization. The effort to make Malcolm X's birthday a holiday involved a series of political calculations, since the wave of school absenteeism that accompanied Karenga's call served as both an organizing technique and a testament to the growing influence of the group. The most successful example of *Dhabihu*, of course, is *Kwanzaa*, the weeklong festival held during the last week of the year. Observed today in millions of homes, *Kwanzaa* is perhaps the most visible celebration of African and African American culture held in the United States.[63]

Widespread support for the holiday, however, grew slowly. At the time, the group's most successful initiative was the Taifa Dance Troupe, a jointly conceptualized vision of Karenga and the South African musicians Letta Mbulu and Caiphus Semanya. Taifa, or "nation" in Swahili, grew from a mutual meeting of minds. Semanya had come into contact with African American radicals while performing at the Watts Summer Festival, and Karenga was anxious to expand his knowledge of Southern African culture. The Taifa troupe performed a modified version of the boot dance performed by South African miners. Scot Brown notes that whereas the typical instrumentation among South Africans was limited to guitars, the version developed by US incorporated congas in a Pan-African bid to link the band to the percussive traditions of West Africa and the Caribbean. These elements were further strengthened by the inclusion of a dance and chant dedicated to Shango, the Yoruba symbol of royal authority. During 1968, the dance troupe was the most visible of the organization's initiatives, performing live on the *Rosie Greer Show* as well as at the Watts Summer Festivals and appearing at a black arts festival held at the Los Angeles County Museum of Art.[64]

Musicians made two attempts to merge jazz with Karenga's blend of cultural nationalism. Both of these were first and foremost the creation of James Mtume, a student at Pasadena City College who joined the US organization soon after its founding in 1965. The biological son of the jazz musician Jimmy Heath, Mtume was the only actual member of the organization to appear on either record. Other performers appearing on *Kawaida* included Herbie Hancock, Don Cherry, Albert Heath, and Billy Bonner.[65]

Kawaida and a second album, *Alekebulan*, represented an attempt to link cultural nationalism and free jazz. The use of collective improvisation, extreme saxophone registers, shifting and open rhythmic patterns, and nontraditional instruments (the first song on Kawaida, dedicated to Amiri Baraka, used only wooden flutes) showed a group working within parameters commonly associated with free jazz. Cognizance of the difficulties posed by the attempt to convey a specific ideological message within an instrumental form led to the inclusion of vocal tracks. The song "Kawaida," for example, featured seven freeform flutes collectively improvising against the vocal recitation of

FIGURE 39 Judson Powell and Noah Purifoy, co-directors of the Watts Towers Art Center, with Mayor Sam Yorty at Watts Easter Week Art Festival, March 25, 1967. *Herald Examiner* Collection, Los Angeles Public Library.

the seven core principles of cultural nationalist ideology developed by Karenga.[66] Other tracks featured voices muttering, shouting, or reading passages lifted directly from *The Quotable Karenga*. While these occasionally seemed overlaid on the music, the voices did at times achieve a rhythmic integration into the larger project.[67]

As was the case with the recordings of the Black Panther Party leader Elaine Brown, Mtume saw the group's creation as fulfilling an essentially political role. Mtume took steps toward making greater provision for creative innovation, noting that the "revolutionary artist" must be both musically innovative and politically dedicated. Terming his music "the continuing process of nationalist consciousness manifesting its message within the context of one of our strongest resources," Mtume warned that "music must not go so far out that it transcends the ability of the people to grasp its meaning and message." Mtume's evaluation of his own success in doing this was absent in his essay. Also missing was a discussion of precisely what message listeners were supposed to grasp, given that both *Kawaida* and *Abelekutan* were primarily in-

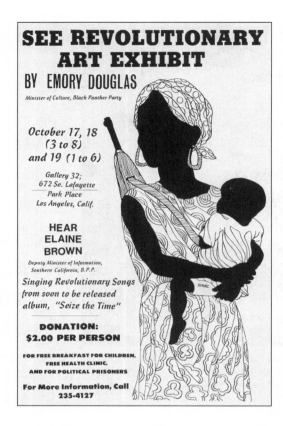

SEE REVOLUTIONARY
ART EXHIBIT
BY EMORY DOUGLAS
Minister of Culture, Black Panther Party

October 17, 18
(3 to 8)
and 19 (1 to 6)

Gallery 32;
672 So. Lafayette
Park Place
Los Angeles, Calif.

**HEAR
ELAINE
BROWN**

*Deputy Minister of Information,
Southern California, B.P.P.*

Singing Revolutionary Songs
from soon to be released
album, "Seize the Time"

**DONATION:
$2.00 PER PERSON**

FOR FREE BREAKFAST FOR CHILDREN,
FREE HEALTH CLINIC,
AND FOR POLITICAL PRISONERS

For More Information, Call
235-4127

FIGURE 40 Emory Douglas exhibition flyer for an event held at Gallery 32, with music by Elaine Brown, 1969. The event took place shortly before the release of Brown's collaboration with Horace Tapscott. Courtesy Center for the Study of Political Graphics.

strumental affairs broken only by statements uttered in a language foreign to nearly all African Americans.[68]

The Black Panther Party developed multiple cultural initiatives, as well. Emory Douglas's drawings formed a cornerstone of the party's political outreach. With several hundred images printed in the pages of the party newspaper, Douglas's drawings became, with the possible exception of the bodies of party activists, the most visible visual representation of the Black Panthers.[69] Douglas consistently maintained that the revolutionary potential of art demanded particular imagery. Although he described the "civil rights" art of the renowned artist Charles White as largely positive, he contended that White's imagery lacked the force required of "pictures that will make people go out and kill pigs." Holding that the advanced nature of the liberation struggle required total commitment—the Black Panther Party held that fascism had essentially arrived in the United States by 1970—Douglas maintained that the intensity of political struggle necessarily filtered down to the level of cultural production.[70]

Poetry formed another cornerstone of this effort. Readings at rallies and other events were common, with party leaders often included among the participants. Bunchy Carter was regarded as among the party's best writers, and his poems continued to attract attention following his death in February 1969. Between its inception in 1967 and 1970, the *Black Panther* newspaper generally featured a page of poetry, which included works by party members and allies such as James Forman and Stokely Carmichael. Transcriptions of lyrics taken from Elaine Brown's *Seize the Time* album were also reprinted.[71]

Brown's album represented another party initiative. Featuring compositions and arrangements by Horace Tapscott, *Seize the Time* contrasted sharply with James Mtume's *Kawaida*. While Mtume's effort sought to link cultural nationalism and the jazz avant-garde, the music on *Seize the Time* eschewed dissonance, used conventional jazz instruments, remained in steady 4/4 time, and otherwise conformed to Brown's vision of a "hard and concrete" product shorn of "abstract, esoteric messages." The production of a record without abstraction represented a definitive break with both the breadth of Horace Tapscott's work and the style of jazz commonly championed as representing a turn toward nationalist radicalism within jazz. Brown's singing overwhelmed Tapscott's subdued arrangements. With the exception of two songs, "Poppa's Come Home" and "Very Black Man," the record gravitated more toward a folk stylization than jazz or even rhythm and blues. Lyrically, the album contained anthemic expositions of party positions clearly audible over Tapscott's score. Brown cast this as the basic aim of the project, claiming, "This album won't free Elaine Brown, but it will allow us a means of expression, a new means of telling our story to the people."[72]

Jane Rhodes has described the Black Panther Party's multifaceted struggle to "tell its story" on its own terms. In her account, despite the party's skill at manipulating the terrain of public presentation, the image it sought to convey created a host of problems. Most pressing of these was the issue of armed struggle. Asserting both the right and necessity of self-defense made the Panthers an aggregate symbol of a generation. But arms breed militarism, and militarism trumps less coercive forms of politics, ensconces male domination, and turns off potential supporters who, in the words of the late Kwame Ture, may not be "ready for revolution." Certainly, listening to one of the Black Panther Party's highest-ranking women proclaiming, "We'll just have to get guns and be men," must have raised more than one pair of eyebrows. My point is not to join in the chorus of those piling on the Panthers or to posit that artists "got it" in a way that "politicals" did not. Far from it. Rather, it is worth noting the gaps—aesthetic as well as political—between the two, for they explain something about the richness of a distinct historical moment and the limitations that adhered to a social movement that was destroyed before it could recognize its ultimate potential and goals.

Thus, despite the importance of the Panther–Arkestra collaborations in the larger history of cultural and political confluence in Los Angeles, the points of divergence between Brown and Tapscott deserve illustration. By the time the pair recorded again in 1971, the musical dissonance on *Seize the Time* had become a political gap as well. Tapscott arranged Brown's second album, a self-titled offering released on Motown's spoken-word subsidiary Black Forum. Having previously distanced himself in part from the Black Panther Party by stating his aversion to violence, Tapscott expressed serious reservations regarding the song "Can't Go Back." The song, meant as a revolutionary nationalist dismissal of Afrocentric cultural nationalist views, ran against Tapscott's interest in Pan-Africanism as a musical, political, and ethno-racial framework. Brown's lyrics explicitly dismissed the idea of Africa as a home for black Americans. As Steven Isoardi writes, however, Tapscott got in the last word, punctuating the song with heavy percussion whose polyrhythmic evocation of the continent was unmistakable and concluding the song with French horns blasting notes meant to recall the trumpeting of elephants.[73]

As popular arts with broad lyrical latitude, music and poetry constituted artistic forms conducive to the promulgation of ideas regarding revolutionary nationalism. As rappers would discover a generation later, however, albums and journals operated as mediated forms in which political messages were not always sufficiently clear for an organization taking pains to distance itself from its closest competitors. Indeed, as Suzanne Jackson's comments and Horace Tapscott's compositions showed, the Panthers occasionally had to struggle with some of their closest allies on ideological questions that the party considered basic and settled. Partially as a result, the Panthers sought a more effective means of putting forth their ideas, including a cinematic collaboration with the Newsreel Collective, a predominantly white group of radical filmmakers affiliated with a breakaway faction of the Students for a Democratic Society. This represented a continuation of efforts begun in New York, Detroit, and San Francisco, where members of the collective had already produced one film, *The Black Panther*, describing the campaign to secure Huey Newton's release from prison. The L.A. film was initially meant as a documentary exposé of the differences between revolutionary and cultural nationalism. As such, it contained scenes that juxtaposed the Panthers' community-service programs with the militant pageantry of the us Organization. Featuring a soundtrack containing compositions by Ornette Coleman and Horace Tapscott, *Repression*, as the film came to be called, depicted speeches by the Southern California party leaders Elaine Brown and Masai Hewitt, footage of the free breakfast program, and the aftermath of a massive police attack on the party's Central Avenue headquarters.[74]

A number of the formal properties in *Repression* can be seen when set alongside other films that emerged within and around black Los Angeles during the 1970s. Much as Charles Burnett and Billy Woodberry would, the members of the Newsreel Collective incorporated the urban landscape as a critical component, with each offering montages of street scenes that evoke a wide range of working-class black activity within the geographic specificity of South Los Angeles. As did *Killer of Sheep*, *Repression* used nondiegetic music, nonlinear storytelling, stark black and whites, and open-frame shots to convey a sense of somber unease and foreboding. As in Larry Clark's *Passing Through*, free jazz is incorporated as an integral element in black radical politics. As Clark would do in the film featuring Horace Tapscott and Clarence Muse, the Newsreel Collective blended montages of African revolutionary struggles in an effort to cast black liberation as an inherently international prospect. In contrast to Stax Records' big-budget concert film, *Wattstax*, which offers a hyper-stylized and unbroken depiction of black unity that one commentator derided as "prefab," *Repression*, like the films of the Los Angeles school, highlights the black community as a place plagued by serious internal schisms.[75]

Indeed, much as films like *Killer of Sheep*, *Bless Their Little Hearts*, and *Menace II Society* would, *Repression* shows a community under siege. Discussions of politics are held indoors. Police invariably share the screen when the Panthers are shown outside, and with the exception of a single scene that highlights the breakfast program, most of what is shown outside conveys the appropriateness of the film's title. Archival footage shows a litany of black oppression: Field hands chop cotton, a chain gang ambles down a road, a man killed by police is carried away, unemployed men stand on a corner. The narrative of the film dovetails with the imagery. Bobby Seale is heard speaking at a funeral, warning, "We know that when you step out, and stick your neck out, you only have one thing coming." The idea of black pride as a sufficient basis for black politics is explicitly rejected, with images of Ron Karenga juxtaposed with a photo of François Duvalier, the brutal Haitian dictator known for manipulating a *noiriste* agenda of black pride. The effect is to highlight the lack of unity, the omnipresent violence, and the importance of political differences in the attempt to find a path toward political liberation.

Repression was filmed throughout 1969 and 1970. Initial treatments of the collaboration between the Black Panther Party and the Newsreel Collective focused heavily on the struggle between the Panthers and us. As noted earlier, relations between the organizations, which had been tense throughout 1967 and 1968, exploded in February 1969 when members of the us Organization shot and killed two leading figures in the Southern California Black Panther Party following a dispute over the direction of the black studies program at the University of California, Los Angeles. Spurred by an active and illegal counterintelligence operation directed by the FBI, violence between the two organizations spiraled throughout 1969 and 1970, leaving a half-dozen members of each organization dead and twice that number wounded, and forcing each group to divert further resources to security and legal defense.[76]

Widely blamed for instigating the violence, the us Organization witnessed a precipitous drop in its influence. Among the organizations denouncing Karenga's group was the Watts Writers Workshop, which published a short missive condemning us as "either traitors or fools."[77] Fear of retaliation exacerbated struggles within the organization, leading to the loss or reassignment of members. These losses directly affected us's ability to continue its cultural projects. James Mtume left the organization in 1969. Following the conviction and incarceration of Ron Karenga in June 1971, Clyde Halisi assumed the chairmanship of us, and his writing increasingly shifted from poetry to articles and pamphlets dedicated to winning Karenga's release from prison. Flaring violence also curtailed public performances by the Taifa Dance Troupe, as a majority of us members were detailed for security tasks. The overall result was a loss of prestige, membership, and initiative that saw the us Organization supplanted by efforts elsewhere as the standard bearers of organized cultural nationalism.[78]

The fortunes of the Black Panther Party in Southern California also declined sharply as a result of the conflict. Police violence played a greater role than was the case with Karenga's group, leading to persistent suspicions that members of the us Organization were in league with the FBI and local police. Police agencies in Southern California accounted for nearly half of the deaths of members of the Black Panther Party across the United States between 1967 and 1970. After 1969, Los Angeles police repeatedly raided local party strongholds, with the assault on the Central Avenue headquarters different only in its extreme severity. The combination of police repression and internecine conflict sent a significant percentage of local party members underground, and while Los Angeles maintained several active cells affiliated with the Black Liberation Army, the Black Panther Party had largely ceased aboveground operations by 1973.[79]

The decline of nationalist organizing coincided with a broader retreat of cultural activism in South Los Angeles. As the examples of Horace Tapscott, John Outterbridge, and the Watts Writers Workshop show, the radical milieu that fostered nationalist activity in Southern California provided inspiration for black artists working and living there. Black radical activity contributed to, and in turn was shaped by, the creative energy of committed artists. Although exchanges between artists and activists often forced each group to acknowledge concrete points of disagreement, interacting with movement organizations and the demands of radical activists unquestionably altered the intellectual and creative processes of Southern California's black artists. The high tide of nationalist agitation coincided with the period of greatest activity among artists concerned with the link between aesthetics and politics.

Seen from this vantage point, widespread support for radical groups could be said to have expanded the social base of black Angelenos interested in pursuing, experiencing, or producing any form of consciously "black" artistic activity. This was as true for institutions and groups sympathetic to black nationalism, such as the Underground Musicians Association and the Mafundi Institute, as it was for more ambivalent institutions, such as the Inner City Cultural Center and the Watts Writers Workshop. But while the rising tide of nationalist agitation lifted the boats of all cultural radicals, the countervailing pressures of sectarian violence and police repression carried potential danger for cultural activists. Audiences that had seen Horace Tapscott play a benefit for Angela Davis or had seen the Taifa Dance Troupe perform as part of a Black Arts Council lecture series might decide that cultural activists were somehow mixed up in the spreading violence. Or they might have decided that it was simply too dangerous to see the Pan Afrikan People's Arkestra at South Park or enroll a child in a drama workshop at the Mafundi Institute.

The decline of black cultural radicalism after 1973 illustrates something of the difficulties faced by cultural movements when the political context that shapes them dissipates. Between 1965 and 1973, black expressive culture became a highly contested site of struggle among artists as well as between revolutionary factions, liberals committed to urban reform, and local government. The combination of severe police repression and intense internal squabbling led to a precipitous collapse of the fortunes of militant organizations. Both the us Organization and the Black Panther Party, moreover, saw the bulk of their leadership killed, imprisoned, or driven into exile.

Politics and culture can shift in unison or in turn. In the case of Los Angeles, a brief set of transitional remarks helps to clarify the nature of this change. The period between 1965 and 1973 marked a distinct moment whose ending deeply altered the possibilities of a radical democratic movement toward creative and political autonomy. The devolution from Johnson's War on Poverty to Nixon's politics of "law and order" was less deadly for musicians and painters than for avowed revolutionists. The formal abandonment of the war on poverty, however, did result in a shift of funding priorities that crippled many of the most visible cultural institutions in South Los Angeles. Casualties of the period between 1972 and 1975 included many of the most successful local black arts institutions, including the Mafundi Institute, the journal *Uprising*, the Compton Communicative Arts Academy, the Watts Writers Workshop, and the Black Arts Council. Institutions that survived increasingly consolidated their offerings as funds for all manner of social spending declined. Although public funds for arts education increased during this time, the destruction of Southern California's industrial base and the migration of affluent African Americans created new challenges for resource-poor institutions serving an increasingly desperate population.

Despite the decline of political radicalism and its corresponding cultural forms, art remained critical to black politics after 1973. The election of Tom Bradley as mayor brought forward a new era in the political mobilization of African American culture. As the structures of segregation came under attack during the 1940s and 1950s, the arts were part of a common, if contested, antiracist platform. In the time of the Arkestra, Mafundi, and the Community Alert Patrol, the arts offered a platform for displaying unity and difference within a mobilized and radicalized community. In the time of Bradley, the arts would showcase the divergent fortunes of African Americans during a time of supposed progress.

PART III

Festivals
and
Funerals

AN INTIMATE ENEMY   Culture and the Contradictions of Bradleyism

When the axe came into the forest, the trees said,
"the handle is one of us."
—PROVERB

Today Mayor Bradley urged us to stay home, stay off
the streets and watch "The Cosby Show." We believe we
need this time [as] a cooling-off period . . . to remember
what our Thursday nights were like before this all began.
—JESS MARLOW, ANCHOR, NBC-TV, DURING THE
FIRST NIGHT OF THE RODNEY KING RIOTS

There is a photograph by Willie Middlebrook in the John Outterbridge papers
at the Smithsonian Institution Archives of American Art. It shows Bob Marley
standing next to Outterbridge, who was then working as the director of the
Watts Towers Art Center. With a crowd of figures in the background, and
Marley looking outside the photograph's frame, Middlebrook's composition
has the feel of a spontaneous snapshot rather than a composed piece. Intentional or not, the effect of the photo is in keeping with the nature of the event.
Marley was in Los Angeles on tour and had asked to see something of the area
that had achieved worldwide notoriety following its explosion in 1965. A tour
of the area was hastily arranged, and a stop at the Watts Towers was made.
When asked for a comment on the visit, the reggae icon replied, "It takes
millions of watts to light up the world, but only one Watts to light up Los
Angeles."

Consider a second image, from a different archive: a photograph from the
Los Angeles Times from 1980 that shows Outterbridge with thirteen Watts

FIGURE 41 Bob Marley and John Outterbridge at Watts Towers, not dated. Photograph by Willie Middlebrook, Smithsonian Institution, Archives of American Art, Washington, D.C.

Towers Art Center instructors. The group stands inside the Watts Towers site, under a seashell-encrusted concrete and metal arch. Along the right side of the frame, the art center building is visible beneath a tall tree. The photographer, Larry Davis, captured the towers as a living, vibrant site, staffed by smiling instructors whose faces reflect the multiethnic makeup of the Watts district and Los Angeles more generally. The overall sensibility is one of affirmation, an affective portrait of unity, multiculturalism, and positivity that suggests the towers as the property of the city as a whole.

Taken together, the two photos illustrate a change in the character of black cultural politics in South Los Angeles during the 1970s and 1980s. The nature of this change was both geographic and ideological, in that it made the Watts district increasingly synonymous with black Los Angeles even as it shifted the terms through which African American culture was discussed. During this time, the Watts Towers emerged as a primary locus for the celebration of black expressive culture, in no small measure as a result of a financial commitment to the site on the part of the state and municipal leadership. Taking place amidst the waning of the broader Black Arts Movement, the decline of insurgent urban politics, and the paring of cultural offerings throughout South Los Angeles more generally, the rise of the towers as a pre-eminent site of black

FIGURE 42 John Outterbridge and the staff of the Watts Towers Art Center, 1980. Los Angeles Times Photographic Archive (Collection 1429), Department of Special Collections, Charles E. Young Research Library, University of California, Los Angeles.

cultural activity illustrates the newly important role of the city government in fostering black expressive culture.

With the backing of distinct levels of municipal leadership, celebration became the primary lens for describing the cultural contributions of black Angelenos. As a general orientation, celebration called for different sorts of cultural projects than the more confrontational ones that had been prevalent in an earlier moment. Over the course of his two decades in office, Thomas Bradley and his aides developed an incorporative municipal multiculturalism in which sites such as the Watts Towers Art Center played a crucial role. This chapter explores this process. My focus in this regard is not meant to suggest that the appropriative aspects of governmental cultural policy constitute the only black arts activity in the city during this time. Far from it. The 1970s and 1980s saw continued vitality on the part of institutions like the Inner City Cultural Center, the development of a critical cinematic avant-garde, and the arrival on the scene of new poetic voices such as Wanda Coleman and Will

Alexander. But with visual artists (David Hammons), musicians (Arthur Blythe), and poets (Jayne Cortez) moving east, institutions such as the Mafundi Institute and the Watts Writers Workshop shutting their doors, and other standouts such as the Underground Musicians Association reducing their public activity, artistic partnerships with the city government are critical for understanding the dominant direction of black cultural politics on the local level after 1973.

Part of this story has been told elsewhere—namely, how the use of arts as an engine of economic growth and spatial exclusion served as a cultural corollary to the undemocratic, socially divided "carceral" city described by Mike Davis in his landmark study *City of Quartz*.[1] My analysis builds on these observations, examining how African American culture became one site where elected officials could demonstrate an affinity with and support for black residents of South Los Angeles. The narrative turns to the link between cultural policy and the architectural renovation of downtown Los Angeles. I then document the formation of a new branch of city government, the Cultural Affairs Department (CAD), and argue that the policies and proclivities of CAD combined the two central concerns of Bradley's administrations: the incorporation of minority communities and the construction of a "world city" of international renown.[2] Ultimately, the story of the Cultural Affairs Department highlights how inclusion and exclusion formed part of a dialectical exercise of power that functioned as an intermittent reinforcement capable of deflecting popular concerns while allowing unabated upward transfer of cultural and financial capital.

Thomas Bradley played a fundamental role in each part of this process. Elected in 1973, Bradley remained in office until 1993. Like Richard Daley, Henry Loeb, and Fiorello La Guardia, Bradley helped to bring about a fundamental transformation in the basic orientation of the city he governed. Roger Keil describes Bradley's tenure as marked by two central goals: a wide-ranging alliance with transnational capital and the incorporation of previously excluded minority populations into public employment at all levels.[3] For black Angelenos, particularly those with college degrees, public-service employment provided a major economic boost. Upward of one-quarter of all black men, and nearly one-third of all black women, worked in the public sector at some point during the 1970s. At the same time, Bradley presided over an economic bifurcation of black Los Angeles, with the emergence of a new middle class standing in sharp contrast to the experiences of a black working class beset by economic restructuring, the rise of the crack cocaine epidemic, and the militarized policing of the Los Angeles Police Department.[4] Thus, as in cases outside the United States, the process of "globalization" included as a central element the expansion of poverty and widening gaps along the outside ends of the socioeconomic spectrum.

For black Los Angeles, the sharp social and economic polarization during these twenty years suggests a fundamentally different political and economic moment than either the interval between the Second World War and the explosion of Watts or the radical interlude between the riot and Bradley's election eight years later. As noted in the earlier sections of this book, each of these three moments coincided with distinct patterns of cultural activism as well. In the first instance, artists played critical roles in desegregating employment and other common arenas of racial inequity. Seeking the transformation of material conditions and racial representations alike, these efforts led to new patterns of organization on the part of artists, including black-owned galleries, union activism, and novel community arts projects. After 1965, black arts activity became a mass movement in its own right as hundreds of creative personalities participated in an ongoing search for creative control, community mobilization, and aesthetic experimentation. During this time, cultural politics became increasingly central to the broader enterprise of black politics as a whole, dividing activists and artists along a number of conceptual and organizational fault lines.

Responding to vastly different political and economic circumstances, the period after 1973 looks quite different. Between Bradley's mayoral victory and his departure from office two decades later, black cultural politics moved in contradictory directions. As a kind of shorthand, these might be characterized as a "practice of celebration" and an "aesthetics of survival." These directions, I would argue, correspond to class positions within the African American population that shaped a broader sensibility toward understanding the place of African Americans within the urban setting. The first of these is the subject of this chapter, while the second subject is treated at length in chapter 8. Taken together, they illustrate a dominant fact of black political and cultural life in the aftermath of the civil-rights and black power periods: the parting of ways between the black middle class and the black poor.

THE ROUGH JEWEL

Located in the geographic center of a five-county metropolitan area whose economic activity exceeds the gross domestic product of Mexico or Australia, and where tourism employs nearly a half-million wage earners, the Watts

Towers constitute the primary—and, for some, the sole—attraction for drawing outsiders to South Los Angeles. Fodor's guidebook for Southern California calls the towers "the jewel of rough South L.A.," though they fail to make the list of "great itineraries" suggested for visitors.[5] Somewhat more bravely, the *Lonely Planet* guide to Los Angeles lists Leimert Park's arts offerings, Exposition Park's museums, and the Watts Towers as "South Central" sights worth seeing, though not before warning visitors that "gangs, drugs, poverty, crime and drive-by shootings are just some of the negative images—not entirely undeserved—associated with this district."[6] In contrast to the towers, the first two destinations can easily be reached by freeways that connect to other likely tourist destinations, and both sit within valuable real-estate zones long since subject to rapid and thoroughgoing gentrification. The towers, by contrast, stand alone, far to the south. The *Rough Guide to Los Angeles* includes a map of the city that shows the towers as the only point of interest for fifteen miles in any direction, making them easily the most isolated of suggested sights. And while the "rough" guide does suggest a trip to see the spiraling sculptures, readers are told that "Watts provides only one compelling reason to visit—and only during the day."[7]

Such prose, with all of its racist undertones, is far from unfamiliar to the residents of South Los Angeles. In his foreword to Leon Whiteson's study *The Watts Towers of Los Angles*, Mayor Tom Bradley cited the structures as a positive force in a community "known more for arson than art."[8] City Councilwoman Joan Milke Flores noted her frustration at having to respond to inquirers who inevitably brought up 1965 when she described the boundaries of her district. "What I try to express," she said," is that Watts is a community, not a riot."[9] Bradley and Milke Flores were responding in part to the perception, cited repeatedly in the *Los Angeles Times*'s commentary on the state of the city, that "the very name [of Watts] has become almost synonymous in Los Angeles with the word ghetto and the negative things it implies."[10] Much as other cities await the periodic return of cicadas, Mardi Gras parades, World Series triumphs, or other perennial events, years ending in either zero or five (1970, 1975, 1980, 1985, 1990) invariably become the occasion for a series of articles assuring readers that South Central Los Angeles continues to decline, with Depression-era unemployment, exploding gang violence, and a host of other ills (insufficient public transportation, poor public health, a lack of affordable housing) that exceed the levels present in 1965.[11]

In such a context, the existence of a recognized, if neglected, art treasure of global fame offered a unique opportunity to effect at least a partial redefini-

FIGURE 43 Watts Towers at night, 2001. Photograph by Thomas Meyer. Los Angeles Public Library.

tion of the Watts district before the city at large. The strategic utility of the towers was further facilitated by the growing dearth of alternative avenues for officially representing Watts as a center of creativity or positive action. The Watts Summer Festival, which had previously served as one forum for bringing media and spectators to South Los Angeles in a celebratory way, had declined throughout the 1970s before finally being suspended in 1985 after county officials refused to issue a permit, citing ongoing financial problems, gang violence, and declining attendance. The decline of Model Cities and Comprehensive Education and Training Act funds, as well as the aforementioned consolidation of arts offerings in South Los Angeles, further contributed to a sense that South Los Angeles was worse off culturally in 1975 or 1985 than in the years immediately preceding or following the initial revolt.

The story of the municipal acquisition and restoration of the Watts Towers highlights the twin imperatives of inclusion and containment that constituted a central element of local cultural policy between 1973 and 1992. Although municipal oversight over the Watts Towers and the Watts Towers Art Center involved few of the financial imperatives present in the formation of the Museum of Contemporary Art or the staging of the Olympic Games, the acquisition and restoration of the towers allowed Bradley to demonstrate anew a commitment to his constituents in South Los Angeles. For the towers, this meant yet another chapter in a long history of contentious external efforts to put them to some larger use. The historian Sarah Schrank charts the passage of the towers as an architectural treasure, a symbol of black Los Angeles, a public nuisance, and a tourist destination.[12] After 1975, the representational history of the towers conveys a shift from ambivalent neglect to quasi-celebration. Along the way, one finds a familiar discussion about the paucity of cultural resources in Southern California, as well as a growing metaphoric affiliation between the originality, durability, and creativity of the artwork and the surrounding neighborhood. One example, drawn from an article in the *Los Angeles Times* describing a meeting of major local cultural institutions, is typical: "The lacy, sky-clutching, arrogantly beautiful Watts Towers, sculpted from flotsam and jetsam through the sheer chutzpah of one man, are a symbol to the people of Watts."[13] What is critical to recall in revisiting this process is the extent to which the history of the representation and preservation of the Watts Towers is also a history of cultural policy—that is, of politics, choices, and debates.

But first, a description. Containing glass fragments, salvaged soda bottles, steel bars bent using nearby railroad ties for leverage, seventy thousand seashells, and more than one hundred thousand pounds of concrete, the Watts Towers were the creation of a single man, the Italian immigrant Simon Rodia, who began working on them in 1921 and labored on them for more than thirty-three years. Comprising seventeen structures in all, including seven towers, a gazebo, a ship, and a one hundred forty-foot wall, the towers occupy a triangular corner lot set amid low-slung bungalow houses on 107th Street in Watts. Bottles, fan-shaped shell patterns, and colored glass mosaics lace the sides of the site, which is dominated by two central towers that rise to a height of nearly one hundred feet. Following the completion of the towers in 1954, Rodia abandoned the project and the city, moving to a suburban area of San Francisco. For the next two decades, the towers were private property and came under municipal ownership in 1975.

Having survived repeated bouts of neglect, Rodia's spires are today regarded as a signal piece of Los Angeles's creative infrastructure. The architect and cultural critic Rayner Banham described the Watts Towers as "unlike anything else in the world," as "unique as they are proper in Los Angeles," and as constituting "almost the only public architecture in the city—public in the sense that it deals in symbolic meanings the populace at large can read."[14] Banham's comments attest to the critical about-face, facilitated in part by the success of Southern California's "junk" art movement of the early 1950s, that has seen the towers redefined from a "bizarre hobby" of an alcoholic foreigner to an "aesthetic triumph of the highest order," symbolizing "the chance democracy offers the lowliest citizen to achieve greatness through his own efforts."[15]

In the course of the journey from nuisance to treasure, Rodia's towers have become strongly identified with the surrounding community and, by extension, with African American Los Angeles as a whole. This was not, however, always the case. Prior to their threatened demolition in 1959, the towers attracted little attention from anyone, including local blacks. Sold to a neighbor in 1954, the towers were later purchased by two men, Bill Cartwright and Nick King, who saw them as vital to the city's cultural heritage. Indeed, the effort to preserve the towers from demolition by the city largely turned on the issue of their value as one of Southern California's only indigenous monuments. Paralleling the efforts by Kenneth Ross, director of the Municipal Arts Department, to develop greater citywide appreciation for the arts, preservation efforts were thus emblematic of a larger process of cultural maturation taking place throughout Southern California during the 1950s.[16]

Slated for destruction by the city's Department of Building and Safety, the towers were preserved following a concerted campaign waged by a coalition that included the new property owners, local artists, gallery owners, officials in the Municipal Arts Department, and more than a few foreign observers. Following the protestations of several hundred letter writers, engineers from the Department of Building and Safety agreed to submit the towers to a test meant to simulate the effects of winds and seismic activity. Following a public hearing in which Deputy City Attorney W. E. Wilder lambasted the "poor workmanship" of the structures, city engineers developed a five-ton "stress" test—captured in an odd silent film—in which incremental amounts of pressure were applied in an effort to jump start the city's effort to tear the structures down. After the tests, held in October 1959, proved insufficient to damage the towers, the site was declared a cultural monument by the state. The preservation coalition—the Committee for Simon Rodia's Towers in Watts—then began to seek funds for restoration and renovation.[17]

Initial efforts to save the towers elicited little attention in the surrounding community. None of the principal figures involved in the preservation committee was a local resident or an African American. The local black press ignored the ongoing debate regarding the structures, and only one of the more than one hundred letters sent to Josh Gibson, the black city councilman responsible for Watts, came from a local resident. Despite this, the successful salvage effort would prove of lasting importance to the surrounding area. For the first time, an area in South Los Angeles was seen as the cultural heritage of the entire city. Preservation led to renovation, and attempts to put the towers to better use resulted in the creation of a nearby art center. The location of the new art center implied increasing participation from the surrounding community, and the Towers Committee actively sought black applicants for staff jobs and the director's post. Opening in 1961 under the directorship of two local African American artists, Judson Powell and Noah Purifoy, the Watts Towers Art Center and affiliated teen post hosted a variety of classes for children, teenagers, and adults. Although it was hampered by its total dependence on private funds, the Watts Towers Art Center was nevertheless one of the first black-directed community arts centers in Los Angeles. Without the preservation of the towers, it is unlikely that the arts center would have been proposed at the site. And without a pre-existing facility, it is doubtful that Watts would have displaced the South Park area, or even Altadena, as the primary site of community-based cultural institutions after 1965.[18]

The ultimate fate of the towers remained uncertain, however. The declaration of the towers as a historical monument worthy of preservation in 1963 offered little more than a stay of execution, and despite warnings regarding the danger to the towers of continued exposure to the elements, Mayor Sam Yorty rejected a proposal made in 1967 for city stewardship over the site. The election of Tom Bradley proved a turning point, albeit a somewhat prolonged one, in efforts to preserve the towers and their adjacent art center as an integral part of what the "cultural master plan" (1991) for Los Angeles termed an "equitable" urban artistic infrastructure.

Throughout his mayoral tenure, Tom Bradley repeatedly championed the towers as a cultural resource for the city as a whole and as "a symbol of hope for an entire community."[19] Arguing that he placed "great importance" on the matter, Bradley urged the City Council to vote to acquire the towers, despite the likelihood of significant costs amid tight municipal budgets. Partially as a result, the City Council voted, first 8-3, and later 11-1, to accept ownership of the Watts Towers and to begin a city-sponsored restoration project.[20] For Bradley, who presided over a gala reopening in 1985 sponsored by Salem cigarettes, the restored site served as a showcase for linking Watts—and, by extension, black Angelenos—with the city at large. Much as the Watts Summer Festival—defunct as of the reopening of the towers—once had, the restored and city-run Watts Towers site also allowed a "positive" image of South Los Angeles to be broadcast to external observers. This official, top-down politics of representation was critical for a black mayor intent on maintaining a governing majority in a city where black voters constituted less than a fifth of the electorate, and where the memory of considerable urban unrest was fresh.

The process took a decade. Control over the site passed from the Committee on Simon Rodia's Towers in Watts (CSRTW) to the city in 1975. Restoration lasted a decade and unfolded amid charges of waste and mismanagement. Placed under the jurisdiction of the Bureau of Public Works rather than the Municipal Arts Department, the towers continued to deteriorate. Both state and federal sources contributed restoration funds, with the U.S. Department of Housing and Urban Development awarding $250,000 under the terms of the federal Historic Preservation Act in April 1977. A year later, the State of California added $207,000. Despite infusions of cash, the quality of the repair work remained substandard. Noting that the contractor selected for the job had little previous experience relevant to the task at hand, Ross observed acidly, "You don't repair a work of art like a storm drain."[21] Although he conceded, "Sure, pieces of tile have fallen off," the director of Public Works showed no inclination to speed up the repair. Moreover, he openly criticized the idea of restoring the site at all, arguing instead that child-care centers offered a more deserving destination for scant municipal funds.[22] Following the public closure of the towers "for reasons of public safety" in March 1978, the CSRTW sued the city, charging mismanagement of the site.[23] Following a series of legal battles ultimately decided by the California Supreme Court, ownership of the towers passed to the State of California, which completed a $1.2 million renovation before returning ownership to the City of Los Angeles in 1985.

The renovation of the Watts Towers took place during a brief window in which funding for the arts expanded on a variety of governmental levels. Following his election in 1974, Governor Jerry Brown began a reorganization of California's arts policy that culminated in 1976 in the replacement of the California Arts Commission with the California Arts Council. The new council, which for the first time included artists among its leadership, oversaw a significant transfer of monies to community-based arts projects and facilitated the creation of the California Afro-American Museum (CAAM). Although as a state facility its opening was formally unconnected to the Los

FIGURE 44 Watts Towers undergoing repairs, circa 1983. Photograph by James Ruebsamen. *Herald Examiner* Collection, Los Angeles Public Library.

Angeles Olympic Games, CAAM's debut took place during the 1984 Olympiad, furthering the sense of the Olympics as a moment of municipal support for South Los Angeles.[24] Located in Exposition Park, a South Los Angeles venue that includes a number of county museums as well as the University of Southern California campus, CAAM holds a collection that includes major works of Los Angeles–based black visual artists, as well as collections drawn from throughout the African Diaspora; a research library and archive; and educational and outreach programs.[25]

The success of CAAM is particularly impressive when set against the general decline in funding for the arts for minority communities and for cities as a whole. Federal and state funds for all three grew scarce with the election of the Republicans Ronald Reagan and George Deukmejian in 1980 and 1982. Most devastating, however, was the passage in 1978 of Proposition 13, a voter initiative that curtailed property-tax revenues and caused a sharp decline in revenue at the municipal level. In 1978, the Los Angeles Unified School District employed eight hundred art teachers in a district of approximately five hundred and eighty-four thousand students. Fifteen years later, the number of art teachers had declined to two hundred, although enrollments had risen to more than six hundred and forty thousand. Arts funding in the schools would remain miniscule until a brief uptick in the early twenty-first century. Prior to this, those avenues for art instruction that did survive, such as the Watts Towers Art Center, saw declining resources, as well.[26] In 1975, the operating budget of the art center was sixty thousand dollars, an amount expected to cover staff salaries, materials, publications, and outreach. Nearly two decades later, in 1993, the annual budget was still the same. Partially as a result, the center began to charge for classes that previously had been free.[27]

Between 1975 and 1992, John Outterbridge served as director of the Watts Towers Art Center, a timeline that is nearly identical with Bradley's tenure in office. As director, Outterbridge sought a means to shepherd an underfunded, city-affiliated center through the budgetary and ideological constraints of the Reagan era. He did so with some measure of success, developing annual jazz and Day of the Drum festivals, running a full schedule of arts classes, and otherwise ensuring that South Los Angeles retained at least one arts institution. The presence of one such institution provided resources for locals and a site for external visitors interested in seeing Watts, a fact that explains the presence of figures such as Bob Marley and Nina Simone in the art center's archives.[28]

During Bradley's long mayoral tenure, city funds supported a number of cultural organizations directed by African Americans, including the Brockman Gallery and Inner City Cultural Center; arts centers, including the William Grant Still Art Center; and festivals, including the Central Avenue Jazz Festival. The Watts Towers, however, remained the primary site of arts activity and the dominant target of financial support. For these reasons, it serves as a fitting example of the cultural politics of both inclusion and containment. Under the direction of Outterbridge, the Watts Towers Art Center mobilized dozens of instructors who offered a range of classes, at nominal fees, for the children of the surrounding neighborhood. Given the evisceration of arts funding in schools during the 1970s, exacerbated by the effects of Proposition 13, the persistence of even one dogged remnant of an arts program focused on children constitutes an achievement. Yet the description of the Watts Towers Art Center as a "survivor" representing the "rather old-fashioned idea" that art "can make a positive difference in social conditions" is perhaps apt.[29] Even as support for a restored towers site grew, the larger fabric of community-based cultural institutions began to fray. Certainly, one can discern a shift in the fortunes of institutions such as Studio Watts, which shifted its mission to low-income housing after 1969; the Mafundi Institute and Watts Writers Workshop, which shut down in 1973 and 1975, respectively; and the Pan Afrikan People's Arkestra, which entered a temporary eclipse with the death of Linda Hill and prolonged illness of Horace Tapscott during the early 1980s.

After 1985, the Watts Towers had the effect of centralizing black expressive culture under city management and of shifting the primary targets of the fostering of creative talent from adults to children. The dual effect of these shifts was a transformation of black cultural politics from revolution to affirmation, a difference that tended to move the focus of artistic activity to celebration from change. And so, while both the efforts of dedicated figures such as Outterbridge and the expending of political capital on the part of Bradley in the end are laudable, they also represent a departure from a previous politics of communitywide activity generated by independent radical organizations to a more spatially bound exhibition of black creativity funded by and tied to the city government.

MOCA: CULTURAL REVOLUTION FROM ABOVE?

Taking place in the uncertain financial climate that followed the passage of Proposition 13 and set amid competing claims on municipal coffers, the $1.2 million restoration and estimated annual maintenance cost of $150,000 for the Watts Towers and the Watts Towers Art Center led proponents and detractors to characterize the renovation project as a significant expenditure of state and local funds. The fiscal year (1986–87) that followed the reopening of the towers, however, saw "one of the most powerful and least-known" sections of the city government spend more than $150 million on downtown redevelopment projects in which arts policy played a central role.[30] The costs represented debt servicing, new acquisitions, and ongoing expenses relating to the redevelopment projects associated with the central business district and one of its crown jewels, the Museum of Contemporary Art (MOCA). The contrast offers a tale of more than competing priorities, for the story of MOCA, downtown redevelopment, and the rapid rise of a real-estate-driven "high-culture" boom in Los Angeles of the 1980s offers a salient window into the place of expressive culture in the exercise of local power. Constituting a kind of cultural revolution from above, the arts-centered downtown redevelopment served as an impetus for the transfer of vast sums, the enactment of new patterns of spatial separation under the aegis of intensely aggressive policing, and a shift in cultural resources from underdeveloped areas of the city to its increasingly parasitic center. Beyond highlighting the particular materiality of cultural policy, the mayor's strong support for a pattern characterized by one observer as "an epiphenomenon of the larger social polarization that has revitalized Downtown and enriched the Westside at the expense of vast debilitated tracts of the inner city" suggests the importance of a broader discussion of the social location of black expressivity in the context of the ostensible political access of the Bradley period.[31]

Initially, the Mayor's Office demonstrated little interest in the arts, focusing instead on diversifying municipal employment, strengthening public safety, and implementing a strategy for economic development that would lead to increasing links between California and the rest of the Pacific Rim. Inattention, however, proved short-lived. Citing the need to consolidate the city's cultural offerings and administrative units in his second inauguration speech, Bradley began 1977 by outlining the two central pillars of mayoral cultural policy. The first offered a continuation of an earlier history of local cultural boosterism, reviving the pattern of public–private partnerships used to highlight flagship institutions and events designed to enhance the image of the city and pique the interest of potential investors. Where previous efforts such as the opening of the new Los Angeles County Museum of Art in 1965 and the 1932 Olympiad had been meant to suggest either the growing urbanity or commercial viability of the region, cultural policy after 1973 facilitated the presentation of Los Angeles as a core center of global capital. If the staging of the 1984 Olympiad—still the most commercially successful such venture in the history of the modern Olympic movement and the model for every festival since—offers the clearest example of this strategy, the ongoing work of the Community Redevelopment Agency (CRA) forms a more permanent presence on the political and cultural landscape. The CRA, founded in 1948, describes its main task as lending "a hand to investors willing to take risks for a more vibrant city." A municipal agency administered by mayoral appointees, the CRA maintains authority to redirect local tax revenue to eradicate urban "blight."[32]

Among the agency's legacies are two "overweening arts acropolises": MOCA and the Walt Disney Concert Hall. Both institutions are housed in buildings designed by internationally famous architects—Arata Isozaki and Frank Gehry—and boards of directors that reflect local corporate leadership direct both institutions. The music center sits on a site that has excited the interest of culturally minded elites with an eye toward real-estate profits for more than a

FIGURE 45 National Guard soldiers near the Museum of Contemporary Art during Rodney King riots, 2 May 1992. Photograph by Gary Leonard. Los Angeles Public Library.

half-century, while the opening of MOCA was intended all along as an integral aspect of downtown real-estate redevelopment. Indeed, the CRA's initial blueprint for downtown redevelopment included an open square marked "culture" to be filled in later. As Jo-Anne Berelowitz observes in a study of internal CRA documents, the alliances that created MOCA came about as a direct result of the perception on the part of city leaders that "for Los Angeles to qualify as a 'world city,' it would need more than big buildings, busy trade, and apartment complexes. It would also need *Culture*."[33]

Such aspirational language highlights the extent to which culture became a concern of regional elites.[34] Throughout the postwar period, both the location and the nature of culture-based development have served as one locus for the playing out of intra-elite skirmishes between competing ruling groups—one located downtown, led by the dynastic publishers of the *Los Angeles Times*, and rooted economically in real-estate development and industry and manufacturing; and the other based on the Westside and tied to the rising real-estate values of West Los Angeles and the entertainment industry. In such a schema, the almost simultaneous opening of two institutions, the Dorothy Chandler Pavilion downtown and the Westside County Museum of Art, symbolized the ongoing gulf "separating new money from old, Jew from Gentile, transplanted New Yorker from hereditary Pasadenan."[35] Moreover, as Davis notes, the explosion of Watts and the consequent fear of an urban core abandoned to black and brown people provided the primary impetus for an elite consensus around the need to reclaim, rebuild, and retain Los Angeles's heretofore neglected and scorned central business district. In line with this vision, an arts policy built around MOCA linked sympathetic ears in city government with a broad section of "somewhat self-appointed" local elites, as the attorney and MOCA partisan William Norris described his museum-seeking cohort.[36]

The CRA emerged as integral to this process. Among the most ill-named branches of city government, the CRA functioned less as a body dedicated to developing the many areas of the city in need of infrastructural and other assistance than as an agency concerned primarily with using its power of seizure through eminent domain to bring about a wide-ranging building spree that made downtown Los Angeles a center of international finance for the first time.[37] Development projects often linked social categories or concerns (such as ethnicity or "high" culture) with real-estate windfalls, as in the case of the decade-long effort to redevelop Little Tokyo more as a center of transpacific big business than as a living testament to local Japanese and Japanese American history.[38] In marked contrast to the prevailing regional preference for lower-density, spread-out development, the CRA concentrated its efforts on the seemingly quixotic task of resurrecting a downtown central business district. To this end, the greatest share of the CRA's resources were spent on parcels inside Bunker Hill, defined as the area bounded by First Street on the north, Hill Street on the east, Fifth Street on the south, and the Harbor Freeway on the west, and the surrounding central business district, originally marked off as the area within the Harbor (west), Santa Monica (south), and Hollywood (north) freeways and the Los Angeles River (south). Between 1986 and 1989, for example, expenditures and appropriations for Bunker Hill and the central business district accounted for $529,589,700 out of $1,007,594,000 spent citywide.[39] These funds helped turn the Bunker Hill of Raymond Chandler and John Fante into a center of corporate capital, adding more than twelve million square feet of commercial space in two decades. Publications such as the CRA's undated *Development Offering: Remaining 8.75 Acres of Bunker Hill* openly championed the concentration of corporate capital downtown at the expense of other projects, citing the building of the Arco oil company's twin office towers, a subterranean shopping complex, and at least four bank headquarters—alongside a host of other corporate office developments—and noting that "the whole development of the western [central business district] as a financial and corporate center has been positively influenced by Bunker Hill's growth."[40]

Under the leadership of successive chief administrators, the CRA remained an active supporter of anchoring downtown redevelopment through the addition of a cultural institution. In a letter to the attorney William Norris, Donald Cosgrove, acting administrator of the CRA, expressed strong support for the selection of MOCA as a centerpiece of Bunker Hill development, affirming the view that "the lack of a modern art museum in Los Angeles is a glaring void" and offering the service and assistance of the agency. In citing his belief that "locating the museum of modern art in the Los Angeles Central Business District . . . will enhance the image of downtown as an emerging regional cultural center," Cosgrove predicted that the addition of a "well-located" museum might create a broader activity center on a par with Manhattan's Lincoln Center.[41] Linking the development of one of the city's richest parcels of land with a high-profile cultural showpiece was only one aspect of the CRA's involvement in a financially oriented arts policy. The agency also administered a 1.5 percent "culture tax" on new development. While this amount was intended to ensure sufficient support for citywide arts activity, the funds were generally used to commission works of art on private property that few urban residents saw or to generate tax savings for businesses to acquire expensive pieces of fine art. Whether used to facilitate the development of a facility committed to exhibiting internationally recognized contemporary art or to underwrite the purchase of privately owned art collections, the effect of the CRA's efforts on the cultural infrastructure of Los Angeles might be summarized as a kind of "trickle up" of resources away from minority communities and toward the business district downtown.

The offices of Mayor Bradley participated actively in fostering a regional cultural policy of dubious utility for the vast majority of African Americans. Bradley told the *Los Angeles Times* that he had "encouraged" a group of interested parties and had "arranged to meet them at [his] office."[42] Much as with the incipient Department of Cultural Affairs, the creation of a mayor's committee of interested private parties gave semiofficial sanction for the interaction between interested individuals and the CRA. The mayor asked William Norris to chair the body. Norris's wife, Merry, had been among those who initially had pushed for the creation of the museum, and Norris had been part of the transitional team that recommended initial leadership appointments for various city bureaus when Bradley took office in 1973.[43] Bradley placed

FIGURE 46 *"Dime con quién andas y te diré quién eres,"* 25 July 1984. From left to right: Harry Usher and Paul Ziffren of the Los Angeles Olympic Organizing Committee; Mayor Tom Bradley; Juan Antonio Samaranch, president, International Olympic Committee; Peter Uberroth, president, Los Angeles Olympic Organizing Committee. Photograph by Guy Crowder. *Herald Examiner* Collection, Los Angeles Public Library.

unconnected but interested individuals in touch with the initial MOCA brain trust and met with artists in a studio in Venice, California, before adding another Mayoral Advisory Committee or artists.[44] As he had with his support for the 1984 Olympiad, Bradley insisted that no city funds be used in the course of the project, a stance that pleased opponents of tax levies but that also created opportunities for moneymaking on the part of wealthy and connected local figures.

The success of this vision of a public–private partnership pursuing cultur-ally oriented urban redevelopment remained contingent on reclaiming sec-tions of downtown that had become economically marginal following decades of decentralized development. Put simply, central Los Angeles had to be re-claimed as a public space for affluent Angelenos generally uninterested in traveling downtown after dark. Like the counterinsurgency language of "clear and hold" military operations, this was a multilayered process. The first of these involved the enactment of new technologies of exclusion, from the aggressive policing of nonwhite youth on the part of the militarized police department to the herding of the city's exponentially increasing homeless population into shrinking areas along the eastern edge of downtown. The physical destruction and reconstruction of public space, from the shape of bus benches to parking patterns, formed a core element of the "push" aspect of this process. A second part, however, involved developing a strategy for "pulling" the affluent to an area that had long been denigrated as an empty "demilitarized zone" devoid of human activity after standard business hours. Construction began during the 1980s and continued well after Bradley left office in 1993. Significant construction of housing in the form of living-and-working lofts and condominiums, the designation of a section of downtown as an "artists' colony," and the arrival of the central business district's first supermarket would wait until the start of the twenty-first century. By this time, condo conversions of former single room occupancy hotels (SROS) and manufacturing plants, compounded by what the federal government agreed was an illegal and racist local transit policy, ensured that vast sections of downtown Los Angeles were well on the way to becoming places where working-class people, mostly people of color, could no longer live or work and could reach only by public transportation through arduous, and often dangerous, journeys.

From the point of view of working-class, inner-city, black residents of Los Angeles, Bradley-era cultural policies concerned with facilitating downtown redevelopment might be said to have comprised the more unhelpful of governmental activities between 1973 and 1992. As one example, redevelopment-agency funds, as well as the power of eminent domain, were used in the demolition of the building that housed the Ebony Showcase Theater. As Bradley had done elsewhere in the city, City Councilman Nate Holden's office chose to erect a new performing-arts facility closely tied with the councilman rather than seek landmark status and rebuild Stewart's site. Thus, while cultural offerings remained the primary point of the site, building contracts and other financial gains in Holden's district could be brought in by the assistance of the CRA. At the groundbreaking ceremony held at the site, the ninety-year-old Stewart protested from his wheelchair as Holden; Bradley's successor, Mayor Richard Riordan; and CRA employees looked on.[45] The institution that eventually emerged was named after Councilman Holden, although it markets itself using the name of the cultural institution evicted from the site. The story of the replacement of the Ebony Showcase Theater with the Nate Holden Performing Arts Center offers a fitting epilogue to the larger story of the CRA.

Characterized by limited transparency, open soliciting of international capital, and the participation of self-appointed groups of powerful citizens, the cultural dimensions of efforts to build a "world city" served as a de facto transfer of resources away from South Los Angeles. Even when resources were directed to black areas of the city, it was done so in ways that erased or repudiated the participation of individuals who had worked in those areas for decades. The formation of MOCA and the attendant cultural policies that surrounded its opening thus constituted an almost diametrically opposite form of cultural policy from that symbolized by the restoration of the Watts Towers.

INSTITUTIONALIZING DIVERSITY

If the reorganization of the Watts Towers under municipal management might be said to encompass that aspect of Bradley-era cultural policy tasked with representing City Hall as favorable to grassroots black concerns, and if the outpouring of effort aimed at securing a cultural anchor for the lucrative redevelopment of the central business district offers a stark example of the fiduciary–cultural nexus equally central to municipal concerns, then the creation of a new city department of cultural affairs might be termed—to borrow one of Los Angeles's booster slogans—the place where "it all comes together." In linking the twin preoccupations of ethnic representation and the adequate inclusion of the arts within local economic-growth strategies, the first decade of activity on the part of the Cultural Affairs Department symbolized both the fusion and fissure of liberal governance in Los Angeles.

Since its inception in 1980, the Cultural Affairs Department has grown into an integral part of the larger municipal bureaucracy. With an annual budget just under $10 million and sixty-nine full-time and several hundred part-time employees, the CAD, alongside an advisory cultural-affairs commission, oversees separate divisions of community arts (which supervises eighteen neighborhood cultural centers), marketing and development, public art (which runs a murals program and manages the city's collection of 2,300 works of art), grants, facilities, and youth arts and education. Though dwarfed by the annual appropriations for fire, police, building and safety, and a host of other city departments, CAD nonetheless occupies an important strategic niche in the exercise of local governance. In a city defined in no small measure by questions of ethnic relations, CAD serves as a critical municipal node for managing ethnic affairs. Offering more than four hundred annual festivals, nearly all organized along ethnic lines, as well as sponsoring a host of other place- and group-based events, CAD constitutes a core means by which a diverse and ostensibly tolerant city can be represented at large.

The following discussion of the Cultural Affairs Department traces the period from its initial mention as a goal of Mayor Bradley's second term (1977) through the publication of a "cultural master plan" for the city fourteen years later. In the time since, successive administrations have placed their own imprimaturs on the department, while demographic transformation, the social unrest of 1992, and other social questions have altered somewhat the patterns of departmental activity. Increased support for local artists as well as for collaborations linking various communities are one manifestation of this shift. Despite these changes, given the importance assigned to the formation and development of CAD by Bradley and a number of his political associates, a basic analysis of the department during its formative years fits within a broader study of the politics associated with African American culture during the postwar period.

First mentioned in his second inaugural address, the establishment of the Cultural Affairs Department represented a major initiative on the part of the second Bradley administration (1977–81).[46] As an initial step, the Mayor's Office organized a deliberative body, the Mayor's Advisory Committee on Culture, that included, among others, City Councilman Joel Wachs and Councilwoman Pat Russell; the visual artist Charles White; Stan Sanders, a former official with the Watts Summer Festival; Margo Albert, director of the board of directors of the Plaza de la Raza arts center; Gordon Davidson, head of the downtown Mark Taper Forum; and Robert Fitzpatrick, president of Cal Arts. This body solicited the opinions of a variety of figures in the entertainment industry and in sections of the city government, including representatives of the American Federation of Musicians Local 47, the Screen Actors Guild, the American Federation of Television and Radio Artists, the International Alliance of Theatrical Stage Employees, and the AFL-CIO, as well as of Universal Studios, the Recreation and Parks Department, the Municipal Arts Department, the Municipal Arts Commission, and the Public Works Department.[47] Recommending the establishment of a new department, the committee suggested consolidating previously unconnected elements of the city's cultural activity, including the efforts of the Municipal Arts Department, the Recreation and Parks Department, and the Los Angeles Film Development Committee, into a voluntary advisory body concerned with "economic development" issues related to "the business and industry of filmmaking" and not "with the cultural aspects of film as an art form."[48] Municipal Arts supported the recommendations, while Recreation and Parks and the Film Development Committee objected.

Despite the mayor's popularity and the strong support of City Councilman Joel Wachs, the proposed department faced initial difficulties. The passage of Proposition 13 radically altered municipal budget calculations, and anti-tax advocates criticized the costs that administrative consolidation and start-up funds for the new department would require. But more ideological opposition existed. Internal correspondence between Bradley aides described slow, plodding resistance to the proposed department. Some proponents grew angry with Bradley, whom they accused of retreating from visibility after initially championing the establishment of the new department. Initial unease on the City Council centered on an allegation that the new department would effectively transfer power from the council to the Mayor's Office.[49] Accused by the *Times* of acting with undue slowness, City Administrative Officer C. Erwin Piper conceded the merits of the proposal but argued against making the city the primary facilitator of local cultural policy.[50] The Parks and Recreation Department, meanwhile, launched a series of behind-the-scenes efforts to forestall the new initiative, offering an eleventh-hour quarter-million-dollar bid to refurbish a theater in Venice in what was viewed as an attempt to sway the vote of Westside Councilwoman Pat Russell and allegedly threatening to fire a Recreation and Parks official expected to testify before the City Council in favor of the CAD proposal.[51] Opponents distributed a fact sheet listing their points of objection, many of which were read as a series of paid public-service announcements on local news radio stations. Organized in the language of fiscal conservatism, consumer advocacy, and law and order, the fact sheet attacked the mayor, City Council, and something called the "Art's Mafia" as operating a deceptive, secretive, and fiscally irresponsible "rip-off."[52] Nevertheless, when the ultimate vote was taken, the City Council voted 11–1 in favor of the proposal, and Bradley signed the new department into existence in May 1980.[53]

As noted, the establishment of the new department consolidated existing cultural offerings at the same time that it inaugurated a new set of cultural policies. Programs from two city departments and two advisory committees were brought under one roof. Nearly twenty existing city-run facilities and programs were consolidated, as well, including the Watts Towers and Watts Towers Art Center; Barnsdall Arts and Crafts Center; and mural, theater, and grants programs. In addition to directing these facilities, CAD included a grants program and a cultural affairs commission tasked with overseeing the cultural effects of signage, real estate development, and other construction on city-owned property. An initial budget of $1.8 million was allocated, of which approximately $250,000 was awarded as grants. By the 1988–89 fiscal year, the overall departmental budget had grown to slightly over $4.1 million, with funding for salaries ($2.487 million) and grants to cultural organizations ($1.038 million) constituting the largest expenses. Twenty-five thousand dollars in departmental funds underwrote nine festivals, including the Watts Towers Jazz Festival, the Watts Towers Drum Festival, and an East Los Angeles Art Festival.[54] Over the course of three sequential budget years (1986–87, 1987–88, 1988–89), CAD grants were awarded to more than two hundred groups, a fourfold increase from a decade earlier.[55]

Despite the expansion of programming into underserved communities, the use of art as an economic "multiplier" was more than a rhetorical conceit during Bradley's mayoral tenure. Something of this can be gleaned from the pages of a "cultural master plan" commissioned by the city and completed by the consulting firm of Morris McNeill. Published as a work of 180 pages, as well as half a dozen preliminary reports, the master plan provided a blueprint for a municipal cultural policy grounded in the twin concerns of diversity and economic growth articulated throughout the Bradley period. While one of the core contentions cited by principal investigators Karen Hill-Scott and Alice Walker Duff was the idea that Los Angeles "should distinguish itself as an international center through the development of a multicultural character," the plan argued that the city government should recognize the arts as an important industry that contributed to "the economic vitality" of Los Angeles. Indeed, among the recommendations used to conclude the first full section of the plan was a statement asserting that increased city funding for the arts formed an integral part "of the goal of becoming an international *economic* and *cultural* center" (my emphasis). Quoting a report issued in 1985 by the Los Angeles Chamber of Commerce, the report argued that the arts served as an economic "multiplier" returning twice the amount of initial investment through the growth of retail spending, property values, business investment, and tourism.[56]

While it is certainly possible to read the inclusion of economic justifications for increasing funding for the arts as a strategic choice adopted by arts advocates seeking proactively to deflect criticism of the arts as unimportant, the frequency with which economic questions entered discussions of cultural policy suggests the central import finance played within all facets of elite governance. At the very least, the fact that the primary public purpose of the arts was now to be raising money rather than, say, generating positive social activity or employing the young, suggests the values of a new age. This becomes even clearer with a more complete survey of the funding patterns, programming, and areas of emphasis of the first decade of activity on the part of the Cultural Affairs Department. During Bradley's first two administrations, the Municipal Arts Department continued to prioritize funding for choral programs, classical concerts, and juvenile arts programs whose genesis lay in concerns about youth delinquency of the 1950s. In a similar vein, a series of grant-writing workshops meant to inform artists about the availability of CAD grants was parceled out in such a way as to recall, almost exactly, the social geography of the all-city arts festivals originally designed by Kenneth Ross. Decentralizing arts programming and meeting artists more or less where they were embodied a laudable effort to avoid the over-centralization of arts policy. Still, placing grant workshops in a San Pedro recreation center, Barnsdall Park, and a library in West Los Angeles, along with obligatory stops in South and East Los Angeles, reflects the persistence, intentional or otherwise, of a social geography rooted in the era of widespread urban segregation.[57]

Moreover, a summary of the grants programs of the Cultural Affairs Department revealed funding practices that continued to privilege individual white artists and artistic genres associated with mainstream organizations at the expense of nonwhite artists and arts organizations. Acting in part on the suggestions of the large numbers of artists, many of them people of color, the cultural master plan of 1991 called for a quarter of all municipal arts funding to be set aside as part of an "arts equity" program meant to expand offerings for underserved "ethnic" communities.[58] An overview of the awards made during CAD's first decade, however, revealed a more limited commitment to "diversifying the arts." A survey of local arts funding between 1985 and 1990, completed as part of the "master plan," revealed a pattern in which private money (52 percent), federal grants (27 percent), and California state sources (15 percent) all dwarfed municipal (5 percent) funding for the arts. "In every year, and for every funding agency," the survey noted, "grants to Anglo/white artists and arts organizations exceeded grants to all the other ethnic groups combined." Commenting on the gross discrepancy between funding choices and the ethnic composition of Los Angeles, the survey noted that CAD, although better than private sources or either the federal or state government, nevertheless regularly directed between 60 percent and 80 percent of its individual and organizational awards to Anglos or whites. Beyond these general tendencies, white artists and groups received all of the money directed to "policy, planning and research" grants, as well as 90 percent of "challenge grants," "design arts," and opera and musical theater, as well as approximately 75 percent of photography, literature, music, and performing arts. Hence, while CAD's mission and orientation retained a strong rhetorical commitment to diversity and the equitable allocation of money and other cultural resources, actual arts policy between 1981 and 1993 remained focused on white artists, predominantly white arts organizations, and traditional, "high," culture. The overall effect was a form of diversity that showcased minority creativity and promised access without actually bringing about a transfer of power, wealth, resources, or cultural authority.

A related critique might be made of the ethnic festivals that constituted a centerpiece of municipal multiculturalism during this period. Today, the Cultural Affairs Department of the City of Los Angeles sponsors more ethnic arts festivals than there are days in a year. County-sponsored festivals add to the total, as do separate events paid for by the numerous surrounding small cities. Periodic one-time events are held, as well, as are ongoing projects such as the California Plaza summer music series and the jazz Thursdays at the Museum of Contemporary Art. These events represent a sizeable expansion in absolute number, but also an ideological continuity with cultural planning begun during the first decade of municipally funded cultural-affairs planning. Perhaps half of these festivals and events are ostensibly identified by ethnicity, a pattern also established during the tenure of Mayor Thomas Bradley. Thus, in addition to periodic art walks, car shows, concert series, and film festivals, the city celebrates Aztec, Chinese, Japanese, Jewish, and Eastern Orthodox New Years. Los Angeles publicly commemorates the flight of the Afro-indigenous Garifuna from St. Vincent to Belize, symbolically erects an "African marketplace" on the playground of a South Los Angeles High School, and holds several annual festivals that have common themes, such as sacred music or ethnic arts.

As the cultural critic Lisa Lowe notes, the celebratory vision of urban multiculturalism enacted primarily through presentations of ethnic festivals functions "as a mode of pluralist containment and a vehicle for intervention" on the part of subordinated populations. According to Lowe, contemporary mechanisms of inclusion fix the cultural practices of the dominant center as the normative ideal, leaving the cultural production and practices of the overwhelming majority of Angelenos little more than a temporary cultural garnish. Moreover, municipal multiculturalism systematically erases the social contradictions that structure urban life—namely, by suggesting that groups actually possess a degree of access and social recognition that rarely extends past a given festival weekend. The result is a deeply disingenuous erasure of "the displacement and disidentification that are the historical products of racialization, immigration and capitalist exploitation."[59]

Plus, some of these narratives are just plain wrong. One event re-enacts "a Greek picnic *believed* to have taken place in the 1920s in Los Angeles."[60] "Garifuna Settlement Day" on 16 November describes the exodus of the Afro-indigenous population from St. Vincent as having taken place "for the purposes of keeping their rich culture intact."[61] No mention is made of the fact that the "exodus" was a forced deportation of a doggedly resistant maroon population who refused to allow the British to re-enslave them. Nor do festival organizers regard the event as a means of bridging the social, linguistic, and political differences that divide Central Americans. The festival's description speaks only of migration to Belize, leaving aside Honduras and Guatemala, two other destinations for the deported "black Caribs." As with many attempts at municipal multiculturalism, the rich polycultural life and political identity of the Garinagu is muzzled in favor of a more limited event. Indeed, an even more fundamental problem with multicultural practice is the inability of this vision of sealed tolerance to capture accurately the fluidity of urban life. Set against the backdrop of homogeneous ethnocultural communities, Latino and Asian American interest in hip hop culture, a putatively "black" form for many, is increasingly understood as "crossing over," despite the importance of Asian Americans, Latinos, and West Indians in the formation of hip hop culture. This vision of ethnic authenticity fails to account for the existence of prewar multiracial communities or to capture accurately the cultural history of Los Angeles.

The attempt to celebrate African American music within an appropriate spatial and temporal frame provides a vivid example of the problem. The city's annual showcase of the region's extensive jazz history is beset by a number of serious ideological limitations. Taking place on Central Avenue opposite the partially renovated Dunbar Hotel that provided housing to famous musicians and other black celebrities during the period of urban segregation, the annual Central Avenue Jazz Festival regularly ignores Los Angeles's pioneering prewar jazz history or the role of the city in the development of the jazz avant-garde. With the occasional exception, scant mention is made of figures as diverse as Kid Ory's Creole Orchestra or Don Cherry. Moreover, Central Avenue today is nearly 80 percent Latino. Rather than allowing this fact to serve as a point of departure for a discussion of the historical importance of Los Angeles within Latin music circuits—or even the myriad points of connection between African American, Afro-Cuban, and Chicano musicians —periodic insertions of Latin jazz interrupt recurring panel discussions about jazz in Los Angeles during the 1940s and early 1950s. Most of them fail to attract more than an occasional passerby. This is not to say that the story of Central Avenue is unimportant. It is. But the attempt to fix jazz and African American Los Angeles in a specific location creates more silences than clarity and squanders opportunities to retrace historical connections with an eye toward precisely the sort of interconnected urbanity that such festivals seek to obtain.

From this perspective, the municipal multiculturalism of the Cultural Affairs Department fulfills a form of ideological encapsulation akin to that achieved through municipal support for small, ethnically based arts centers but more widely dispersed through the city at large. Of course, as a form of public cultural policy, this marked an improvement over the rank exclusion of black Angelenos, as with the Bureau of Music programs of the early postwar period or the use of the LAPD to impede the bustling jazz scene of Central Avenue. Moreover, certain activities sponsored by CAD in the years since the Rodney King riots, such as the expanded Watts Towers Drum Festival, which combines varieties of indigenous North American, Cuban, West African, Japanese, and other styles, suggest the contours of a public culture capable of linking the historical experiences and creative energies of a wide pool of Southern California residents. In a similar vein, the Japanese American National Museum's exhibition in 2003 on prewar Boyle Heights, which focused on telling the interethnic history of a mixed Japanese, Jewish, Russian, and Latino community, might be said to offer a powerful, if mostly implicit, critique of a more familiar, sealed variety of multiculturalism. Such efforts, still very much in the minority (no pun intended), speak to the possibilities of defining new approaches to navigating the complicated currents of contemporary urban life.[62]

A similar conclusion might be drawn for the Bradley period as a whole. During his two decades in office, Tom Bradley opened new paths to access for African Americans on a variety of levels. Yet movements toward inclusion generate parallel patterns of containment, and the Bradley years coincide with the beginning of the end of a vibrant and viable black community life in Southern California. Here, Councilman Nate Holden's role in facilitating the CRA-funded razing of the building that housed the Ebony Showcase Theater offers one example of the gap between the politically established black middle class and popular forces and their creative representatives.

A narrative of partial inclusion implies the existence of parallel populations left on the outside. Bradley's tenure saw an increasingly austere economic order characterized by a growing gap between the black poor and the black middle class. For the former, an aggressive, militarized police force; a fratricidal war between neighborhood youth; and the waning of employment opportunities won at great cost all combined to produce an increasingly desperate urban world. Mayor Bradley's exhortation that rioting crowds should remain indoors and watch the finale of *The Cosby Show* rather than vent their rage at the acquittal of the LAPD officers Laurence Powell, Timothy Wind, Theodore Briseno, and Sergeant Stacey Koon offers another suggestion of just how large the class chasm among African Americans had become. If changing these conditions remained beyond the means of working class black politics, it was not for a lack of analytic clarity. For as we shall see, South Los Angeles in the epoch of Bradleyism was subject to a wide-ranging cultural critique produced by a new iteration of the black avant-garde: the community of Third World filmmakers active locally during the 1970s and 1980s.

HOW TO SURVIVE IN SOUTH CENTRAL   Black Film as
Class Critique

In LA heroes don't fly through the sky of stars
they live behind bars
and everybody's doin' a little dirt
and it's the youngsters putting in the most work
so be alert and stay calm
as you enter the concrete Vietnam
you say the strong survive
shit—the strong even die
in South Central.
—ICE CUBE

Everyone is paranoid and rightfully so.
—CHARLES BURNETT

A critical account of the Bradley years might identify 1973, 1984, and 1993 as the key dates for understanding the period as a whole. The first year corresponds to Bradley's initial election and was for many in South Los Angeles a moment of hope and expectation. The second coincides with the staging of the 1984 Olympiad, an event widely understood as a financial and organizational triumph that signaled the rise of Los Angeles to world city status. The ultimate date, meanwhile, marks Bradley's exit from office amid the rubble and recrimination of the Rodney King uprising. Taken together, these years symbolize both the promise and the limitations of integration and political access after the civil-rights era.

Beyond this broader context, these years saw a trio of films that offered an incisive critique of the socioeconomic situation of South Los Angeles during the Bradley epoch. Filmed in 1973 and released four years later, *Killer of Sheep* tells the story of Stan, an industrial worker who struggles to keep his sanity, job, and family together amid the mounting pressures of daily life. *Killer of Sheep* provides a stark glimpse into the lives of ordinary black Angelenos coping with the initial stages of a generation-long implosion of working-class black life. By the time that Billy Woodberry's *Bless Their Little Hearts* (1984) appeared, a number of the more salient aspects of this transformation could be seen. A tale of family dissolution and individual alienation, *Bless Their Little Hearts* extends and transforms the subject matter and themes of Burnett's film, following the unemployed protagonist Charlie as he struggles to maintain his dignity in the face of constant rejection. Concurrent with the worst period of deindustrialization in South Los Angeles, the rise of hundreds of dueling Crip and Blood sets, and the more or less full-scale flight of the black professional class, the period between the release of *Killer of Sheep* and *Bless Their Little Hearts* offers a stark rejoinder to the optimism of Bradley's "impossible dream."[1] And so, while *Killer of Sheep* seems at first blush a harshly unsentimental window into communal atomization and self-destruction, constituting what one critic calls "an aesthetic appropriate to conditions," both the interpersonal relations and larger social conditions depicted in the film seem benign in contrast to the world depicted in Woodberry's film.[2]

A third film continues this devolutionary trend. Albert and Alan Hughes's *Menace II Society*, a realist snapshot of South Los Angeles in the early 1990s, seems at first glance an unlikely candidate for inclusion alongside the works of Charles Burnett, Billy Woodberry, and the other members of the "Los Angeles" school of independent black filmmakers. Where *Killer of Sheep* was made for less than $10,000, used a nonprofessional cast and crew, and saw only limited theatrical release, *Menace II Society* involved a host of known black talent, cost more than $3 million, and opened nationally on 464 screens.[3] Combining two established genres of American film—the gangster tale and blaxploitation— *Menace II Society* traded on images of black criminality long familiar to U.S. audiences. In contrast, *Killer of Sheep* and *Bless Their Little Hearts* emerged from a lineage that incorporated British documentary realism, Italian neo-realism, and the "imperfect" cinema of the revolutionary Third World.

Still, as we will see, a number of important links bind *Killer of Sheep* and *Bless Their Little Hearts* to *Menace II Society*. Like the former films, *Menace II Society* emerged as part of a distinct moment in independent black filmmaking. Although the Hughes brothers, John Singleton, Spike Lee, Matty Rich, and others never constituted a coherent movement in any distinct sense of the word, they nonetheless operated as part of a wide-ranging outsider effort aimed at transforming the place of black filmmakers within the entertainment industry. As with other moments of black cultural activism discussed earlier, the "new urban cinema" of the early 1990s functioned in a highly intertextual and intergeneric manner, linking music and film while referencing other historical moments and cultural forms.

Beyond the shared setting of South Los Angeles, each film incorporates the urban landscape as both a character and a theme. All three feature working-class male protagonists, and each film suggests no higher possibility than mere survival. All three employ documentary-style realism, non-diegetic use of music, and experimental approaches to storytelling.[4] Each uses shot composition that foregrounds feelings of containment and immobility. None possesses an identifiably linear narrative, although each finds a way to mark the passage of historical time as an explanatory effect. The riots of 1965 and the physical destruction of South Los Angeles form a common point of departure, whether captured in grainy riot footage or panning shots of vacant lots and dilapidated houses. Eschewing sentimentality, all three films grapple with "realness," leaving even *Menace II Society* far from standard Hollywood fare. Indeed, critical elements of what the film scholar Clyde Taylor identifies as part of a "de-colonized" African American cinema, including historicity, orality, musicality, and an orientation toward the "real," can be found as readily in the Hughes brothers' film as in the avant-garde works of Burnett, Woodberry, Haile Gerima, Larry Clark, and Ben Caldwell.[5]

Most important, *Killer of Sheep*, *Bless Their Little Hearts*, and *Menace II Society* offer an implicit class critique of both the social conditions of the Bradley period and its cultural-policy choices. As experimental works within a common field of reference, these films illustrate how certain forms can emerge as particularly trenchant archives of a given moment. Much as jazz became *primer inter pares* among expressive forms during a preceding period of insurgent politics, film offers the most striking examination of the post-movement years. In the case of the period between 1973 and 1993, these films depict the struggle to maintain dignity on the part of working-class black men confronting an increasingly austere economic and social climate. If, as Stuart Hall once observed, "race is the modality through which class is lived," the films of Charles Burnett, Billy Woodberry, and the Hughes brothers illustrate racialized masculinity as the modality through which class is lived at the moment of economic restructuring, deindustrialization, and the rise of a parasitic carceral state.[6]

Viewed historically, the three films provide an important chronicle of black working-class life during the 1970s and 1980s. A wealth of social-science research has done much to detail the profound transformation of the economy of Los Angeles during this time. Considerations of space preclude a full recapitulation of the contours of urban restructuring, though a brief description taken from Edward Soja, Rebecca Morales, and Goetz Wolff offers a helpful précis. They write:

> These changes have juxtaposed substantial aggregate economic growth and expanding concentrations of affluence against extensive job layoffs and plant closures, deepening poverty and unemployment, the re-emergence of industrial sweatshops reminiscent of the nineteenth century, the intensification of ethnic and racial segregation, and increasing rates of urban violence and homelessness.[7]

Over the course of three decades, Los Angeles has undergone a long march toward an economic structure characterized by a "flexible" integration into the Pacific Rim. Almost exactly a century after Karl Marx wrote "California is very important for me because nowhere else has the upheaval most shamelessly caused by capitalist centralization taken place with such speed," a massive shift away from Fordist industry to financial and other services, textile and other light manufacturing, and various elements of high-technology and real-estate speculation have made Southern California into a comparatively rare "regional success story of American capitalism." Roger Keil notes the creation of more than one million jobs in Southern California between 1970 and 1980, observing moreover that while the Los Angeles area contributed more than a fifth of total U.S. industrial growth during this time, these jobs were overwhelmingly concentrated in non-unionized light manufacturing plants.[8] From the point of view of working people, "success" meant out-migration and suburban marginality or defense employment for whites, economic dislocation and social upheaval for blacks, and the proliferation of low-wage, non-union jobs for a mostly Latino and Asian immigrant workforce. Moreover, as Ruth Gilmore shows, "success" has masked the overall decline of American capitalism, with surplus populations, falling rates of profit, declining tax revenues, and the consequent implosion of state services signaling the shift from a redistributive New Deal state to a "military Keynesian" state in which prisons have become the primary institution with which working-class people of color interact.[9]

Illustrating the peculiar effect of these processes on African American residents of Los Angeles, David Grant, Melvin Oliver, and Angela James describe an expanding social differentiation and economic bifurcation of black Los Angeles along class lines. They identify a broad rise in the economic fortunes of black women, whose incomes grew more than 60 percent between 1969 and 1989. Although gains for black men were smaller, rising 13.6 percent over the same period, this number exceeded gains realized by whites (10.4 percent), Latinos (3.2 percent), and Asians (7.9 percent). Using public-sector employment as a primary motor, an unprecedented number of African Americans have transitioned into the amorphous category of the "middle class." At the same time, Grant, Oliver, and James note bleaker trends among lower-income and less well-educated African Americans.[10] These individuals have seen employment rates drop and indexes of segregation and the concentration of poverty rise and have largely been left outside the areas of private-sector job growth that by 2001 had made the five-county Southern California region into an economy larger than that of Mexico, South Korea, India, or Brazil.[11] "And," to quote Gil Scott-Heron, "if all that shit wasn't enough," the rise of a globalized Los Angeles coincides precisely with the eruption of the city's own Thirty Years' War between a dizzying patchwork of rival youth gangs.

All of this took place amid a vast transformation of black political life. As with metropolitan areas across the United States, Los Angeles saw both the rapid rise of a new cohort of black elected officials and the waning of grassroots radicalism. In the aftermath of a liberation politics in which expressive culture played a fundamental role, two distinct forms of cultural politics arose. The first of these, discussed earlier, took the urban landscape as a site of celebratory diversity and community cohesion. A second view instead took survival as a core concern. The chapter that follows argues that the latter form of cultural politics offered a class critique of the first, in which film served as an aesthetic mediation of a specifically black male experience of economic dislocation and social conflict. As protagonists, Stan, Charlie, and Caine are simultaneously surplus people, struggling to make sense of the meaning of their lives at a moment when this country seeks neither their labor nor their creative or political input. This is not a good place to be, and to the extent that municipally supported cultural politics group around the concept of celebration, it is possible to take the cultural critique of *Killer of Sheep*, *Bless Their Little Hearts*, and *Menace II Society* as a rejection of the vision of community coherence enshrined in the Watts Towers site as well as the idea of multiethnic tolerance on which multiple aspects of Bradley-era cultural politics were based. By class critique, I mean not simply the rejection of celebration, however, but a more profound questioning of the premise of black economic advancement, political representation by elected officials, or the possibility of thriving community.

Killer of Sheep, *Bless Their Little Hearts*, and *Menace II Society* illustrate the worldview of the black working class over the course of two decades. In large measure, they do so by telling stories that stand in sharp contrast to the official depiction of Los Angeles as a place moving forward, globalized and capable of meeting the needs of its resident population. To be sure, this critique was more a matter of analysis and critique than of organization or action. Still, these films captured in unique ways the sentiments of those African Americans left behind by the economic transformations of the 1970s and 1980s. For these reasons, they make sense both as intertextual projects and as archives of a particular historical moment.

Beyond seeing these films as connected to each other and to the social history of South Los Angeles, it is important to understand Charles Burnett, Billy Woodberry, the community of black filmmakers based at UCLA, and the Hughes brothers as part of the larger history of the Black Arts Movement on the West Coast. In his discussion of an African American cinema pursuing "determined resistance to the film ideology of Hollywood," Taylor suggests common areas of emphasis between the independent cinema of the early 1970s and the broader Black Arts Movement's focus on a "self-determining cultural identity."[12] In line with this book's core concern with extending the temporal and spatial boundaries of the Black Arts Movement, I would argue that the community of black filmmakers based in California and active during the 1970s should be seen not as inheritors of or successors to the Black Arts Movement but as a part of that movement's long trajectory. Indeed, Toni Cade Bambara's assertion that family, women, history, and folklore form the critical thematic concerns of black independent cinema extends easily to a discussion of the kinds of visual art produced by Betye Saar, the poetry of Jayne Cortez, or the music of the UGMA.[13] Interpersonal links suggest one reason why. Neighborhood friends of Charles Burnett were members of the Watts Writers Workshop. Larry Clark's *Passing Through* included two cast members drawn from distinct moments of black cultural radicalism in Los Angeles: Clarence Muse and Horace Tapscott. Common orientations suggest another reason. Much as Tapscott and his fellow musicians John Carter and Bobby Bradford spoke of film-studio work with open opprobrium, the participants in the UCLA cohort of black filmmakers regarded Hollywood more as a target of critique than as a possible site of employment. Beyond a negative attitude toward the culture industry, the "Los Angeles" school of black filmmakers showed the same concerns with establishing a multilayered creative community linking artists both with each other and with a broader community, as well as producing films whose content, circumstances of production, and formal choices revealed the dynamic triptych of aesthetic experimentalism, communalist politics, and artistic self-organization around which the Black Arts Movement coalesced.

THIRD WORLD WITHIN

In a letter addressed to his friend Arna Bontemps dated 1926, Langston Hughes declared, "Only a subsidized Negro Film Institute, or the revolution, will cause any really good Negro pictures to be made in America."[14] Although the 1970s arrived without the revolution in tow, something akin to the former took hold with the development of a community of independent black filmmakers affiliated with the University of California, Los Angeles, film school. Known variously as the "L.A. School," the "L.A. Rebellion," or simply as an informal grouping of African and African American film students present and active in Southern California between 1970 and 1982, this creative cohort marked a milestone in black cultural politics in general and the history of black arts in California in particular. For while poetry projects, jazz collectives, and community arts projects existed throughout the country, only Southern California produced a sustained, multigenerational community of black artists working in the medium of film. Beyond this, the working-class, Third Worldist orientation of the Los Angeles school, its dual concerns of experimental aesthetic strategies and openness to radical politics, and its commitment to developing a black cinema beyond and opposed to commercial filmmaking content and techniques, affected a fundamental transformation in the character of black efforts to contest the visual representation of African Americans by Hollywood.[15]

The general outline of the Los Angeles school has been told elsewhere and requires only brief recapitulation here. As Ntongela Masilela notes, the Los Angeles school incorporated two overlapping groupings that took hold following the establishment of the ethno-communications program at UCLA. The first included Burnett, Haile Gerima, Ben Caldwell, Larry Clark, Jama Fanaka, Pamela Jones, and Abdosh Abdulhafiz, among others, while the second, later, cohort included Billy Woodberry, Julie Dash, Alile Sharon Larkin, Zeinabu Irene Davis, Barbara McCullough, and Jacqueline Frazier.[16] Generating approximately two dozen films between 1970 and 1982, the Los Angeles school achieved an unusually direct link between African America and the revolutionary energy of the Third World. Incorporating elements drawn from post-revolutionary Cuba and Brazilian Cinema Novo, as well as British documentary realism and Italian neo-realism, the films of the Los Angeles school were produced in an explicitly politicized context characterized by excitement at the films emerging in the course of the worldwide struggle for national liberation, a parallel disgust with the blaxploitation fare of Hollywood, and ongoing intellectual engagements with Third Worldist theorists such as Frantz Fanon and Amilcar Cabral, as well as critical European thinkers such as Georg Lukács and Bertolt Brecht.

As nearly all of the scholarly studies on the Los Angeles school observe, the films made by this cohort demonstrate a relationship with the revolutionary engagements of third cinema.[17] As an artistic form developed by cultural producers embedded within an unfolding moment of mass political activity, third cinema shares more than a few points with the history of avant-garde jazz. Like free jazz, third cinema was cast as inherently revolutionary in both content and form. Like proponents of free jazz, proponents of third cinema produced manifestos, challenged the economic structures that retarded artistic production, and proposed a redefinition of the artist from an individual to a part of the collective. Both set ideological standards that proved difficult, ultimately, to achieve. Both cast originality as a fundamental imperative. Bob Bradford and John Carter decided to play original compositions exclusively. In a similar vein, Charles Burnett recalled the "tremendous pressure" to be original that he and his peers placed on each other, describing the sanction they placed on those who came back with "a film that was a cliché or ordinary or something that someone had seen before."[18] Both third cinema and avant-garde jazz established links between Third World decolonization and the antiracist struggle of the internal colonies of North America, and it is relatively easy to draw a link between the affinity of a figure such as Haile Gerima for black America's "historical credentials of revolt" and the inspiration artists such as Ahmed Abdul Malik, John Carter, and Horace Tapscott found in Africa. It is unsurprising, then, that the works of the jazz avant-garde would occupy an important place in the films of Billy Woodberry, Larry Clark, and Barbara McCullough.

Perhaps more important, third cinema sought to turn unequal circumstances of production from a disadvantage into a principle. Rejecting both the commercialization of Hollywood and the quest for artistic "perfection" of the European avant-garde, filmmakers such as Julio García Espinosa called for an "imperfect" cinema for "those who struggle" that would highlight the process of social contradiction over the celebration of results.[19] Part of this process would involve the broadening of who would make films, how they would be made, and by which criteria they would be evaluated. Films concerned with social reality were more than likely to have a documentary dimension and to use lighting, shot composition, and editing choices that reflected the financial and material conditions of their production. Here it is easy to see a link between third cinema and Burnett and Woodberry, with their semiprofessional casts, nontraditional cinematography, and narrative irresolution. It is also easy to understand how a *New York Times* critic could dismiss *Killer of Sheep* as "amateurish" and "arid." Americans are as unused to films about real people as they are to dignified and serious depictions of African Americans. Even before the inclusion of atypical forms of cinematic presentation, the combination was too much.[20]

The films of the Los Angeles school thus emerged from a setting in which the possibilities for an art of liberation, as well as the boundary between "art" and "life," could be debated and assessed. The latter concern animated the formal properties and circumstances of production. As Clyde Taylor and James Snead observe, Los Angeles police officers interposed themselves as extras in Haile Gerima's production *Bush Mama* (1979). In a film partially about police repression, LAPD officers searched and interrogated the cast and crew as they set up their equipment one day, unwittingly providing a cinema verité opening for the film.[21] Mike Murashige has criticized the scholarly tendency that cites this anecdotal aspect of Gerima's production at the expense of assessing the full complexity of representational strategies in the film.[22] Although this critique has merit, the story of the LAPD's interference with Gerima's film is important, both because it reflects the continuing problem of a police force bent on behaving as an army of occupation and because it reflects a long history of police interference in the affairs of black artists. Without great effort one can find fifty years of organized hostility, whether in the form of Chief Parker's assaults on the interracial jazz world of Central Avenue, police surveillance of the Pan Afrikan People's Arkestra, or the FBI's ill-fated and embarrassing effort to intimidate the rap group N.W.A. following the release of the song "Fuck tha Police."[23]

One of the most important aspects of the cinematic movement that flourished locally during the 1970s was its ability to arrive at a cultural politics of self-determination through a multilayered depiction of the interior life of African Americans. Burnett's films touch on working-class alienation (*Killer of Sheep*), class tensions (*My Brother's Wedding*), and magico-spiritual power (*To Sleep with Anger*). Larry Clark's *Passing Through* places jazz at the center of black life as a force for community unity and political transformation. Gerima's early films *Hour Glass, Bush Mama,* and *Child of Resistance,* as well as later works such as *Harvest: 3,000 Years* and *Ashes and Embers,* explore issues of imperialist war, domestic repression, sexual violence, psychological trauma, and the connections between African and African American liberation. Ben Caldwell's *I and I,* Julie Dash's *Four Women,* and Zeinabu Irene Davis's *Recreating Black Women's Media Image* trace particular contours of working-class black women's lives. As David James notes, Barbara McCullough's four-minute-long *Water Ritual #1: An Urban Rite of Purification* is itself a kind of inter-artistic work that combines collage, the avant-garde jazz of the Los Angeles native Don Cherry, and themes of history, folklore, magic, and the specificity of black feminism.[24] *Daughters of the Dust,* Dash's celebrated multigenerational window into the world of Gullah women, functions as both a statement on cultural resiliency and an indictment of Hollywood's treatment of black women as a kind of background scenery.

Heterogeneous as these films are, they center on two critical points: They show, first and foremost, ordinary working-class black folks, and they showcase the intersections of race, class, and gender in their lives. Despite a shared sense of the limitations of the film industry and an interest in the emerging cinemas of the revolutionary Third World, few of the pioneering directors associated with UCLA's film school held anything resembling a common aesthetic or political program. This variety goes a long way in explaining the reticence of Burnett, Woodberry, Gerima, and others to identify the films produced by students affiliated with UCLA as constituting a singular tendency, movement, or school. And yet in the case of *Killer of Sheep* and *Bless Their Little Hearts,* common questions of narrative, genre, and form can be discerned. Noting these choices, and relating them to the material and human conditions of life in 1970s-era Los Angeles facilitates an investigation into how film illustrated the decidedly mixed legacy of civil rights and black power on the urban stage.

THINGS FALL APART

Killer of Sheep is perhaps the best-known film to emerge from the creative cohort of UCLA-affiliated independent black filmmakers. The film follows Stan, a middle-aged black worker, through a world of overlapping alienation.[25] An insomniac who works in a slaughterhouse, Stan struggles to keep his family together, his job tolerable, and a sense of purpose amid a growing fear that "I have worked myself into my own hell." Unable to rest, uninterested in sex, and at a loss to understand feelings that other characters seem oblivious to, Stan struggles to connect meaningfully to those around him. They do not provide much help. As he finishes telling his friend Oscar about his mental unease, Oscar replies, "Why don't you kill yourself? You'll be a lot happier." Although Stan is the film's central character, *Killer of Sheep* shifts through a variety of intersecting vignettes. Neighborhood kids skirmish with rocks across abandoned lots; Stan works, slicing sheep, hosing blood off floors, cleaning meat hooks; Stan and his wife, played by Kaycee Moore, move toward and away from each other; neighborhood associates trace itineraries that seem to circle back to the kids, or the factory floor, or the people waiting, arguing, fighting, laughing. Languid and circular, the film ranks among the most incisive and subtle depictions of black life produced in any artistic medium during the twentieth century.

Though fictional, *Killer of Sheep* shows a community known intimately by Burnett. Born in the South (Mississippi), like many of his black arts cohort, Burnett had moved with his parents to Watts as a child. Burnett's adolescence coincided with the decline of South Los Angeles amid the ravages of Vietnam, the initial demise of regional heavy industry, and the post-1965 flight of the burgeoning black middle class. After transferring to UCLA from multiracial, working-class Los Angeles City College, Burnett connected with Eliseo Taylor, a former U.S. Army cinematographer and one of the only black faculty members affiliated with the film school. One of only four black students in the film department at UCLA, Burnett was a key figure, along with Taylor, in the development of the ethno-communications program that served as an impetus for the genesis of a new independent black cinema and for parallel movements among Chicanos, Native Americans, and Asian Americans.[26]

Opposed equally to the racist inanity of mainstream movies and the naïve, but no less false, portrayal of working-class life as one victorious labor conflict away from beneficent resolution, Burnett described his animating impulse as arising "because I wasn't happy with the people I saw on the screen. I couldn't identify with the stories or the characters." Burnett completed *Killer of Sheep* as a requirement for his Master of Fine Arts degree on a shoestring budget using university equipment. He also used a mostly nonprofessional cast, he said, "of people who owed me favors" and recruited neighborhood children as sound personnel.[27] Shot on weekends over the course of eight weeks, shown mostly in universities and film festivals, and unreleased commercially, *Killer of Sheep* remained unavailable for purchase until late 2007. Critical commentary generally assigns the film an Italian neo-realist stylistic debt, although Burnett cited the influence of the British social-documentary filmmaker Basil Wright, one of his teachers at UCLA, and an engagement with the revolutionary third cinema of Africa, Cuba, and Brazil as influencing his project. Whichever genealogy one adopts, *Killer of Sheep* exists as a work of politically engaged art that is simultaneously open to formal experimentation and social critique.

The aspects of nontraditional cinematic technique Burnett used have garnered widespread critical attention. Ignoring conventions of narrative, form, and genre common to most American films, *Killer of Sheep* incorporates stylistic devices borrowed from documentary and neo-realist cinema. A back and forth between diegetic and non-diegetic sound heightens an overall sense of ambiguity, while the film's characters lack clearly defined roles as heroes or villains. The protagonist Stan is portrayed less as a figure demanding the sympathy of the viewer than as a man struggling to maintain his equilibrium amid the dehumanization of his job and the grinding poverty that surrounds him. Burnett shows, but he does not tell. The director's refusal "to resolve his situation by imposing artificial solutions" avoids the happy ending—or any ending—American audiences expect. The use of a predominantly nonprofessional cast reinforces the film's everyday-life sensibility. Eschewing linear narration, *Killer of Sheep* unfolds episodically as a series of moments whose connections are left unexplored, further calling attention to the alternative sense of timing and temporality the film presents. With much the same sensibility that animated John Outterbridge's assemblage work "Song for My Father," Burnett's film shows movement without progress.[28] Ultimately, although Stan's days move forward, they do so in a meandering, circular fashion meant to convey Burnett's interest in showing structure without a conventional plot and in highlighting "that there is no end to struggle. In order to survive, you are always going to be resolving some issues while new issues begin."[29]

Moreover, this narrative irresolution is linked to a series of filming choices that highlight a larger sense of social immobility on the part of all the characters in the film. As Paula Massood explains, the claustrophobic shot composition of the indoor work conveys a sense of the emotional paralysis that grips Stan. One scene, featuring two shady characters who try to enlist Stan in a criminal escapade, is filmed in such a way that Stan is entrapped between the duo and his wife, who argues with the men from the top of her steps. The camera rarely focuses on individual faces; instead, it brackets characters in such as way that the camera presses them in without the actors' seeming to move closer to each other.[30] As Clyde Taylor argues, Burnett's use of the open

FIGURE 47 Two young boys transform urban space in the absence of official recreational opportunities following the passage of Proposition 13, 12 August 1978. *Herald Examiner* Collection, Los Angeles Public Library.

frame, in which characters enter and exit from top, bottom, and sides, marks the film as more akin to European, Japanese, or Third World works than the films produced in the major studio facilities that are only a short drive from Watts.[31] Both indoor and outdoor scenes are filmed using long takes that heighten the sense that the viewer has been dropped in from outside to watch scenes that capture the absolute banality of daily life. A creepily sexualized job offer from a homely and domineering white shopkeeper has the feel of a conversation that takes place every time Stan enters the store. At work, we see sheep being killed, gutted, and skinned in a way that is neither sensationalized nor sanitized, and we watch as Stan and his friend Gene struggle to maneuver a secondhand engine down a rickety staircase. Life unfolds, but most people are not going anywhere.

South Los Angeles is depicted as a locale unconnected to the rest of Los Angeles. The city at large is wholly absent; missing are images of freeways and other symbols of contact, noticeable landmarks (the Hollywood sign, beaches, downtown, the Watts Towers), or people from outside Watts, with the exceptions of the white shopkeeper and Stan's supervisor and co-workers at the slaughterhouse.[32] Black immobility is reinforced by Burnett's treatment of transit. One scene features an overloaded sedan that breaks down on its way to the racetrack, forcing the occupants to curtail their outing and roll laboriously home on three wheels and a rim. Another scene features a quartet sitting in a car. A can of beer sits on the hood. As the group prepares to set off, leaving the viewer to wait for the furor that will follow when the beer crashes to the ground, a hand reaches through the nonexistent windshield to grab the can from atop the hood. The camera then zooms back to reveal that the car's occupants are sitting in little more than a metal shell, a car without wheels transformed from a conveyance into a four-person bar. A third scene follows Stan and a friend as they struggle to move an automobile engine bought secondhand out of a second-floor apartment and into a pickup truck. The two men maneuver the engine block down a set of dilapidated wooden stairs and onto the bed of the pickup truck. As they drive off, the engine falls out the back and onto the pavement, where it breaks. Beyond the implicit critique of the possibilities of financial gain through the ordinary petit-bourgeois activity of buying something, fixing it, and selling it again, this scene, like those of immobile trains and broken and overloaded bikes combines to show a community defined by the inability to escape.

A work of experimental filmmaking, *Killer of Sheep* is also a work of radical politics. Unlike the interspersed images of Attica and of the Organizacíon de Solidaridad con los Pueblos de Asia, Africa, y América Latina (OSPAAAL) posters featured in Larry Clark's *Passing Through* or in *Bush Mama*, Haile Gerima's depiction of South Los Angeles as an internal colony shaped by police violence, bureaucratic hostility, and racist contempt, the politics present in *Killer of Sheep* are understated. The distinction is purposeful, for Burnett explicitly sought to portray characters like those he knew growing up, with the limitations, complexities, and questions that ordinary black people have. As an inquiry into "a man who was trying to hold on to some values that were constantly being eroded by other forces," *Killer of Sheep* was meant as a triple critique: of the exploitation of Hollywood, of the destructive sweep of the invisible hand across black lives, and of the limitations of a romantic, middle-class leftism in which "Boom, you get your worker's rights, and everybody is happy."[33] Equally as apt in the days of Ellington, Himes, Still, and the old left as in the moment of party building, the end of the war in Vietnam, and the Weather Underground, Burnett's critique posits black survival as a revolutionary answer to life in non-revolutionary times.

Killer of Sheep is a story of survival. But it is also a story of what survival means for poor black people. It is a film about black particularity, expressed *culturally*—through games, jokes, style, speech. It offers a window into a world that few outsiders see, and it offers a reminder that for those trapped inside the four freeways that provide easy access for the National Guard to South Los Angeles, the rest of the city *are* outsiders. If we take seriously Burnett's statements to the effect that he made the film because he wanted to show people who were not shown on screen, and not because he had any particular audience in mind, we find a politics different from those ascribed to the film by critics. Although his examination of the "minority cinemas" of Los Angeles is perhaps the most comprehensive overview of the Los Angeles school published to date, David James's argument that *Killer of Sheep* puts forth a "liberal humanist appeal for sympathy and understanding—if not pity—from the hegemony, rather than a historical analysis or a militant call to contestation" is wrong, as is his contention that this liberal humanism "partially explains why the film has been primary distributed, not in the black community, but in the white institutions of liberal humanism, in festivals, schools, and museums."[34] As Budd Schulberg noted more than a decade before Burnett finished his film, Watts has no facilities for showing movies of any kind; nor, by the mid-1970s, were there more than a handful of suitable alternative venues in which film screenings could take place. Beyond this, the lack of a black audience for the film says more about black political and aesthetic underdevelopment in the time of Mayor Bradley, Governor Reagan, and President Nixon than it suggests an affinity between the filmmaker and the cultural institutions, such as universities, that provided scant resources for the film's production. The absence of a larger audience for revolutionary black art—a subject treated at other points in this volume—hardly makes the content, form, or message of *Killer of Sheep* one of liberal humanism.

Indeed, in place of liberal humanism's focus on the individual, Burnett's film highlights black collectivity as constituting an important aspect of the overall theme of survival. Take, for example, the scene in which people are drinking beer in the unmoving car. As dramatic evidence that what the historian Earl Lewis elsewhere describes as "turning segregation into congregation" extends beyond the temporal and spatial boundaries of the Jim Crow South, this simple snippet of daily life demonstrates an interaction between human creativity and the built environment that is arguably as rich as that being developed concurrently across town by Jay Adams, Stacey Peralta, Tony Alva, and the like. But if the skateboarders who were transforming urban space in

Venice were trying something new, Burnett was linking to something very old. Listen to the voices that he provides. In one scene, a man challenges his son to come to the aid of his brother, reacting with incredulity as the young man insists that his brother started the fight. In another scene, Stan and Angela join a trio headed for a drive outside the city. As they squeeze into the car, Bracy tells a rambling story about a woman who loses her "cascade" (wig) when a pimp named Boulevard "fires to her jubs" (hits her in the mouth). All of this takes place as the storyteller tries to explain the changes in the neighborhood to a man who has recently been released from prison after serving fifteen years "for being felonious." This is the *Hepster's Dictionary*, two generations on, a continuing update attesting to the specificity of our entries in the book of human language.

A soundtrack that sweeps across a broad expanse of African American history further heightens this sense of black particularity and togetherness-within-difference. *Killer of Sheep* enlists a catalog of black musical history—from William Grant Still's "Afro-American Symphony" and Robeson's "The House I Live In" to Dinah Washington's "This Bitter Earth"—that links Stan to other places and times. The non-diegetic musical choices incorporated by Burnett are critical to touch on, because they suggest both an engagement with black particularity and the broader class-based cultural critique present in all three films. They also shed a different light on the *New York Times* film critic Janet Maslin's complaint about the dialogue being "buried under a soundtrack of vintage blues, making it doubly hard to follow."[35] In the scene that features Robeson's voice, we see children in a vacant lot improvising toys from urban litter as the baritone sings of "the children in the playground / the faces that I see / all races and religions / that's America to me." In the America of *Killer of Sheep*, the children have no playground, and the faces that we see are not "all races and religions." They're all black. There is a tendency to find irony here, or to view the way Burnett sets Robeson's intonation of a multi-ethnic nation against the de facto segregation and poverty of children as illustrating "that the Popular Front dream of racial inclusion has been abandoned, nearly obliterated."[36]

While I do not disagree with this framing, I do find it incomplete. For one thing, Robeson provides a specific representational association when set alongside Dinah Washington and William Grant Still. Given Burnett's stated unease with a facile, workerist leftism of the sort that proliferated in the early 1970s as mass movements gave way to sectarian middle-class cells, Robeson's presence may say less about the decline of racial inclusion than about its permanent impossibility. Such a view would more precisely align the music heard with the camera choices and shot composition of Watts as an inescapable space. Burnett's Robeson may well lament the political defeat of antilynching legislation, Operation Dixie, and Henry Wallace. But the ghostlike baritone may also be vamping on the limits of a white left to comprehend black people as they actually are—and here we come back to the alienated and doubting Stan—as opposed to selfless, proletarianized agents of revolutionary transformation. In juxtaposing blackness and America this way, the disjuncture between sound and image that Burnett constructs recalls the end of that other great cinematic treatment of black masculinity from the early 1970s: Melvin Van Peebles's *Watermelon Man*. Certainly, one can find in Robeson's ballad an echo of Van Peebles's brilliant "Love, That's America," with its refrain, "Where can I be / this ain't America, is it / nah, this ain't America / you can't fool me."

"Without history you are nothing," Burnett told the interviewer Aida Hozic. Given this view, Burnett's musical choices are interesting, for the past that he mobilizes through music is a highly specific one. William Grant Still, Paul Robeson, and Dinah Washington lived at particular moments, recorded in different musical styles, and maintained distinct political orientations. Yet in bringing them together, Burnett achieves an effect akin to the sort of "Great Black Music" developed by the Chicago-based Association for the Advancement of Creative Musicians. *Killer of Sheep* moves from Still's effort to find Africa through and against European art music (a counterculture of modernity?) to Robeson's broken promise of the Popular Front, to the stark rootedness of Dinah Washington's blues ("What good is love / that no ones shares / And if my life is like the dust / That hides the glow of a rose / What good am I / Heaven only knows"). As it moves, this music reflects historical experience, political histories, and communal outlines. It captures, in words that the composer John Gray wrote fifty years before Burnett's film, "the outline of a people" provided by their songs.[37]

Beyond the persistence of community and the framing structure of music, *Killer of Sheep* adopts a collective approach as it shows the intellectual life of a black worker. As Stan assiduously tries to make sense of what is happening to him, he engages others, holding his coffee mug to his cheek as he waxes about affection, describes his sleeplessness, and expresses his financial anxieties. The overall effect is a politics that privileges subjectivity, of black people acting rather than being those who are acted upon. The film ends with mixed allegories of irresolution. A crippled neighborhood woman reveals her long-hoped-for pregnancy; Stan and Angela reconcile sexually; Dinah Washington's voice returns; Stan again herds sheep across the killing floor. The film ends powerfully and ambivalently, offering a complicated portrait of the constraints of everyday life for black Americans in the decade after the end of formal, legal discrimination.

"I CAN'T MAKE THEM PEOPLE GIVE ME NO JOB"

The human cost of survival amid declining possibilities forms a primary theme in Billy Woodberry's *Bless Their Little Hearts* (1984). Although his film has received far less critical attention than Burnett's work, *Bless Their Little Hearts* offers a similarly incisive treatment of black family life in Los Angeles. Part of the second cohort of independent black filmmakers affiliated with UCLA, Woodberry directed and produced the film for which Charles Burnett wrote the screenplay and served as a cameraman. *Bless Their Little Hearts* features a documentary, neo-realist style like that of *Killer of Sheep*, and, like the earlier film, featured a mostly nonprofessional cast. The actress Kaylee Moore joined the cast of *Bless Their Little Hearts*, as well, playing Andais Banks, the wife of Charlie Banks, an unemployed worker who is arguably the film's central character. As in *Killer of Sheep*, music is employed non-diegetically, as when songs by Carla Bley and Charlie Haden and then Archie Shepp play in the background as a quartet of unemployed black men, including Charlie, try their hand at selling catfish caught in the Los Angeles River to passing motorists.[38] *Bless Their Little Hearts* adopts a slightly more aestheticized camera style than *Killer of Sheep*, although long shots, open frames, and the lack of a central narrative or anything resembling resolution inscribe firmly the overall avant-garde sensibility.

In addition to sharing formal characteristics, cast members, and circumstances of production, *Bless Their Little Hearts* takes up themes similar to those in *Killer of Sheep*. Where the early film centered on the figure of an alienated individual, however, the focus in Woodberry's film is more collectively familial. *Bless Their Little Hearts* circles through the lives of the Banks family as they try to hold together amid Charlie's unemployment, his wife's anger at her growing responsibility for the entire unit, and the surrounding decline of the neighborhood. *Bless Their Little Hearts* offers a unique examination of how the growing poverty of inner-city life in black Los Angeles affected family dynamics, thus extending and altering somewhat the focus of Burnett's earlier work.

Indeed, despite many commonalities, critical differences mark a distance between the two films. In *Killer of Sheep*, Stan is employed, while Woodberry's protagonist has lacked regular work for a decade. Largely as a result, the gap between husband and wife, resolved in part at the end of Burnett's film, constitutes an unbridgeable gulf in *Bless Their Little Hearts*. The finances of the two families attest to the change in circumstances. Whereas Stan underscores his class anxiety by insisting that since he gives money to the Salvation Army, he cannot be poor, the family at the center of *Bless Their Little Hearts* cooks using a stove held together with baling wire. Stan is shown engaged in a variety of remodeling projects, an activity that suggests a nervous energy dedicated to improving his surroundings. By contrast, Andais and her children never seem to erase the physical grime in their home, though we see them cleaning time and again. The surrounding neighborhood, too, shows increased physical decline. As noted earlier, *Killer of Sheep* makes extensive use of unreliable automobiles as a symbol of a lack of community mobility or forward progress. In *Bless Their Little Hearts*, it is not cars but buildings that show signs of collapsing. Returning from a day of manual labor, Charlie rides in a truck past long stretches of torn-down and gutted factories. On another occasion, he goes outside to remove gang graffiti spray painted on a garage wall. Beyond an oblique reference to the ominous arrival of the Avalons, East Side Crips, and Brims, we see Charlie engaged in a variety of menial, unconnected tasks. In contrast to Stan's alienating but steady employment, *Bless Their Little Hearts* depicts work options as reduced to a series of casual, ill-paid odd jobs such as clearing vacant lots. Indeed, even as both films portray black men involved in efforts to find other ways to earn money, striking differences are revealed: *Killer of Sheep* shows Stan and a friend attempting to repair and resell an automobile engine; *Bless Their Little Hearts* features men selling catfish on the side of a road. Though the films are set only about a decade apart, they illustrate a starkly different labor landscape. Burnett portrays black employment as a question of dirty, dangerous, and mentally damaging work. Woodberry depicts the decline of industrial employment, by contrast, as leading almost to the return of preindustrial pursuits such as clearing land and catching fish.

Whether portrayed as family relations, the built environment, or working conditions, the different imagery of *Killer of Sheep* and *Bless Their Little Hearts* is anything but accidental, for the interval between the two films coincides with a critical moment in the social history of black Los Angeles. After a period characterized by brief gains in industrial employment, a wave of factory closures swept black Angelenos out of work. Between 1978 and 1982, nearly seventy thousand industrial jobs were lost in auto, tire, steel, glass, and civilian aircraft manufacturing. In 1980 alone, at least sixteen thousand jobs were lost to plant closures, with an additional two and a half jobs placed in jeopardy for each lost. Two auto plants in South Los Angeles closed in 1980, eliminating fifty-four hundred jobs, many of them held by black and Latino workers.[39]

While black workers were hardly alone in confronting deindustrialization, changing conditions harmed them in particular ways. Aircraft and defense manufacturing shifted outside of the county toward areas with few blacks. The boom in high-tech manufacturing required educational backgrounds that became more difficult to acquire as affirmative action came under direct attack and as state funding for community colleges and inner-city high schools declined in the wake of Proposition 13. Increasing opportunities in light manufacturing, construction, and janitorial services, meanwhile, were concentrated among new immigrant populations employed at lower wage levels and thought of by many employers as more docile and less prone to unionization than African American men. The result was a stunning rise in black unemployment among the young and the poor. Compounding the problem, many gainfully employed African Americans chose to leave increasingly dangerous neighborhoods in historically black sections of Los Angeles for suburban homes in Riverside and San Bernardino counties.[40]

With this as a point of departure, *Bless Their Little Hearts* tracks the interplay between Charlie's lack of work and the deleterious effect of male unemployment on family life. The film begins with Charlie visiting an employment office, perusing the job board, and scribbling down phone numbers even as a worker removes posted listings one by one. Charlie spends much of the film looking for work, reading want ads, and doing casual day jobs. His searches are inevitably in vain and elicit little sympathy from those around. When he stops at a barbershop to ask the proprietor if he has any work, the older man delivers a lecture on the importance of getting up early and acquiring skills that an employer will find useful. When Charlie protests that he can do construction, drive trucks, and operate forklifts before adding that, as a parent of three kids, he gets up early every day, the barber suggests that he is "too choosy" and needs more humility if he is going to make it. The sum of these fruitless searches is a profound, generational moment of despair not captured elsewhere, when tens of thousands of black men in Los Angeles, and millions more around the country, engaged in a futile search for steady work that could provide both individual dignity and enough money for them and their loved ones to live on.[41]

Charlie's inability to find steady work dominates the film's central interpersonal relationships, as well, driving a wedge between Charlie and Andais and contributing to Charlie's fears about his role as a father. As the family prepares to leave for church, Andais pauses in the hallway to give Charlie money to give the children to put in a collection plate, a scene that highlights the private humiliation of publicly maintaining his fatherly role before his children. Andais oscillates between offering Charlie emotional support and expressing her rage at her own overwork, her unrecognized sacrifices, and her lack of enough disposable income to afford anything more exotic than nail polish. Her ultimate responsibility for holding everything together is made clear time and again and is epitomized by her statement on entering the kitchen after a day of work, "Lord have mercy, I would *think* somebody in this house would have hands besides me!" Most of the time, though, she speaks without words, staring at Charlie, who stammers excuses about where he is spending the little money he manages to come across. Part of his resolution is taking up with another woman, Rose, a move that provokes the central dramatic scene of film, a spiraling argument between the husband and wife.

"I'm trying to understand, Charlie," Andais begins. " I mean, I've tried to think that maybe this whole mess is my fault." When Charlie responds by asking, "What's the matter with everybody," Andais retorts, "It isn't everybody, Charlie. It's just me." For the next eight minutes, the couple goes back and forth in a wide-ranging battle over everything from Charlie's affair, his lack of work, her endless work, and the unequal burden of their lives. The argument is largely unscripted and improvised, building and boiling, with Charlie shouting, "I can't make them people give me no job," while she shouts, "I'm tired, Charlie! I'm tired!" Claustrophobic and loud, the couple barely fits in the frame, an unsteady, seemingly hand-held shot that follows the duo around the room as they argue. The scene ends, as the film eventually does, by winding down with only partial resolution. As Charlie announces that he is off to sleep at his friend Duck's house, Andais slumps silently in a corner, unspeaking.

Ending with a scene that aptly captures the accelerating decline and scarcity of options in South Los Angeles, *Bless Their Little Hearts* holds out little of the cautious optimism permitted by the dual suggestions of life that mark the final scenes of *Killer of Sheep*. Woodberry's film ends with Charlie leaving the improvised fish stand his friends have created. As his friends ask him where he is going, Charlie waves his hand dismissively and walks alone across a weed-choked lot. Seen from the back, Charlie alternately hangs his head and marches erect, wordlessly moving between resolution and despair. Leaving off where he began, jobless and uncertain, Charlie's relationships with his wife, children, and friends seemingly mirror the broader collapse that he sees all around him.

RAISING CAINE

The collapse of South Los Angeles serves as the point of departure for Albert and Allen Hughes's film *Menace II Society* (1993). A violent exposition of inner-city life released in the aftermath of the Rodney King riots, *Menace II Society* was arguably the most successful among a group of independently produced films made by a group of mostly young black directors during the early 1990s.[42] Between 1991 and 1993, nearly two dozen films by black directors appeared in theaters: Films such as *Boyz in the Hood* (1991), *New Jack City* (1991), *Straight Outta Brooklyn* (1991), and *Juice* (1992) signaled the rise of a distinct era in black moviemaking. These films emerged from a particular social and filmmaking context, with the successes of Spike Lee, a slump in the financial fortunes of Hollywood, and a broader sense of urban crisis combining to open doors previously shut to black directors. As had been the case with the independent and blaxploitation films of the 1970s, the "hood" films of the early 1990s shared a set of aesthetic, contextual, and narrative aspects. These included a general orientation toward coming-of-age stories, the extensive use of hip hop music, and the inclusion of the urban landscape as part of their storytelling fabric. Politically, these films functioned as a cultural critique in which the totality of the social environment, as opposed to a more narrowly defined contest with a putatively white power structure, shapes the characters' lives.

Ranging throughout South Los Angeles but set primarily in and around the Jordan Downs housing projects in Watts, *Menace II Society* tells the story of Caine "KD" Lawson. The film tracks two basic narrative themes: quotidian patterns of life in South Central and the impossibility of escape. *Menace II Society* offers an oscillating portrait of Caine that alternates between his depiction as a violent, drug-dealing hood governed by the particular ethics of the streets and a more sympathetic character keenly aware of the circumstances he and those around him are forced to navigate. Following Caine, a recent high-school graduate, over the course of a long, hot summer, the film unfolds as a series of interlocking vignettes. Most are problems of Caine's own making. He watches his friend O-Dog gun down a shopkeeper; he shoots a Blood who killed his cousin; he impregnates a girl from another neighborhood, then stomps her cousin when he takes exception to Caine's treatment of the girl.

Along the way, Caine is shot, interrogated by detectives, beaten by policemen, and evicted from his grandparents' house. More positively, he takes up with the girlfriend of his imprisoned mentor, Pernell. Discouraged at the prospect of raising her young son Anthony in the hood, Ronnie encourages Caine to join her in moving to Atlanta. After wavering, he accepts. As they pack her house in preparation for leaving, he is killed in a drive-by shooting.

As with *Bless Their Little Hearts* and *Killer of Sheep*, *Menace II Society* provides a privileged text for understanding a distinct historical moment. More than any of the other films with which it is generally compared, *Menace II Society* portrayed the "hood" in starkly dystopian terms, shedding light on the myriad conflicts (interethnic, intergenerational, gendered, and with the police) that shape black working-class life in era of deindustrialization. Of course, one can critique the portrayal of South Los Angeles as a Hobbesian zone of all against all. The Hughes brothers devote scant attention to the lives of hundreds of thousands of African American Angelenos with jobs, hobbies, and stable families. But the economic decline of central Los Angeles, the social dislocation of the crack cocaine epidemic, and the parallel rise of endemic gang violence were determining parts of the lives of even those who sought to remain above the fray.[43]

Moreover, like the works of Woodberry and Burnett, the Hughes brothers' film archives a particular moment not simply for what it shows but for how it does so. While *Menace II Society* generated many of the same sort of unhelpful and uncomplicated reviews attacking its purported "nihilism" that other works of urban black youth culture had received, a more considered criticism also emerged around the formal choices and storytelling mechanics the directors had chosen. Paula Massood and Paul Gormley argue that the film incorporates a distinct urban aesthetic in which the foreclosing of space links the look of the film with its protagonist. In an interview with the directors, Henry Louis Gates notes both the film's claustrophobic shot composition and its efforts to historicize the conditions it depicted. S. Craig Watkins points out that the extensive use of voiceover by Caine, the persistent use of fade outs, and the flashback-laden storytelling style added up to an approach toward narration uncommon in a studio film. Nor did the ending, with its bloody irresolution, provide what most audiences expected. The filmmakers' confrontational stance vis-à-vis the studio world, like their film's unsentimental ending, nontraditional narrative approaches, and historical perspective, may not add up to a formally "avant-garde" film. Nevertheless, *Menace II Society* looks, sounds, and functions quite differently from regular Hollywood fare.

In a related vein, it is important to note the intertextual aspects of the film. Both directors expressed their animosity toward the sentimentality and filial piety of *Boyz in the Hood*, with Albert Hughes reportedly calling John Singleton's work "an afterschool special with cussing." Indeed, the Hughes brothers seemed in part to have tailored their script to repudiate *Boyz in the Hood*'s moralistic discussions of teenage sexuality, the role of father figures for black boys, the importance of education, and the possibility of finding a way out of the hood. At the same time, the sense of an enclosed space that defies either escape or political transformation links the Hughes brothers with the depictions of South Los Angeles described earlier. One of these is a focus on the city as a character unto itself, with South Los Angeles forming a fixed, bounded terrain. Indeed, Paul Gormley's description of an "overwhelmingly concrete connection between the main protagonist, Caine, and the community of the hood" is just as applicable to Stan and Charlie, both of whom are equally and firmly embedded within the social locations—kitchens, factories, EDD offices, empty lots, front porches—that make up South Central Los Angeles. Politics reveal another connection. Much as Charles Burnett cast *Killer of Sheep* as an effort to depict the sorts of figures he had grown up around, the Hughes brothers made "realness" the primary sensibility they sought to convey. And like Burnett, who expressed disdain for a facile leftism "in which you get your workers' rights and everybody is happy," the dystopian vision of Albert and Allen Hughes resists any temptation to ameliorate or sugarcoat the lives and chances of its subjects, whether through family, education, politics, or relocation.

As it does in *Killer of Sheep* and *Bless Their Little Hearts*, music operates in *Menace II Society* as a critical storytelling element. Like most of the other films that appeared during the same moment, *Menace II Society* has an almost organic relationship with rap music. The late 1980s and early 1990s saw the full flowering of the gangsta rap genre, a style defined in equal measure by its violence, misogyny, West Coast geography, and controversial impact across the wider culture. Like *Juice* (Tupac Shakur), *New Jack City* (Ice-T), and *Boyz in the Hood* (Ice Cube), *Menace II Society* cast rappers (MC Eiht, Too Short) as characters. Rap music provides the soundtrack for all of these, and the films and the musical form take up a common subject matter. For S. Craig Watkins, "hood" films and gangsta rap are of a piece, part of a studio-driven "ghetto-centric imagination" that generates white wealth by trading on voyeuristic aspects of black criminality. Figures such as Dr. Dre, Eazy-E, and Ice Cube are complicit in this project for Watkins, who argues that "the cultural practices of black youth reproduce rather than subvert" the idea of capital accumulation.[44]

Without seeking to negate either the super-profits realized by the entertainment industry as a result of the gangsta rap genre or the complex issues that surround questions of racial representation in an era of unprecedented white access to the internal logics of black American culture, a slightly less Adorno-esque framing probably does more to illustrate the complicated politics of the gangsta genre and its cinematic counterpart. While it is true that the members of N.W.A. spoke clearly about their own accumulatory goals, approaching their cultural production primarily on the basis of the group's own complicated ideological framework risks missing the larger point of how these works fit into public life. Without summarizing the contributions of Brian Cross, Mike Odom, Mike Davis, Robin Kelley, George Lipsitz, and Jeff Chang, to list but an incomplete sample, I would argue in passing that gangsta rap carries an identifiable class politics, a profound urban critique, and, most important, the sonic possibility of a more profound intervention into material and social relations.[45] It is true that N.W.A. showed little interest in redistributing anything on more than an individual level. It is also true, however, that the group's music did more than any other contemporary form to lay bare the multiplicity of contradictions plaguing and shaping working-class black life. On a superficial level, one needs to draw an ideological distinction between, say, the music video for Dr. Dre's "Nuthin' but a 'G' Thang," with its depiction of curbside weightlifters, a house party with a fridge full of malt liquor, and Snoop Doggy Dog ironing his own clothes, and a video in which Jay-Z is waving five hundred €1 notes and drinking Cristal. At the very least, a musical form in which the musicians are threatened by the FBI, investigated by Congress, and denounced by preachers left and right, must, however partially, retain some political import.

As with the music, so, too, with the film. Considered contextually, *Menace II Society* reads as an index of the social dissolution of South Los Angeles during the 1990s. From the opening murder of the Korean storeowner to Caine's gory death ninety minutes later, the film is bracketed by violence. Violence, in fact, structures the entire narrative, with the directors telling the interviewer Skip Gates that part of the intentional "chemistry" of the film was that a violent act should take place every fifteen minutes.[46] Along the way, a procession of armed robberies, shootings, and beatings offer a constant reminder of the limited prospect of escaping the hood alive. The script is violent, as well, with the word "fuck" uttered, muttered, or shouted at least three hundred times. Partially as a result of its use of language, including the equally ubiquitous usage of "bitch" and "nigga," *Menace II Society* generated considerable opprobrium among a sizeable group of black academics, reviewers, and everyday people.

At the same time, the violent imagery and the violent language are integral to both the content and the form of the film. The film opens with a murderous interethnic altercation between O-Dog and two Korean shopkeepers. In another scene, police arrest Caine and Sharif for no discernible reason, then beat them with nightsticks as they lie handcuffed in a squad car. The cops drop them in a neighborhood far from their own—a common police practice of the time. Caine and Sharif are left in an alley full of Chicano *eses*, on the assumption that, as Caine says, "We would get our ass kicked even more." Most probably as a result of their own parallel experiences, the Latinos instead take Caine and Sharif to the hospital. Beyond ethnic antagonisms, *Menace II Society* highlights the intergenerational animosity between Caine and his grandparents. In contrast to the portrayals of family life as tense but ultimately sustaining found in the work of Burnett and Woodberry, the hood of *Menace II Society* is depicted as a place where relations between men and women are almost nonexistent. When Caine begins a relationship with the partner of his incarcerated mentor, their romance stands in stark contrast to the interactions between the other men and women in the film.

Earning money, too, is nearly synonymous with violence, whether one works selling drugs, boosting cars, or pursuing any of the other relatively few financial opportunities present in the hood. We learn through Caine's voice-overs that, while his father worked occasionally as a plumber, construction worker, or electrician, he primarily sold drugs. Drugs kill both of Caine's parents—his mother in an overdose; his father in a deal gone wrong. Eight years later, dealing remains the most lucrative and, in the parlance of economists, "rational" of economic activities. Here, too, *Menace II Society* offers a narrative of declension. In ways unimaginable in the era of powdered cocaine, crack cocaine by the early 1980s had begun a devastating sweep through South Los Angeles.[47] The result was a local economy in which drugs occupied an increasingly central role. In contrast to the violence of work in *Killer of Sheep* —a violence that (at least to human beings) is primarily emotional—what passes for the labor process in *Menace II Society* is contingent on doing harm to others.

The primary violence shown in the film, however, is the fratricidal struggle between young black men. Of the six murders that take place in the film, five involve black men killing other black men. This, too, is a part of the realism of the film. During the 1980s, Los Angeles became world famous as the place where hundreds of street gangs, loosely grouped into the larger Crip and Blood confederations, waged war across an area of the city larger than Manhattan and San Francisco combined. The most detailed chronicler of the history of area street gangs notes that the number of black gang sets grew from 18 in 1972 to 60 in 1978 before nearly tripling to 155 by 1982. The latter interval, it is worth recalling, coincides with the sharpest period of decline in local manufacturing. At the same time, one should resist the temptation to attribute the spiraling violence to an entirely economic causality: The shift away from large-scale job-training programs, the educational devastation wrought by Proposition 13, and the decline of the Black Power Movement highlight the importance of politics to this moment, as well. Between 1979 and 1988, nearly 3,000 "gang-related" homicides took place in the City of Los Angeles. These years were a precursor of things to come, with numbers rising sharply from 1988 (452) to 1989 (554), 1990 (690), 1991 (771), and 1992 (803). For purposes of comparison, it is helpful to recall that gang violence in Los Angeles between 1988 and 1993 alone claimed more lives than thirty years of conflict in Northern Ireland or the first Palestinian Intifada. As violence spilled into previously untouched areas such as Westwood Village (adjacent to the campus of UCLA), Hollywood, and Venice Beach, newspapers and television broadcasts were filled with breathless accounts of an urban army of hundreds of thousands of well-armed, homicidal teenagers poised to overrun the entire Southland.[48]

Official efforts to respond to the devastating conflict between the Crips and Bloods revealed an identifiable class politics in which those elements once thought to make up the shock troops of revolutionary nationalist politics were ruthlessly suppressed with the full agreement of the entire political spectrum. Indeed, rather than the image of Tom Bradley and Daryl Gates facing each other uneasily that adorns one book that traces these years, a more apt rendering of the time would show the men shaking hands.[49] The 1980s saw the flowering of a generational war on youth.[50] Within Los Angeles, police who spoke openly of counterinsurgency missions made recurring efforts to block gang truces from taking hold.[51] The widespread fear of gang violence prompted a section of the black political establishment, acting on the wishes of a segment of its constituency, to take police violence as the lesser of two evils. These were years when groups such as the Coalition against Police Abuse received interference and excuses rather than support from Mayor Bradley. Mike Davis illustrates the political stakes present in the city attorney's continuously rising estimates of the local gang population, a population that more than once has threatened to exceed the number of young African American men present in Los Angeles County. Comparing the "gang scare" to earlier moments of anti-tramp and anti-red hysteria—and here we might add contemporary accounts of "terrorists"—Davis argues that the specter of the migration of gang violence outside the spatial limits of the inner city provided the spark for a wide-ranging police regime whose systematic brutality and indiscriminate targeting more or less guaranteed the outcome of 29 April 1992.[52]

Along the way to Florence and Normandie, the Los Angeles Police Department launched arguably the most active phase in its sixty-year history of acting as an army of occupation. Led by Chief Gates, whose repeated racist statements and defense of officers accused of police brutality made him a fitting heir to William Parker, the LAPD developed a series of multimillion-dollar efforts aimed at demonstrating their control over the streets of Los Angeles. To this end, surplus military equipment was purchased for use as a rolling "battering ram" to destroy suspected crack houses. This particular development was satirized in 1985, with the rapper Toddy-Tee calling the mayor "crazy, and half-way wack / to legalize something that works like that."[53] Semiautomatic rifles and incredibly lethal expanding (dum-dum) ammunition found its way into squad cars. And thousands of police rolling four deep to a car were sent to detain, interrogate, and frisk a generation of young black men "suspected"—as nearly all were—of membership in the Crips or the Bloods. Given names like Operation Hammer and CRASH (for Community Resources against Street Hoodlums), anti-gang efforts resulted in mass arrests, few of which ended in charges being filed. In one weekend in April 1988, 1,453 such arrests were made, with the parking lot of the Memorial Coliseum used as an impromptu internment facility. By 1990, more than 50,000 people had been arrested in gang sweeps, though only a fraction would ever be charged or tried. Of the 2,152 complaints of excessive force made between 1986 and 1990, LAPD investigators found only 42 warranted.[54] Speaking as my own native informant, these were years when going outside on the weekend more or less guaranteed that you would be detained, always harassed, sometimes humiliated, and occasionally slapped around.

For the historian, as for the black resident of Los Angeles, there is a profound temptation to see the patterns of policing that developed in the years before the Rodney King beating through the lens of historical time. While sufficient empirical grounds exist to develop a larger theory of policing tactics, history, and the ethnogenesis of a particular identity on the part of black Angelenos along the lines of the one proposed in a parallel context by Ed

FIGURE 48 Members of the 88th Street Avalon Crips consider the text of a peace treaty, 15 November 1988. Photograph by Steve Grayson. Herald Examiner Collection, Los Angeles Public Library.

Escobar, it is important to recall what was distinct and new about this time, as well.[55] If the interval between *Killer of Sheep* and *Bless Their Little Hearts* constitutes the years during which the industrial base of South Los Angeles underwent its most profound demolition, the period between Woodberry's film and the release of *Menace II Society* coincides with the explosion of prison construction and the mass incarceration of black youth. Between 1982 and 2000, California's prison population grew by nearly 500 percent, and the state built twice as many prisons in eighteen years as it had in the previous hundred years. Mandatory sentencing guidelines and some two thousand new laws fueled the growth in the prison population, which also saw a shift in prison demographics from a white plurality (prior to 1986) to a black plurality (1986–92) and then to a brown plurality (1992–present). Ruth Gilmore describes the perverse logic of this time. Despite falling crime rates, prisons have become the only answer offered in response to the dual question of what is to be done with surplus public investment capital—and workers idled by the economic dislocation of "globalization"—in an era when redistributive claims have been delegitimized through the victorious politics of an ascendant right.[56]

This is the context for *Menace II Society*, and many of the favorable accounts of the film focus on the realism conveyed by these scenes. While important, these somewhat journalistic discussions risk obscuring the film's conscious political choices. Alongside its omnipresent violence, *Menace II Society* is unsparing in its systematic repudiation of each of the primary alternatives open to the kinds of youths whose lives the film portrays. Beyond the depiction of disappeared work, imploded families, poisoned gender relations, and abusive police and omnipresent violence, *Menace II Society* openly rejects black nationalism, religion, education, and out-migration away from Los Angeles. Examining how the film does so exposes the limits of the critique of *Menace II Society* as an unbridled celebration of nihilistic violence and points to the limits of a criticism that tracks only the issue of realism. The larger refusal of redemption that the film shows highlights its importance as a social critique of a moment that is both concurrent and consecutive with that of Burnett and Woodberry.

Menace II Society twice dismisses organized religion as a source of strength amid chaos. Caine's grandparents are mocked for their Christian faith by O-Dog and Caine alike, with the latter dismissing his grandfather for praying to a white Jesus while O-Dog adds, "Man, black people got too damn much religion as it is." Their comments follow an exchange between Caine and his grandfather, in which the grandfather reminds Caine that the Bible prohibits killing. When Caine protests that he has never killed anyone, the older man replies, "Oh, I doubt that." While Caine's and O-Dog's rejection of Christianity is helpful in bringing to light the intergenerational tone-deafness that divides elders from the young, the film's treatment of African American Islam is more important for staking out the overall politics of the film. Sharif, a close friend of Caine's and O-Dog's, is described as an "ex-knucklehead turned Muslim" who is "so happy to be learning something he liked, he kept coming at us with it. He thought Allah could save black people . . . yeah, right." Among the film's more sympathetic characters, Sharif gains no traction in his efforts to politicize his friends. The early 1990s were a time of rapid growth for the Nation of Islam, with support from rap musicians and the broader decline of black radical politics sparking a dramatic renewal in the fortunes of a group that had steadily lost influence since the death of Elijah Muhammad in the mid-1970s.

Los Angeles proved fruitful terrain for the Nation of Islam, and throughout much of South Los Angeles young men can still be seen hawking papers and pies. Gerald Horne and Taylor Branch note the multiple reasons that the Nation of Islam grew in Southern California during an earlier moment.[57]

During the 1990s, the group made extensive efforts to ameliorate gang violence, and while the masculinist and petit-bourgeois aims of the organization
were subject to widespread critique, the Nation of Islam managed to build an
undeniable political base. That it did so during a time when ordinary black
folks could find few other organizational expressions of an anti-systemic critique meant that the Nation of Islam often had the field to itself. I can recall,
for instance, seeing Louis Farrakhan address a crowd of at least twenty thousand at the Los Angeles Coliseum in 1990. Farrakhan spoke on the heels of the
23 January killing of the Nation of Islam member Oliver X. Beasley by Los
Angeles police officers, an incident that recalled a similar event in 1962.[58]
Farrakhan's visit came following a year during which the number of gang
killings had exceeded five hundred for the first time. There were plenty of
Crips and Bloods in the stands that day, and members of both groups listened
attentively as Farrakhan urged them to stop fighting each other and unite
against a common foe. Soon enough, the ideological limitations of the group
—whose economic strategies ignore both the basic character of American
capitalism and the entrenched difficulty black Americans have in securing
capital for small business—ensured that, as in the early 1960s, the appeal of the
Nation of Islam would wane. But if one recalls the importance of the Nation of
Islam within inner-city black communities during the late 1980s and early
1990s, both the inclusion of the character of Sharif and his isolation from his
peers signal a particular political attentiveness on the part of the directors.

At the same time, *Menace II Society* makes clear the inescapability of the
hood. Ronnie has a job offer in Atlanta and encourages Caine to leave with her.
A skeptical Caine tells her, "Ain't nothing gonna change in Atlanta. I'm still
gonna be black." When she presses him further, he retorts, "You act like Atlanta
ain't in America." The conversation reflects a dominant demographic fact of
black life in South Los Angeles during the 1980s and 1990s: the increasing
migration of African Americans out of central Los Angeles. Considerable out-
migration had taken place between 1975 and 1980 as more prosperous blacks
bought homes in surrounding suburban counties while African Americans
across the class spectrum began to reverse longstanding patterns by beginning
to return to the South. Between 1975 and 1980, approximately 73,316 African
Americans left Los Angeles, and while nearly 90,000 new arrivals took their
place, the dissolution of an identifiably black community began to unfold.[59]

Between 1990 and 2000, the black population of the City of Los Angeles
declined by 52,303. While much of this migration was voluntary, a significant
portion was not. As David Grant and his co-authors describe, upward of a

quarter of black out-migrants from Los Angeles during the second half of the 1980s departed on California Department of Corrections buses headed for the growing archipelago of prisons that dot the interior landscape of the state.[60] When coupled with the increase of migration from Asia and Latin America, the result was a stunning remaking of Los Angeles from a fairly black and white city of the 1960s to a multinational, polylingual metropolis in which "traditionally black" neighborhoods retained Latino majorities.[61] Whether black Angelenos were seeking better jobs, safer neighborhoods, bigger houses, or some combination, out-migration became an active strategy for a group of people whose ancestors had initially come west seeking the same things that their descendents now sought elsewhere. The Hughes brothers' response to the idea of escaping to greener pastures outside Los Angeles is clear: *Menace II Society* ends with the killings of both Caine, who is preparing to leave for Atlanta, and Sharif, who has decided to follow another friend to Kansas.

In the end, neither physical relocation nor collective action offers a way out. It is this overall sense of immobility and its consequent dearth of solutions that places *Menace II Society* in conversation with *Killer of Sheep* and *Bless Their Little Hearts*. In each case, working-class male protagonists try, with varying degrees of success, to survive in the face of mounting obstacles and declining resources. Survival, in its way, suggests a diametrically different understanding of life in Los Angeles from the celebratory aspects of multi-culturalism or the language of opportunity that emerged alongside black electoral victories. In contrast to the political moments defined by cultural struggles for access or autonomy, the post-civil-rights moment of "late" black politics might be seen in part as one in which even describing the basic outline of what was going on constituted a terrain of critical struggle. To be sure, the character of the cinematic critique offered in this moment was largely one of negation. Burnett, Woodberry, and the Hughes brothers did more to illustrate the nature of the crisis than to suggest possible solutions. But this, too, was part of the point. Burnett himself argued that "for a film to act as an agent for altering people's behavior . . . an ongoing process [of] politicization must be taking place."[62]

To the extent that *Killer of Sheep*, *Bless Their Little Hearts*, and *Menace II Society* posed blackness, masculinity, and class as key modalities for under-standing American urban life at a crisis point, one might conclude that film after 1973 solidifies a view of black cultural production as providing a key diagnostic tool for understanding the larger direction and parameters of black political struggles. While such a view would be in keeping with one of this book's larger arguments regarding the strategic centrality of culture within political movements, it tells only half of the story. Jorge Sanjines suggested that "revolutionary art will always be distinguished by [how it] embraces whole communities of people, with their own particular ways of thinking, of conceiving reality and loving life."[63] In this vein, I would like to suggest that the social diagnostic of politically engaged black art is ultimately less important than its success in reflecting a kind of communal interiority, the "continuing development of a collective consciousness informed by the historical struggles for liberation and motivated by the shared sense of obligation to preserve the collective being."[64]

This is the tie that binds *Killer of Sheep*, *Bless Their Little Hearts*, and *Menace II Society*. These films track the black working class from its tenuous industrial foothold to its postindustrial idling. There is a kind of changing same here, a tale of the same people, in the same place, at different times. By 1992, this was a kind of ghost story, the aftermath of efforts "to make impossible the future we live today."[65] Completed in the absence of both a black liberation movement and an effective welfare state, these films depict the children of those who fought to redefine Watts as a "Freedom City" and who "built street theaters with school drop-outs, junk hunts down the railroad track with pre-schoolers, back yard paintings with amateurs and professionals together."[66] They show the grandchildren of those who came west to build the death machines of democracy and who made movie theaters, playbills, and musicians' unions into sites of dignity and self-definition. While the direction in which they point may not be forward, these films show dignity and defiance as the property of those for whom dissonance is a way of life.

Above all, they show the unfinished effort to define a meaningful black freedom in urban America.

EPILOGUE

On the afternoon of Wednesday, 29 April 1992, following the announcement that ten verdicts of "not guilty" had been reached in the case of four Los Angeles police officers accused of savagely beating the black motorist Rodney King, a western corner of South Central Los Angeles erupted. Lacing outward from a single intersection, rioting spread across the city. Three days later, nearly every police officer and deputy sheriff in Southern California, reinforced by more than thirteen thousand active-duty and reserve military personnel, had managed to establish an uneasy order. When the number of dead, wounded, and arrested was finally tallied, Los Angeles had suffered, for the second time in less than thirty years, one of the worst urban disturbances in American history. As tempers and embers cooled, the full accounting of events began to unfold.

The cultural responses to the uprising could fill a volume in their own right. A partial listing might begin by noting the ongoing revitalization of community arts within the Leimert Park area. A bohemian enclave set within a leafy subdivision, Leimert Park divides middle-class black areas such as Ladera Hills, Baldwin Hills, and View Park from a number of working-class black areas in and around the larger Crenshaw district. Easily accessible by freeway and surface streets, Leimert Park began as a racially restricted neighborhood designed for white homeowners before giving way before the determined homebuyers of the black middle class. The plaza at the center of the area sits astride Degnan Boulevard, a block-long commercial strip that once featured the Brockman Gallery as a prominent tenant. Since 1992, Degnan and parallel streets have hosted a thriving urban village of coffee shops, second-hand stores, galleries, and performance spaces. More recently, Eso Won

Books, one of the largest black-owned bookstores in the United States, has taken up residence.

Much of this transformation is the result of the work of black artists with ties to the avant-garde of the 1950s, 1960s, and 1970s. Several years before the Rodney King uprising, the drummer Billy Higgins and the word musician Kamau Daáood founded the World Stage, a multi-arts improvised music and poetry space. Before his passing in 2001, Higgins recorded on hundreds of jazz records, and he was one of Ornette Coleman's original percussionists. Daaood, meanwhile, had been a member of the Watts Writers Workshop and the Pan Afrikan People's Arkestra. Around the corner from the World Stage is KAOS Network, a digital arts and multimedia resource center where youth interested in new media receive technical training and can showcase their work. KAOS Network is the brainchild of Ben Caldwell, a film professor at CalArts who passed through the UCLA film program with Charles Burnett, Haile Gerima, and Larry Clark.

Beyond Leimert Park, the years after the Rodney King rebellion brought renewed attention to artists who had struggled to remain visible amid the arid political climate of the Reagan years. Pan Afrikan People's Arkestra gigs became a more regular occurrence, as did solo piano and small group combo performances by Horace Tapscott. Many of the former featured the vast vocal range of singer Dwight Tribble, the brilliant horn playing of Michael Sessions, and the dazzling bass work of Roberto Miranda. Tapscott began to record again, releasing *Aiee! The Phantom* (1996) and *Thoughts of Dar es Salaam* (1997). Critical attention arrived, as well, leading to a number of rare tours and a long-delayed performance at Lincoln Center. For the pioneering forerunners of rap, the Watts Prophets, the 1990s brought a new measure of attention and acclaim. Nineteen ninety-seven saw the trio release their first record since 1971, entitled *When the 90s Came*. In 2005, meanwhile, a career retrospective appeared, marking the first time that material from their albums *The Black Voices: On the Streets in Watts* (1969) and *Rappin Black in a White World* (1971) had appeared on compact disc. This moment saw additional resources flow toward the California African American Museum and Watts Towers Art Center, as well, and both acquired directors (John Riddle and Mark Greenfield) with links to the earlier moment of community-based cultural activity.

Most impressive, the cultural flowering centered in Leimert Park linked these veteran voices with a new generation of creative talent. At the World Stage, Michael Datcher mentors a new cohort of writers who make up the Anansi Writers Workshop. Many of the interested youths who pass through the doors of KAOS Network, meanwhile, arrive on Thursday evenings for the underground hip hop ciphers at Project Blowed, whose co-founders, Aceyalone (Eddie Harris) and Abstract Rude (Aaron Pointer), emerged from an open-mic night at the now defunct Good Life health food store. There, Freestyle Fellowship, Jurassic 5, the Pharcyde, and other groups honed their skills. Inside and beyond Leimert Park, visual artists and plastic artists such as Noni Olabisi, Edgar Arcineaux, and Ramsess continue to invigorate and redefine the parameters of black art.

More episodic, but important nonetheless, has been the proliferation of theatrical and literary examinations of black Los Angeles. Anna Deavere Smith's one-woman play *Twilight Los Angeles* sought to make sense of an uprising that defied easy summary within the familiar language of black rage. Drawing on one hundred seventy-five interviews conducted after the riots, Deveare Smith's play is a collage of pointillist character sketches in which live audiences might see the riots from the point of view of an immigrant Asian grocer, a Latina juror, a Crip working to establish a gang truce, a radical white intellectual, the chief of police, a former Black Panther, or a badly beaten white truck driver. In a more autobiographical vein, Paul Beatty's acerbic *White Boy Shuffle* offered a cutting examination of adolescent coming of age in riot-torn South Los Angeles. Beatty's depiction of present-day absurdity found bookends in efforts to examine the future (Octavia Butler) and past (Walter Mosley) of black Los Angeles. On a more minor level, the post-rebellion years saw an outpouring of research on black Los Angeles, including the appearance of major interview series with local musicians and visual artists.

Community stands as a common thread in all of these projects: the hip hop huddles inside the darkened cavern of Project Blowed; Ramsess's stained-glass portraits of Josephine Baker, Thelonious Monk, and Prince; Kamau's and Datcher's second-generation writers' workshop; Gunnar Kaufman, Lauren Olamina, Easy Rawlins; even the Central Avenue Sounds series of oral histories conducted by UCLA. All of these question and seek, search for and build, *community*. For its resident artists, as for the visitors who fill its sidewalks, Leimert Park offers something rare in Los Angeles and rarer still for black Angelenos: a safe, pedestrian-friendly, arts-centered zone of optimism, unity, and creativity. Small wonder, then, that an anonymous passerby could comment in Jeanette Lindsay's 2006 film *Leimert Park: The Story of a Village in South Central Los Angeles*, that "Leimert Park is like an exception to the whole Los Angeles area. It is a little oasis, so to speak."

The dedication that Leimert Park inspires should hardly surprise us. Many of the artists involved have worked to bring art to South Los Angeles for decades. The markers of culture, community, and identity that the arts district symbolizes reflect ongoing despair at the failures, limitations, and unanswered problems that persisted throughout the historical moments described in this book. After 1992, the destruction of the rebellion was only the most proximate of these. Fatigue with the omnipresent violence of the 1980s; the generational decline in the economic fortunes and broader life chances of everyday black people after 1970; the growing class chasm among African Americans; the rapid transition of inner-city neighborhoods from black to brown—all of these factors have produced widespread feelings of generalized anxiety. In this context, the presence of an identifiably black arts district is seen by many as a kind of lifeline that proves that African Americans can find emotional and geographic togetherness in Southern California.

Yet those things that make Leimert Park special are symptomatic of larger problems. As of the 2000 census, the Leimert Park area was 91 percent African American. This marks a striking contrast with the rest of South Los Angeles, where African Americans now hover somewhere around 40 percent of the total population. Given its location at the intersection of working-class and affluent black neighborhoods, Leimert Park promises something that is otherwise absent in Los Angeles: an overwhelmingly black area of varied economic levels, where black people of all walks can mingle and mix. This is the kind of neighborhood that used to exist, during a time that many remember with fondness and nostalgia. Given Abbie Hoffman's apocryphal quote about nostalgia being a mild form of depression, it is perhaps worth dwelling on some of the implications of the Leimert-centered post-rebellion renaissance of community arts.

To begin with, it is hard not to see the atavism implicit in building a self-described "village" in the most populous county in the United States. And while the search for community in the idea of geographic continuity is basic to most forms of human collectivity (social-networking websites notwithstanding), the defense of a few square blocks of racialized space represents a pronounced turnaround from the vision of a Black Arts Movement that spread well beyond the entirety of South Los Angeles. Inside the village itself, we find competing agendas—business versus art being the most important—that highlight the continuing ideological clash between the petit-bourgeois vision of a nascent black capitalism and the conviction that creative endeavors are integral to community life.

Beyond this lack of a unified vision for the area that much of the city seems invested in designating as *the* black space, it is worth asking what answers the cultural vision of Leimert Park provides to black residents of Los Angeles at large. Put most succinctly, in a predominantly Latino city where relations between black and brown constitute perhaps the single most important social and political question, does an all-black arts district help us to find the way forward? If, as this book has tried to argue, part of the salience of cultural politics is in the way that creative works force us to confront the urban landscape, what are we to make of the dogged, persistent, beautiful, and contradictory effort to use "black arts" as a path toward community, identity, and politics in twenty-first-century Los Angeles? Going forward, perhaps there is a space to be found between nostalgia for a different demographic and political time and the unalloyed abrogation of black distinctiveness into the multiethnic tableau. As Duke Ellington reminded us long ago, we are more than part of somebody's larger whole, whether that whole is the one envisioned by George Bush or Ozomatli. We are also not here alone, no matter how much we try to confuse ourselves into wishing we were. We are inside and apart, integral and invisible. The challenge for the next iteration of black urban cultural radicalism will be to find a vision that is both within and without, that gives voice to our peoplehood while serving as a building block of something larger, and better, than what we find today.

This book has explored expressive culture as a modality of black politics. It has argued that art provides a unique vantage point for comprehending the how and why of popular struggle along the axes of class, gender, and race. It has shown how successive historical moments facilitated distinct approaches to cultural politics, and how new political contexts generated new forms of expression. This view provides distinct insight into the concerns that animated integrationists and nationalists, elected officials and urban insurgents, everyday people and extraordinary individuals alike. Following both racial unity and class conflict, I have argued that expressive culture has provided insight into the changing character of black life since the years of the Second World War. At the same time, I have argued that culture highlights commonalities present across the arc of a half-century of black self-activity within a single metropolitan site.

Bearing in mind these observations about continuity and change, I would suggest several lessons that the cultural field may hold for black social movements as a whole.

CULTURAL POLITICS ARE MATERIAL

Throughout this text, I have sought to demonstrate that contests over resources and rights invariably have required cultural work, in part by showing how cultural work was itself a struggle over the material conditions of production and access. William Grant Still's decision to quit work on the *Stormy Weather* score; union amalgamation; the founding of the Black Arts Council; the rise of a cohort of independent black filmmakers—each of these arose from specific disputes over the lives of artists. In each case, transforming the working conditions of artists led to collective organization, and, more often than not, to mass politics. One lesson of cultural politics might therefore be that the issues raised by the problems facing creative personalities take place within industries, neighborhoods, and informal networks that can be changed only through a process that redistributes power and wealth.

CULTURAL POLITICS ARE COLLECTIVE

Art, we sometimes learn, is an individual act, a private truth by a singularly creative being. The artists surveyed throughout this book broke decisively with this view. The communitarian humanism of Charles Burnett; the un-yielding dedication of Horace Tapscott and John Outterbridge; the collective process of creation and debate inside Art West Associated and the Watts Writers Workshop—in each case, the Black Arts Movement demonstrated that what is valuable about any of us is learned through interaction with others. A vast project of democratization lay at the heart of this vision, based on the conviction that art was the property of all rather than the private repository of the few.

CULTURAL POLITICS ARE HOLISTIC

This book has approached the idea of a Black Arts Movement as though each of its constituent terms formed a necessary part of the whole. The movement aspect could be found in dozens of organizations and hundreds of activists. The arts aspect could be found in the search for new forms of expression, whether in jazz, assemblage art, theater, or film. And the black in this Black Arts Movement was to be found in lived experience and conscious articulation, in social being and social consciousness alike. I hasten to add that to speak of *black* art, of *black* people, or of a *black* movement does not trap us within an unquestioning celebration of essentialist unity. On the contrary, the variety of visions charted here—from Billy Woodberry to Jayne Cortez—give voice to a diverse and eloquent reply to the question posed by Cesaire that opened this book: Who and what are we?

CULTURAL POLITICS ARE DEMOCRATIC

Strong people, Ella Baker once said, "don't need strong leaders." But not everyone starts out strong. Some of us start out marginalized and confused, ignorant and downpressed. To become strong people, we need conscious individuals who extend the abilities of those around them. This is the missing link in a time of useless spokespeople, self-appointed leaders, and the unorganized, inchoate masses. A Nick Stewart or a Ruth Waddy; the actor who builds sets by hand and pays his student's Actors' Equity dues; the woman who founds an arts collective and studies nights to master the questions of form her colleagues want to discuss. Clyde Taylor, quoting Tina Turner, is right: We don't need another hero. We need a new heroism that teaches us that leadership is building the capacity of others. This is a kind of heroism that black artists have often proved adept at showing, and it is worth reflecting on the reasons why.

CULTURAL POLITICS ARE IMAGINATIVE

Liberation and imagination are inseparable. Political transformation begins with the belief in a different reality, an achievable vision of life better than what currently exists. It stands to follow that activities that force us to rethink perceptions, boundaries, and limitations objectively advance other struggles for change. Have not the great revolutions of human history been accompanied, however temporarily, by a new art? Vodun after Bois Caïman? Constructivism? Mexican muralism? Third Cinema? Free jazz? Hip hop? That our revolution was defeated before we saw the full flowering of its creative energies should not prevent us from remembering that human problems have human solutions and that these solutions require us to develop the fullness of our own potential, the totality of our being, the unreached-for limits of our collective selves. To paraphrase Buenaventura Durruti, we carry a new world in our art. In the cipher or the cell, in the studio or in the street, that world is growing this instant.

NOTES

Introduction

Epigraphs' sources: Aimé Cesaire, *The Collected Poetry* (Berkeley: University of California Press, 1983), 50; Charles Wright and the Watts 103rd Street Rhythm Band, "Express Yourself," Warner Brothers Records 1864 (1970).

1. In seeking to highlight the spread of ideas and the political salience of creative personalities in the context of California, my narrative incurs an intellectual debt to the work of Richard Cándida Smith: see Smith, *Utopia and Dissent*, xix. Of late, a number of archival collections, autobiographies, documentary films, and other sources have combined and expanded the quantity of material available to students of black cultural production in Los Angeles. We can hope and expect that groups treated quickly, or not at all, in this volume will receive extended analyses in subsequent projects.
2. Rogin, "Democracy and Burnt Cork."
3. Lawrence Christon, "Arts Department Nears Reality," *Los Angeles Times*, 10 May 1979.
4. The art historian Judith Wilson uses creative community to capture the specificity of creative endeavor while preserving a place for social contexts and "the indirect involvement of numerous other people": Wilson, "Garden of Music," 25; Wolff, *The Social Production of Art*, 118–19.
5. Smethurst, *The Black Arts Movement*, 14.
6. Isoardi, *The Dark Tree*.
7. Henry Louis Gates Jr., "Black Creativity: On the Cutting Edge," *Time*, 10 October 1994, 74–75.
8. Kelley, "Dig They Freedom," 18.
9. Sell, *Avant-Garde Performance and the Limits of Criticism*, 228–31.
10. Kobena Mercer, *Welcome to the Jungle*, 238. For a basic introduction to a multidisciplinary black arts criticism, see, on visual art, Driskell, *African American Visual Aesthetics*; Lewis, *Art*; Patton, *African American Art*; Powell, *Black Art and Culture in the 20th Century*; on music, Lewis, "Improvised Music after 1950"; Moten, *In the Break*; Porter, *What Is This Thing Called Jazz?*; Stanyek, "Transmissions of an Interculture"; Thomas, "Ascension"; Weheliye, *Phonographies*. For an important recent over-

view dealing with literature, theater, and community arts, see Smethurst, *The Black Arts Movement*. On literature, see Brown, *Performing the Word*; Henderson, *Understanding the New Black Poetry*; Nielsen, *Black Chant*; idem, *Integral Music*; Redmond, *Drumvoices*; Thomas, *Extraordinary Measures*. For comparative, cross-generic analyses, see, Benston, *Performing Blackness*; Boyd, *Wrestling with the Muse*; Sell, *Avant-Garde Performance and the Limits of Criticism*; Young, *Soul Power*.

11. Porter, *What Is This Thing Called Jazz?*, xvi.

12. Sell, *Avant-Garde Performance and the Limits of Criticism*.

13. David Lionel Smith has spoken of the Black Arts Movement as "emanating from various local responses to a general development within American cultures of the 1960s": see Smith, "The Black Arts Movement and Its Critics," as quoted in Smethurst, *The Black Arts Movement*, 9.

14. Noah Purifoy, "Art in the Community," notes for a speech prepared for the seminar "A Day with the Experts in the Arts," 26 October 1974, Noah Purifoy Papers.

15. Williams, *The Politics of Modernism*, 174–75.

16. In discussing creative personalities as the antithesis of the new industries of mass communication, Cruse sought to extend both C. Wright Mills's exploration of the emergence of new social groups in the United States and the Marxist notion of the industrial proletariat as the force produced by, and capable of destroying, capitalism: Cruse, *The Crisis of the Negro Intellectual*, 64–65.

17. Biondi, *To Stand and Fight*; Countryman, *Up South*; Joseph, *The Black Power Movement*; Ogbar, *Black Power*; Self, *American Babylon*; Sugrue, *The Origins of the Urban Crisis*; Theoharis and Woodard, *Freedom North*, 2–6; idem, *Groundwork*; Woodard, *A Nation within a Nation*.

18. Saul, *Freedom Is, Freedom Ain't*, 9.

19. For an introductory overview of this ever-expanding literature, see Crouch, *The Artificial White Man*; idem, *The All-American Skin Game*; Gilroy, *Against Race*; McWhorter, *Losing the Race*; Reed, "Black Particularity Reconsidered"; Wilson, *The Declining Significance of Race*.

20. Marx, *The Eighteenth Brumaire of Louis Bonaparte*, 47.

21. A number of studies that take Marxism as a method, though not as an ideology, have done much to illustrate the salience of class within African American life. See, e.g., Cruse, *The Crisis of the Negro Intellectual*; Gomez, *Exchanging Our Country Marks*; Robinson, *Black Marxism*; Singh, *Black Is a Country*.

22. Baraka, *The Black Arts Movement*, 11. Although Baraka is often identified by critics as a "Maoist," a term seldom used by those influenced by the theoretical contributions of Mao Zedong, his language in this instance is redolent of that strain of Marxist criticism represented by, for example, Valentin Volosinov: see Volosinov, *Marxism and the Philosophy of Language*, 23.

23. Green, *Selling the Race*; Gregory, *Black Corona*; Woods, *Development Arrested*.

24. Denning, *The Cultural Front*, 57.

25. The most complete examination of Bradley's tenure as mayor is in Sonenshein, *Politics in Black and White*.

26. Churchill, "To Disrupt, Discredit, and Destroy," 96.

27. Smith, *Utopia and Dissent*.

28. Lewis, "Improvised Music after 1950," esp. 91–94, 112–17.

29. Moten, *In the Break*; Sell, *Avant-Garde Performance and the Limits of Criticism*, 281–83; Taylor, "Decolonizing the Image."

30. Franklin, *Black Self-Determination*. Originally published with the subtitle "A Cultural History of the Faith of the Fathers," Franklin's study, like Sterling Stuckey's *Slave Culture*, offers a framework for comprehending the national (and supranational) character of African American collective identity in the absence of a bounded, territorial frame. Franklin's excavation of resistance as one dialectical component of black cultural identity can be adapted to the twentieth century and, one imagines, beyond.

31. I have in mind here two important recent studies. For the prewar period, there is Flamming, *Bound for Freedom*. For the postwar period, see Sides, *L.A. City Limits*.

32. Willard, "Nuestra Los Angeles," 810.

33. McWilliams, *Southern California*, 49.

34. For an introduction to the recent historical literature that takes race as an analytic frame for studying Mexican or Mexican American and Anglo Los Angeles, see Escobar, "The Dialectics of Repression"; Molina, *Fit to Be Citizens?*; Pagan, *Murder at the Sleepy Lagoon*; Sanchez, *Becoming Mexican American*; Villa, *Barrio-Logos*.

35. Noah Purifoy, "Art in the Community," 1974, Noah Purifoy Papers.

36. For interethnic approaches that connect the histories of local communities of color, see Alvarez, *The Power of the Zoot*; Kurashige, "The Many Facets of Brown"; Pulido, *Black, Brown, Yellow, and Left*; Sanchez, "What's Good for Boyle Heights Is Good for the Jews"; Wild, *Street Meeting*.

37. Alvarez, *The Power of the Zoot*; Macías, *Mexican American Mojo*.

38. Rodney, *A History of the Guyanese Working People*, 179.

39. Ibid.

40. Gerald Horne uses the term "the new leadership" in his discussion of the rise of groups such as the Nonviolent Action Committee, the Nation of Islam, the Black Panther Party, and the US Organization after the Watts riot of 1965: see Horne, *The Fire This Time*, 185–212.

41. Cabral's speech was originally delivered on 20 February 1970 as part of the Eduardo Mondlane Memorial Lecture Series at Syracuse University, Syracuse, New York, under the auspices of the Program of Eastern African Studies. It was translated from the French by Maureen Webster.

1. Hollywood Scuffle

Epigraph source: Glen C. H. Perry, *"Dear Bart": Washington Views of World War II* (Westport, Conn.: Greenwood Press, 1982), 184.

1. Ellington, *Music Is My Mistress*, 175.

2. *Jump for Joy* remains relatively unknown among Ellington's works. Patricia Willard's essay, which accompanies the Smithsonian's partially restored recording, constitutes the primary source regarding the musical: Patricia Willard, *Jump for Joy* (Smithsonian Institution, 1988).

3. Ibid., 17–18. See also Emory Holmes II, "The Duke of L.A.," *Los Angeles Times*, 25 April 1999. For a contemporary account that places *Jump for Joy* within the context of Ellington's subsequent examination of African American history, *Black, Brown, and Beige*, see Ulanov, *Duke Ellington*, 239–61. See also Cohen, "Duke Ellington and *Black, Brown, and Beige*."

4. During their brief stay in Los Angeles in 1941, Ellington's band recorded "Moon over Cuba," and "Bakiff": see Lambert, *Duke Ellington*, 101–2.

5. Nicholson, *Reminiscing in Tempo*, 234.

6. Lawrence, *Duke Ellington and His World*, 305.

7. Ellington, *Music Is My Mistress*, 176.

8. The transcriptions of lyrics are from Willard, *Jump for Joy*, 14. Stephen Collins Foster, one of the most important American composers, composed numerous minstrel songs describing an idyllic vision of antebellum life.

9. Tyler, *From Harlem to Hollywood*, 110.

10. Maurice Zolotow, "Duke Ellington's Forgotten L.A. Musical," *Los Angeles Magazine*, February 1982, 179–81.

11. Herb Jeffries, quoted in Nicholson, *Reminiscing in Tempo*, 234.

12. Ellington, *Music Is My Mistress*, 175–76.

13. "Jump for Joy closes in L.A.," *Courier* (Pittsburgh), 4 October 1941.

14. Lawrence, *Duke Ellington*, 305.

15. Davis's columns are discussed in Ulanov, *Duke Ellington*, 242.

16. Ellington, *Music Is My Mistress*, 175.

17. Michael Denning examines *Jump for Joy* as a signature example of Popular Front theater: see Denning, *The Cultural Front*, 312–19. On Ellington's Popular Front political links, see ibid., 317. Ellington's FBI file has been publicly released under the auspices of the Freedom of Information Act: see Edward Kennedy (Duke) Ellington, FBI file 100-HQ-434443, esp. entry 100–7060–977.

18. Duke Ellington, "We, Too, Sing America," speech delivered at Annual Lincoln Day Services, Scott Methodist Church, Los Angeles, 9 February 1941, and published as the "Speech of the Week" in the *California Eagle*, 13 February 1941; reprinted in Tucker, *The Duke Ellington Reader*, 147; John Pittman, "The Duke Will Stay on Top," reprinted in Tucker, *The Duke Ellington Reader*, 148–51.

19. Ellington, "We, Too, Sing America," 147–48.

20. Prewar black politics and culture often oscillated between binaries such as protest–accommodation and folk–urban, while the dominant political framework of the period, racial uplift, was itself an internally bifurcated framework that divided African Americans along class-bound cultural patterns. For important assessments, see Carby, *Reconstructing Womanhood*; Gaines, *Uplifting the Race*; Mitchell, *Righteous Propagation*.

21. Gunnar Myrdal to Floyd Covington, letter, National Urban League, Los Angeles Chapter Records, Special Collections, UCLA, box 2, folder 4. I first became aware of this source through Kurashige, "The Many Facets of Brown."

22. Chester Himes, "Lunching at the Ritzmore," in Himes, *Black on Black*, 182. The essay was originally published in *Crisis*, October 1942.

23. Williams, "My Man Himes," 60.

24. After a prolonged period of critical neglect, Chester Himes has undergone a major rediscovery. For work that discusses Himes's time in California, see Lipsitz, *A Rainbow at Midnight*; Glasrud and Champion, "No Land of the Free"; Skinner, "Streets of Fear"; Fabre and Margolies, *The Several Lives of Chester Himes*.

25. Himes, *If He Hollers Let Him Go*, 79.

26. Ibid., 167.

27. For representative examples of a wit that is simultaneously expansive, dry, and very much racially marked, see Himes's depiction of the argument between male and female black workers regarding the presence of white women on crews (ibid., 135).

28. Ibid., 153. Note Himes's backhanded signification on Van Vetchen.

29. Himes, *The Quality of Hurt*, 76.

30. Bunch, " A Past Not Necessarily Prologue"; Collins, *Black Los Angeles*; De Graaf, "The City of Black Angels," and "Significant Steps on an Arduous Path"; Sandoval, "Ghetto Growing Pains"; Smith, "Black Employment in the Los Angeles Area, 1938–1948"; Williams, "Ecology of Negro Communities in Los Angeles County." The literature on wartime black Los Angeles is excellent and growing: see De Graaf, "Negro Migration to Los Angeles, 1930 to 1950"; Kurashige, "Transforming Los Angeles"; Leonard, "In The Interest of All Races"; Sides, *L.A. City Limits*; Taylor, *In Search of the Racial Frontier*.

31. For a comprehensive analysis of the struggle for economic and social equality during Second World War–era Los Angeles, see Kurashige, *The Shifting Grounds of Race*.

32. Although African Americans constituted approximately 7.1 percent of the population, they held only 5.3 percent of industrial jobs. When one considers that working-age men were over-represented among the newly arrived, the extent of under-representation becomes clearer: "Says Bias Deprives Nation of Minority Contributions," NOW, vol. 2, no. 15, February 1945, 6, quoted in Leonard, "Brothers under the Skin?"

33. The African American struggle for industrial employment in Los Angeles during the Second World War has been covered in some depth. See, e.g., Nash, *The American West Transformed*, 90–94; Sides, *L.A. City Limits*, 57–81; Starr, *Embattled Dreams*, 138–39; Taylor, *In Search of the Racial Frontier*, 254–56.

34. This was a national process. For an important early overview, see Dalfiume, "The 'Forgotten Years' of the Negro Revolution." For a contemporary account of changes to the racial landscape during the war, see James et al., *Fighting Racism in World War II*.

35. Frances Williams, "Varied Relaxation Offsets Taxation," *War Worker*, August 1943. Founded in 1915, Karamu House is the oldest African American theater in the United States.

36. Bakan, "Way out West on Central."

37. Williams, "Varied Relaxation Offsets Taxation."

38. Supervisor John Anson Ford sponsored a county-funded exhibition of Negro art at the county-owned Museum of Art, as well: see John Anson Ford to Beulah Woodard, letter, 13 November 1953, John Anson Ford Papers, box 76.

39. Horne, *Class Struggle in Hollywood*, 61–65. The strike figures and quote regarding the Hollywood Writers Mobilization are in Denning, *The Cultural Front*, 404, 417. On the CIO in California, see Lichtenstein, *Labor's War at Home*, 60–62. On the growth of progressive forces in Hollywood, see Buhle and Wagner, *Radical Hollywood*.

40. Denning, *The Cultural Front*, 16–19.
41. For a representative account of Robeson's wartime presence in Los Angeles, see "Coming of Robeson Stirs Interest Here," *California Eagle*, 3 September 1942.
42. Pagan, *Murder at the Sleepy Lagoon*, 205; Smith, *Becoming Something*, 156. The multiracial mobilization for the defense of seventeen Mexican Americans accused of participating in a murder at a grassy urban reservoir known popularly as Sleepy Lagoon became one the most visible manifestations of Popular Front cultural politics on the West Coast. The riots took place in the broader context of major rioting elsewhere in the country and within the city itself. October 1943 alone saw multiple minor altercations across the city, with cafes, streetcars, and public dances serving as the sites of violent confrontations over urban segregation. Historical accounts regarding zoot culture can be divided into roughly three types. For accounts that place the zoot phenomenon within the context of Mexican American history, see Escobar, *Race, Police, and the Making of a Political Identity*; Mazón, *The Zoot Suit Riots*; Pagan, *Murder at the Sleepy Lagoon*. For accounts that explore the zoot suit within a predominantly African American framework, see Cosgrove, "The Zoot-Suit and Style Warfare"; Robin D. G. Kelley, "The Riddle of the Zoot: Malcolm Little and Black Cultural Politics during World War II," in Kelley, *Race Rebels*; Lott, "Double V, Double-Time." For pioneering accounts that examine the intercultural dimensions of zoot culture, see Alvarez, *The Power of the Zoot*; Daniels, "Los Angeles Zoot"; Leonard, "Brothers under the Skin?"; Nash, *The American West Transformed*, 96. For a discussion of public transportation as a site of radical spontaneity and informal political activity, see Robin D. G. Kelley, "'Congested Terrain': Resistance on Public Transportation," in idem, *Race Rebels*, 55–75.
43. Smith, *Becoming Something*, 157.
44. "Plan 'Salute to Russia' Sunday," *California Eagle*, 5 November 1942.
45. "Hollywood Thrills to Russia Benefit," *California Eagle*, 23 April 1942.
46. For a primer on political conservatism in prewar California, see McWilliams, *Southern California*, 274–94. For an account of the role of white supremacy in the construction of a local industrial base, see Davis, "Sunshine and the Open Shop."
47. On *Star of Ethiopia*, see Flamming, *Bound for Freedom*, 212–13, 267–70. On the Ink Slingers, see Tyler, *From Harlem to Hollywood*, 35–37. Flamming explains that *Star of Ethiopia* generated a major intergenerational skirmish among NAACP activists.
48. "Local Artists Quit Festival Arts Committee: Charge of Segregation Causes Wholesale Resignations," *California Eagle*, 31 May 1934.
49. Membership booklet, Allied Arts, Thomas Bradley Administrative Papers, box 5049, file 4. See also "Society Matrons Present Artists," *California Eagle*, 16 January 1952.
50. On Miller's political trajectory, see Tyler, *From Harlem to Hollywood*, 39–41; see also Loren Miller, "How 'Left' Is the N.A.A.C.P.?" *New Masses*, 16 July 1935.
51. Owing in significant measure to the objections to the script raised by Hughes, the film never got off the ground. Miller accompanied Hughes on part of Hughes's tours through Soviet Central Asia: see Langston Hughes, *I Wonder as I Wander*, 72–82. For background on the Communist Party of the USA, the Soviet Union, and the politics of African American culture, see Robin D. G. Kelley, "'Afric's Sons with Banner Red':

African American Communists and the Politics of Culture, 1919–1934," in idem, *Race Rebels*; Mullen, *Popular Fronts*; Naison, *Communists in Harlem during the Great Depression*.

52. Loren Miller, "Uncle Tom in Hollywood," *The Crisis*, November 1934, 329.

53. "Form Film Committee," *California Eagle*, 31 March 1938. The distinction between "Eastside" and "Westside" constitutes a primary marker of historical social geography in Los Angeles. African Americans, Japanese Americans, Mexican Americans, and whites have each had Eastsides and Westsides that have changed over time. For African Americans, the boundary between east and west has shifted steadily westward with the pace of integration. Today, the Harbor (110) Freeway constitutes the most common boundary, while during the period of the Second World War, Central Avenue would have been the line dividing east and west. This geography, moreover, is social and political. The black "Westside" is thought to have been more affluent, with a larger pool of professionals who worked in mixed, if not fully integrated, contexts. The "Eastside" leadership mentioned here would coincide with a traditional black bourgeoisie whose economic basis was principally in its monopolistic relationship with a spatially bound community. Beyond the familiar categories of morticians, beauticians, and other personal-services providers were advertisers, publishers, and much of the established political leadership of black Los Angeles.

54. "Film Society Is Launched to Aid Protection of Race Dignity in Screen Portrayals," *California Eagle*, 20 January 1938.

55. Allen, "When Japan Was 'Champion of the Darker Races' "; Lipsitz, "Frantic to Join . . . the Japanese Army."

56. Taylor, *In Search of the Racial Frontier*, 265.

57. "Louise Beavers Urges Women 'Organize,' " *California Eagle*, 26 September 1943.

58. "Race Celebs Will Cavort at 'V' House," *California Eagle*, 25 December 1942.

59. As it did in the South and Northeast, public transportation emerged as a locus of racial contestation: See Sides, *L.A. City Limits*, 62. For representative examples regarding public transportation as a site of racial radicalism, class politics, and the limits of nonviolence, see Kelley, "Congested Terrain."

60. DeVeaux, *The Birth of Bebop*, 387–88; Sherrie Tucker, " 'They Got Corns for Their Country': Hollywood Canteen Hostesses as Subjects and Objects of Freedom," paper presented at the American Studies Association Annual Meeting, Atlanta, 13 November 2004.

61. Eastman, "Central Avenue Blues" 22.

62. Hal Holly, "L.A. Band Briefs," *Down Beat*, 15 July 1945, 6.

63. DeVeaux, *The Birth of Bebop*, 388.

64. Goia, *West Coast Jazz*, 16–18.

65. For efforts to address *The Birth of a Nation*, see Flamming, *Bound for Freedom*, 88–90. For a link between *The Birth of a Nation* and the rabidly anti-Asian film *The Cheat*, see Widener, "Perhaps the Japanese Are to Be Thanked?"

66. Cripps, *Making Movies Black*, 102–25. See also Rogin, "Democracy and Burnt Cork"; Koppes and Black, "Blacks, Loyalty, and Motion-Picture Propaganda in World War II."

67. Tyler, *From Harlem to Hollywood*, 99.

68. Federal Writers' Project of the Works Progress Administration under the supervision of Hugh Harlan, "The Story of the Negro in Los Angeles County" (n.p., 1936), 41. See also Floyd Covington, "The Negro Invades Hollywood," *Opportunity*, October 1929.

69. "Washington" refers here to Booker, not George. On Walter White, see Cripps, *Making Movies Black*, 53, 62.

70. "Hattie McDaniel Selects Nine Noted Artists to Help in War Programs," *California Eagle*, 4 June 1943.

71. Herman Hill, "Change in Attitude in Hollywood Observed: Walter White Is Winning His Fight for Better Roles," *Pittsburgh Courier*, 8 August 1942.

72. Duberman, *Paul Robeson*, 227; White, *A Man Called White*, 202–3.

73. Vada Somerville was the wife of John Somerville, owner of the Dunbar Hotel. The couple were close associates of W. E. B. Du Bois: see Flamming, *Bound for Freedom*, 348–49.

74. *Writers' Congress*, 629–30. Some observers found the gathering at UCLA less impressive. Frances Williams criticized the paucity of panels given over to issues of concern to nonwhite communities, as well as the composition of the panel that included Trumbo and McWilliams.

75. Dalton Trumbo, "Minorities and the Screen," in *Writers' Congress*, 497.

76. For an in-depth discussion of Still's life in Los Angeles, see Catherine Parsons Smith, "Finding His Voice: William Grant Still in Los Angeles," in Smith, *William Grant Still*.

77. William Grant Still, "The Negro and His Music in Films," in *Writers' Congress*, 279.

78. Denning uses the "laboring" of American culture as framework for discussing the growing salience of social-democratic cultural politics during the 1930s: see Denning, *The Cultural Front*, xvi–xvii. The quote on the inescapability of mass culture is from Adorno and Horkheimer, "The Culture Industry," 2.

79. Still went on to issue a frank call for what he termed "propaganda" aimed at improving the image of the race: see, e.g., "Time for Negro to Start Propaganda Campaign— Still," *Spotlight* (Los Angeles), 17 July 1944. This call formed part of a bevy of commentary written by Still over the course of three decades. For a comprehensive listing of Still's editorial output, see Still et al., *William Grant Still*.

80. "Artists Assail Dancer's Article as Thoughtless," *California Eagle*, 30 January 1943.

81. "Actor Muse Will Sue Tribune," *California Eagle*, 28 October 1943.

82. "On the Film Front, the War Goes On and On," *California Eagle*, 23 April 1942.

83. Ralph Matthews, "The Truth about Hollywood," *Afro-American* (Baltimore), 9 January 1943.

84. Harry Levette, "Race Screen Stars Idle while Hollywood Ponders on Roles," *California Eagle*, 17 June 1943.

85. Carlton, *Hattie*, 116.

86. Kurashige describes how black women, responding to official claims that their scarcity within defense industries could be attributed to their preference for domestic work, rallied by the thousands in July 1942 to demand industrial work and accessible job training programs: see Kurashige, *The Shifting Grounds of Race*, 142.

87. "200 Race Artists Working in Film," *Pittsburgh Courier*, 30 January 1943; "Actors Ask [Office of War Information] to Scrap MGM's 'Tennessee Johnson,'" *California Eagle*, 18 December 1942; "Film, 'Tenn. Johnson,' Smears Negroes," *California Eagle*, 2 February

1943; "Protest Forthcoming MGM Film as Distortion of Post-Civil War Life," *California Eagle*, 3 September 1942; "U.S. Cracks Down on MGM Race Hate Film," *California Eagle*, 24 September 1942.

88. Still, "The Negro and His Music in Films," 279.

89. *California Eagle*, 7 November 1946; *Los Angeles Sentinel*, 19 September 1946.

90. "Major Studio Representatives Discuss Negro Actor Unemployment," *California Eagle*, 11 November 1950.

91. "Giant Show Business Step Forward," *California Eagle*, 10 January 1952.

92. "TV Attacks Talmadge," *California Eagle*, 17 January 1952.

2. The Negro as Human Being?

1. "Lynchings Fading, Legal Killing Rise," *California Eagle*, 31 December 1953.

2. "Workshop Play Portrays Negro as Human Being," *California Eagle*, 18 August 1950.

3. Starr, *Embattled Dreams*, 339. On the rise of a regional military-industrial complex, see McGirr, *Suburban Warriors*, 25–27.

4. Letter to the Los Angeles City Council, filed 24 December 1951, Council file no. 50460, Los Angeles City Archives. On visual art during the Cold War, see Eva Cockcroft, "Abstract Expressionism, Weapon of the Cold War," *Artforum*, vol. 12, no.10, June 1974, 43–54; Max Kozloff, "American Painting during the Cold War," *Artforum*, vol. 11, no. 9, May 1973, 43–54; Saunders, *The Cultural Cold War*.

5. For a comprehensive overview of the rise of Southern California as a pillar of the American political right, see McGirr, *Suburban Warriors*.

6. On the City Council hearings into subversion, see Schrank, "Art and the City," 180–94. For an overview of the State of California's hearings, see Barrett, *The Tenney Committee*.

7. "Housing Row Echo Heard in Art Talk: City Councilman's Ill Humor Bounces Back in Near Revival of Fracas over Paintings," *Los Angeles Times*, 15 January 1952.

8. Irving Mosely, "A Negro Actor Looks for Work," *California Eagle*, 22 January 1953.

9. The term "multicultural urban civility" appears in Macías, "Bringing Music to the People." On whiteness and the cultural politics of postwar Los Angeles, see Avila, *Popular Culture in the Age of White Flight*, esp. 20–65.

10. For an overview of early efforts to develop a local arts infrastructure, see Moure, "The Struggle for a Los Angeles Art Museum." See also Paul Karlstrom, "Art School Sketches: Notes on the Central Role of Schools in California Art and Culture," in Barron et al., *Reading California*, 85–113.

11. Harby continued to battle Ross. By 1955, he had shifted tack, attacking Ross's financial stewardship of the Municipal Arts Department rather than the content of his programs. These efforts proved more successful and resulted in a sharp curtailing of Ross's funding. As a result, a full-scale, citywide arts program would remain moribund until late in the first term of Mayor Tom Bradley: see chapter 8 of this book, and "City Takes New Approach to Art," *Los Angeles Times*, 23 April 1951.

12. Macías, "Bringing Music to the People," 711.

13. Ibid., 698.

14. Hickman, "Civic Music Administration in Los Angeles," 21; Frank Lachman, "The Los Angeles Bureau of Music," *Choir Guide*, November 1949, 12.

15. Macías, "Bringing Music to the People," 698–700.

16. "Percy McDavid Concert Music at South Park," *California Eagle*, 26 August 1954.

17. Avila, *Popular Culture in the Age of White Flight.*

18. McWilliams, *The Education of Carey McWilliams*, 21.

19. On the racial repercussions of the postwar construction of the Los Angeles freeway system, see Avila, *Popular Culture in the Age of White Flight*, 189–91, 210–15. See also Avila, "The Folklore of the Freeway." For a contrasting view, see Brodsley, *L.A. Freeway.*

20. U.S. Bureau of the Census, *Census of the Population, 1950*, vol. 2, *Characteristics of the Population*, part 5, 100–103; Special Census of Los Angeles; *Census of the Population, 1970*, vol. 1, *Characteristics of the Population.*

21. McGirr, *Suburban Warriors*, 25–27; Sides, *L.A. City Limits*, 81.

22. Sides, "You Understand My Condition."

23. For information on the development of civil rights in Los Angeles during the 1950s, see Horne, *The Fire This Time*, 171–95. Mike Davis uncovers a hidden history of clashes between black and white students, as well as between black students and the police. In one such instance, dozens of black youths rained bottles on the heads of the LAPD while proclaiming that Los Angeles "wasn't Alabama": Davis, "Wild Streets."

24. Wilson, *Parker on Police*; Thomas, "I Have No Use for this Fellow Parker."

25. Horne, *The Fire This Time*, 91–92.

26. William Parker, "The Police Role in Community Relations," in Wilson, *Parker on Police*, 155–57; Parker, *Police Chief William H. Parker Speaks*, 9.

27. Davis, *City of Quartz*, 294.

28. Mina Yang describes an abrupt rise in the number of narcotics arrests during this time: Yang, "A Thin Blue Line down Central Avenue."

29. Collette, in "Central Avenue Sounds," Oral History Program, 148.

30. Woodman, 101.

31. Art Farmer, interview by Steven Isoardi, in "Beyond Central Avenue," audio recording, tape 1, transcript, 57–58, 106–107.

32. Bob Bradford, interview by Steven Isoardi, in "Beyond Central Avenue," audio recording, tape 1, transcript, 184.

33. Spellman, *Four Lives in the Bebop Business*, 105.

34. "Artist Stopped by Cop, Told 'No Negroes' Here," *California Eagle*, 26 September 1952.

35. "Jimmy Witherspoon Beaten Up by Police," *California Eagle*, 24 January 1952.

36. Otis, *Upside Your Head!*, 68.

37. Tom Stoddard, *Jazz on the Barbary Coast* (Essex: Storyville Publications, 1982), 60, quoted in Michael Bakan, "Way out West on Central," 23.

38. Gordon, *Jazz West Coast*, 55.

39. Porter, *What Is This Thing Called Jazz?*, 118–19.

40. Gioia, *West Coast Jazz*, 309; Harold Land, *Harold in the Land of Jazz* (Contemporary Records, 1958); B. Case, "Unfortunate, Like a Fox," *Wire*, no.1, 1982, 8; Kernfield, *New Grove Dictionary of Jazz*, 675.

41. Yang, "A Thin Blue Line down Central Avenue," 228–29.

42. Cox, *Central Avenue*, 24. Cox's book is a unique resource that combines a narrative monograph and two dozen pathbreaking oral histories. Nothing else like it is available

for the researcher concerned with the community life of prewar black Los Angeles. Membership estimates in the *California Eagle* and *Los Angeles Sentinel* range from a low of four hundred to a high of eight hundred. Amalgamation activists repeatedly described the "more than 600" members of Local 767 in their advertisements and editorials.

43. In 1943, *International Musician* listed total AFM membership at approximately 200,000. In 1945, film studios employed 5,518 musicians, composers, arrangers, and music librarians. In 1948, James Petrillo, president of the AFM, claimed that fewer than 10,000 of his union's 225,000 members had ever been featured on a recorded album. Radio, television, and film networks and studios, he added, increasingly employed musicians only as temporary employees, resulting in widespread job losses. By 1953, film and television work provided primary employment for fewer than 300 musicians: see *International Musician*, June 1945, April 1953. Moreover, white musicians were in a better position to land studio work. The headquarters of Local 47 was on Vine Street in Hollywood, almost next door to several television and film studios. Local 767, meanwhile, was several miles to the southeast. Given the smaller percentage of private car ownership and Southern California's spotty public transportation, geographical constraints further compounded the effects of direct discrimination. On the AFM's most successful job action, a wartime ban on recorded music, see DeVeaux, "Bebop and the Recording Industry."

44. Frank Kofsky, "Is Shelley Manne Secretly a Harpist? Does Andre Previn Cut Cecil Taylor?" *Los Angeles Free Press*, 2 December 1966. Of course, Manne also recorded as a drummer for Ornette Coleman, so one has to take a fairly catholic view of the issue of race, representation, and power during this time.

45. Collette with Isoardi, *Jazz Generations*, 111.

46. Callendar and Cohen, *Unfinished Dream*, 107; Hampton with Haskins, *Hamp*, 28–29.

47. Anthony Macías, conversation with the author, 20 August 2002.

48. Advocates and detractors alike used the term "amalgamation" to describe union desegregation. I have followed their usage throughout the chapter.

49. Maury Paul, "From the Board Room," *Overture*, September–November 1952.

50. The literature that takes music as the central organizing principle on which collective identity on the part of people of African descent is built is considerable, ideologically diverse, and growing. For an introduction to several of the key positions, see Jones, *Blues People*; Stuckey, *Slave Culture*; Gilroy, *The Black Atlantic*; Floyd, *The Power of Black Music*. For a theoretical overview of the debate, see Salaam, "It Didn't Jes Grew."

51. Works that treat musicians as activists and intellectuals form a logical corollary to the works by Baraka, Gilroy, Stuckey, and Floyd cited earlier. For a work on the period discussed here, see Saul, *Freedom Is, Freedom Ain't*. For a longer view, see Johnson, "*Cinquillo* Consciousness."

52. Collette with Isoardi, *Jazz Generations*, 113–16, 121–22; Maurice Zam, "Jazzics versus Classics," *Overture*, 5 July 1952.

53. White members of Local 47 involved in the initial informal merger meetings included George Kast, Gail Robinson, Seymour Sheklow, Roger Segure, Joe Eger, Henry and Esther Roth, Erica Keen, and Emma Hardy Hill: *Overture*, December 1988.

54. Gerald Wilson, "Central Avenue Sounds," 337–41.

55. Marl Young, *Central Avenue Sounds*, 386.

56. Lewis, *In Their Own Interests*, 91.

57. John Gray, "In the Music World," *California Eagle*, 29 February 1924.

58. The politics of racial uplift and racial respectability constitute an area of inquiry for scholars of African American political ideology and practice. For an introduction, see Gaines, *Uplifting the Race*; Higginbotham, *Righteous Discontent*; Mitchell, *Righteous Propagation*.

59. Cox, *Central Avenue*, 10.

60. John Gray, "The Wilkins Recital," *California Eagle*, 2 July 1921.

61. Bakan, "Way out West on Central," 47.

62. "Musicians to Battle over 'Merger' Vote," *California Eagle*, 4 December 1952.

63. Ibid.

64. "Musicians in Merger OK by 274–127," *Los Angeles Sentinel*, 15 January 1953.

65. "Musicians Vote to End Jim Crow, Vote One Big Union," *California Eagle*, 18 December 1952.

66. Bennet L. Carter, "Statement Read to Committee of Local 767 and 47 re: Amalgamation," *Overture*, March 1952.

67. Amalgamation proposals and counterproposals appeared monthly in *Overture* between August and November 1952.

68. "Amalgamation Will Not Cost You One Cent," *Overture*, October 1952.

69. *Overture*, February 1953; *International Musician*, April 1953.

70. "Musicians to Battle," *California Eagle*, 4 December 1952.

71. Nick Stewart, interview by Dan Pasternack, 20 June 1997, tape 1, Academy of Television Arts and Sciences, Archive of American Television (hereafter, ATAS/AAT).

72. Ibid., tape 2.

73. Ibid., tape 3.

74. The term "aural minstrelsy" is in Savage, *Broadcasting Freedom*.

75. For an overview of the campaigns against the *Amos 'n' Andy* show in radio and television, see Ely, *The Adventures of Amos 'n' Andy*. See also "Why the *Amos 'n' Andy* TV Show Should Be Taken off the Air," *NAACP Bulletin*, 15 August 1951. In the context of criticism directed at the organization for its supposed class bias, it is interesting to note the specific mention the NAACP made concerning the portrayal of black professionals.

76. Stewart interview, tape 2, ATAS/AAT.

77. In addition to the Negro Art Theater, founded in 1937 with the assistance of Langston Hughes, local thespians inspired by one of the nation's oldest black theaters opened a Southern California Karamu House theater. Both efforts were short-lived, with neither lasting beyond a year.

78. Edna Stewart, "Memories of Nick Stewart's Incredible Life," manuscript, copy in author's possession.

79. John L. Mitchell, "Reflections of a Black Actor: *Amos 'n' Andy* Left Far Behind," *Los Angeles Times*, 28 November 1982.

80. "Nick Stewart and *Amos 'n' Andy* Timeline," ATAS/AAT.

81. "Ebony Showcase Theatre Seeking Greater Support of 'Neighborhood' People," *California Eagle*, 25 February 1954.

82. "Clubs Rally to Support of Ebony Showcase Stage Project," *California Eagle*, 19 March 1953.

83. "Ebony Showcase Theater Night," *California Eagle*, 7 October 1954.

84. " 'Anna Lucasta' Still Drawing Rave Notices," *California Eagle*, 19 February 1953.

85. "Anna Lucasta to Close after Next Week's Run," *California Eagle*, 5 March 1953.

86. "Ebony Showcase Change: 'Norman, Is That True?' " *Los Angeles Times*, 17 March 1977.

87. Among those whose careers began under the tutelage of Stewart were the film and television actors Juanita Moore, Al Freeman Jr., Debby Morgan, John Amos (*Good Times*), Greg Morris (*Mission Impossible*), Isabel Sanford (*The Jeffersons*), and Nichelle Nichols (*Star Trek*). The *Anna Lucasta* cast members Mauri Lynn and Rosalind Hayes received studio interviews as a result of their roles at the Ebony Showcase.

88. "Louise Beavers in Star Role in 'Anna Lucasta,' " *California Eagle*, 18 December 1952; Stewart interview, tape 4, ATAS/AAT.

89. *California Eagle*, 14 April 1952, 9 July 1953, 16 July 1953; " 'The Negro and American Culture' NAACP Lecture," *California Eagle*, 12 April 1951; "Negro Artists Exhibit in Hollywood," *California Eagle*, 19 April 1951.

90. Weir, *Singlejack Solidarity*, 167–84.

91. Curtis Tann, interview by Karen Anne Mason, in "African American Artists of Los Angeles," Oral History Program, audio recording, tape 1, transcript, 25–28, 115, 117, 120, 131.

92. Ruth Waddy, interview by Karen Anne Mason, ibid., audio recording, tape 1, transcript, 18; Tann interview, ibid., 25–28, 106. On Pajaud, see Paul von Blum, *Resistance, Dignity, and Pride*, 96–100. On Biggers, see Wardlaw, *The Art of John Biggers*.

93. LeFalle-Collins, "Working from the Pacific Rim"; Wilson, "How the Invisible Woman Got Herself on the Cultural Map."

94. *California Eagle*, 16 February 1950, 5 October 1950; John Anson Ford to Beulah Woodard, letter, 13 November 1953, John Anson Ford Collection, box 76.

95. Carpenter with Saar, *Betye Saar*, 6.

96. Wilson, "How the Invisible Woman Got Herself on the Cultural Map," 201.

97. Carpenter with Saar, *Betye Saar*, 57.

98. "Speaking of People," *Ebony*, October 1951, 5.

99. Betye Saar, in "African American Artists of Los Angeles," Oral History Program, tapes 1–2.

100. My point is not to argue here that the white artists based in Southern California were not crossing genres, for they were. In fact, figures such as Wallace Berman and Edward Keinholz sought to obliterate form, in part by combining text, sculpture, and performance. However, both the emerging world of experimental galleries located along La Cienega Boulevard and the Venice Beach Beat milieu contained artists who worked primarily in the forms of visual arts, sculpture, or poetry.

101. Wilson, "How the Invisible Woman Got Herself on the Cultural Map."

102. Powell, *Black Art and Culture in the 20th Century*, 152–54. On the early work of Edwards, see Gedeon, *Melvin Edwards Sculpture*.

3. *Writing Watts*

1. James Thomas Jackson, "Watts: From Ashes to Crucible of Black Writing," *Los Angeles Times*, 11 January 1970, N10.

2. Budd Schulberg, "Introduction," in Schulberg, *From the Ashes*, 1–2.

3. The most thoughtful and comprehensive work on the 1965 riots is Horne, *The Fire This Time*, esp. 3, 326–27.

4. Antipoverty efforts in Los Angeles began inauspiciously. Concern about requirements that mandated local matching funds for federal assistance led Mayor Sam Yorty to oppose the selection of Los Angeles as a site for federal aid. This position generated widespread opposition from local African American politicians, including City Councilman Tom Bradley and Congressman Augustus Hawkins. Fissures between elites provided an opening for the development of more popular protest. For an overview of antipoverty efforts in Los Angeles, see Marshall, *The Politics of Participation in Poverty*. See also Bauman, "Race, Class, and Political Power," 12, 257–60. For a work that treats the intersection of black and Chicano responses to antipoverty efforts, see Bauman, "The Black Power and Chicano Movements in the Poverty Wars in Los Angeles."

5. Editorial comment, *Economist*, 21 August 1965.

6. Califano, *The Triumph and Tragedy of Lyndon Johnson*, 62.

7. Ibid., 61.

8. "Get Out of Here, Dr. King," *New York Times*, 19 August 1965; "Dr. King Hears Watts Protest over Heckling," *Los Angeles Times*, 19 August 1965.

9. McGirr, *Suburban Warriors*, 188, 199–202.

10. On the proliferation of black militancy in the aftermath of the riot, see Horne, *The Fire This Time*, 185–212. See also Tyler, "Black Radicalism in Southern California, 1950–1982"; Brown, *Fighting for us*.

11. Patterson, *America's Struggle against Poverty in the Twentieth Century*, 112–21.

12. Katz, *The Undeserving Poor*, 16; Oscar Lewis, "The Culture of Poverty," *Scientific American*, no. 215, October 1966, 19–25.

13. Katznelson, "Was the Great Society a Lost Opportunity?" 196.

14. "Watts Towers Art Center," 3 October 1967, 4 October 1967, 23 January 1968, Watts Writers Workshop Collection, Rockefeller Archive Center (hereafter, www/rac), box 469, folder 4010; Jackson, "Watts."

15. "Accomplishments of Douglass House," n.d., www/rac, box 469, folder 4010; Allan Muir, dir., *Voicepoint* (Watts Writers Workshop/kcet, 1967); *The Angry Voices of Watts* (nbc-tv, 1966), film in author's possession.

16. Horne, *The Fire This Time*, 181.

17. Brown, *A Taste of Power*, 149–51.

18. Stanley Crouch, liner notes, *West Coast Hot*, featuring the John Carter and Bobby Bradford Quartet and the Horace Tapscott Quintet (Novus Records, 1969; reissued by bmg, 1991). Jayne Cortez, former wife of the free jazz avatar Ornette Coleman, was a co-founder of the Studio Watts workspace, a combination gallery, rehearsal, and exhibition space for local black artists. Cortez and Crouch worked together on a

repertory project the former had founded, the Watts Repertory Theater: Jayne Cortez, letter to the author, 20 August 2001.

19. Schulberg, *From the Ashes*, 14. Given the group's nationalist orientation and frequent residence in the Watts Happening Coffee House site, the hostile percussionists may well have been members of the Pan Afrikan People's Arkestra, although this is impossible to state with certainty.

20. "Excerpt from HK's diary," 30 April 1968, WWW/RAC, box 470, folder 4011; "John Carter and Bobby Bradford," interview by Frank Kofsky, reprinted in Rivelli and Levin, *The Black Giants*, 42. During this interview, neither Bradford nor Carter seemed particularly interested in the reasons the Watts Writers Workshop attracted greater attention than other community-based jazz institutions. When pressed, Carter indicated that he thought it had more to do with the difficulty in finding audiences for "out" jazz than any particular bias on the part of media or philanthropic organizations.

21. Budd Schulberg, testimony to the House Un-American Activities Committee, 23 May 1951, in Beck, *Budd Schulberg*, 77–133.

22. U.S. Congress, Senate Committee on Government Operations, Subcommittee on Executive Reorganization, *Federal Role in Urban Affairs*, hearings, 8th Cong., 2nd sess. (Washington, D.C.: U.S. Government Printing Office, 1966–68), 2457, 2477–2483.

23. Robert Semple Jr., "Ghetto Described at Senate Inquiry," *New York Times*, 10 December 1966.

24. Stanley Crouch, "When Watts Burned."

25. Foucault, *Power/Knowledge*, 51.

26. Governor's Commission on the Los Angeles Riots, *Violence in the City—An End or a Beginning?* (Sacramento: State of California, 1965), 3, 27–37, 85–86.

27. Blauner, "Whitewash over Watts"; Elizabeth Hardwick, "After Watts," *New York Review of Books*, 31 March 1966; Fogelson, "White on Black"; Rustin, "The Watts 'Manifesto' and the McCone Report" (originally published in 1966 in *Commentary* magazine).

28. Strategies for helping the poor often turned on the tasks of identifying, measuring, and otherwise assessing the poor. The War on Poverty thus involved social scientists in no small measure. For an introduction to this literature, see Katz, *The Undeserving Poor*, 79–123; Levitan, *Programs in Aid of the Poor for the 1970s*, 1–18; Russell, *Economics, Bureaucracy, and Race*. For two works that treat the specific issue of social-science research, poverty, and public policy, see Aaron, *Politics and the Professors*; Moynihan, *On Understanding Poverty*. For three very different critiques of the politics of knowledge production as they relate to power, poverty, and race, see Michel Foucault, "Governmentality," in Burchell et al., *The Foucault Effect*, 87–104; Kelley, *Yo' Mama's DisFUNKtional*, 16–18; Wolf, *Europe and the People without History*. Foucault offers an examination of how social science and government use knowledge in the creation of regulatory social structures; Kelley's critique centers on the methodological problems that attended contemporary social-science examinations of the inner city; and Wolf notes the deep political history and consequent biases of social-science inquiry, particularly its formative hostility to Marxism.

29. Johnny Scott, "Chaos in a Ghetto Alley," in Schulberg, *The Angry Voices of Watts*, 127.

30. Redmond, *Drumvoices*, 404.

31. K. Curtis Lyle, "Sometimes I Go to Camarillo and Sit in the Lounge," in Lyle, *Electric Church*, 15–17.

32. For a historical overview of the politics of mass transportation in Los Angeles with a particular focus on race, see Labor Community Strategy Center, *A New Vision of Urban Transportation*.

33. Harry Dolan, "The Sand-Clock Day," in Schulberg, *From the Ashes*, 36–39.

34. Ojenke (Alvin A. Saxon), "To Mr. Charles and Sister Annie," in Schulberg, *From the Ashes*, 64.

35. Johnnie Scott, "Watts, 1966," in Schulberg, *From the Ashes*, 135. Scott's poem was among those filmed and included in the *Angry Voices* broadcast.

36. Amde Hamilton, conversation with the author, 15 May 2000.

37. See "Watts Towers Art Center," 4 October 1967, "Account RF 67082–Arts," 13 March 1968, and "Watts Writers Workshop," 23 January 1968, www/rac, box 469, folder 4010.

38. Constance Holden, "Arts and Humanities: Federal Money Is Benefiting Culture," *Science*, vol. 170, no. 3963, 11 December 1970, 1181.

39. Jackson, "Watts"; Schulberg, *From the Ashes*, 20–21.

40. Gerald Freund, "Los Angeles Trip Report," 3 October 1967, www/rac, box 469, bolder 4010, 2.

41. The Rockefeller Foundation funded the American Negro Theater between 1941 and 1965. Grants were made to the Cleveland-based Karamu House between 1940 and 1953, and the Free Southern Theater received assistance from 1967 to 1973: see letter, 12 August 1971, www/rac, box 469, folder 4010. See also Freund, "Los Angeles Trip Report," 1. On the issue of alleged misappropriation of poverty-program funds, see Wolfe, *Radical Chic and Mau-Mauing the Flak Catchers*.

42. Beck, *Budd Schulberg*, 41–44.

43. The iccc is worthy of a monograph in and of itself. In existence between 1965 and 1986, the iccc trained thousands of actors, set designers, technical personnel, and playwrights. The early commitment to cast plays without regard to race and the selection of material by obscure playwrights of color made the theater a pioneer in developing multiculturalism within American theater. Finally, the theater developed important relationships with both the Teatro Campesino of Luis Valdez and the Asian American East West Players, providing a rare interethnic moment linking black, Latino, and Asian American community theater. Articles of Incorporation, Inner City Cultural Center, 15 April, 1966, California Arts Commission Records, F3719:228.

44. Sheffey-Stinson, "The History of Theater Productions at the Los Angeles Inner City Cultural Center, 1965–1976," 25.

45. Gregory Peck, fundraising letter, October 1966, iccc Collection, Los Angeles Theater Center; Los Angeles Theater Clipping Files, Literature Department, Los Angeles Public Library.

46. Cecil Smith, "New Repertory Company for the Underprivileged," *Los Angeles Times*, 6 August 1967. See also Walker, "The Politics of Art," 18–20.

47. James Thomas Jackson, "On Chino, San Bernadino, Altadena and Other Places," www/RAC, box 469, folder 4010.

48. U.S. Congress, *Federal Role in Urban Affairs*, 2481.

49. "Grant in Aid to Douglass House Foundation," 13 March 1968, www/RAC, box 469, folder 4010.

50. "Los Angeles Trip Report," 3 October 1967, www/RAC, box 469, folder 4010.

51. Ibid.; Budd Schulberg, "Progress Report from Douglass House Foundation: April 1 thr[ough] July 31, 1968," 21 May 1969, www/RAC, box 470, folder 4011.

52. Watts Writers Workshop, *Watts Writers Workshop* (Los Angeles, n.d. [ca. 1970s]), Daphne Muse Collection.

53. Schulberg, "Progress Report from Douglass House Foundation."

54. Interoffice correspondence, 20 October 1967, www/RAC, box 469, folder 4010.

55. Letter from Norman Lloyd, 23 August 1968, www/RAC, box 469, folder 4010.

56. Flamm, *Law and Order*.

57. Interoffice correspondence, 20 October 1967, www/RAC; Freund, "Los Angeles Trip Report"; "Watts Area—Watts Happening Coffee House and Budd Schulberg's Writers Workshop at the Douglass House," 30 April 1969, www/RAC, box 470, folder 4011; "Watts Area," excerpt from WLB Diary, 6 April 1970.

58. The concept of maximum feasible participation emerged as among the most contested legacies of the Johnson administration's antipoverty crusade. A major critique can be found in Moynihan, *Maximum Feasible Misunderstanding*. For a contrary view, see Adam Walinsky, "Maximum Feasible Misunderstanding," *New York Times*, 2 February 1969.

59. Beck, *Budd Schulberg*, 68.

60. The Mafundi Institute was a community arts center in operation from 1967 to 1973. "Watts Area," excerpt from WLB diary; Watts 13 pamphlet, www/RAC, box 470, folder 4011.

61. Watts 13 pamphlet.

62. "New Watts Group Stages Black Culture Evening," *Hollywood Reporter*, 30 October 1968; "Watts 13 Founding Holding Benefit Tonight," *Daily Variety*, 1 November 1968.

63. Milton McFarlane, "To Join or Not To Join," in Troupe, *Watts Poets*, 1.

64. Ibid., 1–4; Cortez, *Pisstained Stairs and the Monkey Man's Wares*; Crouch, *Ain't No Ambulances for No Nigguhs Tonight*; Nielsen, *Black Chant*, 62; Redmond, *Drumvoices*, 402–408; Thompson, *Dudley Randall, Broadside Press, and the Black Arts Movement in Detroit, 1960–1995*, 142.

65. Although episodic performances using the workshop's name continued throughout the 1970s, theatrical performances, writing classes, and poetry readings became increasingly intermittent after this time. External funding ceased after 1973, as well.

66. Watts Writers Workshop, "A Choice of Positions," vertical file, 1960s Watts Collection, Southern California Library for Social Research.

67. Roger Rapoport, "Meet America's Meanest Dirty Trickster: The Man the FBI Used to Destroy the Black Movement in Los Angeles," *Mother Jones*, April 1977, 21–23.

68. Schulberg, *From the Ashes*, 8.

4. Notes from the Underground

Epigraph source: Walter Benjamin, "The Author as Producer," *New Left Review* I 62 (July–August 1970): 92.

1. "Horace Tapscott," in "Central Avenue Sounds," Oral History Program, 47.

2. Over the course of its nearly five decades, the Arkestra has existed in several incarnations. For an examination of the history of the Arkestra during the 1980s and in the aftermath of the 1992 rebellion, see Isoardi, *The Dark Tree*.

3. For a selection of works that assess the musical trajectory of the jazz avant-garde within, but also beyond, a political and social context, see Ake, *Jazz Cultures*; Anderson, *This Is Our Music*; Gray, *Cultural Moves*; Lewis, *A Power Stronger than Itself*; Monson, *Saying Something*; Porter, *What Is This Thing Called Jazz?*; Saul, *Freedom Is, Freedom Ain't*.

4. Wilkins, a striking figure given to Stetson hats and a gold-tipped cane, held outdoor weekly piano recitals in the decade before the First World War, directing his students from the porch of a house on Central Avenue and 14th Street: Cox, *Central Avenue*, 15.

5. Bob Bradford, interview by Steven Isoardi, in "Beyond Central Avenue,"audio recording, tape 1, transcript, 151.

6. Cox, *Central Avenue*, 106–108; Horace Tapscott, liner notes, *Songs of the Unsung* (Interplay Records, 1978).

7. Horricks, *The Importance of Being Eric Dolphy*, 18.

8. Tapscott and Isaordi, *Songs of the Unsung*, 36.

9. Gioia, *West Coast Jazz*, 344.

10. See chapter 2 of this book. See also "The Need for Racial Unity in Jazz: A Panel Discussion," *Down Beat*, vol. 30 (1963): 16–21; John Szwed, "Musical Style and Racial Conflict," in Szwed, *Crossovers*, 19–26.

11. Carter and Bradford discuss the issue of studio work in *John Carter and Bobby Bradford: The New Music* (Rhapsody Films, New York, 1986). The Tapscott quote is from "Central Avenue Sounds" Oral History Program, 298.

12. Collette with Isaordi, *Jazz Generations*, 81–82; Simosko and Tepperman, *Eric Dolphy*, 31. Dolphy's composition "GW" appears on *Outward Bound* (New Jazz, 1960). Horace Tapscott's "Ballad for Samuel" appears on *Dissent or Descent* (Nimbus West, 1984). Bradford interview, "Beyond Central Avenue," 151–52.

13. Hawes, *Raise up off Me*, 12. For a general description of the Central Avenue scene, see Cox, "The Evolution of Black Music in Los Angeles, 1890–1955"; Gioia, *West Coast Jazz*, chap. 1.

14. On the transfer of musical ideas through personal contact, see Stanyek, "Transmissions of an Interculture."

15. Gioia, *West Coast Jazz*, 332; Dan Morgenstern, "Charlie Haden: From Hillbilly to Avant Garde, a Rocky Road," *Down Beat*, vol. 34, no. 5 (1967): 20–21, 42; Tapscott, liner notes, *Songs of the Unsung*.

16. Gioia, *West Coast Jazz*, 311–13, 343; Horricks, *The Importance of Being Eric Dolphy*, 23–24.

17. Catalano, *Clifford Brown*, 115–16.

18. Bradford had lived for time as a child in Chavez ravine before moving with his family to Texas.

19. Michael James, "Order and Feeling, Discipline and Fire: An Introduction to the John Carter and Bobby Bradford Quartet," *Jazz and Blues*, April 1973, 6–9.

20. A Watts native who played with Les Hite and Lionel Hampton, Ortega is an underappreciated figure in postwar jazz. He was a pioneering experimentalist who played with Paul Bley until Bley replaced him with Ornette Coleman. Ortega's career, which crossed the amalgamation of Local 47 and Local 767, the expansion of the local Latin music scene in the early 1950s, and the development of free jazz, awaits a full recounting. For an examination of his career, see Macías, *Mexican American Mojo*, esp. 193–200.

21. As noted in passing in chapter 2, Central Avenue declined for a number of reasons. The most important include the financial dislocation of black Los Angeles during the 1950s, the aggressive policing of Parker's LAPD, and the first shifts of the black middle class westward to other sections of the city.

22. Spellman, *Four Lives in the BeBop Business*, 137.

23. Litweiler, *Ornette Coleman*, 91.

24. Ibid., 104; Frank Kofksy, interview with John Carter and Bobby Bradford, in Rivelli and Levin, *The Black Giants*, 42–43; Stanley Crouch, "Black Song West: Horace Tapscott and the Community Cultural Orchestra," *Cricket*, 1967, 22.

25. Crouch, "Black Song West," 25; Kofksy, interview with Carter and Bradford, in Rivelli and Levin, *Black Giants*, 44.

26. Elaine Cohen, "Horace Tapscott Talking: A Legacy to Pass On," *Cadence*, August 1984, 12.

27. Isoardi, *The Dark Tree*, 50.

28. Cohen, "Horace Tapscott Talking," 13; Frank Kofsky, "Horace Tapscott," *Jazz and Pop*, December 1969, 16.

29. Cox, *Central Avenue*, 108–9.

30. Sides, *L.A. City Limits*, 95–97, 120–28.

31. George Lewis has written a scintillating and soulful study of the AACM: see Lewis, *A Power Greater than Itself*.

32. Cohen, "Horace Tapscott Talking," 13; Kofsky, "Horace Tapscott," 16–17.

33. Nielsen, *Black Chant*, chap. 4.

34. John Outterbridge, in "African American Artists of Los Angeles," Oral History Program, 251.

35. Jayne Cortez, letter, 20 August 2001; Daniel Widener and Michael Williard, interview with James Woods, 13 February 2000, audiotape in author's possession.

36. Isoardi, *The Dark Tree*, 52, 184.

37. Jayne Cortez, "In Her Own Words: Jayne Cortez," in Carter, *Watts*, 34.

38. Nielsen, *Black Chant*, 221.

39. Jayne Cortez, "how long has the trane been gone," *Celebrations and Solitudes* (Strada East Records, 1974).

40. Malcolm X, "Message to the Grassroots," 10 November 1963, Paul Winley Records, Cat. #PWIN134LP.

41. There is a growing body of scholarship on the poetics and politics of Jayne Cortez: see Anderson, *Notes to Make the Sound Come Right*; Bolden, "All the Birds Sing Bass"; Kelley, *Freedom Dreams*, 186–90; Melhem, *Heroism in the New Black Poetry*, 181–214; Nielsen, *Integral Music*.

42. Linda Hill's lead sheets, songs, and scores, Horace Tapscott Jazz Collection, 1960–2002, box 65.

43. See the discussion of the Watts Happenings Coffee House in chapter 3 of this book.

44. Ntongela Masilela, "The Los Angeles School of Black Filmmakers," and Toni Cade Bambara, "Reading the Signs, Empowering the Eye: Daughters of the Dust and Black Independent Cinema," in Diawara, *Black American Cinema*, 116, 138

45. Tapscott, in "Central Avenue Sounds," Oral History Program, 381.

46. Ibid., 382.

47. Ted Gioia's pathbreaking revisionist account of jazz in California concludes in 1960, thus omitting the history of the UGMA, the Carter and Bradford ensemble, and the West Coast careers of musicians such as Prince Lasha, James Newton, Arthur Blythe, and Anthony Ortega: see Gioia, *West Coast Jazz*, 331–59. From the other direction, both musicological accounts such as Jost, *Free Jazz*, and more sociologically and politically minded projects such as Litweiler, *The Freedom Principle*, and Wilmer, *As Serious as Your Life*, accord California only brief mention, discussing Ornette Coleman's difficult early days and little more.

48. On free jazz, see Gray, *Fire*; Jost, *Free Jazz*; Litweiler, *The Freedom Principle*; Such, *Avant-Garde Musicians Performing "Out There"*; Wilmer, *As Serious as Your Life*.

49. Gennari, "Jazz Criticism."

50. DeVeaux, "Constructing the Jazz Tradition," 550–51; Merriam and Garner, "Jazz—The Word," 7–31.

51. Litweiler, *Ornette Coleman*, 117.

52. Roberto Miranda, "A View from the Bottom: The Music of Horace Tapscott and the Pan Afrikan Peoples Arkestra," in Isoardi, *The Dark Tree*, 300–301.

53. Ibid., 297.

54. Avotcja quoted in Iosardi, *The Dark Tree*, 110.

55. Litweiler, *Ornette Coleman*, 96.

56. Ornette Coleman, liner notes, *Change of the Century* (Atlantic Records, 1959).

57. Spellman, *Four Lives in the BeBop Business*, xxxii.

58. I am indebted to Robin D. G. Kelley for sharing this story with me.

59. Tapscott interview, "Central Avenue Sounds, 377.

60. Horace Tapscott Jazz Collection, 1960–2002, box 40.

61. Ibid. box 38, item 1, box 39, item 1.

62. Bradford interview, "Beyond Central Avenue," 293.

63. Benston, *Performing Blackness*, 6.

64. Moten, *In the Break*, 18, 82.

65. Amiri Baraka introduces the term "the changing same" in "The Changing Same: R&B and New Black Music," in Baraka, *Black Music*, 180.

66. Porter, *What Is This Thing Called Jazz?* xxi.

67. Such, in part, is the point made in Hobsbawm, *Nations and Nationalism since 1780*.

68. Weinstein, *A Night in Tunisia*, 82–93.

69. Gerald Horne uses the term "the new leadership" in distinguishing the political generation that emerged after the Watts rebellion in 1965 from the previously extant leadership composed of familiar civil-rights groupings such as the NAACP, Urban League,
and Southern Christian Leadership Conference. The new leadership would include
organizations such as the Black Panther Party and the US Organization, along with
independent radicals such as Ron Wilkins and organizations such as SNCC, which
existed before 1965 but moved toward a more systemic critique of American society
during the second half of the decade: see Horne, *The Fire This Time*, 180.

70. Horace Tapscott discography, clipping file, Institute of Jazz Studies, Rutgers University.

71. Weinstein, *A Night in Tunisia*. See also Robin Kelley's forthcoming volume on jazz,
Africa, and the African diaspora.

72. "Partial List of the Black Congress," *Harambe Notes*, 18 November 1968; Black Power
Rally, transcript, February 1968, Pacifica Radio Archives.

73. "Underground Musicians Association," memorandum, 18 December 1967, Los Angeles, FBI, file 157–1950. The file entry is an account of the Western Regional Black
Youth Conference.

74. "Black Power: Protest or Affirmation," pamphlets vertical file, Southern California
Library for Social Research; files on Horace Tapscott, Underground Musicians Asso-
ciation, and Western Regional Black Youth Conference, FBI, Cointelpro (Black Hate
Groups) files 157–1833, 157–6042, 157–3598.

75. Stanley Crouch, interview by the author, 15 May 2001, New York; Tapscott and Isaordi,
Songs of the Unsung, 112–13.

76. Brown, *Seize the Time*. For a longer discussion of *Seize the Time*, see chapter 6 of this
book.

77. Black Panther Party event flyer, Center for the Study of Political Graphics.

78. Michael Zinzun, interview by the author, 1 September 2002, Los Angeles; Ron Wilkins,
interview by the author, 15 March 1999, Los Angeles. Ron Wilkins was kind enough to
share television and film footage of the SWAT assault on the Black Panther Party
headquarters. The rattlesnake story was told to me by a former co-worker at a Los
Angeles community college who had worked as an undercover officer during this
time.

79. See Brown, *Fighting for Us*; Churchill, "To Disrupt, Discredit and Destroy," 108; Roger
Rapoport, "Meet America's Meanest Dirty Trickster: The Man the FBI Used to Destroy
the Black Movement in Los Angeles," *Mother Jones*, April 1977, 21–23. It is important to
recall that police malfeasance targeted Chicano activists, as well: see Escobar, "The
Dialectics of Repression."

80. Underground Musicians Association, memorandum, entries dated 18 December 1967,
29 October 1970, 8 March 1971, 22 January 1973, Los Angeles, FBI, file 157–1950,

81. Tapscott interview, "Central Avenue Sounds," 377.

Epigraph source: Cedric Dover, *American Negro Art*, 44.

1. "Black Artists on Art: New View for Glendale," *Glendale News-Press*, 24 July 1970; "Racists in Glendale," *Los Angeles Free Press*, 17 September 1964.

2. *Glendale News-Press*, 24 July 1970; "Black Artists on Art," dir. Samella Lewis, 1971.

3. Growing organizations, both formal and informal, was a national process that accelerated among black artists throughout the 1960s: see Patton, *African-American Art*, 214–17. On jazz artists' groups, see chaper 2, n. 8, in this volume. On organization among writers, see Redmond, *Drumvoices*.

4. Joan Ankrum's gallery was one of approximately thirty galleries located on or near La Cienega Boulevard. Ankrum was the primary dealer for her nephew, the painter Morris Broderson: Paul Karlstrom, "Interview with Joan Ankrum," 1997, Joan Ankrum Papers.

5. According to Curtis Tann, black students were unwelcome at Chouinard's daytime classes throughout the 1950s. Although Noah Purifoy reported no specific incidents with prejudice while attending the school, Robert Perine's monograph on Chouinard describes the racist leanings of its founder, Nelbert Chouinard: see Perine, *Chouinard, an Art Vision Betrayed*.

6. Gedeon, *Melvin Edwards Sculpture*.

7. Curtis Tann, in "African American Artists of Los Angeles" Oral History Program, 115; Ruth Waddy, ibid., 56; Cecil Fergerson, interview by the author, 21 June 2000; Lowery Stokes Sims, "Melvin Edwards, An Artist's Life and Philosophy," and Samella Lewis, "An Interview with Camille Billops," *International Review of African American Art* 10, no. 4 (1994): 24–38.

8. Ruth Waddy, in "African American Artists of Los Angeles" Oral History Program, 56–60; Waddy, *Prints by American Negro Artists*.

9. Biographical information for the Davis brothers (born in 1942 and 1945, respectively) and for Suzanne Jackson (born in 1944) is from Lewis and Waddy, *Black Artists on Art*; LeFalle-Collins, *19 Sixties*.

10. John Outterbridge, in "African American Artists of Los Angeles" Oral History Program, 240.

11. Suzanne Jackson, ibid., 95, 125–127, 257–259; Tate, "Suzanne Jackson."

12. Jackson, "African American Artists in Los Angeles," 263.

13. Brockman Gallery Productions, event listing, 1974–75, vertical file, Balch Art Research Library, LACMA. Elton C. Fax, "John Outterbridge," in idem, *Black Artists of the New Generation*, 307.

14. Brockman flyer, undated, vertical file, Balch Art Research Library, LACMA.

15. Cecil Fergerson, interview by the author, 3 June 1999.

16. Ferguson, in "African American Artists of Los Angeles," Oral History Program, 162, 191.

17. Statement by John Outterbridge, n.d., Committee for Simon Rodia's Towers in Watts Records, box 18, folder 9.

18. In his study of the US Organization, Scot Brown describes how the Taifa dance, originally a percussive work song and march step developed by South African dia-

mond miners, was reorganized musically and performatively by members of us. New instruments, rhythmic patterns, and dance steps meant to symbolize various members of the organization were developed between visiting African and resident African American musicians and activists: see Brown, *Fighting for us*, 132–36.

19. Black Arts Council flyer, undated, John Outterbridge Papers, box 4.

20. Fergerson, "African American Artists of Los Angeles," Oral History Project, 191.

21. LeFalle-Collins, *Noah Purifoy*, 70.

22. Outterbridge, "African American Artists of Los Angeles," Oral History Project, 237.

23. This section's epigraph is from Richard Cándida Smith, *Assemblage: Poetry and Narration* (Palos Verdes: Palos Verdes Art Center, 1988), unpaginated.

24. For two representative works that connect the jazz avant-garde to black nationalist ideology, see Kofsky, *Black Nationalism and the Revolution in Black Music*; John Sinclair, "Self-Determination Music," *Jazz and Pop*, August 1970. For two examinations of how debates over the relationship between music and politics played out in relation to free jazz, see Porter, *What Is This Thing Called Jazz?*; Radano, "The Jazz Avant-Garde and the Jazz Community."

25. Powell, *Black Art and Culture in the 20th Century*, 152–54.

26. Schrank, "Nuestro Pueblo," and "Picturing the Watts Towers"; Whiting, *Pop L.A.*

27. On the link between the avant-garde and popular culture, see Plagens, *Sunshine Muse*; Smith, *Utopia and Dissent*, xx. On the history of assemblage, see Elderfield, *Essays on Assemblage*; Seitz, *Art of Assemblage*. On Dada and surrealism, see Rubin, *Dada, Surrealism, and Their Heritage*. On the form in California, see *Assemblage in California*; "Forty Years of California Assemblage," Annual Exhibition, UCLA Art Council, Wight Art Gallery, Los Angeles, 1989); Starr, *Lost and Found in California*.

28. Purifoy and Mitchell, *Junk Art*.

29. Brenson, "Lynch Fragments," in *Melvin Edwards*, 27.

30. Lewis, *Art*, 170.

31. LeFalle-Collins, *19 Sixties*, 19–20.

32. Le Falle-Collins, "Keeper of Traditions," 14.

33. Waddy and Lewis, *Black Artists on Art*, 49.

34. Ibid.

35. Woods, *Development Arrested*, 29–39. Woods places the blues as epistemology within a wide critical framework drawn from Marxist political economy, African American history, and critical cultural studies. In taking the blues as a constitutive element of black self-conception, his work offers a further advance along lines laid out by Baraka and Larry Neal, to say nothing of Houston Baker, Richard Powell, and a host of others: see Larry Neal, "The Ethos of the Blues," in Neal, *Visions of a Liberated Future*, 107–18. For works that take the blues as central, though in different ways and for distinct purposes, see Leroi Jones, *Blues People*; Murray, *Stomping the Blues*. For works that extend blues aesthetics beyond music, see Baker, *Blues, Ideology, and Afro-American Literature*; Powell, *The Blues Aesthetic*. This list is obviously neither exclusive nor extensive.

36. Saar, "Unfinished Business," 3.

37. Outterbridge's comment is instructive in that it suggests the extent to which the

members of the Black Panther Party became emblematic of both the black liberation movement and the police repression directed at that movement. For information on the harassment of artists, see Jackson, "African American Artists in Los Angeles," 130–33. The 1962 date reflects the LAPD raid on the Los Angeles branch of the Nation of Islam, an event that signaled the start of armed conflict between black activists and the LAPD.

38. Many of the members of this community would seem to fit Elsa Fine's discussion of "Blackstream" artists, whose styles "responded, emotionally and politically, to the political turmoil of which they are a part with a political statement painted in the styles and techniques of contemporary art." Fine counterpoised these artists to "mainstream artists" with black skin concerned with purely formal questions, on the one hand, and to fully committed and politicized polemicists affiliated with the black Liberation movement on the other, whom she defined as the Black Arts Movement. My treatment of black visual arts partially collapses Blackstream and Black Arts Movement–style artists.

39. Waddy and Lewis, *Black Artists on Art*, 18–20, 84.

40. Conwill, "Interview with Betye Saar."

41. The breadth of Saar's subject matter and formal choices can be seen in two works that offer extended discussions of her more than four decades as a visual artist: see Carpenter with Saar, *Betye Saar*; Steward et al., *Betye Saar*.

42. Purifoy and Mitchell, *Junk Art*, n.p.

43. Ayres, "Objects of Magical Power," 14–15, quote on 15.

44. Purifoy and Mitchell, *Junk Art*, n.p.

45. John Outterbridge, interview by the author, May 1999.

46. Statement by John Outterbridge, Committee for Simon Rodia's Towers in Watts Records.

47. Lewis and Waddy, *Black Artists on Art*, 2, 101.

48. LeFalle-Collins, *19 Sixties*, 19.

49. Edwards's works were part of the exhibition "Los Angeles 1972: A Panorama of Black Artists," exhibition catalogue file, Balch Art Research Library, LACMA. Greg Pitt uses the term "Ogunetwork" to refer to the cadre of "urban blacksmiths" who arose during this time. Pitts includes Purifoy, Edwards, Outterbridge, Riddle, and Ed Love in this group. All were from or had worked in Los Angeles: Greg Angaza Pitts, n.d., John Outterbridge Papers, box 4.

50. For a historical overview describing aspects of the aesthetic relationship between visual and musical creative processes on the part of black artists, see "The Edited Transcript of the Round Table on Integrative Inquiry"; Goldson, *Seeing Jazz*; O'Meally, *The Jazz Cadence of American Culture*; Powell, *The Blues Aesthetic*.

51. Jackson, *What I Love*; Jackson, *Animal* (Los Angeles, 1978).

52. Cortez, letter to the author; Purifoy and Mitchell, *Junk Art*.

53. David James, *The Most Typical Avant-Garde*, 280–81.

54. Powell, "African American Postmodernism and David Hammons," 128–32.

55. *Betye Saar*.

56. Ryan, *Spirituality as Ideology in Black Women's Film and Literature*, 22–27.

57. Hobsbawm, *Nations and Nationalism since 1780*, 65–75.

58. Anderson, *Imagined Communities*.

59. Jerry Raynor, "Artist Claims That Art Is Functional, Public," *Daily Reflector* (Greenville, N.C.), 30 June 1974.

60. In the period before the 1965 riots, almost no government support for community-based African American art activity is to be found. Until their transfer to municipal ownership in 1975, the Watts Towers and arts center were private property. Institutions such as the Underground Musicians Association, the Ebony Showcase Theater, and Studio Watts, as we have seen, were funded through the efforts of the artists involved. In the years after the riot, the situation shifted somewhat, and federal, state, and local funds began to be available in greater measure. In the two years (1973–74) immediately preceding its replacement by the newly organized California Arts Council, the extant California Arts Commission provided funding to the Mafundi Institute, the Compton Communicative Arts Academy, and the R'Wanda Lewis Afro-American Dance Company: see files F3719:307/SP-060–73 (Mafundi), F3719:262/V4–041–73 (Communicative Arts Academy), F3719:227/PA-105–73, R'Wanda Lewis Afro-American Dance Company, California Arts Commission Records. This period, however, was not without its own fiduciary, aesthetic, and political limitations, the process and implications of which are discussed in chapter 7 of this book.

61. Jack Jones, "Antipoverty Chiefs OK Plans for 38 Summer Projects Here," *Los Angeles Times*, 14 May 1968, A1; Margaret Harford, "Youthful Havoc Gives Way to Talents," *Los Angeles Times*, 27 March 1966, B1; Ray Loynd, "Workshop Forges Ghetto Talent," *Los Angeles Times*, 15 June 1969, 028; Jack Jones, "EYOA [Economic and Youth Opportunity agency of Greater Los Angeles] Commits Last of 1968's Poverty Funds to Three Programs," 21 November 1967, 1. Many of the articles that described Stewart's foray into community arts did so using a scarcely concealed liberal racism reminiscent of the discourse surrounding the Watts Writers Workshop.

62. Davis, "Sunshine and the Open Shop"; Kurashige, *The Shifting Grounds of Race*; Nicolaides, *My Blue Heaven*, 272–332.

63. Powell résumé, John Outterbridge Papers, box 4.

64. Prospectus for Communicative Arts Academy, John Outterbridge Papers, box 4.

65. CCA bylaws, John Outterbridge Papers, box 4.

66. Lewis, *Art*, 230. Outterbridge, "African American Artists of Los Angeles," 390–93.

67. "Symposium," *Street Chopper*, April 1972.

68. Communicative Arts Academy presents "Actuality with Reality," event flyer, John Outterbridge Papers, box 4. The ongoing, informal relationship between the CAA and Mechicano was typical of relations between black and Latino community artists in Southern California. Alonzo Davis, for instance, knew the muralist Judith Baca, founder of the Social Political Art Resource Center, from a variety of mural projects, while Outterbridge and Noah Purifoy had relationships to both Mechicano and Self-Help Graphics, the East Los Angeles printmaking workshop founded by a group of young Chicano artists in partnership with a sympathetic Franciscan nun, Sister Karen Boccalero.

69. Funding sources, service donations, and affiliated personnel are listed in Grants—

Communicative Arts Academy, California Arts Commission Records, F3719:262. Budget Estimates and Records, CCA file, John Outterbridge Papers, box 4.

70. Articles of Incorporation of the Inner City Cultural Center, California Arts Commission Records, file PA 138–73.

71. CCA flyer, n.d., John Outterbridge Papers, box 4.

72. Browning résumé, ibid.

6. The Arms of Criticism

1. Baraka, *The Autobiography of Leroi Jones*, 356–60.

2. In selecting the Black Panther Party and the US Organization, I do not mean to participate in a reificatory historiography that treats these organizations, in particular the Black Panther Party, as the sole, main, or most important black nationalist grouping of the time. A burgeoning scholarship, of which Ahmad, *We Will Return in the Whirlwind*, is an excellent example, has done much to reveal a complicated landscape that includes groups such as the Revolutionary Action Movement, the Republic of New Africa, the League of Revolutionary Black Workers, and more. One might well argue, as some have, that SNCC had the greatest effect as a national formation, although some would doubtless disagree. In Los Angeles, the Panthers and US shared the stage with a varied cast of black radical organizations, some national, like SNCC; some local, like the Community Alert Patrol and Self-Leadership for All Nationalities Today; and some ephemeral, like Black Unitarians for Radical Reform, the Black Anti-Draft association, and the United Afro-Asian Nations. The Panthers and the US Organization, however, stand out for the depth of their attention to cultural matters and their lasting local influence.

3. This is a problem endemic to the "production" of historical knowledge. Documents, duly archived, have the effect of fixing contingent and shifting aspects of lived experience into a record that scholars duly assume is permanent and true. Solidifying that which was in effect up in the air creates distortions that partially explain the gap between "history" and "memory." The 1960s as a moment certainly seem to bear this out.

4. Woodard, *A Nation within a Nation*, 71.

5. Horne, *The Fire This Time*, 263.

6. Marable, *Race, Reform and Rebellion*, 110.

7. Indeed, while the wholesale adoption of the language of cultural and political nationalism at least has a basis in the contemporary language used by black radicals, the widespread preference academics continue to demonstrate for interracial and integrationist struggles, as opposed to variants of black nationalist activity, is harder to justify conceptually or empirically. For an example, see Ward, *Just My Soul Responding*, 415. For a critique of this tendency, see Kelley, *Freedom Dreams*, 62.

8. The source of this section's epigraph is Hebdige, *Subculture*, 3.

9. By "seeing like a state," I mean to invoke Scott's discussion of the "legalistic" mechanisms by which populations are assessed, managed, and governed. It is worth noting that the Black Panther Party's survival programs corresponded to those aspects of the welfare state familiar to residents of both the First World and the Second World and that there is very little that was inherently revolutionary in feeding children, providing

assistance to elders, or monitoring the activities of the police. Both the party's stated goal of a plebiscite in which black Americans would voice their preferences for political community and its oft-quoted references to the founding documents of American political life suggest an internal struggle concerning how to steer a course between reform and revolution. Of course, Lenin's comments on the matter are instructive, as he reminds us that

> it would be absolutely wrong to believe that immediate struggle for socialist revolution implies that we can, or should, abandon the fight for reforms. Not at all. We cannot know beforehand how soon we shall achieve success, how soon the objective conditions will make the rise of this revolution possible. We should support every improvement, every real economic and political improvement in the position of the masses.

See Lenin, "Principles Involved in the War Issue," 158–59; Scott, *Seeing Like a State*.

10. Churchill, "To Disrupt, Discredit and Destroy," 108.
11. Hebdige, *Subculture*, 17.
12. It is instructive, for example, to note that Hebdige ends *Subculture* with a discussion of Jean Genet and George Jackson and that much of his book traces the dialectical debt owed to black culture by white youth. Although ethno-national origins (Caribbean versus North America) on the black side and class (working class versus petit-bourgeois) on the white side differ, it is easy to see how critical elements of Hebdige's analysis might be transposed from England to the United States of the late 1960s.
13. Jane Rhodes analyzes at length the contradiction between the Black Panther Party's cultivation of the spectacle and its members' struggle to represent themselves: Rhodes, *Framing the Black Panther Party*, 91–115.
14. Singh, "The Black Panthers and the 'Undeveloped Country' of the Left."
15. For an analysis that links the politics of wartime youth culture and style to a longer history of black and brown self-activity, see Alvarez, *The Power of the Zoot*.
16. For an overview of the style politics of the period, see Van Deburg, *Black Camelot*.
17. Woodard, *A Nation within a Nation*, 147.
18. On the relationship between race, youth, and policing in the zoot-suit riots, the Watts rebellion, and the 1992 Rodney King riots, see Escobar, *Race, Police, and the Making of a Political Identity*, 3–4, 286–87; Horne, *The Fire This Time*, 131–37, 191–95; Davis, *City of Quartz*, 267–316.
19. Bourdieu, *In Other Words*, 9, 61, 77.
20. Mercer, *Welcome to the Jungle*, 100.
21. Davis, "Afro Images," 273.
22. Kelley, "Nap Time," 341.
23. Mercer, *Welcome to the Jungle*, 100.
24. Kelley, "Nap Time," 348–50.
25. Gang culture in Southern Californian continues to exercise an important influence on regional and national trends within youth culture: see Jankowski, *Islands in the Street*; Phillips, *Wallbangin.'*
26. Conot, *Rivers of Blood, Years of Darkness*, 244; Davis, *City of Quartz*, 298–300. For

another discussion of the transition from the black liberation movement to the rise of the Crips and Bloods, see Cle "Bone" Sloan, dir., *Bastards of the Party* (HBO Films, 2007). See also Alonso, "Territoriality among African-American Street Gangs in Los Angeles."

27. Tyler, "The Rise and Decline of the Watts Summer Festival," 64.

28. Conot: *Rivers of Blood, Years of Darkness*, 114–19; Mike Davis, *City of Quartz*, 297.

29. Bobby Seale, speech at the Kaleidoscope, 16 April 1968, in Pacifica Radio Archives, BB 5471; Seale, speech at Free Huey Rally, in Pacifica Radio Archives, BB 4723. CAP was also a contemporary acronym for the Congress of African People.

30. Bright, "Remappings."

31. Testimony of Sergeant Robert J. Thomas before the U.S. Senate Internal Security Committee hearings, Washington, D.C., 20 January 1970, transcript in my possession.

32. As the example of Hoover's FBI makes clear, the state has cultural politics of its own. For an overview of the cultural production used to impede the work of the black liberation movement, see Churchill, *The Cointelpro Papers*, 131, 159.

33. This point becomes even clearer when we consider the formation of Black Panther organizations among the Mizrachim of Israel, the Dalits of India, black British activists, and aboriginal Australians. There is a growing literature on the party, as noted in the bibliography. For a summary of the rapid spread of the Black Panther Party, see Ahmad, *We Will Return in the Whirlwind*, 186.

34. Douglas, "On Revolutionary Culture," 490.

35. George Murray, "For a Revolutionary Culture," *Black Panther*, 7 September 1968.

36. Conversation with Emory Douglas, 28 October 2006, Los Angeles.

37. For a comprehensive overview of Douglas's artistic and intellectual production, see Durant, *Black Panther*.

38. Emory Douglas, "Position Paper 1 on Revolutionary Art," *Black Panther*, 20 October 1968.

39. "Black Revolutionary Poetry," *Black Panther*, 7 September 1968; Linda Harrison, "On Cultural Nationalism," *Black Panther*, 2 February 1969; "The True Culture of Africa and Africans," *Black Panther*, 17 February 1969.

40. Brad Brewer, "Revolutionary Art," *Black Panther*, 24 October 1970; Frank Jones, "Talent for the Revolution," *Black Panther*, 16 March 1969; Emory Douglas, "Revolutionary Art: A Tool for Liberation," speech delivered at the First Revolutionary Artists Conference, Malcolm X College, Chicago, 8 June 1970.

41. Douglas, "Revolutionary Art." On David Hammons, John Outterbridge, Noah Purifoy and Betye Saar, see chapter 5 in this volume.

42. Harrison, "On Cultural Nationalism."

43. *Harambe*, 18 November 1968; On the conflict between the two organizations, see Churchill, "To Disrupt, Discredit and Destroy"; Cox, "The Split in the Party"; Karenga, *The Roots of the U.S./Panther Conflict*.

44. "Boston" Fred Nolan, "Black Cultural Nationalism," *Black Panther*, 21 December 1968. See also Brewer, "Revolutionary Art"; Murray, "For a Revolutionary Culture."

45. Ernest Mkalimoto, "Revolutionary Black Culture," 11–17.

46. On the tenets and principles of the US Organization, see Scot Brown, *Fighting for US*, 38–73.

47. Ibid., 26–28; Ahmad, *We Will Return in the Whirlwind*, 138–40.

48. Horne, *The Fire This Time*, 10–16.

49. Kelly and Esch, "Black Like Mao." Kelley and Esch observe that many of Karenga's ideas on art bear a striking resemblance to Mao's "Talks at the Yenan Forum on Literature and Art." By Western Marxism, I mean those like Regis Debray, the situationists, and Herbert Marcuse, who argued that (and organized as if) the confluence of youth revolt, antiracist struggle, decolonization, and the other new social movements heralded the rise of a new revolutionary subjectivity. I do not mean Althusser, Social Democrat parliamentarians, or the more exclusively academic contributions of later critical theorists.

50. Ngugi wa Thiong'o, *Decolonising the Mind*.

51. Gramsci, *Selections from the Prison Notebooks*, 12.

52. For a discussion of the idea of cultural hegemony, see Lears, "The Concept of Cultural Hegemony." George Lipsitz observes that the construction of hegemony is as much a project of resistance from below as of domination from above and that the very concept of hegemony is useful in part because victory and defeat are never mutually exhaustive categories: see Lipsitz, "The Struggle for Hegemony," 146–50.

53. Baraka, *The Autobiography of Leroi Jones*, 355–58.

54. Suzanne Jackson, "African American Artists of Los Angeles," Oral History Collection, tape 4, side 1.

55. Ibid., 237.

56. *Uprising*, April 1968.

57. James Cunningham, "Ron Karenga and Black Cultural Nationalism," *Negro Digest*, January 1968, 76–78.

58. Beyond viewing the blues as an important historical root of African American culture, a number of scholars have tried to examine the blues as a kind of foundation and ongoing ontology. For a literary study, see Baker, *Blues, Ideology, and African American Literature*; on visual art, see Powell, "Art History and Black Memory"; for the blues as a historical social geography, see Woods, *Development Arrested*.

59. Karenga, "On Cultural Nationalism," in Chapman, ed., *New Black Voices*, 482; Jones, *Blues People*. On jazz figures in Los Angeles and their use of the blues, see chapter 2 in this book.

60. Tyler, "The Rise and Decline of the Watts Summer Festival," 63.

61. Interview with Vantile Whitfield, appendix in Wilkerson, "Black Theaters in the San Francisco Bay Area and in the Los Angeles Area."

62. "Black Hate Groups," Mafundi Institute, Los Angeles, FBI, Special Agent in Charge (SAC) Files 157–7195, 157–8502, copy in my possession.

63. "Observance Set for Malcolm X," *Los Angeles Sentinel*, 3 February 1966; "Riots disrupt Malcolm X Meeting," *Los Angeles Sentinel*, 25 May 1967.

64. Scot Brown, "The US Organization," Ph.D. diss., Cornell University, 1977, 206–8; "Taifa Dance Troupe," 30 November 1968, *Rosie Grier Show*, video recording, UCLA Film and Television Archives; "Black Culture Festival Due Saturday at Art Museum," *Los Angeles Sentinel*, 26 December 1968.

65. Brown, "The US Organization," 213.

66. Idem, *Fighting for Us*, 140.

67. *Kawaida* (O'be Records, 1970).

68. Mtume, "Tripping with Black Music," *Cricket*, 1969, 1.

69. Doss, "Revolutionary Art Is a Tool for Liberation," 175. See also Baldwin, "Culture Is a Weapon in Our Struggle for Liberation."

70. Douglas, "Revolutionary Art"; Doss, "Revolutionary Art Is a Tool for Liberation," 181–83.

71. In addition to the *Black Panther*, see Jennings, "Poetry of the Black Panther Party."

72. Elaine Brown, liner notes, *Seize the Time* (Vault, 1969).

73. Isoardi, *The Dark Tree*, 124.

74. James, "An Impossible Cinema?"; *The Black Panther* and *Detroit I Do Mind Dying*, newsreels, copies in author's possession.

75. Vincent Canby, "Film: 'Wattstax,' Record of Watts Festival Concert," *New York Times*, 16 February 1973.

76. Churchill, "To Disrupt, Discredit and Destroy," 80–83, 104–105. Given the vituperation to which he has been subjected in the aftermath of his commentary regarding the World Trade Center, it is perhaps appropriate to recall here that Churchill has done as much as any scholar to bring to light the role of clandestine bodies and illegal activities in devastating the black liberation movement and its leadership.

77. Watts Writers Workshop, "A Choice of Positions," *Black Panther*, 22 January 1969.

78. Woodard, *A Nation within a Nation*, 116–120; Brown, "The US Organization," 214, 223, 314–15.

79. Churchill, "To Disrupt, Discredit and Destroy," 96. Michael Zinzun, interview by the author, Los Angeles, 1 September 2002.

7. An Intimate Enemy

1. Davis, *City of Quartz*, 70–78; Berelowitz, "Protecting High Culture in Los Angeles." For a different view, see Molotch, "L.A. as Design Product."

2. On the emergence of a "global" Los Angeles, see Abu-Lughod, *New York, Chicago, Los Angeles*; Davis, *City of Quartz*; Rieff, *Los Angeles*; Sonenshein, *Politics in Black and White*. Roger Keil notes that Davis and Sonenshein offer alternative positions on the overall political legacy of Thomas Bradley: see Keil, *Los Angeles, Globalization, Urbanization, and Social Struggles*, 79; Erie, *Globalizing L.A.*

3. Keil, *Los Angeles, Globalization, Urbanization, and Social Struggles*, 56, 73. Erie cautions against reducing the complex political economy of the time to the agency of a single elected official. His point is well taken, although Bradley's role was an influential one: see Erie, *Globalizing L.A.*, 6.

4. Grant et al., "African Americans," 387–98.

5. Chute-Peevers and Vlahides, *Lonely Planet*, 115.

6. Dickey, *The Rough Guide to Los Angeles*, 14, 171.

7. Fodor's, *Fodor's Los Angeles 2006*, 46.

8. Whiteson, *The Watts Towers of Los Angeles*, 5.

9. Ibid., 32.

10. Sandy Banks, "Watts: The Legacy," *Los Angeles Times*, 11 August 1985.

11. Rich Connell, "Watts Called Still Plagued 19 Years after Riots There," *Los Angeles*

Times, 15 January 1985; Cecil Smith, "Watts—Ten Years After," *Los Angeles Times*, 27 June 1985; William Farr, "Inner-City Problems Grow, Panel Warns," *Los Angeles Times*, 9 July 1985.

12. Schrank, "Picturing the Watts Towers," 374. A number of related points are made in Whiting, *Pop L.A.*

13. Maggie Savoy, "The Summit Meeting at Watts Towers," *Los Angeles Times*, 6 July 1970.

14. Banham, *Los Angeles*, 132.

15. For two early articles that mention Rodia's project, see "Flashing Spires Built as Hobby," *Los Angeles Times*, 13 October 1937; "Glass Towers and Demon Rum," *Los Angeles Times*, 28 April 1939. The source for the latter quote is William Wilson, "Watts Towers: Civic Pride or Shame?" *Los Angeles Times*, 23 April 1978. The bibliography of works regarding the towers crosses architecture and art, alongside the news accounts of their shifting states of ownership and repair. For an overview bibliography and a chronology of events relating to the Watts Towers, see Whiteson, *The Watts Towers of Los Angeles*, 82–86. See also Goldstone, *The Los Angeles Watts Towers*. For a history of assemblage and found art in postwar California, see Sandra Leonard Starr, curator, in *Lost and Found in California*.

16. Collection abstract and summary, Committee for Simon Rodia's Towers in Watts Records.

17. On preservation efforts and the stress test, see "Tower 'Art' Passes Test," *San Francisco Chronicle*, 11 October 1959; "Art Group Fights to Save Los Angeles Tower," *Architectural Forum*, July 1959; "Watts Towers Survive Torture Test," United Press International, n.d., in Committee for Simon Rodia's Towers in Watts Records, box 1, folder 11.

18. Letters to Councilman Josh Gibson, in Committee for Simon Rodia's Towers in Watts Records; Information on Towers Art Center programming, ibid., box 30, folders 2, 5.

19. Erwin Baker, "Bradley Urges L.A. to Accept Offer of Watts Towers, Center," *Los Angeles Times*, 29 July 1974.

20. Baker, "Council Votes 8–3 for City Acquisition of Watts Towers," *Los Angeles Times*, 2 November 1974; Kay Cooperman, "Council Agrees to Take over Watts Towers," *Los Angeles Times*, 23 July 1975.

21. Kenneth Ross, letter to the editor, *Los Angeles Times*, 1 October 1978.

22. Judith Michaelson, "Groups Dispute How Fast Watts Towers Are Falling Apart," *Los Angeles Times*, 18 April 1978.

23. Indeed, it is worth noting that the photograph of Watts Towers Art Center staff members discussed earlier was taken while the towers were closed for renovation.

24. At the time, opinion on the desirability of the Olympiad and its effect on South Los Angeles was mixed. Security concerns, aggressive policing, transportation and parking, economic development, and limits on political demonstrations were among the issues addressed in public forums, constituent letters, and City Council hearings: see Thomas Bradley Administrative Papers, box 139, folder 11, boxes 151–53, folders 1–3, box 169, folder 8, boxes 2552–53, folders 1–3, 6–9. A full accounting of the effect of the games on South Los Angeles is still to be written.

25. Created by the California State Legislature in 1977, the museum originally opened in 1981 before moving to a permanent facility in 1984. In 2001, the museum closed for a

multiyear renovation, reopening in 2003. For a summary of CAAM's history, see the website at http://www.caamuseum.org/cah.htm.

26. Catherine Gottlieb, "The Healing Power of Art," *Los Angeles Times*, 18 July 1994; Beverly Beyette, "The Arts Come Back to Class," *Los Angeles Times*, 9 September 2001.

27. López, "Community Arts Institutions in Los Angeles," 55.

28. John Outterbridge, interview by Richard Cándida Smith, 1990, in "African American Artists of Los Angeles" Oral History Program, 1990, audio recording, tape 1, transcript, 439.

29. Suzanne Muchnic, "Home of the Arts Towers in Watts," *Los Angeles Times*, 13 July 1980.

30. Development Offering Community Redevelopment Administration, in Thomas Bradley Administrative Papers, box 1608, folder 3. For the quote on the CRA, see "Little-Known L.A. Agency Sculpts a New Downtown," *Los Angeles Times*, 26 April 1982.

31. Davis, *City of Quartz*, 78.

32. Publications of the Community Redevelopment Agency, *Development Offering: Remaining 8.75 Acres of Bunker Hill: Downtown Los Angeles* (n.d.), unpag., Tom Bradley Collection, UCLA.

33. Berelowitz, "Protecting High Culture in Los Angeles," 150.

34. Schrank, *Art in the City*.

35. Davis, *City of Quartz*, 73.

36. Undated chronology of MOCA, in Thomas Bradley Administrative Papers, box 1608, folder 3. See also Donald Cosgrove to William Norris, letter, 15 June 1979, CRA files, ibid.

37. Roger Keil offers the most complete micro-history of the CRA, noting its centrality to local urban redevelopment and its central position in facilitating the rise of a city tied firmly to transnational circuits of finance capital: Keil, *Los Angeles, Globalization, Urbanization, and Social Struggles*, 153–71. Keil's account takes Mike Davis's poetically acerbic description of the CRA's downtown efforts ("a single demonically self-referential hyperstructure . . . raised to dementia") as a point of departure for an approach that tracks the gradual process of reforming the CRA in a more equitable direction after the 1980s.

38. See Kurashige, *Japanese American Celebration and Conflict*, 193; Suga, "Little Tokyo Reconsidered."

39. City of Los Angeles budget, in Thomas Bradley Administrative Papers, box 4175, folder 6, s-38.

40. Development Offering Community Redevelopment Administration.

41. Cosgrove to Norris.

42. Undated chronology of MOCA.

43. Payne and Ratzan, *The Impossible Dream*, 130.

44. Undated chronology of MOCA.

45. George Ramos, "Groundbreaking for Theater Center Marred by Protest," *Los Angeles Times*, 12 December 2000; Deborah Belgum, "Fighting for a Legacy," *Los Angeles Times*, 26 September 1996.

46. Kenneth Reich, "Bradley Sworn to Second Term, Lists Goals for City," *Los Angeles Times*, 2 July 1977.

47. "Appendix B: Report of Mayor's Advisory Committee on Culture," in Thomas Bradley Administrative Papers, box 2758, folder 6.

48. Los Angeles Film Development Committee to Councilman Gilbert Lindsay, letter, ibid.

49. Internal memorandum, 8 February 1979, in Thomas Bradley Administrative Papers, box 2758, folder 6.

50. C. Erwin Piper, city administrative officer, "Review of the Report by the Mayor's Advisory Committee on Cultural Affairs," 29 June 1979, routing no. 0220–01769, and letter from James Hadaway, general manager, Department of Recreation and Parks, 1 September 1977, ibid.

51. Internal memorandum, 8 February 1979, in Thomas Bradley Administrative Papers, box 2758, folder 6.

52. Friends of Hollywood, Department of Cultural Affairs fact sheet, n.d., in Thomas Bradley Administrative Papers, box 2758, folder 6.

53. Erwin Baker, "Forming of Cultural Affairs Department Voted," *Los Angeles Times*, 4 May 1979; "Cultural Affairs Department Created," *Los Angeles Times*, 29 May 1980.

54. Budget summary, fiscal year 1988–89, in Thomas Bradley Administrative Papers, box 4175, folder 6.

55. Transfer list, Los Angeles. City Archives, boxes 4227, 4239–40, 4242, 4248, 4269. The city's archives show a pattern of funding for community and other local arts projects and festivals during the 1970s. During the period from 1959 through 1965, municipally sponsored fine arts exhibitions and the All City Outdoor Festival are the primary activities: Los Angeles City Archives, boxes 9043, 19339.

56. Morris McNeill Inc., "Los Angeles Cultural Master Plan," in Thomas Bradley Administrative Papers, box 4175, folder 4, 21, 27.

57. Thomas Bradley Administrative Papers, box 1053, folder 3.

58. "Los Angeles Cultural Master Plan," 44–45.

59. Lowe, *Immigrant Acts*, 84–96. For works on globalization and inequality in Southern California, see Bonacich and Appelbaum, *Behind the Label*; Davis, *Beyond Blade Runner*; López-Garza and Diaz, *Asian and Latino Immigrants in a Restructuring Economy*.

60. Thomas Bradley Administrative Papers, box 1053, folder 4; emphasis added.

61. Festival descriptions are taken from an undated copy of a Cultural Affairs Festival guide in author's possession.

62. From the vantage point of interethnic history and cultural policy, the 2002–3 exhibition "Boyle Heights: The Power of Place" marks a watershed. Held at the Japanese American National Museum in Little Tokyo, the exhibition traced the linked ethnic histories of the East Los Angeles neighborhood. An exhibition booklet gives a sense of the project. See Japanese American National Museum, *Los Angeles's Boyle Heights*.

8. How to Survive in South Central

Epigraphs' sources: Ice Cube, "How to Survive in South Central," *Boyz in the Hood* soundtrack, Quest/Warner Brothers; Charles Burnett, "Inner City Blues," 226.

1. Bradley's biographers J. Gregory Payne and Scott C. Ratzan use the term "impossible dream" to indicate simultaneous narratives of personal achievement and social transformation in the career trajectory of their subject: Payne and Ratzan, *Tom Bradley, the Impossible Dream*.

2. Massood, "An Aesthetic Appropriate to Conditions."

3. The *Variety* box-office reports for *Menace II Society* (New Line Cinema, 1993) are from Watkins, *Representing*, 193.

4. Diegetic sound refers to those sounds that have a visible source or whose source is present in the film. These sounds can be heard by the characters in the film. Examples of diegetic sound include the voices of characters and music whose source is apparent and depicted. Non-diegetic, or commentary, sound has an origin not present on the screen. Examples include narration, background music, and other sounds added subsequently.

5. Taylor, "Decolonizing the Image," 168.

6. Hall, "Race, Articulation, and Societies Structured in Dominance," 55.

7. Soja et al., "Urban Restructuring," 195.

8. Karl Marx to Friedrich Sorge, letter, 1880, quoted ibid.; Keil, *Los Angeles, Globalization, Urbanization, and Social Struggles*, 96–97.

9. Gilmore, "Globalisation and U.S. Prison Growth."

10. Grant et al., "African Americans," 384.

11. Erie, *Globalizing L.A.*, 4.

12. Taylor, "Decolonizing the Image," 167.

13. Bambara, "Reading the Signs, Empowering the Eye," 118–22.

14. Nichols, *Arna Bontemps–Langston Hughes Letters, 1925–1967*, 89.

15. For an overview of the history of the Los Angeles school within the broader study of black American film history, see Masilela, "The Los Angeles School of Black Filmmakers." See also Tajima and Willard, "Nothing Lights a Fire Like a Dream Deferred." David James discusses the Los Angeles school in his *The Most Typical Avant-Garde*; see also Young, *Soul Power*.

16. Masilela, "The Los Angeles School of Black Filmmakers," 107–108.

17. Third cinema refers to the body of films that emerged in the course of the struggle against colonialism and neocolonialism during the post–Second World War period. In this schema, first cinema corresponds to the commercialized cinema of Hollywood. Second cinema refers to the "auteur" cinema of the European avant-garde. Much as the political movement of Third Wordlism tended to reject the First World in its entirety while pursuing a more nuanced, though ultimately problematic, relationship with the Soviet-directed Second World, third cinema directors borrowed selectively from the European avant-garde while regarding Hollywood as almost entirely irrelevant or worse.

18. Hozic, "The House I Live In," 478.

19. Espinosa, "For an Imperfect Cinema."

20. For an important overview of third cinema, see Gabriel, *Third Cinema in the Third World*. See also Pines and Willemen, *Questions of Third Cinema*; Janet Maslin, " 'Killer of Sheep' Is Shown at the Whitney: Nonprofessional Cast," *New York Times*, 14 November 1978. Interestingly, in her acerbic review of the film, Maslin complained that "even the slaughter of the sheep is numbingly uneventful." Exactly.

21. Snead, "Images of Blacks in Black Independent Films," 22; Taylor, "Decolonizing the Image," 168.

22. Murashige, "Haile Gerima and the Political Economy of Cinematic Resistance," 187.

23. Midway through 1989, Milt Ahlerich, assistant director and spokesman of the FBI, sent a letter to Priority Records (N.W.A.'s parent company) complaining that the group's lyrics "encouraged violence against and disrespect for the law enforcement officer." Ahlerich's letter offered a number of thinly veiled references to the unity of the law-enforcement community in the face of the group's recordings, a development that generated strong condemnation from a number of members of the House of Representatives given the task of FBI oversight: see Dave Marsh and Phyllis Pollack, "Wanted for Attitude," *Village Voice*, 10 October 1989, 333.

24. James, *The Most Typical Avant-Garde*, 335.

25. Julie Dash's film *Daughters of the Dust* (1991) is better known than *Killer of Sheep*, but *Daughters of the Dust* was completed long after Dash had left UCLA and the West Coast.

26. For biographical information on Burnett, see MacDonald, "Charles Burnett"; Wali, "Life Drawings."

27. Wali, "Life Drawings," 22.

28. See chapter 5 of this book.

29. MacDonald, "Charles Burnett," 113.

30. Massood, "An Aesthetic Appropriate to Conditions," 29–30.

31. Taylor, "Decolonizing the Image," 170.

32. James, "Toward a Geo-Cinematic Hermeneutics," 38–39.

33. MacDonald, "Charles Burnett," 108; Wali, "Life Drawings."

34. James, "Toward a Geo-Cinematic Hermeneutics," 39.

35. Maslin, " 'Killer of Sheep' Is Shown at the Whitney."

36. Young, *Soul Power*, 241.

37. John Gray, "In the Music World," *California Eagle*, 29 February 1924. Writing much later, Paul Gilroy expressed great concern with the limitations of music as a framework for describing a racially coded community, observing in part that "inner secrets and ethnic rules can be taught and learned": Gilroy, "Sounds Authentic," esp. 135. If we recall that Shelly Manne appeared on Ornette's album *Tomorrow Is the Question*, Gilroy's point would appear to be well taken, especially if we add an addendum from George Lewis. He writes, "The process of critiquing racialized notions of authenticity and cultural theft should not obscure the possibility that theft is nonetheless taking place": Lewis, *A Power Stronger than Itself*, 450. In reflecting on the particular musicians selected by Burnett, there is not much doubt about what has been stolen. Dinah, dead before forty; Robeson, pushed into internal exile and driven from history; Still, excised from two separate musical canons. Even in the case of the particular songs Burnett chose, theft is taking place. Frank Sinatra's filmed version of "The House I Live In" offers a didactic (and anti-Japanese) paean to religious and ethnic tolerance in which Presbyterians and Jews come together and blacks are reduced to an aside, while Still's "Symphony #1 (Afro American)" features a third movement that sounds suspiciously like George Gershwin's "I Got Rhythm," which Still claimed was stolen when the other composer heard him working on it during a rehearsal.

38. The inclusion of "Drinking Song" from Charlie Haden's *Liberation Music Orchestra*

provides a link between *Bless Their Little Hearts* and the jazz avant-garde of Los Angeles. The album, which includes Carla Bley extemporizing over lyrics originally composed by Bertolt Brecht, connects to the German exile community of critical theorists who landed in Los Angeles on the eve of the Second World War. Moreover, the inclusion of Haden and Shepp, two artists associated with free jazz; the inter-generic connections of the Black Arts Movement; and the struggle for African libera-tion suggest a move toward a left-inflected class struggle that is more present than in Burnett's film: discussion with Billy Woodberry, 24 May 2007, Los Angeles.

39. Soja, "Urban Restructuring," 217–18.

40. On deindustrialization in Los Angeles and its effect on African Americans, see ibid.; Flusty, "Postmodern Urbanism"; Johnson and Roseman, "Increasing Black Outmigra-tion from Los Angeles"; California Joint Committee of the State's Economy and the Senate Committee on Government Organization, *Problems and Opportunities for Job Development in Urban Areas of Persistent Unemployment*, 29, 50, 58, 94, 108, 111.

41. William Julius Wilson speaks of the transition from "industrial" to "jobless" ghettos as the sine qua non of contemporary urban poverty: Wilson, *When Work Disappears*, 18–19. It is worth noting that James and Grace Lee Boggs anticipated some of the prob-lems that capitalist transformation would entail a generation ago. Anticipating (as we would expect from an autoworker considering automation) the problems of post-Fordism through an analysis of the deleterious effects welfare placed on human sub-jectivity, the Boggses made a stab at suggesting forms of conduct and consciousness that might reimagine "work" in ways appropriate to the kind of economic regime that inner-city black people confront: see Boggs and Boggs, *Revolution and Evolution in the Twentieth Century*, 227–33.

42. Commercially, *Menace II Society* ranked as the fifth most profitable film of 1993. By its sixth week of theatrical release, it had already earned $20 million, or more than six times the $3 million it cost to make: Watkins, *Representing*, 192. Beyond its commercial success, *Menace II Society* proved among the most influential and enduring of the spate of films released during these years, earning a lasting reputation as an "authentic" depiction of ghetto life that continues to draw intertextual references from throughout the pop-culture realm.

43. Media coverage, sociological studies, and common linguistic usage often collapse "gangs and drugs" into a singular site of antisocial behavior. This is unfortunate, and incorrect. Despite evidence of a certain amount of low-level involvement in drug retailing on the part of area street gangs, gangsters and dealers for the most part move in different worlds. One need only recall the vast difference between the lives of Stanley Williams and Rick Ross to make the point clear.

44. Watkins, *Representing*, 71–73.

45. There is an expanding body of literature on Los Angeles–area hip hop. For an intro-duction, see Cross, *It's Not about a Salary*; Robin Kelley, "Kickin' Reality, Kickin' Ballistics: 'Gangsta Rap' and Postindustrial Los Angeles," in Kelley, *Race Rebels*, 183–228; Odom, "Dope Lyrics and Bangin' Beats"; Chang, *Can't Stop, Won't Stop*; George Lipsitz, "The Hip Hop Hearings: The Hidden History of Deindustrialization," in Chang, *Footsteps in the Dark*, 154–83.

46. Gates, "Blood Brothers."
47. Of course, the crack cocaine epidemic was national in scope. To the extent that the global is always local, however, one can identify a number of reasons that Los Angeles became a key node in the wide proliferation of rock cocaine. The presence of a large number of recreational cocaine users in the entertainment industry offers one clue; the massive rise of California as a carceral state provides another. Federal efforts to sustain an anticommunist jeremiad in the face of congressional oversight made the U.S.-Mexican border an important cocaine transshipment point, and this made the imported good slightly cheaper and more widely available in California. One should also mention the human agency of legendary figures such as Ricky "Freeway Rick" Ross. If we consider this incomplete list, it is easy to see the Althusserian overdetermination of the epidemic that in fact occurred. Aqeela Sherrills, the former Grape Street Crip-turned-community organizer, captured the feel of the time, saying, "The whole quality of life in the neighborhood just changed. I mean, all the girls that we were just crazy about when we were kids, that we all looked up to, became strawberries. . . . Folks went to jail for the rest of their life. People got murdered . . . totally devastated the neighborhood": quoted in Chang, *Can't Stop, Won't Stop*, 208–209.
48. Alonso, "Territoriality among African-American Street Gangs in Los Angeles," 19–23.
49. Sonenshein, *Politics in Black and White*, 1993.
50. Gilmore, *Golden Gulag*; Parenti, *Lockdown America*.
51. Joao Vargas and Jeff Chang describe ongoing patterns of police interference with gangs' truce efforts: see Vargas, *Catching Hell in the City of Angels*, 177–209. The account Vargas provides is particularly useful, as he examines the class politics, internal orientations, and differing agendas of the Community in Support of the Gang Truce and Jim Brown's Amer-I-Can foundation: Chang, *Can't Stop, Won't Stop*, 386.
52. Davis, *City of Quartz*, 270–71.
53. Toddy Tee's song "Batterram" (1985) deserves an extended mention, at least insofar as it sought to link Bradley and Gates. Tee raps:

> Mayor of the city, what you're tryin to do?
> They say they voted you in in '82
> But on the next term huh, without no doubt
> They say they gon' vote your jack ass out.
> Because you musta been crazy or half-way wack
> To legalize somethin that works like that
>
> And the Chief of Police says he just might
> Flatten out every house he sees on sight
> Because he say the rockman is takin him for a fool
> And for some damn reason it just ain't cool
> And when he drives down the street, I tell you the truth
> He gets no respect, they call his force F Troop
> He can't stand it, he can't take no more
> And now he's gonna have you all fall into the floor.

54. "Report of the Independent Commission on the Los Angeles Police Department: Summary," Los Angeles, 1991, 13.

55. Escobar, *Race, Police, and the Making of a Political Identity*. Escobar traces the dialectic between police practice and Chicano political consciousness. A similar tale can be told for the black residents of Los Angeles.

56. Gilmore, "Globalisation and U.S. Prison Growth," 171–88.

57. Horne, *The Fire This Time*, 10–16; Branch, *Pillar of Fire*, 3–13.

58. Knight, "Justifiable Homicide, Police Brutality, or Governmental Repression?" Charles Burnett told Minona Wali about the impression the police raid on the Nation of Islam mosque made on him as a youth: see Wali, "Life Drawings," 19.

59. Johnson and Roseman, "Increasing Black Outmigration from Los Angeles," 205–22. See also Brookings Institution Center on Urban and Metropolitan Policy, *Los Angeles in Focus*, 18.

60. Grant et. al, "African Americans," 403.

61. From 1960 to 2000, the African American population of Los Angeles declined from 13.8 percent to 10.9 percent. During this time, the white population of Los Angeles declined by more than half, from 70 percent of the city to about 29 percent, and the Latino population grew from about 10.7 percent to about 50 percent. These figures tell only part of the story. Since 1980, the neighborhoods traditionally considered to make up "South Central Los Angeles" have gone from more than 75 percent black to approximately 75 percent Latino. Many white areas of the city have stayed white. As a result, many African Americans have come to regard immigration from Latin America as having a profound impact on the spatial possibility of an identifiably "black" community. Josh Sides argues that this signals the waning of an opportunity gap between white and black: Sides, *City Limits*, 205. In his estimation, the decline of geographically contiguous neighborhoods signals an end to racial exclusion and thus highlights an objectively beneficial reality. I prefer to remain more agnostic, at least until the possibility of a durable joining of the political aspirations of black and brown appears on the scene.

62. Charles Burnett, "Inner City Blues," in Pines and Willemen, *Questions of Third Cinema*, 223–26.

63. King, *Magical Reels*, 65–66.

64. Robinson, *Black Marxism*, 171.

65. Gilmore, "Globalisation and U.S. Prison Growth," 186.

66. Noah Purifoy, "Art in the Community," notes for speech prepared for the seminar "A Day with the Experts in the Arts," 26 October 1974. Noah Purifoy Papers.

WORKS CITED

Archival and Manuscript Collections

Academy of Television Arts and Sciences, Archive of American Television. Burbank, Calif.

"African American Artists of Los Angeles." Center for Oral History Research, Department of Special Collections, University Research Library, University of California, Los Angeles.

Joan Ankrum Papers, Archives of American Art, Smithsonian Institution. Washington, D.C.

Balch Art Research Library. Los Angeles County Museum of Art.

"Beyond Central Avenue," Center for Oral History Research, Young Research Library, University of California. Los Angeles.

Black Arts Research Center. Nyack, N.Y.

Thomas Bradley Administrative Papers, Department of Special Collections, University of California. Los Angeles.

California Arts Commission Records, California State Archives. Sacramento.

Center for the Study of Political Graphics. Los Angeles.

"Central Avenue Sounds." Center for Oral History Research, Department of Special Collections, University Research Library, University of California. Los Angeles.

Committee for Simon Rodia's Towers in Watts Records, Department of Special Collections, University Research Library, University of California. Los Angeles.

John Anson Ford Collection, Huntington Library. San Marino, Calif.

Institute of Jazz Studies, John Cotton Dana Library, Rutgers, State University of New Jersey. Newark.

Los Angeles City Archives, Office of the City Clerk. Los Angeles.

Los Angeles City College, Martin Luther King Jr. Library. Los Angeles.

Los Angeles Theater Clipping Files, Literature Department, Los Angeles Public Library. Los Angeles.

Daphne Muse Collection, Bancroft Library, University of California. Berkeley.

National Endowment for the Arts and National Endowment for the Humanities, National Archives and Records Administration. Washington, D.C.

John Outterbridge Papers, Papers of African American Artists, Archives of American Art, Smithsonian Institution. Washington, D.C.

Pacifica Radio Archives. Los Angeles.

Noah Purifoy Papers, Papers of African American Artists, Archives of American Art, Smithsonian Institution. Washington, D.C.

Rockefeller Archice Center, Sleepy Hollow, N.Y.

Schomburg Center for Research in Black Culture, New York Public Library. New York.

Southern California Library for Social Research. Los Angeles.

Horace Tapscott Jazz Collection, 1960–2002, Music Library Special Collections, University of California. Los Angeles.

Watts Writers Workshop Collection, Rockefeller Archive Center. Sleepy Hollow, N.Y.

Charles White Papers, Papers of African American Artists, Archives of American Art, Smithsonian Institution. Washington, D.C.

Newspapers and Periodicals

Architectural Forum
Black Panther
Cadence
California Eagle
Choir Guide
Claremont Collegian
Cricket: Black Music in Evolution
Crisis
Coda
Compton Herald Tribune
Daily Reflector
Daily Variety
Down Beat
Ebony
Economist
Glendale News-Press
Harambe Notes
Hollywood Reporter
International Musician
Jazz and Blues
Jazz and Pop
Jazz Magazine
Jet
Los Angeles Free Press
Los Angeles Herald Examiner
Los Angeles Music Guide
Los Angeles Newsletter
Los Angeles Sentinel
Los Angeles Times

Mother Jones
NAACP Bulletin
Negro Digest (continued by *Black World*)
Neworld
New York Review of Books
New York Times
Nigger Uprising
Overture
Pittsburgh Courier
San Francisco Chronicle
Science
Scientific American
Street Chopper
Village Voice
Vogue

Recordings

Carter, John, and Bobby Bradford Quartet. *Flight for Four*. Flying Dutchman FDS-108.
——. *Secrets*. Revelation 18.
——. *Seeking*. Revelation 9.
——. *Self-Determination Music*. Flying Dutchman FDS-128.
Carter, John, and Bobby Bradford Quartet, with the Horace Tapscott Quintet. *West Coast Hot*. Novus Series '70.
Coleman, Ornette. *Free Jazz*. Atlantic 1364.
——. *The Shape of Jazz to Come*. Atlantic 1317.
——. *Something Else!!!! The Music of Ornette Coleman*. Contemporary S7569.
Criss, Sonny. *Sonny's Dream*. Prestige PR 7576.
Land, Harold. *Harold in the Land of Jazz*. Contemporary Records 3550.
Pan Afrikan People's Arkestra. *The Call*. Nimbus NS246.
——. *Flight 17*. Nimbus NS135.
——. *Live at I.U.C.C.* Nimbus NS357.
Tapscott, Horace. *The Dark Tree, Volume 1*. Hat Art CD 6053.
——. *The Horace Tapscott Quintet*. Flying Dutchman FDS107.
——. *Songs of the Unsung*. Interplay IP-7714.
Various artists. *Black California*. Savoy SJL 2215.
Various artists. *Boyz in the Hood*. Warner Brothers. Catalog #926643-2
Various artists. *Project Blowed*. Freestylus 1994.

Published Materials

Aaron, Henry J. *Politics and the Professors: The Great Society in Perspective*. Washington, D.C: Brookings Institution, 1978.
Abrahams, Roger. *Talking Black*. Rowley, Mass.: Newbury House Publishers, 1976.
Abu-Lughod, Janet. *New York, Chicago, Los Angeles: America's Global Cities*. Minneapolis: University of Minnesota Press, 2001.

Adorno, Theodor, and Max Horkheimer. "The Culture Industry: Enlightenment as Mass Deception." Pp. 120–67 in *Dialectic of Enlightenment: Philosophical Fragment*. New York: Continuum, 1976.

Ahmad, Muhammad. *We Will Return in the Whirlwind*. Chicago: Charles Kerr Publishing, 2007.

Ake, David. *Jazz Cultures*. Berkeley: University of California Press, 2002

Allen Jr., Ernest. "When Japan Was 'Champion of the Darker Races': Satokata Takahashi and the Flowering of Black Messianic Nationalism." *Black Scholar* 24 (Winter 1994): 23–46.

Allen, Robert L. *Black Awakening in Capitalist America*. Garden City, N.Y.: Doubleday, 1969.

Alonso, Alejandro. "Territoriality among African-American Street Gangs in Los Angeles." Ph.D. diss., University of Southern California, 1999.

Alvarez, Luis. *The Power of the Zoot: Youth Culture and Resistance during World War II*. Berkeley: University of California Press, 2008.

Anderson, Benedict. *Imagined Communities*. London: Verso, 1991.

Anderson, Iain. *This Is Our Music: Free Jazz, the Sixties, and American Culture*. Philadelphia: University of Pennsylvania Press, 2007.

Anderson, T. J. *Notes to Make the Sound Come Right: Four Innovators of Jazz Poetry*. Fayetteville: University of Arkansas Press, 2004.

Assemblage in California: Works from the Late 50s and Early 60s. Irvine: School of Fine Arts, University of California, 1968.

Avila, Eric. "The Folklore of the Freeway: Space, Culture and Identity in Postwar Los Angeles." *Aztlan* 23, no. 1 (Spring 1998): 15–31.

——. *Popular Culture in the Age of White Flight: Fear and Fantasy in Suburban Los Angeles*. Berkeley: University of California Press, 2004.

Ayres, Anne. "Objects of Magical Power." In *Southern California Assemblage: Past and Present*. Santa Barbara, Calif.: Contemporary Arts Forum, 1986.

Bakan, Michael. "Way out West on Central: Jazz in the African-American Community of Los Angeles before 1930." Pp. 23–78 in *California Soul: Music of African Americans in the West*, ed. by Jacqueline DjeDje and Eddie S. Meadows. Berkeley: University of California Press, 1998.

Baker, Houston. *Blues, Ideology, and African American Literature*. Chicago: University of Chicago Press, 1983.

Baldwin, Davarian. " 'Culture Is a Weapon in Our Struggle for Liberation': The Black Panther Party and the Cultural Politics of Decolonization." Pp. 289–305 in *In Search of the Black Panther Party: New Perspectives on a Revolutionary Movement*, ed. by Jama Lazerow and Yohuru Williams. Durham: Duke University Press, 2006.

Bambara, Toni Cade. "Reading the Signs, Empowering the Eye: Daughters of the Dust and the Black Independent Cinema Movement." Pp. 118–44 in *Black American Cinema*, ed. by Manthieu Diawara. New York: Routledge, 1993.

Banham, Raynar. *Los Angeles: The Architecture of Four Ecologies*. London: Penguin, 1971.

Baraka, Amiri. *The Autobiography of Leroi Jones*. New York: Lawrence Hill, 1984.

——. *The Black Arts Movement*. Atlanta: Self-published, 1994.

Barrett, Edward. *The Tenney Committee: Legislative Investigation of Subversive Activities in California*. Ithaca, N.Y.: Cornell University Press, 1951.

Barron, Stephanie, Sheri Bernstein, and Ilene Susan Fort, eds. *Reading California: Art, Image and Identity*. Berkeley: Los Angeles County Museum of Art and University of California Press, 2000.

Bauman, Alan. "Race, Class, and Political Power: The Implementation of the War on Poverty in Los Angeles." Ph.D. diss., University of California, Santa Barbara, 1998.

Bauman, Robert. "The Black Power and Chicano Movements in the Poverty Wars in Los Angeles." *Journal of Urban History* 33, no. 2 (2007): 277–95.

Bass, Charlotta. *Forty Years: Memoirs from the Pages of a Newspaper*. Los Angeles, 1960.

Beck, Nicholas. *Budd Schulberg: A Bio-Bibliography*. Lanham, Md.: Scarecrow Press, 2001.

Benston, Kimberly. *Performing Blackness: Enactments of African American Modernism*. New York: Routledge, 2000.

Berelowitz, Jo-Anne. "A New Jerusalem: Utopias, MOCA, and the Redevelopment of Downtown Los Angeles." *Strategies* 3 (1990): 202–26.

———. "Protecting High Culture in Los Angeles: MOCA and the Ideology of Urban Re-development." *Oxford Art Journal* 16, no. 1 (1993): 149–57.

Betye Saar. New York: Whitney Museum of Art, 1975.

Biondi, Martha. *To Stand and Fight: The Struggle for Civil Rights in Postwar New York City*. Cambridge: Cambridge University Press, 2003.

Blauner, Robert. "Whitewash over Watts: The Failure of the McCone Commission Report." Pp. 167–88 in *The Los Angeles Riots: Mass Violence in America*, ed. by Robert M. Fogelson. New York: Arno Press, 1969.

Boggs, James, and Grace Lee Boggs. *Revolution and Evolution in the Twentieth Century*. New York: Monthly Review Press, 1974.

Bolden, Jayne. "All the Birds Sing Bass: The Revolutionary Blues of Jayne Cortez." *African American Review* 35, no. 1 (Spring 2001): 61–71.

Bonacich, Edna, and Richard Appelbaum, eds. *Behind the Label: Inequality in the Los Angeles Apparel Industry*. Berkeley: University of California Press, 2000.

Bontemps, Arna, and Jack Conroy. *Anyplace but Here* (rev. ed. of *They Seek a City*). New York: Hill and Wang, 1966.

Bourdieu, Pierre. *In Other Words: Essays toward a Reflexive Sociology*. Palo Alto. Calif.: Stanford University Press, 1990.

Bowman, Rob. *Soulsville, U.S.A: The Story of Stax Records*. New York: Schirmer Books, 1997.

Boyd, Melba Joyce. *Wrestling with the Muse: Dudley Randall and the Broadside Press*. New York: Columbia University Press, 2003.

Branch, Taylor. *Pillar of Fire: America in the King Years, 1963–65*. New York: Simon & Schuster, 1998.

Bright, Brenda Jo. "Remappings: Los Angeles Low Riders." Pp. 89–123 in *Looking High and Low: Art and Cultural Identity*, ed. by Brenda Jo Bright and Elizabeth Bakewell. Tucson: University of Arizona Press, 1995.

Brodsley, David. *L.A. Freeway: An Appreciative Essay*. Berkeley: University of California Press, 1981.

Brookings Institution Center on Urban and Metropolitan Policy. *Los Angeles in Focus: A Profile from Census 2000*. Washington, D.C.: Brookings Institution, 2003.

Brown, Elaine. *A Taste of Power: A Black Woman's Story*. New York: Pantheon, 1992.

Brown, Fahamisa. *Performing the Word: African American Poetry as Vernacular Culture*. New Brunswick, N.J.: Rutgers University Press, 1999.

Brown, Scot. *Fighting for US: Maulana Karenga, the US Organization, and Black Cultural Nationalism*. New York: New York University Press, 2003.

Buhle, Paul, and Dave Wagner. *Radical Hollywood*. New York: New Press, 2002.

Bunch, Lonnie G., III. "A Past Not Necessarily Prologue: The Afro-American in Los Angeles since 1930." Pp. 101–30 in *Twentieth-Century Los Angeles: Power, Promotion, and Social Conflict*, ed. by Norman M. Klein and Martin J. Schiesl. Claremont, Calif.: Regina Books, 1990.

——. *Black Angelenos: The Afro-American in Los Angeles*. Los Angeles: California Afro-American Museum, 1988.

Burchell, Graham, Colin Gordon, and Peter Miller, eds. *The Foucault Effect: Studies in Governmentality*. Chicago: University of Chicago Press, 1991.

Califano, Joseph, Jr. *The Triumph and Tragedy of Lyndon Johnson: The Presidential Years*. New York: Simon and Schuster, 1991.

California Joint Committee of the State's Economy and the Senate Committee on Government Organization. *Problems and Opportunities for Job Development in Urban Areas of Persistent Unemployment*. Sacramento: State of California, 1982.

Callendar, Red, and Elaine Cohen. *Unfinished Dream: The Musical World of Red Callender*. London: Quartet Books, 1985.

Carby, Hazel. *Reconstructing Womanhood: The Emergence of the Afro-American Woman Novelist*. Oxford: Oxford University Press, 1995.

Carpenter, Jane, with Betye Saar. *Betye Saar*. San Francisco: Pomegranate, 2003.

Carson, Clayborne. *In Struggle: SNCC and the Black Awakening of the 1960s*. Cambridge, Mass.: Harvard University Press, 1981.

Carter, Curtis. *Watts: Art and Social Change in Los Angeles, 1965–2002*. Milwaukee: Haggerty Museum of Art, Marquette University, 2003.

Castells, Manuel. *The City and the Grassroots: A Cross-Cultural Theory of Urban Social Movements*. Berkeley: University of California Press, 1983.

Catalano, Nick. *Clifford Brown: The Life and Art of the Legendary Jazz Trumpeter*. Oxford: Oxford University Press, 2000.

Chang, Edward, and Russell C. Leong. *Los Angeles—Struggles toward Multiethnic Community: Asian American, African American and Latino Perspectives*. Seattle: University of Washington Press, 1994.

Chang, Jeff. *Can't Stop, Won't Stop: A History of the Hip Hop Generation*. New York: St. Martin's Press, 2005.

Chapman, Abraham, ed. *New Black Voices: An Anthology of Contemporary Afro-American Literature*. New York: New American Library, 1972.

Chatterjee, Partha. *The Nation and Its Fragments: Colonial and Postcolonial Histories*. Princeton: Princeton University Press, 1993.

Churchill, Ward. *The Cointelpro Papers: Documents from the FBI's Secret Wars against Domestic Dissent*. Boston: South End Press, 1990.

——. "'To Disrupt, Discredit and Destroy': The FBI's Secret War against the Black Panther Party." Pp. 87–117 in *Liberation, Imagination and the Black Panther Party*, ed. by Kathleen Cleaver and George Katsiaficas. New York: Routledge, 2001.

Chute-Peevers, Andrea, and John Vlahides. *Lonely Planet: Los Angeles and Southern California*. Oakland, Calif.: Lonely Planet Publications, 2005.

Cleaver, Kathleen, and George Katsiaficas, eds. *Liberation, Imagination and the Black Panther Party*. New York: Routledge, 2001.

Cohen, Harvey G. "Duke Ellington and *Black, Brown, and Beige*: The Composer as Historian at Carnegie Hall." *American Quarterly* 56, no. 4 (December 2004): 1003–34.

Cohen, Nathan, ed. *The Los Angeles Riots: A Socio-Psychological Study*. New York: Praeger, 1970.

Collette, Buddy, with Steven Isaordi. *Jazz Generations: A Life in American Music and Society*. New York: Continuum, 2001.

Collins, Keith. *Black Los Angeles: The Maturing of the Ghetto*. Saratoga, N.Y.: Century Twenty One Publishing, 1980.

Conot, Robert. *Rivers of Blood, Years of Darkness*. New York: Bantam, 1967.

Conwill, Houston. "Interview with Betye Saar." *Black Art* 3, no .1 (1978): 4–15.

Cortez, Jayne. *Pissstained Stairs and the Monkey Man's Wares*. New York: Phrase Text, 1969.

Cosgrove, Stuart. "The Zoot-Suit and Style Warfare." *History Workshop Journal* 18 (Fall 1984): 77–91.

Countryman, Michael. *Up South: Civil Rights and Black Power in Philadelphia*. Philadelphia: University of Pennsylvania Press, 2006.

Cox, Bette Yarbrough. *Central Avenue—Its Rise and Fall*. Los Angeles: BEEM Publications, 1993.

——. "The Evolution of Black Music in Los Angeles, 1890–1955." Pp. 249–78 in *Seeking El Dorado: African Americans in California*, ed. by Lawrence B. De Graaf and Quintard Taylor. Seattle: University of Washington, and Los Angeles: Autry Museum of Western Heritage, 2001.

Cox, Donald. "The Split in the Party." Pp. 118–22 in *Liberation, Imagination and the Black Panther Party*, ed. by Kathleen Cleaver and George Katsiaficas. New York: Routledge, 2001.

Cripps, Thomas. *Making Movies Black: The Hollywood Message Movie from World War II to the Civil Rights Era*. Oxford: Oxford University Press, 1993.

Cross, Brian. *It's Not about a Salary: Rap, Race and Resistance in Los Angeles*. London: Verso, 1992.

Crouch, Stanley. *Ain't No Ambulances for No Nigguhs Tonight*. New York: R. W. Baron, 1972.

——. *The All-American Skin Game, or the Decoy of Race, the Long and the Short of It, 1990–1994*. New York: Pantheon Books, 1995.

——. *The Artificial White Man: Essays on Authenticity*. New York: Basic Civitas, 2004.

———. "When Watts Burned." Pp. 346–48 in *Voices in Our Blood*, ed. by Jon Meacham. New York: Random House, 2001.

Cruse, Harold. *The Crisis of the Negro Intellectual*. New York: William Morrow, 1967.

Cunningham, James. "Hemlock for Black Artist: Karenga Style," *Negro Digest* (January 1968); reprinted Pp. 483–89 in *New Black Voices: An Anthology of Contemporary Afro-American Literature*, ed. by Abraham Chapman. New York: New American Library, 1972.

Dalfiume, Richard. "The 'Forgotten Years' of the Negro Revolution." *Journal of American History* 55, no. 1 (June 1968): 90–106.

Daniels, Douglas. "Los Angeles Zoot: Race 'Riot,' the Pachuco, and Black Music Culture." *Journal of Negro History* 82, no. 2 (Spring 1997): 201–20.

Dávila, Arlene. *Sponsored Identities: Cultural Politics in Puerto Rico*. Philadelphia: Temple University Press, 1997.

Davis, Angela. "Afro Images: Politics, Fashion, and Nostalgia." Pp. 273–78 in *The Angela Davis Reader*, ed. by Joy James. Malden, Mass.: Blackwell Publishers, 1998.

Davis, Mike. *Beyond Blade Runner*. Westfield, N.J.: Open Pamphlet Series, 1992.

———. *City of Quartz: Excavating the Future in Los Angeles*. London: Verso, 1990.

———. "Sunshine and the Open Shop: Ford and Darwin in 1920s Los Angeles." Pp. 96–122 in *Metropolis in the Making: Los Angeles in the 1920s*, ed. by Tom Sitton and William Deverell. Berkeley: University of California Press, 2001.

De Graaf, Lawrence B. "The City of Black Angels: Emergence of the Los Angeles Ghetto, 1890–1930." *Pacific Historical Review* 30, no. 3 (August 1970): 323–52.

———. "Negro Migration to Los Angeles, 1930 to 1950." Ph.D. diss., University of California, Los Angeles, 1962.

De Graaf, Lawrence, and Quintard Taylor. *Seeking El Dorado: African Americans in California*. Seattle: University of Washington, and Los Angeles: Autry Museum of Western Heritage, 2001.

Denning, Michael. *The Cultural Front*. London: Verso, 1997.

DeVeaux, Scott. "Bebop and the Recording Industry: The 1942 AFM Recording Ban Reconsidered." *Journal of the American Musicological Society* 41 (1988): 126–65.

———. *The Birth of Bebop: A Social and Musical History*. Berkeley: University of California Press, 1997.

———. "Constructing the Jazz Tradition: Jazz Historiography." *Black American Literature Forum* 25, no. 3 (Fall 1991): 525–60.

Diawara, Manthieu, ed. *Black American Cinema*. New York: Routledge, 1993.

Dickey, J. D., ed. *The Rough Guide to Los Angeles*, 4th ed. London: Rough Guides, 2005.

Dje-Dje, Jacqueline, and Eddie S. Meadows. *California Soul: Music of African Americans in the West*. Berkeley: University of California Press, 1998.

Doss, Erica. "Revolutionary Art Is a Tool for Liberation: Emory Douglas and Protest Aesthetics at the *Black Panther*." Pp. 175–87 in *Liberation, Imagination, and the Black Panther Party*, ed. by Kathleen Cleaver and George Katsiaficas. New York: Routledge, 2001.

Douglas, Emory. "On Revolutionary Culture." Pp. 489–90 in *New Black Voices*, ed. by Abraham Chapman. New York: Signet, 1972.

Dover, Cedric. *American Negro Art*. Greenwich, Conn.: New York Graphic Society, 1960.

Driskell, David, ed. *African American Visual Aesthetics: A Postmodernist View*. Washington, D.C.: Smithsonian Institution Press, 1995.

Duberman, Martin. *Paul Robeson*. New York: Alfred A. Knopf, 1988.

Durant, Sam, ed. *Black Panther: The Revolutionary Art of Emory Douglas*. New York: Rizzoli, 2008.

Eastman, Ralph. "Central Avenue Blues: The Making of Los Angeles Rhythm and Blues, 1942–1947." *Black Music Research Journal* 9, no. 1 (Spring 1989): 19–33.

Elderfield, Jon, ed. *Essays on Assemblage*. New York: Museum of Modern Art, 1992.

Ellington, Duke. *Music Is My Mistress*. New York: Da Capo Press, 1973.

Ely, Melvin. *The Adventures of Amos 'n' Andy: A Social History of an American Phenomenon*. Charlottesville: University Press of Virginia, 2001.

Erie, Steven P. *Globalizing L.A.: Trade, Infrastructure, and Regional Development*. Stanford, Calif.: Stanford University Press, 2004.

Escobar, Edward. "The Dialectics of Repression: The Los Angeles Police Department and the Chicano Movement, 1968–1971." *Journal of American History* 79, no. 4 (March 1993): 1483–1514.

——. *Race, Police, and the Making of a Political Identity: Mexican Americans and the Los Angeles Police Department, 1900–1945*. Berkeley: University of California Press, 1999.

Espinosa, Julio García. "For an Imperfect Cinema." *Jump Cut*, no. 20 (1979) 24–26.

Fabre, Michael, and Edward Margolies. *The Several Lives of Chester Himes*. Jackson: University Press of Mississippi, 1997.

Fax, Elton C. *Black Artists of the New Generation*. New York: Dodd, Mead, 1977.

Fine, Elsa Honig. *The Afro-American Artist: A Search for Identity*. New York: Holt, Rinehart and Winston, 1973.

Fischlin, Daniel, and Ajay Heble, eds. *The Other Side of Nowhere: Jazz, Improvisation, and Communities in Dialogue*. Middletown, Conn.: Wesleyan University Press, 2004.

Flamm, Michael. *Law and Order: Street Crime, Civil Unrest, and the Crisis of Liberalism in the 1960s*. New York: Columbia University Press, 2005.

Flamming, Douglas. *Bound for Freedom: Black Los Angeles in Jim Crow America*. Berkeley: University of California Press, 2005.

Floyd, Samuel. *The Power of Black Music*. New York: Oxford University Press, 1996.

Flusty, Steven. "Postmodern Urbanism." *Annals of the Association of American Geographers* 88, no. 1 (March 1998): 50–72.

Fodor's. *Fodor's Los Angeles 2006*, rev. ed. New York: Fodor's, 2004.

Fogelson, Robert M. "White on Black: A Critique of the McCone Commission Report on the Los Angeles Riots." Pp. 111–44 in *The Los Angeles Riots: Mass Violence in America*, ed. by Robert M. Fogelson. New York: Arno Press, 1969.

Fogelson, Roger. *The Fragmented Metropolis: Los Angeles, 1850–1930*. Berkeley: University of California Press, 1967.

Foucault, Michel. *Power/Knowledge: Selected Interviews and Other Writings, 1972–1977*. New York: Pantheon Books, 1980.

Franklin, V. P. *Black Self-Determination: A Cultural History of African-American Resistance*. Brooklyn, N.Y.: Lawrence Hill Books, 1992.

Fuller, Burgess, and Daniela Salvioni, eds. *Art/Women/California: Parallels and Intersections, 1950–2000*. Berkeley: University of California Press, 2002.

Gabriel, Teshome. *Third Cinema in the Third World: The Aesthetics of Liberation*. Ann Arbor: University of Michigan Research Press, 1982.

Gaines, Kevin. *Uplifting the Race: Black Leadership, Politics and Culture in the 20th Century*, Chapel Hill: University of North Carolina Press, 1996.

Gates, Henry Louis. "Black Creativity: On the Cutting Edge," *Time*, 10 October 1994: 74–75.

———. "Blood Brothers." *Transition* 63 (1994): 164.

Gayle, Addison, Jr., ed. *The Black Aesthetic*. Garden City, N.Y.: Anchor Books, 1972.

Gedeon, Lucinda, ed. *Melvin Edwards Sculpture: A Thirty-Year Retrospective, 1963–1993*. Purchase, N.Y.: Neuberger Museum of Art, State University of New York, Purchase, 1993.

Gennari, John. "Jazz Criticism: Its Development and Ideologies." *Black American Literature Forum* 25, no. 3 (Fall 1991): 449–523.

Gilmore, Ruth Wilson. "Globalisation and U.S. Prison Growth: From Military Keynesianism to Post-Keynesian Militarism." *Race and Class* 40, nos. 2–3 (1999): 171–88.

———. *Golden Gulag: Prisons, Surplus, Crisis, and Opposition in Globalizing California*. Berkeley: University of California Press, 2007.

Gilroy, Paul. *Against Race*. Cambridge, Mass.: Harvard University Press, 2000.

———. *The Black Atlantic: Modernity and Double Consciousness*. Cambridge, Mass.: Harvard University Press, 1993.

———. "Sounds Authentic: Black Music, Ethnicity, and the Challenge of a 'Changing' Same." *Black Music Research Journal* 11, no. 2 (Fall 1991): 111–36.

Gioia, Ted. *West Coast Jazz: Modern Jazz in California, 1945–1960*. Oxford: Oxford University Press, 1991.

Glasrud, Bruce, and Laurie Champion. " 'No Land of the Free': Chester Himes Confronts California (1940–1946)." *CLA Journal* 44, no. 3 (March 2001): 391–416.

Goldson, Elizabeth. *Seeing Jazz: Artists and Writers on Jazz*. San Francisco: Chronicle Books, 1997.

Goldstone, Bud. *The Los Angeles Watts Towers*. Los Angeles: Getty Conservation Institute, 1997.

Gomez, Michael. *Exchanging Our Country Marks: The Transformation of African Identities in the Colonial and Antebellum South*. Chapel Hill: University of North Carolina Press, 1998.

Gordon, Robert. *Jazz West Coast: The Los Angeles Jazz Scene of the 1950s*. New York: Quartet Press, 1987.

Governor's Commission on the Los Angeles Riot. *A Report by the Governor's Commission on the Los Angeles Riot*. Los Angeles: Kimtex Corporation, 1965.

Grabbard, Krin, ed. *Jazz among the Discourses*. Durham: Duke University Press, 1995.

Gramsci, Antonio. *Selections from the Prison Notebooks*. New York: International Publishers, 1971.

Grant, David, Melvin Oliver, and Angela D. James. "African Americans: Social and Economic Bifurcation." Pp. 379–411 in *Ethnic Los Angeles*, ed. by Roger Waldinger and Mehdi Bozorgmehr. New York: Russell Sage Foundation, 1996.

Gray, Herman. *Cultural Moves: African Americans and the Politics of Representation*. Berkeley: University of California Press, 2005.

Gray, John. *Fire Music: A Bibliography of the New Jazz, 1959–1990*. New York: Greenwood Publishing Group, 1991.

Gregory, Steven. *Black Corona: Race and the Politics of Place in an Urban Community*. Princeton: Princeton University Press, 1998.

Green, Adam. *Selling the Race: Culture, Community, and Black Chicago*. Chicago: University of Chicago Press, 2007.

Hall, Stuart. "Race, Articulation, and Societies Structured in Dominance." Pp. 16–60 in *Black British Cultural Studies: A Reader*, ed. by Houston A. Baker, Manthia Diawara, and Ruth H. Lindeborg. Chicago: University of Chicago Press, 1996 (1980).

Hampton, Lionel, with James Haskins. *Hamp: An Autobiography*. New York: Warner Books, 1989.

Harrison, Paul, moderator. "The Edited Transcript of the Round Table on Integrative Inquiry." *Lenox Avenue* 1 (1995): 10–44.

Hawes, Hampton. *Raise up off Me: A Portrait of Hampton Hawes*. New York: Thunder's Mouth Press, 1972.

Hebdige, Dick. *Subculture: The Meaning of Style*. London: Methuen, 1979.

Henderson, Stephen. *Understanding the New Black Poetry: Black Speech and Black Music as Poetic References*. New York: William Morrow, 1972.

Hickman, C. Sharpless. "Civic Music Administration in Los Angeles." *Music Journal* 10, no. 4 (April 1952): 21–22, 32–34.

———. "Community Sings in Los Angeles." *Music Journal* 10 (January 1952): 28–29.

Higginbotham, Evelyn Brooks. *Righteous Discontent: The Women's Movement in the Black Baptist Church, 1880–1924*. Cambridge, Mass.: Harvard University Press, 1994.

Himes, Chester. *Black on Black*. New York: Doubleday, 1973.

———. *If He Hollers Let Him Go*. New York: Thunder's Mouth Press, 1945.

———. *Lonely Crusade*. New York: Thunder's Mouth Press, 1986.

———. *The Quality of Hurt: The Autobiography of Chester Himes*, vol. 1. New York: Doubleday, 1972.

Hobsbawm, Eric J. *Nations and Nationalism since 1780*. Cambridge: Cambridge University Press, 1990.

Horne, Gerald. *Black and Red: W. E. B. Du Bois and the Afro-American Response to the Cold War, 1944–1963*. Albany: State University of New York Press, 1986.

———. *Class Struggle in Hollywood*. Austin: University of Texas Press, 2001.

———. *The Fire This Time: The Watts Rebellion and the Sixties*. Charlottesville: University of Virginia Press, 1995.

Horricks, Raymond. *The Importance of Being Eric Dolphy*. Tunbridge: Costello, 1989.

Hozic, Aida A. "The House I Live In: An Interview with Charles Burnett." *Callaloo* 17, no. 2 (Spring 1994): 471–87.

Hughes, Langston. *I Wonder as I Wander: An Autobiographical Journey*. New York: Hill and Wang, 1984.

Isoardi, Steven. *The Dark Tree: Jazz and the Community Arts in Los Angeles*. Berkeley: University of California Press, 2006.

Jackson, Carlton. *Hattie: The Life of Hattie McDaniel*. Lanham, Md.: Madison Books, 1990.

Jackson, Suzanne. *Animal*. Los Angeles: Continuity Transcript & Features, 1978.

———. *What I Love: Painting, Poetry, and a Drawing*. Los Angeles: Contemporary Crafts, 1972.

James, C. L. R., George Breitman, and Edgar Keemer et al. *Fighting Racism in World War II*. New York: Monad Press, 1980.

James, David. "An Impossible Cinema? The Proletarian Avant-Garde in Los Angeles." Pp. 274–75 in *Looking for Los Angeles*, ed. by Charles G. Salas and Michael S. Roth. Los Angeles: Getty Research Institute, 2001.

———. *The Most Typical Avant-Garde: History and Geography of Minor Cinemas in Los Angeles*. Berkeley: University of California Press, 2005.

———. "Toward a Geo-Cinematic Hermeneutics: Representations of Los Angeles in Non-Industrial Cinema—*Killer of Sheep* and *Water and Power*." *Wide Angle* 20, no. 3 (1998): 23–53.

Jankowski, Martin. *Islands in the Street: Gangs and American Urban Society*. Berkeley: University of California Press, 1991.

Japanese American National Museum. *Los Angeles's Boyle Heights*. Charleston, S.C.: Arcadia Publishing, 2005.

Jennings, Regina. "Poetry of the Black Panther Party." *Journal of Black Studies* 29, no. 1 1998: 106–29.

Johnson, James H., Jr., and Curtis C. Roseman. "Increasing Black Outmigration from Los Angeles: The Role of Household Dynamics and Kinship Systems." *Annals of the Association of American Geographers* 80, no. 2 (June 1990): 205–22.

Johnson, Sara E. "*Cinquillo* Consciousness: The Formation of a Pan-Caribbean Musical Aesthetic." Pp. 35–58 in *Literature, Music and Caribbean Unity*, ed. by Tim Reiss. Trenton, N.J.: Africa World Press, 2005.

Jones, Charles, ed. *The Black Panther Party Reconsidered*. Baltimore: Black Classic Press, 1998.

Jones, Leroi. *Blues People*, reprint. ed. New York: Quill, 1963.

Joseph, Peniel. *The Black Power Movement: Rethinking the Civil Rights/Black Power Era*. New York: Routledge, 2006.

Jost, Ekkehard. *Free Jazz*. New York: Da Capo Press, 1994.

Karenga, Maulana. "Black Art: Mute Matter Given Force and Function." Pp. 477–90 in *New Black Voices*, ed. by Abraham Chapman. New York: New American Library, 1972.

———. *The Roots of the U.S./Panther Conflict: The Perverse and Deadly Games People Play*. San Diego: Kawaida Publications, 1976.

Katz, Michael. *The Undeserving Poor: From the War on Poverty to the War on Welfare*. New York: Pantheon Books, 1989.

Katznelson, Ira. "Was the Great Society a Lost Opportunity?" Pp. 185–211 in *The Rise and Fall of the New Deal Order 1930–1980*, ed. by Steve Fraser and Gary Gerstle. Princeton: Princeton University Press, 1989.

Keil, Roger. *Los Angeles, Globalization, Urbanization, and Social Struggles*. Chichester: John Wiley, 1998.

Kelley, Robin D. G. "Dig They Freedom: Meditations on History and the Black Avant-Garde." *Lenox Avenue* 3 (1997): 13–27.

———. *Freedom Dreams: The Black Radical Imagination.* Boston: Beacon Press, 2002.

———. "Nap Time: Historicizing the Afro." *Fashion Theory* 1 (December 1997): 330–51.

———. *Race Rebels: Culture, Politics, and the Black Working Class.* New York: Free Press, 1994.

———. *Yo' Mama's DisFUNKtional: Fighting the Culture Wars in Urban America.* Boston: Beacon Press, 1997.

Kelly, Robin D. G., and Betsy Esch. "Black Like Mao: Red China and Black Revolution." *Souls* 1, no. 4 (1999): 6–41.

Kernfield, Barry, ed. *New Grove Dictionary of Jazz.* New York: St. Martin's Press, 1994.

King, John. *Magical Reels: A History of Cinema in Latin America.* London: Verso, 1990.

Klein, Norman. *The History of Forgetting: Los Angeles and the Erasure of Memory.* London: Verso, 1997.

Klein, Norman, and Martin J. Schiesl. *Twentieth Century Los Angeles: Power, Promotion, and Social Conflict.* Claremont, Calif.: Regina Books, 1990.

Knight, Frederick. "Justifiable Homicide, Police Brutality, or Governmental Repression? The 1962 Los Angeles Police Shooting of Seven Members of the Nation of Islam." *Journal of Negro History* 79, no. 2 (Spring 1994): 182–96.

Kofsky, Frank. *Black Nationalism and the Revolution in Music.* New York: Pathfinder Press, 1970.

Koppes, Clayton R., and Gregory D. Black. "Blacks, Loyalty, and Motion-Picture Propaganda in World War II." *Journal of American History* 73, no. 2 (September 1986): 383–406.

Kurashige, Lon. *Japanese American Celebration and Conflict: A History of Ethnic Identity and Festival, 1934–1990.* Berkeley: University of California Press, 2002.

Kurashige, Scott. "The Many Facets of Brown: Integration in a Multiracial Society." *Journal of American History* 91, no. 1 (June 2004): 56–68.

———. *The Shifting Grounds of Race: Black and Japanese Americans in the Making of Multiethnic Los Angeles.* Princeton: Princeton University Press, 2008.

———. "Transforming Los Angeles: Black and Japanese American Struggles for Racial Equality in the 20th Century." Ph. D. diss., University of California, Los Angeles, 2000.

Labor Community Strategy Center. *A New Vision of Urban Transportation: The Bus Riders Unions' Mass Transit Campaign.* Los Angeles: Labor Community Strategy Center, 2002.

Lambert, Eddie. *Duke Ellington: A Listener's Guide.* Studies in Jazz Series, no. 26 Lanham, Md.: Scarecrow Press, and Institute of Jazz Studies, Rutgers University, 1999.

Lapp, Rudolph. *Afro Americans in California.* San Francisco: Boyd and Fraser, 1979.

Lawrence, A. H. *Duke Ellington and His World: A Biography.* New York: Routledge, 2001.

Lears, T. J. Jackson. "The Concept of Cultural Hegemony: Problems and Possibilities." *American Historical Review* 90, no. 3 (June 1985): 567–93.

LeFalle-Collins, Lizzetta. *19 Sixties: A Cultural Awakening Re-evaluated, 1965–1975.* Los Angeles: California Afro American Museum Foundation, 1989.

———. "Keeper of Traditions." Pp. 7–22 in *John Outterbridge: A Retrospective*, ed. by Lizzetta LeFalle-Collins and Leslie King-Hammond. Los Angeles: California Afro-American Museum, 1994.

———. *Noah Purifoy: Outside and in the Open*. Los Angeles: California Afro-American Museum, 1998.

———. "Working from the Pacific Rim: Beulah Woodard and Elizabeth Catlett." Pp. 38–45 in Carolyn Shuttlesworth, *Three Generations of African American Women Sculptors: A Study in Paradox*. Philadelphia: Afro-American Historical and Cultural Museum, 1996.

Lenin, Vladimir. "Principles Involved in the War Issue." Pp. 152–60 in *Lenin Collected Works*, vol. 23, trans. M. S. Levin et al. Moscow: Progress Publishers, 1964.

Leonard, Kevin. " 'Brothers under the Skin?' African Americans, Mexican Americans, and World War II in California." Pp. 187–214 in *The Way We Really Were: The Golden State in the Second Great War*, ed. by Roger Lotchin. Urbana: University of Illinois Press, 2000.

———. " 'In the Interest of All Races': African Americans and Interracial Cooperation in Los Angeles during and after World War II." Pp. 309–40 in *Seeking El Dorado: African Americans in California*, ed. by Lawrence B. De Graaf, Kevin Mulroy, and Quintard Taylor. Seattle: University of Washington, and Los Angeles: Autry Museum of Western Heritage, 2001.

Levitan, Sar. *Programs in Aid of the Poor for the 1970s*. Baltimore: Johns Hopkins University Press, 1973.

Lewis, David L. *When Harlem Was in Vogue*. New York: Oxford University Press, 1989.

Lewis, Earl. *In Their Own Interests: Race, Class, and Power in 20th Century Norfolk, Virginia*. Berkeley: University of California Press, 1991.

Lewis, George. *A Power Stronger than Itself: The AACM and American Experimental Music*. Chicago: University of Chicago Press, 2008.

———. "Improvised Music after 1950: Afrological and Eurological Perspectives." *Black Music Research Journal* 16, no. 1 (Spring 1996): 91–122.

Lewis, Samella. *Art: African American*. New York: Harcourt Brace Jovanovich, 1978.

Lewis, Samella, and Ruth Waddy. *Black Artists on Art*. Los Angeles: Contemporary Craft Publishers, 1969.

Lichtenstein, Nelson. *Labor's War at Home: The CIO in World War II*. Cambridge: Cambridge University Press, 1982.

Lipsitz, George. *Footsteps in the Dark: The Hidden Histories of Popular Music*. Minneapolis: University of Minnesota Press, 2007.

———. " 'Frantic to Join . . . the Japanese Army': Black Soldiers and Civilians Confront the Asia Pacific War." Pp. 347–77 in *Perilous Memories: The Asia-Pacific War(s)*, ed. by T. Fujitani, Geoffrey M. White, and Lisa Yoneyama. Durham: Duke University Press, 2001.

———. *A Rainbow at Midnight: Labor and Culture in the 1940s*. Urbana: University of Illinois Press, 1994.

———. "The Struggle for Hegemony." *Journal of American History* 75, no. 1 (June 1988): 146–50.

Litweiler, John. *The Freedom Principle: Jazz after 1958*. New York: Quill, 1984.

———. *Ornette Coleman: A Harmelodic Life*. London: Quartet, 1992.

Lock, Graham. *Forces in Motion: The Music and Thought of Anthony Braxton*. New York: Da Capo Press, 1989.

Locke, Alain. *Negro Art: Past and Present*. Washington, D.C.: Associates in Negro Folk Education, 1936.

López, Elizabeth Christine. "Community Arts Institutions in Los Angeles: A Study of the Social and Political Art Resource Center, Visual Communications, and the Watts Towers Art Center." M.A. thesis, University of California, Los Angeles, 1995.

López-Garza, Marta, and David Diaz. *Asian and Latino Immigrants in a Restructuring Economy: The Metamorphosis of Southern California*. Palo Alto, Calif.: Stanford University Press, 2001.

Lott, Eric. "Double V, Double-Time: Bebop's Politics of Style." *Callaloo* 36 (Summer 1988): 597–605.

Lowe, Lisa. *Immigrant Acts*. Durham: Duke University Press, 1996.

Loza, Steven. *Barrio Rhythms: Mexican American Music in Los Angeles*. Urbana: University of Illinois Press, 1993.

Lyle, K. Curtis. *Electric Church*. Venice, Calif.: Beyond Baroque, 2003.

MacDonald, Scott. "Charles Burnett." Pp. 103–122 in *A Critical Cinema 3*. Berkeley: University of California Press, 1998.

Macías, Anthony. "Bringing Music to the People: Race, Urban Culture, and Municipal Politics in Postwar Los Angeles." *American Quarterly* 56, no. 3 (September 2004): 693–717.

——. *Mexican American Mojo: Popular Music, Dance, and Urban Culture in Los Angeles, 1935–1968*. Durham: Duke University Press, 2009.

Marable, Manning. *Race, Reform and Rebellion: The Second Reconstruction in America, 1945–1982*. Jackson: University Press of Mississippi, 1984.

Marshall, Dale Roberts. *The Politics of Participation in Poverty: A Case Study of the Board of the Economic and Youth Opportunities Agency of Greater Los Angeles*. Berkeley: University of California Press, 1971.

Marx, Karl. *The Eighteenth Brumaire of Louis Bonaparte*. New York: International Publishers, 1963 (1869).

Massood, Paula. "An Aesthetic Appropriate to Conditions: *Killer of Sheep*, (Neo)Realism, and the Documentary Impulse." *Wide Angle* 21, no. 4 (October 1999): 20–41.

Masilela, Ntongela. "The Los Angeles School of Black Filmmakers." Pp. 107–17 in *Black American Cinema*, ed Manthieu Diawara. New York: Routledge, 1993.

Maynard, John Arthur. *Venice West: The Beat Generation in Southern California*. New Brunswick, N.J.: Rutgers University Press, 1991.

Mazón, Mauricio. *The Zoot Suit Riots: The Psychology of Symbolic Annihilation*. Austin: University of Texas Press, 1984.

McGirr, Lisa. *Suburban Warriors: The Origins of the New American Right*. Princeton: Princeton University Press, 2001.

McWhorter, John. *Losing the Race: Self-Sabotage in Black America*. New York: Free Press, 2000.

McWilliams, Carey. *The Education of Carey McWilliams*. New York: Simon and Schuster, 1979.

——. *Southern California: An Island on the Land*. New York: American Book-Stratford Press, 1946.

Melhem, D. H. *Heroism in the New Black Poetry*. Lexington: University Press of Kentucky, 1990.

Mercer, Kobena. *Welcome to the Jungle: New Positions in Black Cultural Studies*. New York: Routledge, 1994.

Mitchell, Michelle. *Righteous Propagation: African Americans and the Politics of Racial Destiny after Reconstruction*. Chapel Hill: University of North Carolina Press, 2004.

Mkalimoto, Ernest. "Revolutionary Black Culture: The Cultural Arm of Revolutionary Black Nationalism." *Negro Digest* 19, no. 2 (December 1969): 11–17.

Molina, Natalia. *Fit to Be Citizens? Public Health and Race in Los Angeles, 1879–1939*. Berkeley: University of California Press, 2005.

Molotch, Harvey. "L.A. as Design Product: How Art Works in a Regional Economy." Pp. 225–275 in *The City: Los Angeles and Urban Theory at the End of the Twentieth Century*, ed. by Allen Scott and Edward W. Soja. Berkeley: University of California Press, 1996.

Monson, Ingrid. *Saying Something: Jazz Improvisation and Interaction*. Chicago: University of Chicago Press, 1996.

Moten, Fred. *In the Break: The Aesthetics of the Black Radical Tradition*. Minneapolis: University of Minnesota Press, 2003.

Moure, Nancy. "The Struggle for a Los Angeles Art Museum, 1890–1940." *Southern California Quarterly* 74, no. 3 (Fall 1992): 247–75.

Moynihan, Daniel P. *Maximum Feasible Misunderstanding: Community Action in the War on Poverty*. New York: Free Press, 1969.

Moynihan, Daniel P., ed. *On Understanding Poverty: Perspectives from the Social Sciences*. New York: Basic Books, 1969.

Mullen, Bill. *Popular Fronts: Chicago and African American Cultural Politics, 1935–1946*. Urbana: University of Illinois Press, 1999.

Murashige, Mike. "Haile Gerima and the Political Economy of Cinematic Resistance." Pp. 183–204 in *Representing Blackness: Issues in Film and Video*, ed. by Valerie Smith. New Brunswick, N.J.: Rutgers University Press, 1997.

Murphet, Julian. *Literature and Race in Los Angeles*. Cambridge: Cambridge University Press, 2001.

Murray, Albert. *Stomping the Blues*. New York: Da Capo Press, 1976.

Naison, Mark. *Communists in Harlem during the Great Depression*. Urbana: University of Illinois Press, 1983.

Nash, Gerald. *The American West Transformed: The Impact of the Second World War*. Bloomington: Indiana University Press, 1985.

Neal, Larry. *Visions of a Liberated Future*. New York: Thunder's Mouth Press, 1989.

Nichols, Charles H., ed. *Arna Bontemps–Langston Hughes Letters, 1925–1967*. New York: Dodd, Mead, 1980.

Nicholson, Stuart. *Reminiscing in Tempo: A Portrait of Duke Ellington*. Boston: Northern University Press, 1999.

Nicolaides, Becky. *My Blue Heaven: Life and Politics in the Working-Class Suburbs of Los Angeles, 1920–1965*. Chicago: University of Chicago Press, 2002.

Nielsen, Aldon Lynn. *Black Chant: Languages of African-American Postmodernism*. Cambridge: Cambridge University Press, 1997.

——. *Integral Music: Languages of African American Innovation*. Tuscaloosa: University of Alabama Press, 2004.

Odom, Mychal Matsamela-Ali. "Dope Lyrics and Bangin' Beats: History and Politics of Los Angeles County Hip Hop Music and Gang Proliferation during the Crack Cocaine Epidemic and Beyond, 1984–present." M.A. thesis, University of San Diego, 2004.

Ogbar, Jeffrey. *Black Power: Radical Politics and African American Identity*. Baltimore: Johns Hopkins University Press, 2004.

O'Meally, Roger, ed. *The Jazz Cadence of American Culture*. New York: Columbia University Press, 1998.

Otis, Johnny. *Upside Your Head! Rhythm and Blues on Central Avenue*. Hanover, N.H.: University Press of New England, 1993.

Pagan, Eduardo. *Murder at the Sleepy Lagoon: Zoot Suits, Race, and Riot in Wartime L.A.* Chapel Hill: University of North Carolina Press, 2003.

Parenti, Christian. *Lockdown America: Police and Prisons in the Age of Crisis*. New York: Verso, 1999.

Parker, William. *Police Chief William H. Parker Speaks*. Los Angeles: Community Relations Conference of Southern California, 1965.

Patterson, James. *America's Struggle against Poverty in the Twentieth Century*. Cambridge, Mass.: Harvard University Press, 2000.

Patton, Sharon. *African-American Art*. Oxford: Oxford University Press, 1998.

Payne, J. Gregory, and Scott C. Ratzan. *Tom Bradley, the Impossible Dream: A Biography*. Santa Monica, Calif.: Roundtable, 1986.

Plagens, Peter. *Sunshine Muse: Art on the West Coast, 1945–1970*. Berkeley: University of California Press, 1974.

Perine, Robert. *Chouinard, an Art Vision Betrayed: The Story of the Chouinard Art Institute, 1921–1972*. Encinitas, Calif.: Artra, 1985.

Phillips, Susan. *Wallbangin': Graffiti and Gangs in L.A.* Chicago: University of Chicago Press, 1999.

Pines, Jim, and Paul Willemen, eds. *Questions of Third Cinema*. London: British Film Institute, 1989.

Porter, Eric. *What Is This Thing Called Jazz? African American Musicians as Artists, Critics, and Activists*. Berkeley: University of California Press, 2002.

Porter, James. *Modern Negro Art*. New York: Arno Press, 1969.

Powell, Richard. "African American Postmodernism and David Hammons: Body and Soul." Pp. 121–36 in *African American Visual Aesthetics: A Postmodern View*, ed. by David Driskell. Washington, D.C.: Smithsonian Institution Press, 1995.

——. "Art History and Black Memory: Toward a Blues Aesthetic." Pp. 228–43 in *The Jazz Cadence of American Culture*, ed. by Robert G. O'Meally. New York: Columbia University Press, 1998.

——. *Black Art and Culture in the 20th Century*. London: Thames and Hudson, 1997.

——. *The Blues Aesthetic: Black Culture and Modernism*. Washington, D.C.: Washington Project for the Arts, 1989.

Pulido, Laura. *Black, Brown, Yellow, and Left: Radical Activism in Los Angeles*. Berkeley: University of California Press, 2005.

Purifoy, Noah, and Ted Mitchell. *Junk Art: 66 Signs of Neon*. Los Angeles: 66 Signs of Neon, 1967.

Radano, Ronald. "The Jazz Avant-Garde and the Jazz Community: Action and Reaction." *Annual Review of Jazz Studies* 3 (1985): 71–79.

——. *New Musical Figurations: Anthony Braxton's Cultural Critique*. Chicago: University of Chicago Press, 1993.

Redmond, Eugene. *Drumvoices: The Mission of Afro-American Poetry*. Garden City, N.Y.: Anchor Press, 1976.

Reed, Adolph. "Black Particularity Reconsidered." *Telos* 39 (1979): 71–93.

Reed, Tom. *The Black Music History of Los Angeles, Its Roots: A Classical Pictorial History of Black Music in L.A. from 1920–1970*. Los Angeles: Black Accent on LA Press, 1992.

Rhodes, Jane. *Framing the Black Panther Party: The Spectacular Rise of a Black Power Icon*. New York: New Press, 2007.

Rieff, David. *Los Angeles: Capital of the Third World*. New York: Simon and Schuster, 1991.

Rivelli, Pauline, and Robert Levin. *The Black Giants*. New York: World Publishing, 1970.

Robinson, Cedric. *Black Marxism: The Making of the Black Radical Tradition*. London: Zed Books, 1983.

Rodney, Walter. *A History of the Guyanese Working People, 1881–1905*. Baltimore: Johns Hopkins University Press, 1981.

Rogin, Michael. " 'Democracy and Burnt Cork': The End of Blackface, the Beginning of Civil Rights." *Representations*, no. 46 (Spring 1994): 1–34.

Rosenthal, David. *Hard Bop: Jazz and Black Music, 1955–1965*. New York: Oxford University Press, 1993.

Rubin, William S. *Dada, Surrealism, and Their Heritage*. New York: Museum of Modern Art, 1967.

Russell, Judith. *Economics, Bureaucracy, and Race: How Keynesians Misguided the War on Poverty*. New York: Columbia University Press, 2004.

Rustin, Bayard. "The Watts 'Manifesto' and the McCone Report." Pp. 145–64 in *The Los Angeles Riots: Mass Violence in America*, ed. by Robert M. Fogelson. New York: Arno Press, 1969.

Ryan, Judylyn S. *Spirituality as Ideology in Black Women's Film and Literature*. Charlottesville: University of Virginia Press, 2005.

Saar, Betye. "Unfinished Business: The Return of Aunt Jemima." P. 3 in Betye Saar, *Workers and Warriors: The Return of Aunt Jemima*. New York: Michael Rosenfeld Gallery, 1998.

Salaam, Kalamu ya. "It Didn't Jes Grew: The Social and Aesthetic Significance of African American Music." *African American Review* 29, no. 2 (Summer 1995): 351–75.

Salas, Charles G., and Michael S. Roth, eds. *Looking for Los Angeles*. Los Angeles: Getty Research Institute, 2001.

Sanchez, George J. *Becoming Mexican American: Ethnicity, Culture, and Identity in Chicano Los Angeles, 1900–1945*. Oxford: Oxford University Press, 1993.

———. " 'What's Good for Boyle Heights Is Good for the Jews': Creating Multiculturalism on the Eastside during the 1950s." *American Quarterly* 56, no. 3 (September 2004): 633–61.

Sandoval, Sally Jane. "Ghetto Growing Pains: The Impact of Negro Migration in the City of Los Angeles, 1840–1960." M.A. thesis, California State University, Fullerton, 1973.

Saul, Scott. *Freedom Is, Freedom Ain't: Jazz and the Making of the Sixties*. Berkeley: University of California Press, 2003.

Saunders, Frances Stonor. *The Cultural Cold War: The CIA and the World of Arts and Letters*. New York: Free Press, 2000.

Savage, Barbara. *Broadcasting Freedom: Radio, War and the Politics of Race*. Chapel Hill: University of North Carolina Press, 1999.

Schrank, Sarah L. "Art and the City: The Transformation of Civic Culture in Los Angeles, 1900–1965." Ph.D. diss., University of California, San Diego, 2002.

———. *Art in the City: Civic Imagination and Cultural Authority in Los Angeles*. Philadelphia: University of Pennsylvania Press, 2008.

———. "Nuestro Pueblo: The Spatial and Cultural Politics of Los Angeles' Watts Towers." Pp. 275–312 in *The Spaces of the Modern City: Imaginaries, Politics, and Everyday Life*, ed. by Gyan Prakash and Kevin Kruse. Princeton: Princeton University Press, 2008.

———. "Picturing the Watts Towers: The Art and Politics of an Urban Landmark." Pp. 373–86 in *Reading California: Art, Image, and Identity, 1900–2000*, ed. by Stephanie Barron, Ilene Fort, and Sheri Bernstein. Berkeley: University of California Press, 2000.

Schulberg, Budd, ed. *From the Ashes: Voices of Watts*. New York: Meridian Books, 1967.

Scott, Allen, and Edward W. Soja, eds. *The City: Los Angeles and Urban Theory at the End of the Twentieth Century*. Berkeley: University of California Press, 1996.

Scott, James. *Seeing like a State: How Certain Schemes to Improve the Human Condition Have Failed*. New Haven: Yale University Press, 1998.

Scott, Mel. *The States and the Arts: The California Arts Commission and the Emerging Federal–State Partnership*. Berkeley: Institute of Government Studies, University of California, 1971.

Seitz, William Chapin. *Art of Assemblage*. New York: Museum of Modern Art, 1961.

Self, Robert. *American Babylon: Race and the Struggle for Postwar Oakland*. Princeton: Princeton University Press, 2003.

Sell, Mike. *Avant-Garde Performance and the Limits of Criticism: Approaching the Living Theatre, Happenings/Fluxus, and the Black Arts Movement*. Ann Arbor: University of Michigan Press, 2005.

Sheffey-Stinson, Sanid. "The History of Theater Productions at the Los Angeles Inner City Cultural Center, 1965–1976." Ph.D. diss., Kent State University, 1979.

Sides, Josh. *L.A. City Limits: African American Los Angeles from the Great Depression to the Present*. Berkeley: University of California Press, 2004.

———. " 'You Understand My Condition': The Civil Rights Congress in the Los Angeles African-American Community, 1946–1952." *Pacific Historical Review* 67, no. 2 (May 1998): 233–57.

Sidran, Ben. *Black Talk*. New York: Holt, Rinehart, and Winston, 1971.

Simosko, Vladimir, and Barry Tepperman. *Eric Dolphy: A Musical Biography and Discography*. Washington, D.C.: Smithsonian Institution Press, 1974.

Singh, Nikhil. *Black Is a Country: Race and the Unfinished Struggle for Democracy*. Cambridge, Mass.: Harvard University Press, 2004.

——. "The Black Panthers and the 'Undeveloped Country' of the Left." Pp. 57–103 in *The Black Panther Party Reconsidered*, ed. by Charles E. Jones. Baltimore: Black Classic Press, 1998.

Sitton, Tom, and William Deverell, eds. *Metropolis in the Making: Los Angeles in the 1920s*. Berkeley: University of California Press, 2001.

Skinner, Robert. "Streets of Fear: The Los Angeles Novels of Chester Himes." Pp. 227–238 in *Los Angeles in Fiction: A Collection of Essays From James Cain to Walter Mosely*, ed. by David Fine. Albuquerque: University of New Mexico, 1995.

Smethurst, James. *The Black Arts Movement: Literary Nationalism in the 1960s and 1970s*. Chapel Hill: University of North Carolina Press, 2005.

Smith, Alonzo Nelson. "Black Employment in the Los Angeles Area, 1938–1948." Ph.D. diss., University of California, Los Angeles, 1978.

Smith, Catherine Parsons. *William Grant Still: A Study in Contradictions*. Berkeley: University of California Press, 2000.

Smith, David L. "The Black Arts Movement and Its Critics." *American Literary History* 3, no. 1 (Spring 1991): 93–110.

Smith, Mona. *Becoming Something: The Story of Canada Lee*. New York: Faber and Faber, 2004.

Smith, Richard Cándida. *Utopia and Dissent: Art, Poetry, and Politics in California*. Berkeley: University of California Press, 1995.

Smith, Suzanne. *Dancing in the Street: Motown and the Cultural Politics of Detroit*. Cambridge, Mass.: Harvard University Press, 1999.

Snead, James A. "Images of Blacks in Black Independent Films: A Brief Survey." Pp. 16–25 in *Black Frames: Critical Perspectives on Black Independent Cinema*, ed. by Mbye Cham and Claire Andrade-Watkins. Cambridge, Mass.: MIT Press, 1988.

Soja, Edward. *Postmodern Geographies: The Reassertion of Space in Critical Social Theory*. New York: Verso, 1989.

Soja, Edward, Rebecca Morales, and Goetz Wolff. "Urban Restructuring: An Analysis of Social and Spatial Change in Los Angeles." *Economic Geography* 59, no. 2 (April 1983): 195–230.

Sonenshein, Raphael. *Politics in Black and White: Race and Power in Los Angeles*. Princeton: Princeton University Press, 1993.

Spellman, A. B. *Four Lives in the BeBop Business*. New York: Pantheon Books, 1966.

Stanyek, Jason. "Transmissions of an Interculture: Pan-African Jazz and Intercultural Improvisation." Pp. 87–130 in *The Other Side of Nowhere: Jazz, Improvisation, and Communities in Dialogue*, ed. by Daniel Fischlin and Ajay Heble. Middletown, Conn.: Wesleyan University Press, 2004.

Starr, Kevin. *Embattled Dreams: California in War and Peace*. Oxford: Oxford University Press, 2002.

Starr, Sandra Leonard. *Lost and Found in California: Four Decades of Assemblage Art, the First Generation, 1940–1962*. Santa Monica, Calif.: James Corcoran Gallery, 1988.

Steward, James Christen, Deborah Willis, Kellie Jones, Richard Cándida Smith, and Lower Stokes Sims. *Betye Saar: Extending the Frozen Moment*. Berkeley: University of California Press, 2005.

Still, Judith Anne, Michael J. Dabrishus, and Carolyn Quin. *William Grant Still: A Bio-Bibliography*. Westport, Conn: Greenwood Press, 1996.

Stimson, Grace Heilman. *Rise of the Labor Movement in Los Angeles*. Berkeley: University of California Press, 1955.

Stuckey, Sterling. *Slave Culture: Nationalist Theory and the Foundations of Black America* (1987). Reprint ed. Oxford: Oxford University Press, 1988.

Such, David. *Avant-Garde Musicians Performing "Out There."* Iowa City: University of Iowa Press, 1993.

Suga, Miya Shichinohe. "Little Tokyo Reconsidered: Transformation of Japanese American Community through the Early Redevelopment Projects." *Japanese Journal of American Studies*, no. 15 (2004): 237–55.

Sugrue, Thomas. *The Origins of the Urban Crisis: Race and Inequality in Postwar Detroit*. Princeton: Princeton University Press, 1996.

Szwed, John. *Crossovers: Essays on Race, Music and American Culture*. Philadelphia: University of Pennsylvania Press, 2005.

Tajima, Renee, and Tracey Willard. "Nothing Lights a Fire Like a Dream Deferred: Black Independent Filmmakers of Los Angeles." *Independent* 7, no. 10 (November 1984): 18–21.

Tapscott, Horace, and Steven Isaordi, eds. *Songs of the Unsung: The Musical and Social Journey of Horace Tapscott*. Durham: Duke University Press, 2001.

Tate, Mae. "Suzanne Jackson." *Black Art* 4, no. 3 (1979): 3–21.

Taylor, Clyde. "Decolonizing the Image: New U.S. Black Cinema." Pp. 166–78 in *Jump Cut: Hollywood, Politics, and Counter Cinema*, ed. by Peter Steven. New York: Praeger, 1985.

——. *The Mask of Art: Breaking the Aesthetic Contract—Film and Literature*. Bloomington: Indiana University Press, 1998.

Taylor, Quintard. *In Search of the Racial Frontier: African Americans in the American West, 1528–1990*. New York: W. W. Norton, 1998.

Theoharis, Jeanne, and Komozi Woodard. *Freedom North: Black Freedom Struggles Outside the South, 1940–1980*. New York: Palgrave Macmillan, 2003.

Theoharis, Jeanne, and Komozi Woodard, eds. *Groundwork: Local Black Freedom Movements in America*. New York: New York University Press, 2005.

Thomas, Charles. " 'I Have No Use for This Fellow Parker': William H. Parker of the LAPD and His Feud with J. Edgar Hoover and the FBI." *Southern California Quarterly* 87, no. 2 (2005): 171–98.

Thomas, Lorenzo. "Ascension: Music and the Black Arts Movement." Pp. 256–74 in *Jazz among the Discourses*, ed. by Krin Gabbard. Durham: Duke University Press, 1995.

——. *Extraordinary Measures: Afrocentric Modernism and Twentieth Century American Poetry*. Tuscaloosa: University of Alabama Press, 2000.

Thompson, Julius. *Dudley Randall, Broadside Press, and the Black Arts Movement in Detroit, 1960–1995*. Jefferson, N.C.: McFarland, 1999.

Thompson, Robert Farris. *Flash of the Spirit: African and Afro-American Art and Philosophy*. New York: Vintage Books, 1983.

Troupe, Quincy, ed. *Watts Poets: A Book of New Poetry and Essays*. Los Angeles: House of Respect, 1968.

Tucker, Mark. *The Duke Ellington Reader*. New York: Oxford University Press, 1993.

Tyler, Bruce. "Black Radicalism in Southern California, 1950–1982." Ph.D. diss., University of California, Los Angeles, 1983.

——. *From Harlem to Hollywood: The Struggle for Racial and Cultural Democracy, 1920–1943*. New York: Garland Publishing, 1992.

——. "The Rise and Decline of the Watts Summer Festival." *American Studies* 31, no. 2 (Fall 1990): 61–81.

Tyson, Timothy. *Radio Free Dixie: Robert F. Williams and the Roots of Black Power*. Chapel Hill: University of North Carolina Press, 1999.

Ulanov, Barry. *Duke Ellington*. New York: Creative Age Press, 1946.

Van Deburg, William L. *Black Camelot: African American Cultural Heroes and Their Times, 1960–1980*. Chicago: University of Chicago Press, 1997.

Vargas, João H. Costa. *Catching Hell in the City of Angels: Life and Meanings of Blackness in South Central Los Angeles*. Minneapolis: University of Minnesota Press, 2006.

Villa, Raul. *Barrio-Logos: Space and Place in Urban Chicano Literature and Culture*. Austin: University of Texas Press, 2000.

Volosinov, V. N. *Marxism and the Philosophy of Language*. Cambridge, Mass.: Harvard University Press, 1986 (1929).

von Blum, Paul. *Resistance, Dignity, and Pride: African American Artists in Los Angeles*. Los Angeles: CAAS Publications, 2004.

Waddy, Ruth. *Prints by American Negro Artists*. Los Angeles: Cultural Exchange Center, 1965.

Waldinger, Roger, and Mehdi Bozorgmehr, eds. *Ethnic Los Angeles*. New York: Russell Sage Foundation, 1996.

Wali, Minona. "Life Drawings: Charles Burnett's Realism." *Independent* 8, no. 11 (October 1988): 16–22.

Walker, Victor. "The Politics of Art: A History of the Inner City Cultural Center." Ph.D. diss., University of California, Santa Barbara, 1989.

Ward, Brian. *Just My Soul Responding: Rhythm and Blues, Black Consciousness, and Race Relations*. Berkeley: University of California Press, 1998.

Wardlaw, Alvia. *The Art of John Biggers: View from the Upper Room, New York*. Houston: Harry N. Abrams and Museum of Fine Arts, 1995.

wa Thiong'o, Ngugi. *Decolonising the Mind: The Politics of Language in African Literature*. Portsmouth, N.H.: Heinemann, 1986.

Watkins, S. Craig. *Representing: Hip Hop Culture and the Production of Black Cinema*. Chicago: University of Chicago Press, 1998.

Weheliye, Alexander. *Phonographies: Grooves in Sonic Afro-Modernity*. Durham: Duke University Press, 2005.

Weinstein, Norman. *A Night in Tunisia: Imaginings of Africa in Jazz*. New York: Proscenium Publishers, 1992.

Weir, Stan. *Singlejack Solidarity*. Minneapolis: University of Minnesota Press, 2004.

Wheeler, B. Gordon. *Black California*. New York: Hippocrene Books, 1993.

White, Walter. *A Man Called White: The Autobiography of Walter White*. New York: Viking Press, 1948.

Whiteson, Leon. *The Watts Towers of Los Angeles*. Oakville, Calif.: Mosaic Press, 1987.

Whiting, Cécile. *Pop L.A.: Art and the City in the 1960s*. Berkeley: University of California Press, 2006.

Widener, Daniel. 'Perhaps the Japanese Are to Be Thanked?' Asia, Asian Americans, and the Construction of Black California." *Positions* 11, no. 1 (Spring 2003): 135–81.

Wild, Mark. *Street Meeting: Multiethnic Neighborhoods in Early 20th Century Los Angeles*. Berkeley: University of California Press, 2005.

Wilkerson, Margaret. "Black Theaters in the San Francisco Bay Area and in the Los Angeles Area: A Report and Analysis." Ph.D. diss., University of California, Berkeley, 1972.

Willard, Michael. "Nuestra Los Angeles." *American Quarterly* 56, no. 3 (September 2004): 807–43.

Williams, Dorothy Slade. "Ecology of Negro Communities in Los Angeles County: 1940–1959." Ph.D. diss., University of Southern California, 1961.

Williams, John A. "My Man Himes." Pp. 25–94 in *Amistad 1: Writings on Black History and Culture*, ed. by John A. Williams and Charles F. Harris. New York: Vintage, 1970.

Williams, Raymond. *The Politics of Modernism*. London: Verso Press, 1989.

Wilmer, Valerie. *As Serious as Your Life: The Story of the New Jazz*. Westport, Conn.: Lawrence Hill, 1980.

Wilson, Judith. "Garden of Music: The Search for Creative Community in the Art and Life of Bob Thompson (1937–1966)." Ph.D. diss., Yale University, New Haven, Conn., 1995.

——. "How the Invisible Woman Got Herself on the Cultural Map." Pp. 201–16 in *Art/Women/California: Parallels and Intersections, 1950–2000*, ed. by Diana Burgess Fuller and Daniela Salvioni. Berkeley: University of California Press, 2002.

Wilson, O. W., ed. *Parker on Police*. Springfield, Ill.: Thomas, 1957.

Wilson, William Julius. *The Declining Significance of Race: Blacks in Changing American Institutions*. Chicago: University of Chicago, 1980.

——. *When Work Disappears: The World of the New Urban Poor*. New York: Vintage Books, 1997.

Wolf, Eric. *Europe and the People without History*. Berkeley: University of California Press, 1982.

Wolfe, Tom. *Radical Chic and Mau-Mauing the Flak Catchers*. New York: Farrar, Straus and Giroux, 1970.

Wolff, Janet. *The Social Production of Art*. New York: St. Martin's Press, 1981.

Woodard, Komozi. *A Nation within a Nation: Amiri Baraka and Black Power Politics in Newark*. Chapel Hill: University of North Carolina Press, 1999.

Woods, Clyde. *Development Arrested: The Blues and Plantation Power in the Mississippi Delta*. New York: Verso, 1998.

Writers' Congress: The Proceedings of the Conference held in October 1943 under the Sponsorship of the Hollywood Writers' Mobilization and the University of California. Los Angeles: University of California Press, 1943.

Yang, Mina. "A Thin Blue Line down Central Avenue: The LAPD and the Demise of a Musical Hub." *Black Music Research Journal* 22 (2002): 217–40.

Young, Cynthia. *Soul Power: Culture, Radicalism, and the Making of a U.S. Left*. Durham: Duke University Press, 2006.

INDEX

Abdulhafiz, Abdosh, 256
Abreau, Lazaro, 204
abstract expressionism, 53–54
Actor's Equity Association, 76
"Acts of Culture," 17–18
African culture: Afrocentrism, 207, 214; cultural nationalism and, 205; idioms of, in visual art, 166–68, 171–72; as influence, 63, 139, 147–48, 205
Afrocentrism, 207, 214
Afrological vs. Eurological improvisation, 13–14
Albert, Margo, 242
Alekebulan, 210–12
Alexander, William, 82, 223–24
Allen, Ernest, 204
Allied Arts League, 36
Alvarez, Luis, 15
Amos 'n' Andy, 9, 75–76
Amy, Curtis, 130
Anansi Writers Workshop, 284
Anderson, Benedict, 175
Anderson, Eddie "Rochester," 38–39, 42
Anderson, John, 67
Anderson, Marian, 48
Angry Voices of Watts, The, 95–97, 101–3
antiracist politics, 30, 35, 38, 88, 218, 257
Ark, the (Pan Afrikan People's Arkestra). *See* Underground Musicians Association
Armstrong, Louis, 74

Art West Associated, 87, 120, 134, 155–56, 159, 288
Ash Grove, 144, 149
Asian Americans, 30, 35, 247, 253–54, 274, 275
assemblage and "junk" art, 7, 16, 82, 86, 103, 162–76, *164*, 178, 261; Watts Towers as, 163, 225–29
Associated Film Audiences, 37
Association for the Advancement of Creative Musicians (AACM), 128, 266
Association for the Study of Negro Life and History, 36
"aural minstrelsy," 75
authenticity, 47–48, 247, 325n37
autonomy, creative, 2, 4, 111, 144–47; artists and, 132, 218, 225; in *Passing Through*, 134–36; self-definition and, 99–102, 141–42; union amalgamation vs., 71–72
Ayers, Anne, 171
Ayers, Roy, 121

Baca, Judy, 202
Baker, Chet, 62, 63, 124, 125
Baker, Ella, 119, 289
Baker, Herbert, 119
Baker, Josephine, 67
Bambara, Toni Cade, 255
Banham, Rayner, 228–29
Baraka, Amiri, 13, 66, 188, 189, 200, 206–9

Barr, Catherine, 36

Bartlett, Elmer, 67

Bass, Charlotta, 35, 38, 43, 44, 46

beach and surf culture, 53, 57

Beasley, Oliver X., 280

Beat milieu, 82

Beatty, Paul, 285

Beavers, Louise, 39, 42, 44, 48, 80

Benjamin, Walter, 117

Benston, Kimberly, 133, 142

Benton, Walter, 123

Berelowitz, Jo-Anne, 236

Berg, Billy, 40

Berman, Wallace, 163

big-band music, 62, 121, 123–25, 139–40, 143

Bigger, John, 84

Billops, Camille, 156, 173, 174

"Bird and Diz" (Riddle), 167–69, *168*, 173, 178

Birth of a Nation, The, 35, 40, 46

"black," 6

Black Artists Alliance (BAA), 159

Black Arts Council, 4, 134, 159–62, 179, 218, 288

Black Arts Movement, 142, 255–56; "Blackstream artists" and, 314n38; collective organization and, 5–6, 88, 155–56, 288; cultural identity and, 158, 288; decline of, 17, 222–23; politicization of, 3–7, 16–17, 49–50, 146, 188, 200; as social movement, 184, 186

Black Congress, 148

"Black Girl's Window" (Saar), 172

Black Liberation Army, 152, 217

black liberation movement, 7, 118, 141–42, 162–63, 169, 182, 189; style politics within, 192–93, 203–4

Blackman, William, 82

blackness, 88, 171; as critical stance, 6; cultural particularity and, 142, 175; masculinity and, 11, 266, 281; political activism and, 192–93

Black Panther (newspaper), 201, 213

Black Panther, The (film), 214–15

Black Panther Party, 4, 8, 12, 16–17, *191*, 199, *202*, 316n2; Black Arts Movement and, 152; collapse of, 152, 216–18; cultural initiatives of, 187–88, 209, 212–18; cultural theory and ideology of, 198–206, 316n2; economic critiques by, 147; FBI vs., 150–51, 216–17; international culture of resistance and, 200–206; LAPD vs., 12, 150–51, 190–91, 216–17; liberation art and, 199–200; as male-dominated, 213–14; revolutionary culture and, 189, 199–200; SNCC and, 148–49, 203; style politics and, 192–95; UGMA and, 149–50, 188, 214, 217; US Organization vs., 187–88, 194–95, 204, 207, 215–18; Watts riots as context for emergence of, 93–94

Black Power Movement, 4, 9, 113, 120, 146, 147, 171, 276

black press, 43–44, 73–75, 79. See also *California Eagle*

"Blackstream artists," 314n38

Blackwell, Ed, 120, 125, 138

Blauner, Roger, 100

Bless Their Little Hearts (film), 17, 215, 251–55, 259, 267–71, 278, 281–82

Bley, Carla, 125, 267

Bley, Paul, 125, 138

blues, 60–61, 140, 141, 149, 167–68, 208, 313n35

Blythe, Arthur, 118, 120, 223

body, the, 165, 194

Bogart, Humphrey, 38–39

Bohanon, Gloria, 154, 180

Bola Press, 132

Bonds, Margaret, 181

Bonner, Billy, 210

Bontemps, Arna, 36, 37, 256

Booker, Claude, 134, 159, 161–62, 180

bop, 40, 63, 123, 125

Bowron, Fletcher, 56

boycotts, 35, 40, 43, 48

Boyz in the Hood, 271, 273

Bradford, Bobby: creative autonomy and, 145–46, 257; on film studio work, 255; as member of LA jazz network, 120–21, 124–27, 134, 138–39, 144, 208; police harassment of, 60; on politics of jazz, 139; on UGMA, 142

Bradley, Thomas, 15, *239*, 241–49; CAD and consolidation, 224, 243–44, 248; career of, 3, 11–12, 72, 152, 224, 250; cultural policy of, 3, 12, 223, 233, 235, 238–39; diversity institutionalized in policies of, 8; economic policies of, 12, 224, 238, 244–46; redevelopment of downtown and, 234–41; Rodney King unrest and, 221, 249; role of black art in governance, 17; Watts Towers and, 226–28, 230–31, 233–34, 243, 254, 284

Branch, Taylor, 279–80

Brantley, Florence Cardrez, 71

bricolage, 171, 192. *See also* assemblage and "junk" art; cross-genre art

Brockman Gallery, 134, 158–59, 176, 186, 233

Brown, Clifford, 125

Brown, Edmund "Pat," 99

Brown, Elaine, 97, 112–13, 149–52, 188, 211, *212*, 213, 215

Brown, Everett, 149

Brown, H. Rap, *195*

Brown, Jerry, 231

Brown, Scot, 210

Browne, Samuel, 67, 70, 121, 124, 128–29, 139–40

Browning, Robert, 181

Bryant, Clara, 60

Bryant, David, 120, 123, 127

Bulosan, Carlos, 35, 46

Bunche, Ralph, 44, 52

Burnett, Charles, 17, 135, 158, 250, 255–61, 284, 288. See also *Killer of Sheep*

Burroughs, Margaret, 84, 194

Bush Mama (film), 258, 259

Byrd, Donald, 181

Cabin in the Sky (film), 74

Cabral, Amilcar, 17–18, 201, 257

Caldwell, Ben, 256, 259, 284

California Afro-American Museum (CAAM), 231–32

California Eagle (newspaper), 36–37, 48, 52, 71–73, 75, 78–79

California Institute for Men, Chino, 107

Callendar, Red, 35, 65, 67

Calloway, Cab, 25, 45, 74

car culture, 23, 197

Carter, Alprentice "Bunchy," 195–96, 213, 255, 257

Carter, Benny, 42, 48, 67, 71, 146

Carter, John, 120, 125, 130, 134, 138, 144–46, 164, 257

Cartwright, Bill, 229

Casey, Bernie, 160

Cayton, Revels, 45

celebratory model of cultural politics, 225, 234, 236, 241–49, 254

Césaire, Aimé, 1, 10, 142, 288–89

Chaney, Lon, 41

"Chaos in a Ghetto Alley" (Scott), 100

Cherry, Don, 120–22, 124, 210

Chicanos and Latinos (Mexican Americans), 14–15, 107–8, 247, 253–54, 281, 315n68; antiracist politics and, 35; hip-hop culture and, 247; jazz and Latin music, 123, 248; Mechicano Art Center, 179, 316n68; racial discrimination against, 65

Churchill, Ward, 12, 150, 191

Cinema League of Colored People, 37–38

City of Quartz (Davis), 224

civil rights and civic equality, 52–59

Clark, John Henrik, 7–8

Clark, Larry, 134–36, 255, 256, 284

class, social, 7–8, 15, 17–18, 36; cultural policy and, 236–37, 239–40; cultural radicalism and, 11, 89, 91, 198; demographics and, 2, 12, 32, 57–58, 128, 176, 181, 247, 260, 280–81; elite control of cultural development, 236–37, 239–40; film as critique of, 17, 215, 252–55; gangs and gangsta rap and politics of, 274–77; middle class and arts and activism, 37–38, 78, 159, 265–66; tensions and African-

class, social (*cont.*)
   American, 10–11; vulnerability to racism
      and, 30–31, 101, 198; working-class art-
      ists, 16, 30–31, 82, 91, 137, 152, 175–76. *See
      also* economics
Cole, Nat "King," 67, 121
Coleman, Ornette: film work and, 215; as
   jazz innovator, 124–25, 138–39, 141; as
   member of LA jazz network, 40, 118, 120,
   130, 145, 284; police harassment of, 60–
   61; on venues, 126
Coleman, Wanda, 223–24
collective organization, 4–6, 139–41, 155–62,
   170–71, 288; Black Arts Movement and, 88;
   in Burnett's films, 264; communal interiority and, 282; community-based cultural politics and, 2, 104, 119; creativity as
   process of, 13, 24, 26, 104; critiques of, 281;
   economic drivers for, 127–29; female artists and, 86–87; film production and, 214–
   16, 256–57; form and content exploration
   and, 104; jazz as collective art form, 119,
   145, 210–11; nationalist ideologies and
   framing of, 207–8; Nguzo Saba and principle of, 205; social drivers for, 129; Tapscott's communitarian politics and, 6, 97,
   117–20, 127–30, 137, 143, 148, 288; visual
   and plastic artists and, 155–62, 176. *See also*
   unions, labor
Collette, Buddy, 60, 65–67, 71, 121–23, 125
Collier, John, 46
Colored Spade (film), 174
Coltrane, John, 125, 127, 132–33, 135, 139, 147
Committee for the Promotion of Colored
   People in Motion Pictures, 37–38
communism, 54, 97–98, 106, 147, 189, 201
community, 4, 282, 285–87
Community Alert Patrol (CAP), 8, 93, 196–
   97, 218
Community Redevelopment Agency
   (CRA), 235–40, 248–49
Community Symphony Orchestra (CSO),
   66–67, 123
Compton, 176–86

Compton Communicative Arts Academy
   (CCAA), 134, 154, 178–81, *182–85*
Concholar, Dan, 158
Congress of Industrial Organizations
   (CIO), 58
Congress of Racial Equality (CORE), 148
Connell, Will, 140–41
Conner, Bruce, 163
conservative politics, 53–55, 99, 110, 218
Containment series (Outterbridge), 165–66
Conwill, Houston, 163
"cool," 25
cool jazz (West Coast jazz), 53, 73, 124, 138,
   139
Cortez, Jayne, 130–35; arts education and,
   87, 96–97; politicization of, 13, 17, 255;
   relations of, with other artists, 11, 130–
   32, 173–74, 255; theatrical training of,
   9, 80; UGMA and, 129. *See also* Studio
   Watts
Cosgrove, Donald, 238
Covington, Floyd, 29, 33
Craft, Henrietta, 86
Crawford, Ernest, 123
Criminal Conspiracy Section (CCS), 150
Crisis, The, 29
Criss, Sonny, 70, 121, 123, 125
cross-genre art, 6, 103, 120, 129, 133, 134–36,
   141–42, 168–71, 173–74
Crouch, Stanley, 10, 97, 99, 112–13, 133, 149,
   208
Cruse, Harold, 7–8, 28
Cultural Affairs Department (CAD), 224,
   243–44, 248
cultural democracy, 28, 34, 41, 45–46, 66,
   80, 89, 137
cultural policy, 56–57; Bradley and municipal, 3, 12, 223, 233, 235, 238–39, 241–49;
   class and, 15, 236–37, 239–40
cultural politics, 241–49, 288–89; celebratory
   model of, 225, 234, 236, 254; survival aesthetics model of, 225, 254, 263–64. *See also*
   celebratory model of cultural politics
Cunningham, James, 207–8

Daáood, Kamau, 103, 113, 133, 284–85
Dancer, Earl, 38, 47–48
Dandridge, Dorothy, 22
Dash, Julie, 135, 256, 259
Datcher, Michael, 284–85
Davidson, Gordon, 242
Davis, Almena, 24
Davis, Alonzo, 134, 157–61, 180
Davis, Angela, 150, 194, 206–7
Davis, Bette, 39
Davis, Dale, 134, 154, 158, 180
Davis, Doris, 178–79
Davis, Larry, 222
Davis, Leo, 67, 71
Davis, Mike, 60, 224, 237, 276–77
Davis, Sammy, Jr., 80
Davis, Zeinabu Irene, 256, 259
Dedeaux, Richard Anthony, 113
defense industry, 32–33, 39, 52–53
Denning, Michael, 11, 26
desegregation, 39, 50–51, 54–55; of culture
    industry, 28–29; as distinct from im-
    proved opportunity, 73; social mixing,
    60, 61; union, 63–68, 71–73, 122–23,
    301n43
Desmond, Paul, 124
Deveaux, Scott, 40, 139
diegetic and non-diegetic sound, 135, 215,
    252, 261, 265, 324n4
dissonance, 26
diversity or multiculturalism, 3, 8, 17, 233,
    241–49
documentaries, 95–97, 101–3, 136, 171, 214–
    15; influence of, on new urban cinema,
    252, 257–58, 261, 267
Dolan, Henry, 97–99, 98, 101–3, 112
Dolphin, John, 60
Dolphy, Eric, 121–25, 127, 135; employment
    and training of, 65, 67, 70; free jazz and,
    138–39, 145; as member of LA jazz com-
    munity, 118, 120, 162
"Door, The (Admissions Office)" (Ham-
    mons), 165–66, 166
Dorothy Chandler Pavilion, 236

Douglas, Bill, 67
Douglas, Emory, 150, 158, 169, 188, 199–207,
    212, 212, 214
Douglass Foundation and Frederick Doug-
    las House, 107–8, 110, 112, 151
Dover, Cedric, 153
Down Beat (magazine), 39, 62–63, 122, 124
drugs, 60, 142, 224–25, 272, 275, 326n43,
    327n47
Du Bois, W. E. B., 35
Duff, Alice Walker, 244
Dunham, Katherine, 33
Duran, Bob, 202
Durrati, Buenaventura, 289

Eagle. See California Eagle
Easy-E, 18
Ebony Showcase Theater, 74, 76–81, 88, 176,
    186; cast members of, 78; demolition of,
    240, 248–49; influence of, on artists, 9,
    80, 130, 132, 181
Eckstine, Billy, 35
economics, 4, 52–53, 128–31, 224–25, 245–
    46, 254–55, 276; of arts funding, 232–33,
    315n60; black creativity and, 132–36; cap-
    italist, 147, 253; of commercial film in-
    dustry, 257–58; cultural investment and,
    237–38, 244; of deindustrialization, 181,
    251, 252, 269, 272, 275; globalization and
    local, 10, 12, 235, 253–55, 278; of jazz, 62,
    126–27, 147; race and, 46–47, 65, 89, 181–
    82, 225; value of arts, 12, 234–36, 242–45.
    See also poverty, urban
education, cultural, 84, 130, 155, 160–61,
    232–34, 244; community-based cultural
    projects and, 33–34; cultural policy and
    access to, 55–56; liberation culture and,
    200–201; militancy alleviated by, 95, 107,
    205; Proposition 13 and, 269, 276; public
    schools and, 107, 121; racial uplift and,
    68–69, 153; social reform and, 177–78;
    Watts Towers Art Center and, 176–77,
    181–82, 186, 221–23. See also music edu-
    cation

Educational Laboratory Theater Project, 107

Edwards, Desireo, *96*

Edwards, Jimmy, 80

Edwards, Melvin "Mel," 88, 132–33, 155, 165, 173–74

Edwards, Teddy, 125

Eleven Associated Artists, 83–84

Ellington, Edward Kennedy "Duke," 3, 16, 31, 41, 49, 74, 121, 123, 141, 287; on black particularity and inclusion, 27; *Jump for Joy* and, 21–22; with Franklin, *27*; political activism of, 26

employment, 32, 41, 53, 86, 224; arts as vocation, 64–65, 68–69, 80–81, 90–91, 106–7, 181, 306n43; in defense industry, 39, 52–53; deindustrialization and loss of, 181, 251–52, 269, 272, 275; racial discrimination in, 29–32, 40–41, 46–47, 65; as subject of art works, 101–3, 153–54, 165, 267, 281; of women, 39, 130–31

entertainment industry, 2–3, 42–43; desegregation of, 50–51; Himes's works as critique of, 30; racial discrimination in, 29–31, 40–41, 73; stereotypes in, 16, 33, 37, 40, 43–46, 48–49, 75. *See also* film, film industry; music; television

Esch, Betsy, 205–6

Escobar, Ed, 277–78

Eso Won Books, 283–84

Evans, Emmery, 112

Fair Employment Practices Commission (FEPC), 32

Fanaka, Jama, 256

Fanon, Franz, 203, 257

Farmer, Addison, 125

Farmer, Art, 60, 125

Farrakhan, Louis, 280

Fast, Howard, 42–43

Fax, Elton, 158

Feather, Leonard, 62

Federal Bureau of Investigation (FBI), 26, 35, 150–52, 198, 216–17, 258, 274

Ferguson, Cecil, 134, 157, 159–62, 180

festivals, 36; community-based and artist-organized, 81, 84, 85, 159, 233; as film venues, 159, 260, 264; as jazz venues, 119, 129, 144, 233; municipal sponsorship of, 55, 235, 241–48; Watts Summer Festival, 108–9, 157, 188, 196, 208, 210, 227, 231

"Festivals and Funerals," 17

film, film industry, 17, 41, 46–47, 135, 174, 251–58, 264; as cultural criticism, 37–38; diegetic and non-diegetic sound elements and, 215, 261, 265, 324n4; employment in, 64–65; independent filmmaking, 37–38, 43, 288; on masculinity, 266, 269–70, 275–76, 281–82; music and soundtracks in, 265–67, 273–74; neo-realist cinema, 7, 260–61, 267; Newsreel Collective, 214–15; race and, 3, 40–41, 48–49; Third Worldism and, 251, 262, 324n17; urban landscape in, 215, 261–63, 271. *See also* *Bless Their Little Hearts*; *Killer of Sheep*; *Menace II Society*

Fitzgerald, Ella, 74

Fitzpatrick, Robert, 242

Flash (journal), 36

Flores, Joan Milke, 226

Ford, John Anson, 34, 44, 86

Forman, James, 5

Foucault, Michel, 99

Franklin, V. P., 14

Frazier, Jacqueline, 256

"Freedom City," 147, 148, 282

free jazz, 119, 124–26, 138–41, 144–49, 163, 210–11

Fritzhand, Harriet, *85*

From the Ashes (poetry anthology), 103, 112

Gafford, Alice Tayford, 82, 84, 86, 169

Gallery 32, 86, 87, 157–58, 162

gangs, 195–96, 254, 275–77; conflation of, with drug retailing, 326n43; filmic treatment of, 271–82; violence of, 193, 196, 226, 227, 272, 280

gangsta rap, 273–74

Garner, Fradley, 139
Gates, Daryl, 276–77, 327n53
Gates, Henry Louis, Jr., 5, 272
Gayle, Addison, 163
Gehry, Frank, 235
Gerima, Haile, 252, 256–59, 263, 284
Giant Is Awakened, The (album), 147–48
Gibbs, Marla, 131, 134
Gibson, Josh, 230
Gibson, Kenneth, 193
Gillespie, Dizzy, 40, 168
Gilmore, Ruth, 253, 278
Gilpin Players, 83
Gilroy, Paul, 10, 325n37
globalization, 10, 12, 225, 235, 254–55, 278
Gone With the Wind (film), 42, 46
Gordon, Dexter, 70, 121
Gordon, Robert, 62
Gormley, Paul, 272
Gorz, Andre, 119–20
Go West Young Man (film), 74
Gramsci, Antonio, 6, 28
Grant, David, 254, 280–81
Granz, Norman, 39–40
Graves, Jesse, 48
Gray, John, 36, 38, 67–68, 70, 121, 266
Gray, Wardell, 125
Green, Bill, 123
Green, Wendell, 72–73
Greenaway, Gladyse, 36
Greenfield, Mark, 284
Greer, Sonny, 22
Gregory, Andre, 106–7
Griffin, Booker, 208
Griffith, T. L., 38
Griffith Park exhibition, 53–54

Haden, Charlie, 120, 124–25, 138, 267
Hahn, Kenneth, 78
hair, style politics of, 193–94, 203
Halisi, Clyde, 216
Hall Stuart, 252
Hamilton, Amde, 104, 113, 151
Hamilton, Chico, 121

Hammons, David, 151, 154, 160–61, 163, 165, *166*, 171, 173–74, 201–2
Hampton, Lionel, 65, 121
Hancock, Herbie, 210
Handy, W. C., 36, 70, 121
Harby, Harold, 53–54, 299n11
Harden, Marvin, 169
Harlem on the Prairies (film), 38
Harris, Eddie (Aceyalone), 285
Harris, Kerrie, Steve, and Virginia, *202*
Hawes, Hampton, 62, 120, 125
Hawkins, Coleman, 40
Heath, Albert, 210
Hebdige, Dick, 8, 190, 192
Henry, Calvin, 141
Herms, George, 163
Hewitt, Masai, 204, 215
Higgins, Billy, 120, 122, 124, 138, 284
Hightower, Alma, 70, *70*
Hill, Andrew, 125
Hill, Linda, 87, 112–13, 118, 120, 128, 130–34
Hill, Tony, 34
Hill-Scott, Karen, 244
Himes, Chester, 3, 16, 29–31, 33, 45, 49
Hines, Al, 127, 131
history, cultural, 33–34, 36, 316n3; Afro-centrism and, 207; Burnett's use of, 266; "celebratory" festivals and revision of, 247; demolition of Ebony Showcase Theater and, 240–41; of jazz, 124, 139, 141, 247; oral history projects and, 285; publications as archive and community memory and, 134; UGMA and, 130
Hobsbawm, Eric, 175
Hodek, Antonin, 181
Hoijer, Harry, 46
Holden, Nate, 240–41, 248–49
Holiday, Billie, 35
Holly, Hal, 63
Hollywood Victory Committee, 42, *43*, 74
Hollywood Writers Mobilization, 45–47
Hope, Elmo, 124, 125
Hopkins, William, 50
Horne, Gerald, 16, 59, 146, 194, 279–80

Horne, Lena, 38–39, 45, 74
housing, 32, 37, 54–58, *58*, 128, 232
How I Wonder (play), 52
"How Long Has Trane Been Gone" (Cortez), 132–33
Hubert, René, 22
Huggins, John, 148, 188
Hughes, Allen and Albert, 17, 255, 272. See also *Menace II Society*
Hughes, Langston, 24, 26–27, 36, 256

"I, Too, Sing America" (Hughes), 26–27
ice cube, 250
identity, 7, 137, 174–75; masculine, and employment, 269–70; names as expression of, 195, 204–5; self-definition and, 28, 141–43, 255; style politics and, 190–98
If He Hollers Let Him Go (Himes), 30, 32
improvisation, 141–42; Afrological vs. Eurological, 13–14; assemblage or junk art as, 163–65; cultural nationalism and, 175, 192, 208, 210; cultural politics as imaginative, 289; free jazz and collective, 62, 139–40; poetry and, 100; of subjectivity, 7
Ink Slingers, 36
Inner City Cultural Center (iccc), 1–2, 4; arts education and vocational missions of, 81, 106–7, 181, 306n43; founders of, 134, 209; politics and, 151, 217; support of, 157, 176, 233
Inner City Institute for the Performing and Visual Arts, 181
integration, 4, 9–10, 39, 51, 60–61, 71–73
Islam, 148. *See also* Nation of Islam
Isoardi, Steven, 5, 131, 214
Isozaki, Arata, 235

Jackson, C. Bernard, 106
Jackson, Faye, 33, 36
Jackson, James Thomas, 107
Jackson, Suzanne, 86, 87, 150, 157–58, 162, 169, 174, 207, 214
Jacquette, Tommy, 208
James, Angela, 254

James, C. L. R., 81–82
James, David, 259, 264
jazz, 7, 62–63; as agent of freedom, 259; blues tradition and, 167–68; as collective art form, 119; cool or "West Coast," 53, 73, 124, 138, 139; cultural nationalism and, 210; economics of performance of, 126–27; educational networks and development of community of, 120–21; evolution of, 125; in film, 257; history as flawed or incomplete, 124, 139, 141, 247; integration of nightclubs linked to, 39–40; venues for, 126. *See also* free jazz
Jeffries, Herb, 22, 24
jive, 25
Johnson, Charles, 35–36
Johnson, Daniel LaRue, 87
Johnson, Dorothy, 78
Johnson, Lyndon Baines, 92–93
Jones, Frank, 201
Jones, Pamela, 256
Jump for Joy, 16, 21–26, *25*, 50
junk art. *See* assemblage and "junk" art

kaos Network, 284–85
Karamu House Theater, 83–84
Karenga, Ron, 148, 188–89, *195*, *196*, 204–11, 215–16
Kaufman, Gunnar, 285
Kawaida (album), 187–88, 210–12
Kawaida (doctrine), 206–7, 209
Keil, Roger, 224
Keinholz, Ed, 163
Kelley, Robin, 5–6, 194, 205–6
Kennedy, Vallejo, 112
Killer of Sheep (film), 17, 251, 259–67
Kimbrough, Jesse, 36
King, Martin Luther, Jr., 93, 110
King, Nick, 229
King, Rodney. *See* Rodney King riots
King Christophe, 142
Knepper, Jimmy, 125
Kofsky, Frank, 97, 126–27
Kotto, Yaphet, 181

Kuller, Sid, 24
Kurashige, Scot, 15
Kwanzaa, 210

Land, Harold, 63, 125
Lange, Ted, 134, 135
language as cultural product, 25, 137, 175, 265, 274, 316n7
Larkin, Alile Sharon, 256
Lasha, Prince, 125, 138
Lawrence, Jacob, 34
League for Industrial Democracy, 37
League of Revolutionary Black Workers, 147, 199, 316n2
LeBlanc, Thomas, 36
Lee, Arthur, 18
Lee, Canada, 35, 41, 45–46
LeFalle-Collins, Lizette, 172
Leimert Park, 158–59, 283–87
Leimert Park (film), 285
Levette, Harry, 48
Lewis, Earl, 264
Lewis, Genevieve Barnes, 67
Lewis, George, 13–14
Lewis, Joseph, *61*
Lewis, R'Wanda, 134
Lewis, Samella, 11, 87, 160, 165
liberalism, 34–42, 53–54, 91, 97–98, 265–66, 273
"Liberation of Aunt Jemima" (Saar), 165, 169–70, 174
liberation politics, 138
Lincoln, Abbey, 194
Lindsay, Gilbert, 78
"Lino's Pad" (Tapscott), 128, 130, 140
Liston, Melba, 70
Litwiler, John, 126
Local 47 (musicians' union), 39, 54, 56, 64–68, 71–74, 122, 242, 301n43
Local 767 (musicians' union), 33, 56, 64, 67–68, 71–73, 301nn42–43
Lonely Crusade (Himes), 30, 32
Los Angeles, 2, 11–14; as carceral city, 224, 252; cultural policy in, 55–56, 223, 233, 235, 238–39, 241–49; cultural politics in, 28; demographics of, 32, 57–58, 128, 176, 181, 247, 260, 280–81, 328n61; downtown renovation and economic development of, 52–53, 224, 234–38, 240; as fragmented cultural environment, 87, 234, 245; racial discrimination as reality in, 29–31; urban blight and poverty in, 98–99. *See also* Los Angeles Police Department
Los Angeles County Museum of Art (LACMA), 159–62, 179
Los Angeles Negro Art Association, 84
Los Angeles Police Department (LAPD), 12, *61*, 150–52, 276–78; artists and, 60–62, 169, 258–59, 325n23; Black Panther Party and, 12, 190–91; brutality and abuse of power by, 3, 6, 72, 99–100, 193, 197; CAP monitoring of, 8, 93, 196–97, 218; CCS use of rattlesnakes and, 150; as film subject, 258; Gates and, 327n53; institutionalized racism in, 59–61, 277; militarization of, 53, 59, 277; Nixon's "law and order" platform and, 110–11; Parker and, 59–61, 93; Rodney King case and, 249; spatial separation and, 234; Watts riots and, 99–100
Lowe, Lisa, 246–47
"Lunching at the Ritzmore" (Himes), 29
Lyle, K. Curtis, 100–101, 103, 112
"Lynch Fragments" (Edwards), 88, 165, 173–74
lynchings, 52

Macías, Anthony, 15, 65
Mafundi Institute, 112, 151, 176, 188, 209, 217–18, 224, 234
Makeba, Miriam, 194
Malcolm X, 7–8, 10, 132
Malik, Ahmed Abdul, 257
Manne, Shelly, 126
Mao Zedong, 147, 187, 189, 201, 204
Marable, Manning, 189
Marley, Bob, 221–22, 222, 233

Marshall, Gen. George C., 21
Marshall, William, 134, 142
Marvin X, 200
Marxism, 47, 189, 199, 205–6, 253, 319n49
masculinity, 17, 269–70, 281–82; blackness and, 11, 266; employment and, 102; filmic treatment of, 266, 275–76; militarism and, 213–14
Masiela, Ntongela, 256
Maslin, Janet, 265
Mason, Biddy, *85*
Mason, Fred, 163
Mason, Karen Ann, 158
Massood, Paula, 261, 272
Matthews, Miriam, 11
"Maybe the People Would Be the Times" (Lee), 18
Mbulu, Letta, 210
McCarthyism, 53–54, 99
McClendon, Constance, 82
McCone, John, and the McCone Report, 99–100, 170
McCullough, Barbara, 256, 259
McDaniel, Hattie, 16, 42, *43*, 44, 47–48, 74
McDonough, Gordon, 34, 44
McFarlane, Milton, 112
McGhee, Howard, 40
McGirr, Lisa, 93
McKeller, Sonora, 107
McWhorter, John, 10
McWilliams, Carey, 14, 35
Mechicano Art Center, 179, 316n68
Menace II Society (film), 17, 251–52, 271–79
Mercer, Kobena, 6, 193–94
Merriam, Alan, 139
Mexican Americans. *See* Chicanos and Latinos
Micheaux, Oscar, 37
Middlebrook, Willie, 221–22
militancy, 3, 93, 105, 152, 175, 218; cultural education as antidote to, 95, 107, 205; liberation art and, 200. *See also under names of specific militant organizations*
Miller, Loren, 36–37, 41, 78, 158

Mills, P'lla, 86–87
Mingus, Charles, 62–63, 125; free-jazz and, 138, 141, 171; frustration of, with audience ignorance, 127; as member of LA jazz community, 70, 118, 120–22, 124; as politicized artist, 66–67
minstrelsy, 3, 75
Miranda, Roberto, 140, 284
modernist aesthetics, 88
Moore, Juanita, 80
Moore, Lenora, 82
Morales, Rebecca, 253
Moreland, Mantan, 42
Morgan, Frank, 121, 123
Moss, Carlton, 41
motorcycle clubs, 178–79
Mtume, James, 210–12, 216
Municipal Arts Department, Los Angeles, 55–56
murals, 82, 159, 169, 178, 202, 241, 243
Murashige, Mike, 258
Murray, George, 199–200, 203
Muse, Clarence, 16, 44–48, 135, 255
Museum of Contemporary Art (MOCA), 234–41
music: in film, 46–47, 257, 265–67, 273–74; integration of bands and orchestras, 39; Los Angeles Bureau of Music, 55–56; political activism and musicians, 66; recording industry, 132, 135–36, 144–45, 274; unionization of musicians, 63–68. *See also* music education; *and under names of specific musical artists and genres*
music education, 68–69, *69*, 120–23, 125; in public schools, 128; UGMA and, 136, 140–41
Music Town, 33–34
mutualism, 69–70
Myrdal, Gunnar, 29

Nance, Ray, 22
National Association for the Advancement of Colored People (NAACP), 4, 35, 148

National Association of Negro Musicians, 68

National Endowment for the Arts, 105, 110, 156, 179, 180

National Foundation for the Arts, 105

nationalism, black, 105–6, 111; as context for cultural activism, 217–18; cultural vs. revolutionary, 189, 199–200, 203–4, 215; free jazz and, 147; identity construction and, 175

nationalism, cultural, 2, 148–49

Nation of Islam, 165, 189, 194–95, 196, 279–80, 314n37

Negro Digest (magazine), 204, 207

Negro Motion Pictures Players Association, 50

Nengudi, Senga, 163

New Art Jazz Ensemble, 4, 96, 134, 138, 145

Newman, George, 120, 121

new music. *See* free jazz

newspapers, black, 43–44

Newton, Huey, 150, 165, 203–5, 214–15

Newton, James, 120

Nguza Saba, 205

Nichols, Fayard, 42

Nielsen, Aldon Lynn, 129

Nigger Uprising (journal), 4, 83, 87, 111, 113, 134, 207

nightclubs, 123–27, 132–33, 144–45

"Nine Mojo Secrets" (Saar), 172, *172*

Nixon, Richard M., 54, 110, 204, 218

Norman, Maddie, 80

Norris, William, 237, 238

N.W.A., 258, 274, 325n23

Odetta, 194

Ojenke (Alvin A. Saxon), 103, 112

Olamina, Lauren, 285

Oliver, Melvin, 254

Olympiad (1984), 8, 235, *239*

Organization of African American Unity, 7–8

Ortega, Anthony, 121, 125, 309n20

O'Solomon, Otis, 113

Otis, Johnny, 61

Our Authors Study Circle, 84

Outlook (journal), 36

Outterbridge, John, 130, 158, *222*, *223*, 288; arts education and, 134, 154, 177–78, 186, 202, 221–22, 233–34; as member of LA visual arts community, 13, 82, 154, 158, 162–63, 172–73, 175; as politicized artist, 153–54, 157, 160, 163, 165–67, 169, 171; works of, 153–54, 157, 165–67, *167*, 172

Pajaud, William "Bill," 82–85, 87–88, 162, 180

Palfi, Marion, 181

Parker, Charlie, 40, 101

Parker, William, 59–61, 93, 276–77

particularity, 9–10, 14, 26, 28, 47, 142–43, 264, 287

Passing Through (film), 134–36, 255, 259

Paul Robeson Players, 181

Peace Action Council, 149

Peck, Gregory, 106–7

Performing Arts Society of Los Angeles (PASLA), 111, 176, 208

Perry, Darthard, 113, 151

Petrillo, James, 67–68

Philharmonic Orchestra, Los Angeles, 39–40

Pinkney, Elliot, 178, 180

Piper, C. Erwin, 243

Plagens, Peter, 163

poets, poetry, 7, 130, 132, 173–74

Pointer, Aaron (Abstract Rude), 285

Polacheck, Charlie, 181

police, policing. *See* Los Angeles Police Department

Popular Front, 24, 26, 28, 35–37, 58, 84, 265

Porter, Eric, 6

Porter, Roy, 125

Pot, Pan, and Skillet, 22

poverty, urban, 73, 94, 304n4; cultural programs as tactic against, 90–91, 97–99, 104–5, 109; War on Poverty and, 100, 218, 305n28

Powell, Benny, 179

Powell, Judson, 9, 120, 163, *177*, *211*; arts education and, 177, 230; as member of LA
art community, 134, 154; Watts Towers
Art Center and, 134, *211*, 230; works by,
164–65, 170–71, 174

Powell, Petsye, 179

Powell, Richard, 88, 163, 174

Pratt, Elmer "Geronimo," 150, 195

prisons, 107–8, 135, 278, 281

Progressive Music Organization (PMO), 123

Project Blowed, 285

propaganda, 34, 38–39, 42–43, 54, 187, 198,
200

Proposition 13, 232–34, 243, 269, 276

Pulido, Laura, 15

Purifoy, Noah, 120, 162, 170–71; on art as
instrument for reform, 7, 14–15; career
of, 82, 86; as politicized artist, 163, 165,
168, 202; Watts Towers Art Center and,
134, 154, *211*, 230; works by, 165, 168, 172–
74

Quotable Karenga, The, 207, 210

radicalism, 146–47, 217–18, 287

radio, 8, 56, 73, 75, 301n43

Rag Man series (Outterbridge), 166–67;
"Case in Point," *167*

Ramsess, 285

Randolph, A. Philip, 78

Randolph, Lilian, 42

rap, 113, 258, 273–74, 279, 284

Reagan, Ronald, 93, 232, 264

recording industry, 132, 135–36, 144–45

Redmond, Eugene, 100–101

Reed, Adolph, 10

Reese, Lloyd, 67, 70, 121–22

religion, 22; African American religiosity,
137, 205; Christianity, 165, 205, 265, 279;
political activism and, 148; spiritual imagery in art, 172, 174–75. *See also* Islam;
Nation of Islam

representation, racial, 43–50: autonomy

and self-definition, 142–43; Black Panther Party and, 213–14; discrimination
and, 30–31; film and, 40, 258; identity
politics, 137; *Jump for Joy* as critique of,
23–24; minstrelsy, 3, 75; self-definition
and, 91, 101, 137, 142–43, 266; stereotypical, 16, 33, 37, 40, 75; style politics and,
192–96

Repression (film), 174, 215–16

Republican Party, 40, 54–55, 232–33

Revolutionary Action Movement, 205

Rhodes, Cecil, 141, 213

Rhodes, Jane, 192

rhythmic innovation in free jazz, 139–41,
210–11

Ribicoff, Abraham, 99

Richards, Beah, 84, 181

Riddle, John, 160–61, 167–69, 178, 284

Riordan, Richard, 240

riots, 44, 110; after Rodney King beating
(1992), 1, 193, 221, *236*, 248, 271, 277, 283–
84; zoot-suit riots (1943), 45, 193

Roach, Max, 125

Roberts, Fred, 36

Robeson, Paul, 24, 33, 35, 38, 41–43, 47–48,
265–66

Robinson, Bill, 45, 48, 74

Robinson, Jackie, 52

Robinson, Leroy "Sweetpea," 123

Robinson, Lester, 140–41, 149

Rockefeller Foundation, 97, 103–5, 108–12

Rodia, Samuel, 163, 228–29

Rodney, Walter, 15

Rodney King riots, 1, 193, 221, *236*, 248–49,
271, 277, 283–84

Rogers, Bob, 132

Roosevelt, Franklin D., 45

Ross, Kenneth, 55–56, 85, 229, 231

Royal, Ernie, 121

Royal, Marshall, 121

Russell, Pat, 242, 243

Rustin, Bayard, 100

R'Wanda Lewis Dance Company, 176

Ryan, Judylyn, 175

Saar, Betye, 82, 86–88, 165, 169–70, 172–76, 202; as member of LA arts community, 11, 154; as politicized artist, 154, 163
Samaranch, Juan Antonio, 239
Sanchez, George, 15
Sanchez, Sonia, 200
"Sand Clock Day" (Dolan), 101–3
Sanders, Stan, 208, 242
Sanjines, Jorge, 282
Saunders, Ridhiana, 11, 87, 112–13, 134, 160, 207–8
Saunders, Stan, 160
Savage, Archie, 33
Schrank, Sarah, 163, 228
Schulberg, Budd, 91–98, 95, 103–13, 134, 146, 264. See also Watts Writers Workshop
Scott, Johnny, 97–100, 98, 103–4, 107
Scott-Heron, Gil, 254
Screen Actors Guild (SAG), 51, 76
Seale, Bobby, 150, 165, 200, 203, 215
Second World War, 3, 16, 32–34, 38–39, 44, 45
segregation, 12–13, 29, 56–61, 234–35, 277. See also housing; integration
Seize the Time (album), 149, 187–88, 213, 214
"self-determination music," 119–20, 146–47
Self-Leadership for All Nationalities Today (SLANT), 93–94, 148
Sell, Mike, 6
Semanya, Caiphus, 210
"separate but equal" civic arts policy, 56
Sessions, Michael, 284
Shabazz, Betty, 200
Sheffield, Maceo, 38
Silvera, Frank, 80
Simone, Nina, 194, 233
Singh, Lal, 33
Singh, Nikhil, 192
Singleton, John, 251–52, 273
"Sir Watts" (Purifoy), 165, 168
"66 Signs of Neon" (exhibition and poetry anthology), 170–71, 174
Slater, Van, 154, 169, 177

Smalls, Danny, 74
Smethurst, James, 4
Smith, Anna Deavere, 285
Smith, Gladys Owens, 85
Smith, Richard Cándida, 13, 162
Smith, William E., 82, 84
SNCC (Student Non-Violent Coordinating Committee), 132, 148–49, 195–97, 203, 316n2
Snead, James, 258
social formation, 7
socialism, 47, 189, 199, 205–7, 253, 316n9
Soja, Edward, 253
Somerville, Vada, 44
"Sometimes I Go to Camarillo and Sit in the Lounge" (Lyle), 100–102
"Song for My Father" (Outterbridge), 153–54
Song of the South (film), 9, 75–76
Songs of the Unsung (recording, Tapscott), 124
Sons of Watts, 148, 196, 209
Spanish-Mexican culture. See Chicanos and Latinos
Spellman, A. B., 141
Spikes, Benjamin "Reb," 33, 62, 68
Spikes, John, 36, 68
Spohn, Clay, 163
Star of Ethiopia, 35
Steinbeck, John, 105
St. Elmo's Village, 1–2
Stewart, Donald Ogden, 52
Stewart, Edna, 11, 76
Stewart, Horace Winston (Nick), 9, 42, 44, 74–77, 77
Still, William Grant, 45–47; as composer, 129, 265; as music educator, 70, 121; as politicized artist, 5, 16, 41, 49, 265–66, 288
Stitt, Sonny, 125
Stormy Weather (film), 44–45, 67, 74, 288
Strayhorn, Billy, 22
Stuckey, Sterling, 66
Student Non-Violent Coordinating Committee (SNCC), 132, 148–49, 195–97, 203, 316n2

Studio Watts, 87, 97, 111–12, 120, 130, 132, 134, 176, 234
survival aesthetics model of cultural politics, 225, 254, 263–64
symphony orchestras, 65, 66, 123

Taifa Dance Troupe, 160, 210, 216–17, 312n18
Tales of Manhattan, 33, 43
Talmadge, Herman, 50–51
Tann, Curtis, 82–88
Tapscott, Celia, 130
Tapscott, Horace, 5, 13, 117–22, 127–30, 139–43, *144*, 147–49, 255; communitarian politics of, 97, 137, 288; as composer, 135, 208, 213–15; creative autonomy and, 111, 145; critical reception of works by, 124, 145; CSO and, 67; FBI surveillance of, 150–52; in *Passing Through*, 135–36; recordings by, 119, 124, 143–45, 284; UGMA and, 16, 87, 128–29, 134, 137, 150, 175
Tatum, Art, 35
Taylor, Clyde, 252, 255, 258, 261–62, 289
Tee, Toddy, 327n53
television, 50–51, 64–65, 75, 95–96
Tenney, Jack, 54
Theoharis, Jeanne, 9
Third Worldism, 135, 195, 199, 206, 209; filmmaking and, 251, 256–59, 262
Thomas, Lorenzo, 163
Thompson, Noah, 36
Three Brothers (play), 141–42
Thurman, Wallace, 36, 37
Tizol, Juan, 22
"To Mister Charles and Sister Anne" (Ojenke), 103
touring, by musicians, 127
transit system, 98, 101–3, 240, 263
Tribble, Dwight, 284
Tristano, Lennie, 141
Troupe, Quincy, 103, 112
Trumbo, Dalton, 35, 46–47
Tucker, Marcia, 174
Ture, Kwame, 213–14

Turner, Joe, 22
Twilight Los Angeles (Deavere), 285
Tynam, John, 124

Ueberroth, Peter, *239*
Underground Musicians Association (UGMA), 16, 96, 111, 133–37, 139–41; audience for, 145, 151; Black Panther Party and, 149–50, 188, 214, 217; coalitions and participation, 148–49; as collective community-based organization, 128–30; economics of performance and, 129, 152; emergence and organization of, 128, 134; Hill and, 87, 112–13, 118, 120, 128, 130–31, 234; identity politics and, 142–43; mission of, 143–44; as multigenerational, 129; musical training of members of, 123; politics of, 146–50
Union of God's Musicians and Artists Ascension (UGMAA). *See* Underground Musicians Association
unions, labor, 8, 32, 39, 58, 63–68; amalgamation of, 71–73, 122–23, 137, 288, 301n42; desegregation of, 54–55; membership in, 301nn42–43; in Second World War, 34–35. *See also* Local 47; Local 767
United Service Organization (USO), 39
Urban League, Los Angeles, 36
Usher, Harry, *239*
US Organization, 4, 16–17, 113, 187–88, 192–95, 215–18, 316n2; Black Panther Party vs., 204, 207; cultural initiatives of, 209–12, 217–18; cultural nationalism and, 205–9; cultural theory and ideology of, 198, 203–4, 206–9, 316n2; style politics and, 205; Watts riots and, 93–94

violence, 275–77; gang violence, 196, 226–27, 272, 280; "legal killings," 12, 52, 72, 150; police brutality, 3, 6, 72, 99–100, 197. *See also* Los Angeles Police Department; riots
visual and plastic arts, 81, 153–59, 161–74;

"blackness" as concept in, 88; Studio Watts and education in, 130. *See also* assemblage and "junk" art

Wachs, Joel, 242, 243
Waddy, Ruth, 86, 87; Art West organized by, 120, 134, 289; employment and training of, 82, 156, 173; as member of LA arts community, 11, 162; as politicized artist, 160
Wahad, Dhoruba Bin, 191
Walt Disney Concert Hall, 235
Warner, Jack, 29–30
Washington, Dinah, 265–66
Washington, Timothy, 160, 161
Waters, Ethel, 45
wa Thiong'o, Ngugi, 206
Watkins, S. Craig, 272
Watts Happening Coffee House, 96, 96–97, 111, 134, 141, 144, 151
"Watts 1966" (Scott), 103
Watts 103rd Street Rhythm Band, 1
Watts Poets (anthology), 112–13, 134
Watts Prophets, 9, 113, 129, 133, 284
Watts Repertory Theater, 130, 134
Watts riots: casualties and damages from, 92, 93; cultural politics and, 3, 16, 91–92; emergence of political "new leadership" after, 311n69; McCone Commission Report on, 99–100, 170
Watts Summer Festival, 108–9, 157, 188, 196, 208, 210, 227, 231
Watts Towers and Watts Towers Art Center, 176–77, 186; artists affiliated with, 9, 120, 134, 174, 177, 221–23, 223; Bradley's cultural policy and, 226–28, 230–31, 233–34, 243, 254, 284; cultural education and, 181–82, 221–23, 233–34; pictured, 223, 227, 232; renovation and preservation of Towers, 229–32, 234; Rodia's Towers as assemblage art, 163, 225–29
Watts Writers Workshop, 4, 83, 90–93, 95, 129, 224, 288; closure of, 218, 234; employment and, 94; FBI investigation of,

151; funding for, 104–5, 108, 110–12, 157, 181, 216, 218; as high-profile project, 99, 104; members of, 95; mission of, 103–4; political ideology and conflicts within, 97, 112–14, 217; riots as context for founding of, 99; Schulberg and, 97, 106, 111–14, 134; Watts Happening Cafe as facility for, 96
Webster, Ben, 22
Welles, Orson, 35
West, Mae, 74
Western Regional Black Youth Conference, 149
Westminster Neighborhood Association, 96, 103, 107, 208
Westside County Museum of Art, 236
What Makes Sammy Run (Schulberg), 91, 106
Whipper, Leigh, 42
Whitaker, Leon, 44
White, Charles, 82, 84, 154–55, 157, 160–61, 212, 242
White, Paul, 23
White, Walter, 37, 40–41, 45–47
White Boy Shuffle (Beatty), 285
Whiteson, Leon, 226
Whiting, Cécile, 163
Whitman, Ernest, 48
Wilder, W. E., 229
Wilkins, Ron "Crook," 195–97
Wilkins, William, 69, 69, 121
William Grant Still Art Center, 233
Williams, Bessie, 67
Williams, Frances, 11, 33–34
Williams, Paul, 38
Williams, Raymond, 7–8
Willkie, Wendell, 40, 45
Wilson, Gerald, 67, 123, 129, 139–40
Wilson, William Julius, 10, 157
Witherspoon, Jimmy, 61
Wolff, Goetz, 253
women, 36, 39, 86, 130–34, 213–14
Woodard, Beulah Ecton, 11, 82, 84, 85, 86, 88

Woodberry, Billy, 17, 215, 251–52, 255–59, 267–68, 281
Woodman, Britt, 60, 67, 121
Woodman, Coney, 60
Woods, Clyde, 167–68
Woods, James, 97, 120, 130
Woods, Margo, 130, 134
Woodson, Carter G., 36, 71
Woodward, Komozi, 9, 189
World Stage, 284
World War Two, 3, 16, 32–34, 38–39, 44–45
Wright, Charles, 1, 180
Wright, Jimmy, 61

Wright, Richard, 84, 142
Wyatt, Richard, Jr., *131*

Yang, Mina, 63
Yergan, Max, 33
Yorty, Sam, 98, *211*, 230, 304n4
Young, Marl, 67–68, 71
youth subcultures, 55, 192–96, 244. *See also* gangs

Ziffren, Paul, *239*
zoot culture, 22, 44, 45, 193

DANIEL WIDENER is an associate professor of
history at the University of California, San Diego.

Library of Congress Cataloging-in-Publication Data
Widener, Daniel.
Black arts West : culture and struggle in postwar
Los Angeles / Daniel Widener.
p. cm.
Includes bibliographical references and index.
ISBN 978-0-8223-4667-8 (cloth : alk. paper)
ISBN 978-0-8223-4679-1 (pbk. : alk. paper)
1. African American arts—Political aspects—
California—Los Angeles—History—20th century.
2. African American artists—Political activity—
California—Los Angeles—History—20th century.
3. Los Angeles (Calif.)—Race relations—History—
20th century. I. Title.
NX512.3.A35W534 2010
700.89'96073079494—dc22   2009043379